CALIFORNIA

After the Revolution

After the Revolution
Studies in the Contemporary
Jewish American Imagination

MARK SHECHNER

INDIANA UNIVERSITY PRESS
Bloomington & Indianapolis

Manufactured in the United States of America

Library of Congress Cataloging-in-Publication Data

Shechner, Mark.
    After the revolution.

    Bibliography: p.
    Includes index.
    1. American literature—Jewish authors—History
and criticism.   2. Jews—United States—Intellectual
life.   3. Jewish radicals—United States.   I. Title.
PS153.J4S48   1987   810'.9'8924   85-45977
ISBN 0-253-30450-4

1 2 3 4 5 91 90 89 88 87

Contents

PREFACE   vii

1. Introduction   1
2. The Paradox of the Fortunate Fall   14
3. The Aftermath of Socialism   32
4. From Socialism to Therapy, I: *Sigmund Freud*   58
5. Psychoanalysis and Liberalism: *The Case of Lionel Trilling*   71
6. From Socialism to Therapy, II: *Wilhelm Reich*   91
7. Preserving the Hunger: *Isaac Rosenfeld*   102
8. Down in the Mouth with Saul Bellow   121
9. Memoirs of a Revolutionist: *Norman Mailer in the '50s*   159
10. Allen Ginsberg: *The Poetics of Power*   180
11. The Road of Excess: *Philip Roth*   196
12. Conclusion   239

NOTES   243
INDEX   257

Preface

A BOOK is never really finished, it has been said, only abandoned, and only the author knows how much he has left unsaid, how many puzzles he's left unsolved and mysteries unexamined, and how many loose ends he's left untied. That is inevitable, especially if the personal agenda behind the book remains open and the author's ideas are still in flux, even as he is shipping the manuscript off to the publisher. The best a writer can hope is that he has been skillful enough to create an illusion of closure so that the book itself may have the firm and rounded complexion his thoughts lack.

This book, I suspect, falls a little short of that ideal. It is not a history so much as it is a sequence of discrete windows on a history, which, for all my efforts to give them continuity, are slightly discontinuous. In attempting a broadly conceived study such as this one, the writer has to choose between coverage and focus, and I've consistently chosen the latter, electing to dispense with comprehensiveness in the interests of concentrating more sharply upon the subjects at hand. The result is a book whose asymmetries are obvious, the longest chapter, for example, dealing with Philip Roth, who is a generation apart from the other writers under study and whose example, as the illustration of a thesis, must be understood as symbolic rather than historical.

The book has singular contours, then. It is not a survey but the arc of an emotion, a long slow ellipse of thought that brought me from unformed intuitions through a tangled history to idiosyncratic conclusions. Though that pursuit of my own intuitions may present the reader with occasional questions that the book does not answer, it has made for a more exciting, more personal, and more open-ended project to pursue. Finally, any work of scholarship is bound to be as much about the scholar who wrote it as it is about the figures under study, and this one is no exception.

The author of a scholarly book spends so much of his time alone in the library or in his study or before his typewriter (or in my case the word processor) that he may become afflicted by an overwhelming sense of mental and social isolation. After lower back trouble, loneliness is the major health hazard of scholarship. And yet, though we work alone, our work develops a social rhythm that brings us into touch with others whose scholarship parallels our own. By degrees, our solitary effort blends into a group project, and I have been blessed with professional colleagues and friends who, over the years, have traded manuscripts with me, battled their way through my hectic first drafts, and suffered in turn my hasty comments on theirs. Not being a historian, I have had constant recourse to historians, whose research is more competent than my own and whose historical understanding is far more comprehensive. Without their support this manuscript would be not only a mass of errors but a far thinner work of historical reconstruction. It may still be plagued with errors, but at least I know how much embarrassment their timely and honest criticism has saved me. Most deserving of thanks for their scholarship, advice, and friendly disagreement are Bill Chace, Fred Crews, Andy Gordon, Mark Krupnick, Stephen Longstaff, Sanford Pinsker, Taylor Stoehr, Alan Wald, Stephen Whitfield, and Adi Wimmer.

The chapter on Isaac Rosenfeld involved me in more correspondence than all the others combined, and I was surprised, and touched, by all the correspondents who were willing to share some reminiscences of Rosenfeld with me: Dr. George Sarant, Mrs. Vasiliki White, Ted Solotaroff, Irving Howe, Albert Glotzer, Milton Klonsky, Seymour Krim, Ray Rosenthal, David Bazelon, the late Dwight Macdonald, Samuel Freifeld, Saul Bellow, Jerome Greenfield, and Dr. Laura Perls, who sent me an unpublished short story entitled "A Peg to Hang my Hat on (Requiem for Isaac Rosenfeld)." To George Sarant, Rosenfeld's son, I am especially grateful for his making it possible for me to see and quote extensively from his father's journals.

These projects also demand a degree of financial support, and I owe thanks to the American Council of Learned Societies which provided me with a research fellowship for the year 1977–78, to the State University of New York at Buffalo for two sabbatical leaves to devote to this project, and to the State University of New York Research Foundation which lent welcome support in the form of a summer stipend.

Finally, I owe my greatest appreciation to my wife, Anne, who has been my closest reader, my sanest critic, and my best friend, and who for years told everyone that her husband was on the verge of finishing a book until I was forced to come through at last in order to salvage her credibility. I am also thankful to my daughter, Sarah, who can't recall when her father wasn't writing a pictureless book whose words she couldn't understand and he wouldn't explain. What can "Bolshevism" and "world-historical" and "therapeutic" mean to an eleven-year-old anyway? She has put up with me heroically. The loneliness of scholarship has its compensations after all, the best of them being the discovery of new friends and the love of old ones.

1. Introduction

SEVERAL YEARS AGO, at the end of a course in the contemporary Jewish-American novel, I asked my students to supply me with a brief written summary of what they'd learned about the literature and in particular to identify those common threads that had given the course whatever coherence it had for them. The students were not in the least shy about finding common elements and gave me answers that were remarkably uniform and comparatively simple. The recurring themes of Jewish fiction, they agreed, are sex, selfishness, and misogyny. One student, who had either been reading back issues of *Partisan Review* or had been keeping notes on my own vocabulary, remarked that the literature was about "the self" and "alienation," though having put her views in so formal a language she let it be known that she had little affection for the alienated selves she had encountered.

This was a standard course, whose like may be found in college curricula around the country. It sprang no surprises, gave the students no Ludwig Lewisohn or Meyer Levin or Edward Dahlberg to ponder, and even steered away from such estimable writers as Herbert Gold, Mark Harris (I had already assigned Bernard Malamud's *The Natural* and thought one Jewish baseball book sufficient for the season), Cynthia Ozick, and Elie Wiesel. It was a course in the Big Five: Saul Bellow, Bernard Malamud, Philip Roth, Norman Mailer, and I. B. Singer, with novels by Joseph Heller and E. L. Doctorow added to lend a semblance of coverage. In short, it was a class in mainstream, bestselling American novelists who just happened to be, by birth and God-knows-what else, Jewish or, to be more exact, of Jewish descent.

The course's themes were the difficult Jewish rapprochement with America and the problem of Jewish identity within American culture, and there are few better guides to those matters than the Jewish writers who have established careers upon long and fragile negotiations with America and been rewarded for their efforts in terms any American might envy: fame, money, and literary power. One aspect of the students' reactions, then, came as no great surprise: no one saw anything markedly Jewish in any of the books save Singer's and even then, being unfamiliar with Kabbalah and Yiddish folklore, my students were uncertain of what was so Jewish about all the mystical rigmarole. (For which they are forgiven. A good many Yiddishists have exactly that problem with Singer.) More striking was the near unanimity of their displeasure, which was strongest among the women in the class, most especially the Jewish women. The Jews, naturally, had the greater liberty of their feelings, while the others were more circumspect and their responses somewhat chastened by the sense of being in unfamiliar and possibly hazardous territory.

This repulsion was not exactly foreign to the spirit in which the course was taught. The literature was presented to the students as one of storm and stress, in which anxiety and confusion normally reign, and whose peculiar sense of life is drawn in terms of humiliation, guilt, and general spiritual vexation. The course, then, was decidedly *not* a prolegomenon to Jewish morals: the last things we are likely to find in Jewish fiction in our time are moral clarity and a consistent, instructive view of life. But where I had presented the literature as challenging and problematic, as a typically *modern* literature, my students had found it largely irritating. Intricate personal ironies and baffling conundrums of cultural identity that felt so pressing to me did not register with them at all; they belonged to an entirely different school of attention. They were struck by the more personal matters of character and conduct, by what we are now inclined to call the "interpersonal relations" of the characters, and were largely appalled by what they read. They just did not like Roth's Alex Portnoy and Peter Tarnopol, nor did they care much for Bellow's Joseph of *Dangling Man* or Moses Herzog; they did not warm to Malamud's Morris Bober and Frank Alpine and felt a special kind of sexual distaste for Helen Bober. The central characters in Doctorow's *The Book of Daniel* and Heller's *Something Happened* did not charm them. And this was a bright class of undergraduates. It was altogether fruitless for me to instruct them that those refractory turns of character that had so repelled them were critical elements of the literary imagination in our time and the very chevrons of The Modern Novel. They'd have nothing to do with my lectures on the modernist resistance to middlebrow cheerfulness and the obligatory Dostoevskian self-abasement of the modern hero and were fully prepared to despise on sight authors who must be, they felt, just like their major characters. They had a decided preference for people who knew how to get along.

It happened that my class's reactions gained unexpected support about that time from an essay in *The Village Voice,* "Why Do These Men Hate Women?" an angry lead article on Mailer, Bellow, and Roth by a Jewish feminist, Vivian Gornick, who charged them with virtually every crime known to woman, from the humdrum sexisms of home and office right on up to wishing women dead.[1] Though Ms. Gornick liberally misread some scenes from certain books and confessed to an affection for the profascist writer Louis-Ferdinand Céline that she could not muster for Jewish writers, her charges were not readily dismissed. It was not she, after all, who had written *An American Dream* or *Marilyn* or *Herzog* or *Portnoy's Complaint,* in which the shikse is elevated into an object of Jewish worship and terror and the erection into the sternest test of Jewish manhood. In short, it was not by any means unanimous that "the Jewish novel," whatever exactly it might be, was the unalloyed contribution to the moral enrichment of mankind that some of the more academically minded critics were inclined to make it and some of the writers themselves were given to believe. If my students and Ms. Gornick were seeing things plainly, a book on Bellow so buoyantly titled *Saul Bellow: In Defense of Man* might better have been called *Saul Bellow: In Self-Defense.* Who was it—Truman Capote? Gore Vidal?—who charged some years back that the reputations of the Jewish novelists were the inventions of a Jewish literary mafia that had been unduly solicitous of its own? Let them read Gornick on Mailer et al., or Philip Rahv on Mailer, or Irving Howe on Roth and Leslie Fiedler, or Alfred Kazin on Lionel Trilling, or Norman Podhoretz on Bellow's conversion novel of the early 1950s, *The Adventures of Augie March,* or Harold Rosenberg on the "herd of independent minds," or just about everyone on Podhoretz's memoir, *Making It!* It is sometimes hard to tell the Jewish literary scene from gang warfare. Surely it is plain that there are issues aplenty in this literature, issues having the power to pit Jews against Jews in sharp moral combat.

The impatience exhibited by Jewish critics and readers toward writers who presume to speak for "the Jewish experience" tells us something important about the literature itself, and it seems to me now that the way to gain perspective on this literature is to pay close attention to the atmosphere of faction and scrimmage that has enveloped it from the start. The intellectual life in which this fiction initially took root has rarely been anything short of tumultuous, and we get a deceptive picture of Jewish thought and writing if we heed only its monuments and ignore its torments and agitations, its confusions and failures. We need only recall the pungent ozone of battle given off by *Partisan Review* in its heyday and observe now the crisis mentality that prevails in the bunkers at *Commentary* to gain some idea of the conditions of siege in which

Jewish novelists and intellectuals have always worked, and even worked most productively. Intellectual life in New York being what it is, the capacity to arouse a proper degree of scandal, or even loathing, is the surest sign that a writer or a journal is doing its job. Culture, to rephrase Clausewitz, is war by other means.

II

The polemics that have surrounded this literature are framed, largely, by a specific history, a history of crisis and conversion, and all the writers and intellectuals with whom this book deals experienced some version of the crisis and underwent some form of conversion. By the mid-1950s virtually everyone who wrote for *Partisan Review* or those other command posts of politics and culture—*Commentary, The New Leader, Encounter*—was a convert. They had begun their intellectual journeys under the banner of proletarianism or the Popular Front or Trotskyism or alienation and now had to hoist other colors. As Leslie Fiedler once put it, the great experience of the postwar intellectual was to be twice-born, "once as a Bolshevik and once as a human."[2] The 1952 *Partisan Review* symposium, "Our Country and Our Culture," was a collective admission that an entire intellectual class had thrown in the revolutionary towel along with the spirit of rejection that had nourished artists and intellectuals up through the 1930s.[3] "The American artist and intellectual," announced Philip Rahv and William Phillips in their editoral statement, "no longer feels 'disinherited' as Henry James did, or 'astray' as Ezra Pound did in 1913. Van Wyck Brooks himself has by now entirely repudiated the view that 'the national mind has been sealed against that experience from which literature derives its values.'"

Soliciting responses from a cross section of the New York intellectual scene that included Newton Arvin, Jacques Barzun, Richard Chase, Sidney Hook, Irving Howe, Norman Mailer, C. Wright Mills, Arthur Schlesinger, Jr., Delmore Schwartz, and Lionel Trilling, the editors posed the following four questions:

> 1. To what extent have American intellectuals actually changed their attitude toward America and its institutions?
>
> 2. Must the American intellectual and writer adapt himself to mass culture? If he must, what forms can his adaptation take? Or, do you believe that a democratic society necessarily leads to a leveling of culture, to a mass culture which will overrun intellectual and aesthetic values traditional to Western civilization?

3. Where in American life can artists and intellectuals find the basis of strength, renewal, and recognition, now that they can no longer depend fully on Europe as a cultural example and a source of vitality?

4. If a reaffirmation and rediscovery of America is under way, can the tradition of critical non-conformism (going back to Thoreau and Melville and embracing some of the major expressions of American intellectual history) be maintained as strongly as ever?[4]

Clearly, Rahv and Phillips framed these questions in such a way as to suggest that affirmations were in order, and affirmations, by and large, were what they got. However, the symposium was not without its dissenters. Mills, Mailer, and Howe denounced its assumptions, and others, like Mark Schorer, were only slightly less vehement in their skepticism. Still others who might have been expected to behave badly—Dwight Macdonald, Harold Rosenberg, and Paul Goodman—were either not solicited and chose not to respond. Mailer at the time was a lame-duck Trotskyist, still under the tutelage of Jean Malaquais but headed elsewhere, and had just finished his tormented sex-pol novel of rooming house Armageddon: *Barbary Shore.* Howe, ready as ever to lecture on "the exhaustion of capitalism on a world scale," would write an excited rejoinder for *Partisan Review* two years later, "This Age of Conformity,"[5] in which he scourged his fellow intellectuals for insufficient unrest. But the basic mood of the symposium was affirmative, and it was understood by those who kept close tabs on the Zeitgeist that *Partisan Review* was compiling the results of a decade of conversions. As Rahv and Phillips were quick to observe, "For better or worse, most writers no longer accept alienation as the artist's fate in America; on the contrary, they want very much to be a part of American life."

To be part of America without qualification, however, was to melt into the middle class and pay homage to the man in the grey flannel suit and his boss, the capitalist, a surrender that few intellectuals or writers were then prepared to contemplate. (That would have to await the final leg of the intellectuals' argosy, the 1970s, when they charged through the canyons of Wall Street like gold diggers pouring into the Klondike.) If they were going to be a part of American life, some, at least, were going to demand their own terms. The problem was a scarcity of available terms. Rahv and Phillips recommended "the tradition of critical non-conformism going back to Thoreau and Melville" as one might recommend the Junior League to a stymied housewife. And indeed, much of the appeal of American literature for intellectuals lay in their quest for a usable radical past, a tradition of dissent rooted in native soil and bearing an American postmark. They would see themselves as couriers of a

vision proposed by the literary imagination but yet undreamed by society at large. Alfred Kazin's *On Native Grounds* (1942), Leslie Fiedler's
Love and Death in the American Novel (1960, though Fiedler had been
writing steadily about American literature since the 1940s), and Irving
Howe's critical biography of Sherwood Anderson (1951), all sprang
from the desire to paste a Yankee stamp of approval on their Jewish
mutinies.[6]

In such an atmosphere, the dilemma for the artist whose initial sense
of mission had been formed in a revolutionary age was how to discreetly
bury his adolescent Leninism while preserving the avant-gardist's icono-
clasm. How did you go on smashing idols after you'd put down the
Marxist club? It was in the effort to solve that dilemma that a remarkable
history of conversions took place, conversions that shaped the careers of
a generation of writers and left a profound mark on our literature and
our thought.

Let me pose the issue concretely. What do we make of a writer who
started out in the thirties as a youthful revolutionist, a member of the
Spartacus Youth League and the Young People's Socialist League during
the brief period when it was a revolutionary Trotskyist organization, and
wound up thirty years later humoring the public with the antics of Moses
Herzog, failed scholar and convalescent lover, who goes about half-
dazed in a striped jacket and straw boater trying to understand how he
lost out? How do we assess another writer who, in 1949, dismayed his
hosts at a Communist-sponsored conference on "world peace" by denouncing both the Soviet Union and the United States as equally warlike,
equally capitalist states, but who later in life settled down to writing
potboilers by the armful about moon rockets, prize fighters, and Marilyn
Monroe—*twice*—and took potboiling to new heights with a disposable
murder mystery entitled *Tough Guys Don't Dance*. Understand me. I'm
not bemoaning these writers' sellouts any more than I'm cheering their
redemptions. I am simply illustrating the ongoing crisis of spirit that
bedevils the Jewish intellectual in America and the volatility of principle
and instability of self-conception that are its diagnostic symptoms. These
writers and the others under study in this book give us reason to believe
that the dimensions of the political rebirth of the 1940s have been
seriously underestimated. The standard histories and even the memoirs
of the era incline to regard it as no more than a political reorientation, a
simple change of heart about the merits of communism or socialism and
those of capitalism. In the aggregate, that may have been the common
experience, but among writers for whom the allure of politics was secondary to the commandments of the imagination, the experience of

rebirth was often charged with more dangerous voltage. For them, the process of political conversion was a backdrop to something more profound, a crisis of the will that shook them to the foundations of their being, leaving some rejuvenated, others exhausted and drained of their powers. For such people, being twice-born could be a precarious adventure.

This book is a study of the Jewish intellectual's quest for a firm base of judgment and identity and his failure to maintain a steady relation to the world, immune from the shocks of the moment and the short-term fate of values and behavior under conditions of change and uncertainty. It is not merely that writers and intellectuals have been prone to changing their minds; rather they have been prone to changing themselves. To see these changes as simple alterations of opinion is to mistake them thoroughly; they are deeply personal and, it needs be added, deeply political, though the politics is one of culture rather than one of parties or movements. In the case of Bellow and Mailer the politics are those of self-renewal that, strikingly different though they appear in each, as different as Moses Herzog is from the White Negro, are remarkably similar in point of personal need and cultural influence. The politics of self-renewal are as native to the Jewish intellectual today as those of social redemption were two generations ago, and as varied as its forms may be—theatrical, therapeutic, religious—their history exhibits certain universal features. Jewish intellectual life in America since the 1930s has been a mass exodus from the ghettos of revolutionism toward the condos of individualism. The single enabling condition that allowed Jewish writers in our time to emerge as serious *modern* authors was the emergence of a demanding and intricate *self,* a self that was an idea before it could become a social possibility. That self is a compendium of attitudes that became current in the wake of, and as a consequence of, the collapse of the great social ideologies that had held sway among intellectuals, Jews and non-Jews alike, through the end of the 1930s.

III

In an earlier draft, I had titled this book after one of its chapters, *From Socialism to Therapy,* in order to highlight certain opposing cultural codes within which a generation of Jewish intellectuals sought its rules of conduct and principles of affirmation and rebellion in recent decades, and while that title gave a deceptively tidy appearance to a turbulent history, it served to keep certain essential polarities in view. It also kept in view the remoteness of the intellectuals' argosy from the values of traditional Judaism. So alien, indeed, from the norms of Judaism have been certain Jewish enthusiasms of our day that we may tend to see them as wholesale substitutions for it: thoroughgoing efforts to replace an entire religion and code of values and relations root and branch with secular equivalents. It is not mistaken to regard Marxism, at a certain moment of its penetration into Jewish existence, as a substitute Judaism, endowed with all the powers once possessed by halakhic or Orthodox Judaism for interpreting the world, dictating principles, forming character, and regulating conduct. When it collapsed for those intellectuals, the event was no less disorienting for them than the dissolution of traditional Jewish life under Halakha had been for their grandparents.

This drama of revolutionism and recoil was scarcely confined to Jews; it was played out in every corner of the civilized world that had been touched by the tide of revolutionary Marxism that swelled after the Russian revolution in 1917 and receded during the great unmasking, roughly the twenty years from 1936 to 1956, from the Moscow trials to the Hungarian uprising. Jews were caught up in this great cycle together with many others whom the shocks of modern history had set adrift from inherited codes of value and rendered susceptible to revolutionism of one stripe or another. Be it under oath before HUAC, under fear of death before Vishinsky, under personal stress and moral exhaustion before one's own conscience or one's God, the phrases "I confess," "I submit," "I am reborn" were the strains of a new *Internationale* that became as familiar to a generation of chastened revolutionists as the one that starts with "Arise." Yet there were, after all, groups among whom the universal grievances of class were compounded and raised to revolutionary pitch by national grievances, and who brought to their revolutionism agendas that were quite distinct from the international revolt of the masses. History shows—there is no blinking the fact—that Jews, through the end of the 1930s, had subscribed to revolutionism in disproportionate numbers, for reasons of their own tumultuous history and their own precarious position on the world's stage.[7] For Jews, the encounter with Marxism enacted a double drama, uniting them, on the one hand, with the universal progress of Western man toward liberty, or so they imagined, and bringing them, on the other, into fateful confrontation with their own traditions.

For a segment of Jewish intellectuals in the years just following the Second World War, the shadows of 1936 (Spain, the Moscow show trials) and 1939 (Stalin's nonaggression pact with Hitler, the carving up of Poland) loomed even more darkly than those of the death camps in which six million Jews lost their lives. This fact is entirely familiar but no less provoking for its familiarity. It is not self-evident that that fate of Russia should have dealt a blow to Jewish intellectuals more crushing than the destruction of the European diaspora, and yet it is a fact that needs to be fully absorbed if the character of a certain influential group of Jewish writers, the New York intellectuals, is to be properly appreciated. The romance of American communism was at bottom the romance of Russia, an extraordinary enchantment of the heart that occasioned the most passionate devotion by the lovers while it lasted and provoked just as passionate a revulsion when it ended. Had the essential character of this Jewish intelligentsia taken root elsewhere—in Jewish tradition, in the residues of Yiddish culture that yet remained, or in the memorialization of the Holocaust—its character would have been altogether different from what it is and its impact on America a good deal less. But it was the course of events in Russia, not in Warsaw or Auschwitz or Israel or even America, that left the deepest impression on these writers and even brought them to awareness of themselves as a generation, which might be called, for neatness' sake, the class of 1939. No matter what their age at the critical moment—and some of those to be most celebrated later on were scarcely out of knee pants when the Spanish civil war broke out, when the Moscow trials began, when Stalin signed a pact with Hitler, and when the Soviet Army attacked Finland—Jewish intellectuals took on their special character *as* intellectuals at the moment of disillusionment, and everything that followed from that moment was suffused with the energy of recoil that would be their trademark as a generation thereafter.

Disillusionment was discovery. Whether in any individual case the moment of discovery actually came in 1939 or 1936 or 1933 tends to blur in the long view, but the moment, whenever it occurred, was decisive for both Jewish intellectual life *and* American. It gave birth to a generation whose role in American life and letters was established upon its youthful disenchantment, and it set the terms on which Jews could join the American intelligentsia as full partners for the first time: the terms of anticommunism. Like the Christian myth of the fall from paradise that set the stage for the resurrection into glory, this drama could well be termed the paradox of the fortunate fall, since it was the fall from the garden of Marxism that brought Jews into the mainstream of American intellectual life and vaulted them into the empyrean of power that they had dreamed of as revolutionaries but had imagined achieving only as comrades or, perhaps, commissars, but never, never as patriots.

In its broader outlines, this history is entirely familiar, since certain of its consequences have already been well plotted. The essential character of what we call the Jewish novel is keyed to it, as are those influential journals of opinion in our time that have shaped postwar sensibility and ordered the agendas of debate: *Partisan Review, Commentary, The New Leader, Encounter, The Public Interest, Dissent,* and the now-defunct *Reporter.* But it took time for this history to work itself out, and the working out was neither simple nor uniform. Its inner dimensions, especially in their relation to our literature and our thought, remain obscure, and it is as a contribution to bringing some of that obscurity to light that this book is written.

This book, then, is an effort to plot the trajectory of certain key ideas that weave through contemporary thought and provide the unifying factors in it. The Jewish intellectual, as novelist, poet, and critic, as social thinker and cultural strategist, emerges onto the stage of American letters in the 1940s possessed of a style, a history, and a repertoire of obsessive themes that both unite him with the mainstream of American culture, easing his passage into the inner chambers of power, and mark him off sharply as an intruder. Those themes include *alienation, anticommunism, modernism,* and *therapy,* all of which bear the mark of a history of political cataclysm and personal bereavement. The anticommunism of the Jewish intellectuals is lately so overworked a theme that I'll refrain from belaboring it except to note its relation to the other tangents of experience that are more immediate to my concerns. Moreover, since imaginative literature is my point of departure and anticommunism left its impression on our literature only indirectly, it may be safely relegated to the background while those ideas that had more direct impact on literature are more closely examined. Alienation, lately overthrown as a moral standard and sustaining personal ideology, did succeed for a time in being the most widespread and influential idea of all among Jewish writers in the early postwar years, and everything that is initially distinctive about the "Jewish novel"—its note of suppressed grief, its mood of rejection, its plangency and brooding—is founded upon and sanctioned by the alienations that stand behind it.

The therapeutic, as a commanding cultural idea, arises in tandem with alienation, as both remedy for it and highlight: as a way, that is, of insinuating disability as a preferred moral condition. Arising out of the conjunction of international catastrophe and widespread individual disorientation, the therapeutic is necessarily a complex and difficult idea, and Philip Rieff's account of it in his book, *The Triumph of the Therapeutic,*[8] as an ethic of personal remission, a mere flight from the obligations of society, is pure caricature. All variants, however—Freudian (in its late incarnation as tragic theology), Reichian, neo-Freudian, and Lawrencian—reflect a common sense of alarm and press the claim for locating the sources of the worldwide political debacle in the vulnerabilities and imperfections of the individual. Such titles as *Civilization and Its Discontents, Man against Himself, The Neurotic Personality of Our Time, Escape from Freedom,* and *The Mass Psychology of Facism* express plainly the widespread desire to find in psychoanalysis a social reagent that, when titrated into the murky waters of history, would turn them crystal clear and disclose the bedrock of human imperfection beneath all. When writers began taking stock of their situation during the war and just after, many found in psychoanalysis an objective correlative to their state of shock. With its penchant for basic interpretations, its view of the irrational and destructive in human nature, and its intimations of regeneration through wholly individual efforts, psychoanalysis allowed its adherents to grieve in the deepest and most comprehensive terms of all: *for all mankind.*

It is psychoanalysis as a social idea, then, and as a distinct slant on civilization and its disasters, that this book is largely concerned with, and it will have little to say, consequently, about psychoanalysis as an evolving theory of mind or as a therapeutic practice. I'm tempted to say that I intend to deal with psychoanalysis as an ideology, though it is doubtful whether for those who turned to it as a guide to values and conduct it was ever quite so imposing. For all that it shares in common with true ideologies, psychoanalysis in most of its forms normally fails in being a total explanatory system and in arousing in its adherents the same zeal and self-assurance that total explanatory systems are famed for doing. The photographer's viewfinder might be the better analogy, implying as it does a circumscribed field of vision, a mechanism of focus, and a world beyond the frame that is encountered simply by raising one's eyes from the apparatus. Except for those few, mainly Reichians, who have demanded from the therapeutic that it set the world right by vigorous programs of self-reclamation, psychoanalysis has always fallen shy of the explanatory sufficiency and redemptive confidence of a true ideology. Many have argued the necessity of analytic reasoning, but few have come forward to defend its sufficiency. For all but those who have embraced its doctrines out of a personal need for firm doctrines, the skepticism of psychoanalysis has normally been its modulating feature, preserving it as a flexible point of view while preventing it from becoming a dogma.

It goes without saying that these Jewish dramas were performed on an American stage and that it was American culture being challenged and remade, not Jewish. The belief that a man could shed the old skin to release the new Adam was commonplace among American intellectuals in the postwar years; Jews held no patent on it. It may be the most basic American myth of them all, that by will alone a man may break with the past and attain a higher vision of himself, an improved conception of character and life free from guilt and the obligations of custom.[9] The doctrine of the new Adam, that human nature may be recycled and that every man is his own redeemer, is a staple of liberal ideology, which believes in the power of the will over conditions, history, tradition, and guilt. We should not be surprised that Jews in postwar America, given their long history of exile and confinement, their tradition of unfulfilled messianism, their modern romance of political radicalism, and their own stringent codes of personal conduct, should be drawn to revival in substantial numbers. Nor should we be surprised to find that when they do perform their ceremonies of renewal they do so *as Americans*, and that it is in American life and literature that they find their sources and listen for their echoes, for it is their belated passage into America that they are symbolizing. "I am an American, Chicago born," boasts Augie March in that formidable opening line, as though he were speaking for a Dreiser or a Sandburg instead of a Canadian-born Jew from a Yiddish-speaking home.

The particular Jew who bulks large in this study, then, is the "non-Jewish Jew," as Isaac Deutscher once called him, the Jew who, in the middle of the last century, made a sharp break with his own traditions and history and entered the mainstream of European history as intellectual pioneer. Social types more pronounced in Europe, once upon a time, than ever they became in America, these non-Jewish Jews were "born and brought up on the borderlines of various epochs. Their minds matured where the most diverse cultural influences crossed and fertilized each other. They lived on the margins or in the nooks and crannies of their respective nations. They were each in society and yet not in it, of it and yet not of it."[10]

The non-Jewish Jew never did establish himself as the commanding presence in America that Deutscher's examples—Spinoza, Heine, Marx, Luxemburg, Freud—were in Europe, because the international crosscurrents of thought that nurtured him in Europe are feeble here, and the tensions between Jewish culture and American are now so slack that the Jewish community seems hardly anything more distinctive than a large congregation of prosperous Protestants. The pressure of living at the margin of two cultures that helped create such figures is all too easily endured in America. Still, the non-Jewish Jew as artist and thinker is a familiar figure in American letters, with his restlessness, his irritability, his jeremiads, his proclivity for the nooks and crannies of culture, and his belief, not unwarranted, that his particular cranny is more dynamic, more significant, and more in key with developing trends than anything at the cultural center. It is he, finally, who is the inventor of the Jewish imagination in our time and the figure therefore with whom any serious study of that imagination must contend.

2. The Paradox of the Fortunate Fall

> [The Jew] is a specialist in alienation (the one international banking system the Jews actually control). Alienation puts him in touch with his own past traditions, the history of the Diaspora; with the present predicament of almost all intellectuals and, for all one knows, with the future conditions of civilized humanity. Today nearly all sensibility—thought, creation, perception—is in exile, alienated from the society in which it barely manages to stay alive.
>
> —Issac Rosenfeld, "The
> Situation of the Jewish Writer"

I

IT HAS LATELY become a maxim in conservative circles that the creative impulse in America has begun to die back for want of travail and that, to put Edmund Wilson's famed metaphor to a new use, it is only in injured polities, under conditions of maximum duress, that the bow of the imagination is now fully drawn. Thus it is to the Soviet Union and Eastern Europe that some critics now look for the modern Helicon. What lines of sustained creativity, they ask, can America boast in this century to compare with the one that runs from Isaac Babel and Osip Mandelstam to Boris Pasternak, Aleksander Solzhenitsyn, Aleksander Zinoviev, and Nadezhda Mandelstam? Where in the West is the human condition *in extremis* wrestled with so powerfully as it is in the Soviet Union? The most comprehensive formulation of this case for America's imaginative impoverishment by material ease and social justice to date comes from abroad, from George Steiner, who postulates as a modern law of the imagination, an inverse ratio between political justice and exemplary creativity. "There is . . . substantial evidence," he writes, "to suggest that the generation and full valuation of eminent art and

14

thought will come to pass . . . under conditions of individual *anomie,* of anarchic or even pathological unsociability and in contexts of political autocracy."[1] The evidence for such a conclusion is the astonishing creativity to be found in Russia and the Soviet-bloc countries under what are seemingly impossible conditions.

> It is not the "creative writing centres," the "poetry workshops," the "humanities research institutes," the foundation-financed hives for deep thinkers amid the splendours of Colorado, the Pacific coast or the New England woods we must look to for what is most compelling and far-reaching in art and ideas. It is to the studios, cafés, seminars, *samizdat* magazines and publishing houses, chamber-music groups, itinerant theatres, of Krakow and of Budapest, of Prague and of Dresden. Here . . . is a reservoir of talent, of unquestioning adherence to the risks and functions of art and original thought on which generations to come will feed.[2]

If such be the case—and I'm not persuaded that it is—who would not prefer a drab liberty to an aesthetically enhanced state of terror? Who would desire a Russia restored to Stalinism or frozen forever in the neolithic grip of Brezhnevism that we might enjoy (enjoy *is* the word for it) future episodes of Solzhenitsyn's epic of the gulag? Who would wish Czechoslovakia captive for one more day for the gift of Milan Kundera's brittle ironies? And who would wish to see the Jewish people reduced again to wandering and grief that a Kafka, a Mandelstam, a Bialik, or a Sholom Aleichem might nourish his genius with their tears? The American option, concedes Steiner, makes sense. "The flowering of the humanities is not worth the circumstances of the inhuman. No play of Racine is worth a Bastille, no Mandelstam poem an hour of Stalinism."[3] We are stuck, it appears, with freedom and Saul Bellow.

But what if we should pose the question of injury and imagination in purely individual terms; is the answer still so unambiguous? No one, surely, would beg to have his faculties sharpened in a prison camp, but are there not a few who thrill to the thought of having a father as overbearing as Kafka's, an epilepsy as dangerous as Dostoevsky's, a neurasthenia as exquisite as Proust's, that their latent genius might be released by their torment? If tickets went on sale tomorrow for Philoctetes' Lemnos, would not the lines go around the block? The mythos of Romanticism, in whose shadow we still live, holds the artist's power to be a compensatory gift, and rare is the writer who has not felt the lure of the disinherited mind and of the feats of creation and intellect that have been laid at its door. "When a man's breast feels like a cage from which all the dark birds have flown," thinks Moses Herzog, "he is free, he is

light. And he longs to have his vultures back again. He wants his customary struggles, his nameless, empty works, his anger, his affliction and his
sins."[4] Historian Cesar Graña speaks of "an active wish for desolation
and inner injury" at the core of Romanticism, "a will to unhappiness and
. . . search for heartaches" that becomes, in the nineteenth century, a
recurrent feature of the myth that the imagination is honed to a point
only under conditions of rebellion, derangement, even morbidity.[5] Since
the nineteenth century, the appeal of the tumultuous and the disabling
has been a constant for those who court the passions of the mind; what is
subject to the vicissitudes of the age is the number who actually immerse
themselves in the destructive element to seek that pearl of genius that is
said to grow in irridescent rings around a core of affliction. Our age
gives little sanction to such a plunge and small recognition to those who
take it. This is the age of the ready, the muscular, the ambitious, the age
of positive thinking and bustling self-assurance. For those who treasure
such a standard, this is an age of gold, while for those who long for
something more inward and problematic, this is the ice age.

Yet it was scarcely a generation ago that alienation held center stage as
the diagnostic fever of the contemporary artist and literary intellectual.
Whether descanting on their spiritual orphanage or puzzling over their
irrelevance in the grand scheme of things or lamenting the history that
had brought Man into The Modern World, intellectuals turned uner-
ringly to alienation as an omnibus explanatory term as if drawn there by
magnetic force. It was their pole star, their true north. This was especially the case among Jewish intellectuals during and after the Second
World War. Though the sense of being out of harmony with the world is
scarcely of Jewish patent, rootlessness, marginality, and estrangement
have always had a special meaning for the Jews as a dispersed nation,
and never more so than just after the war, when the murder of European Jewry had brought an end to an entire phase of their history, with
its known landmarks and familiar, if not always beloved, portion of the
earth. Intellectuals suffered the general estrangement with an added
poignancy, being doubly alienated, first *as* Jews, second *from* Jews. To
them fell the double disinheritance of having residence in two worlds
and a home in neither. "Even when he succeeds in detaching himself
completely from Jewish life," observed a young Irving Howe in 1946,
"[the Jewish intellectual] exhibits all the restless agonizing rootlessness
that is the Jewish birthmark." But the consolations of Jewish communal
life were unavailable to him; the history that had bestowed upon him his
badge of distinction belonged to a culture in which he played no part

except that of Esau: "He has inherited the agony of his people; its joy he knows only second hand."[6]

Irving Howe's voice is singled out from among the choruses of the postwar alienated for no special reason save his familiarity to us as an interpreter of contemporary Jewish culture and his aptitude, even as a young man, for seeing his own tensions as representative and symptomatic. But I might have quoted a dozen others, since such avowals of uprootedness were practically routine just after the war's end. In the 1940s, Howe and his contemporaries had a weakness for the first-person plural; the pronoun "we" came as easily to their lips as did the semantic beacons of the age: "crisis," "transition," and "alienation."[7] It is not too great an exaggeration to say that homelessness constituted their home, and that, in virtue of their rupture with the past, they looked to their own generation and its collective experience for the ingredients of self-definition that inherited traditions could no longer provide. Thus a young Alfred Kazin would announce in 1944 in a prominent Jewish journal, *Contemporary Jewish Record,* "The writing I have been most deeply influenced by—Blake, Melville, Emerson, the seventeenth-century English religious poets, and the Russian novelists—has no direct associations in my mind with Jewish culture; it has every association, of course, with the fact that, *like many another American, I have had to make my own culture*" (my italics).[8]

Lacking a ready-made culture in which they could submerge themselves unselfconsciously, Jewish intellectuals of Howe and Kazin's generation took their principles of solidarity from the experience they shared in common: the street life they all experienced as children of the ghetto; those special brands of ambition and shame that are endemic to children of immigrants; the books they read in common; the Depression; and the crises of history to which they responded with all the anguish of participants, from Spain to the Moscow trials to the Holocaust, all of which stamped them with an identity as distinctive as anything their fathers had drawn from Torah, Talmud, and the ceremonies of Jewish life. If in the 1930s this shared identity, brimming with the spirit of progressive camaraderie, resolved itself in Marxism of one stripe or another, in the 1940s it found its desolate symbol in alienation, the exile of sensibility, in Isaac Rosenfeld's phrase, "from the society in which it barely manages to stay alive."

Time has dealt harshly with alienation, which has of late fallen out of favor as a symbol of *lacrimae rerum* and come under suspicion of being a fashion, a routine of conspicuous dishevelment that says as much about the condition of the modern mind as the language of Freudian meta-psychology says about the reasons of the heart. "In America," sneered Harold Rosenberg in the late fifties, "philosophers of the void are compelled to disguise themselves as literary critics, sociologists, mental therapists. One examines the text of a novel and discovers it to be a lid on the abyss. . . . Or one charts the daily routines of a suburb and encounters *tohu-bohu* between the cars parked at the shopping center: this is good for a notice in *Time* and appointment to a full professorship."[9] A decade later Lionel Trilling would complain, in *Sincerity and Authenticity*, of the "culture-Philistines" who, "because they see themselves as damned, are saved."[10] And Saul Bellow's Moses Herzog, in a novel that is both a handbook of self-affliction and a tract against making world-historical claims for the merely neurotic, frets continually about "the commonplaces of the Wasteland outlook, the cheap mental stimulants of Alienation, the cant and rant of pipsqueaks about Inauthenticity and Forlornness."[11]

This "Wasteland outlook," a phrase that has passed into the folklore of antimodernism as the definitive summation of some very complex ideas, has become the particular bête noire of certain intellectuals who were once cradled under its sign but have more recently, under a new dispensation, swapped its gray vistas for a sunnier window on the world. Some of them can be grouped under the broad rubric of neoconservative: conservative because they take the mechanisms of the free market for comprehensive social philosophies, and neo because they adopted such views in midlife after tortuous journeys from left field—CCNY or some moral equivalent thereof. "After I had begun writing for it," recalls Norman Podhoretz, striking a characteristic post of *haut* mischief in *Making It*, "my editor at the *New Yorker* once asked me in the dryest possible way whether they had special typewriters in the *Partisan Review* office with entire words like 'alienation' stamped on each key."[12] Lately, Joseph Epstein, editor of *The American Scholar* and a peacetime paratrooper for the neoconservative culture patrol, has made a career of leading missions against the last diehards of alienation, holed up in their redoubts like Japanese snipers on Mindanao. He monotonously drives home the point in essay after essay that contemporary alienation is merely curricular, a routine of the classroom learned entirely from the anthologized monuments of modern art and literature. The spirit of *non serviam*, he holds, that once marked the modern artist's Luciferian revolt against Philistia is now the staple of the research library, where the major in Modern Despair patiently takes notes on the Dark Night of the Soul and applies his magic marker to *Les Fleurs du Mal* in translation.[13]

If this campaign were just an instance of New York intellectual parti pris and ultimately reducible to questions of insular midtown Manhattan politics we could safely take a dim view of it. But there are signs that something fundamental is taking place and that the assault on alienation portends a general revolution in values and taste in all the arts, as spokesmen for antimodernism step forward with complaints against the domestication of extreme experience and the routines of making it new. According to Hilton Kramer, who is just now the most formidable spokesman for the conservative temper in the arts, art and its criticism have begun to veer sharply away from the modernist spirit that has dictated highbrow taste in art since the 1920s. "We are witnessing the final collapse of the great myth that dominated the aspirations of high culture in the West for more than a century—the myth of avant-garde intransigence and revolt that gave to all of modernist culture its aura of moral combat—we are seeing, at the same time, the opening skirmishes of a new contest to determine precisely what the relation of culture to power will be in the postmodernist era upon which we have now entered."[14] Though Kramer addresses himself here to developments in painting and art criticism, which tend to be more volatile than their literary counterparts (as consumables, art and its criticism are more thoroughly creatures of fashion than literature), his argument has obvious implications for literature and, especially, for the institution of criticism, where the prevailing myth of criticism as a progressive endeavor that advances knowledge by consuming its own past is now being called into question. Evidence of skirmishing can be found along a broad front, in literary criticism and the social sciences—right on up, indeed, to the offices of the National Endowment for the Humanities, though it is by no means confined to those sectors patrolled by neoconservatives. Gerald Graff's influential book *Literature against Itself,* a summary of the case against the critical methodologies of alienation and Schadenfreude, appears to be rooted in a Marxist apprehension that literary study at its very leading edges is devoted to dulling our taste for reality and turning us away from the contemplation of institutions, power, and the social arrangements of existence.[15] The Wasteland outlook is now assailed as an ideology of obfuscation and irresponsibility from almost any point of view that stands for reason, critical rigor, problem solving, and moral accountability.

It is no accident that Jewish writers have been heard on both sides of the question of alienation, in promoting it as an American standard in the 1940s and in seeking to disestablish it in succeeding decades. Alienation, as an aesthetic and an attitude toward culture, is closely bound up with modernization as a social process and modernism in the arts; we might look upon it as the cultural component of modernizaton, the agenda of feelings drawn up by artists to place themselves in an advantageous relation to a world in revolution—an Archimedean lever, in a sense, and a place to stand. It needs no arguing here that the impact of the modern world on Jewish life has been enormous since industrialization and the Enlightenment made their belated appearance in the Jewish villages and urban enclaves of Eastern Europe in the middle of the nineteenth century. We need only reflect on the distinction achieved by Jews, some only a generation removed from the ghetto, in modern science and art and in the great surges of revolutionism in thought and politics that mark our century to measure the changes in Jewish consciousness in the last one hundred years. Jewish culture today is a culture of the uprooted, marked in every particular by stress lines and sharp faults. We are not what our parents were, nor were they what their parents were. In less than a century, the Yiddish language, which had been spoken by millions of Jews—as recently, indeed, as forty-five years ago—has virtually disappeared; Jewish folk culture has become a specialty for antiquarians; the great, passionate Jewish religion has been driven into fortified enclaves by the Jews themselves; and Judaism's entire center of gravity has been transported from Eastern Europe and the Pale of Settlement to America and Israel. That Jewish writers and thinkers should continually be measuring the costs and benefits of their escape into modern life should not surprise us: we should wonder, in the light of Jewish history, how they could find time to do anything else.

And yet, despite the Jews' history of flight and devastation, by the second decade after the war and the Holocaust the stresses within Jewish life in its major centers—America, Israel, and Russia—had relaxed substantially, or taken forms at any rate that could no longer sustain ceremonies of individual revolt and self-alienation. In America, the rapid embourgeoisement of the Jews and the consolidation of their status within American society has made the traditional figures through which they had once imagined themselves—the scholar, the Luftmensch, the zaddik, the revolutionary, the schlemiel, the restless cosmopolitan—seem as ancient and mythical as the pharoah or the caveman. One could even believe that such people never existed. There is no more precise barometer of the state of American Jewry these days than *Commentary* magazine, which presents a vastly different image of the Jew today than it did just thirty years ago when, under the editorship of Eliot Cohen, it was a forum for cultural Judaism and what one historian has termed "the cosmopolitan ideal."[16] Even subtracting that portion of *Commentary's* mission that reflects the personalities of its two editors, Cohen and, since 1960, Norman Podhoretz, we are left with a residue of sentiment in the magazine as it is today that points decisively toward the Jews' growing acceptance of the terms of their being in America and their identification with its institutions and power. Seen through the eyes of *Commentary*, Judaism begins to look like twentieth-century Americanism. It is one of the more astonishing indices of our time that the normalization of the Jew has materially closed the gap between the politics of organized American Jewry and those of the American heartland. Who'd have been so bold as to propose, even five years ago, that an evangelical movement out of the Bible Belt, Reverend Jerry Falwell's Moral Majority, might so effortlessly close ranks on all major issues (save, possibly, abortion) with *Commentary*? In the long evolution of the Jews toward Protestantism, which finds its reflection in the Protestant myth of its own origins in Judaism, has there ever been a more startling reconciliation than this: a united front of Christians and Jews in defense of the free market, the nuclear family, the nuclear deterrent, and the state of Israel, and in determined opposition to homosexuality?[17] As the tensions within Jewish life ease, the comic ironies surrounding it seem only to grow, as Christian and Jew resolve their differences in the prosthetic Zion of the new conservatism, where the idea of the Judeo-Christian ethic is fleshed out in rare detail, and the ambiguities of value and allegiance that once tormented the Jewish conscience are clarified in the pure light of stability and nationalism.

Against such a background and in view of the palpable benefits in social ease, material well-being, and peace of mind that accompany the normalization of the Jew and the domestication of his sympathies and politics, it would be churlish to propose that something essential to his imagination may have been lost in the surrender of so fruitless a standard as alienation, a standard that calls into question the Jews' adjustment to America and is as contemptuous of day-to-day politics as it is hostile to ideal constructions of every sort, from traditional religions to progressive utopias. The alienated man is a champion of maladjustment, not a citizen, and whatever else the waiver of alienation has meant for intellectuals who once flew its banner, it has certainly meant the acceptance of citizenship. I am going to be churlish, however, and insist that the affirmative imagination that is the new standard among Jewish intellectuals is impoverished by its very will to affirm. In the exchange of disengagement for full participation, a vital principle of the imagination has been given up, one so vital, indeed, that its loss alone would explain the end of an exceptional chapter in Jewish intellectual history in America, one that spawned not only some of the most vital fiction of our time but also some of the most rigorous and demanding critical thought.

If it is true, as some believe, that the so-called Jewish novel is now dead, that is partly so because the tension between the self and the world, the knot of unregenerate trouble at the heart's core that once supplied the traction and drive of the imagination in *galut* has been soothed in America, where exile is a benign condition with all the conveniences of home. We patiently indulge lingering postures of insurrection, like Norman Mailer's characterization of suburbia as "cancer gulch," since admonitions about the moral degeneracy of our lives are about as provocative when borne upon salt breezes from Provincetown as when arriving in film canisters from Hollywood. We're all in cancer gulch these days and are remarkably unembarrassed about our Land Rovers, our L. L. Bean gear, our season's hockey tickets. Jewish intellectuals were once readily distinguishable from bankers, bartenders, psychotherapists, and other champions of positive thought. They were balding, wore rimless Trotsky glasses, and were disaffected. Now they are no longer disaffected. Their books, by their very titles, make known their preference for enterprise over hand wringing, winning over losing: *Ambition, Making It, Breaking Ranks, Free to Choose, We Must March My Darlings, Two Cheers for Capitalism.* What ever happened to *Death of a Salesman?*

To urge a revival of alienation as a social term and a moral posture, however, we need to do more than just apply for a national change of heart. We need to be clear about what is being proposed, since alienation has long since become an intellectual folk term whose very range of uses serves to obscure any particular one of them. So encrusted has the word become with mannerism and pretense that one hesitates to use it at all except inside a *cordon sanitaire* of quotation marks, to signal one's ironic intentions.[18] Alienation strikes us as an anachronism, a relic of a more sentimental age when intellectuals put a higher premium on wounded feelings than we now deem beneficial. This is an age of hard-boileddom, and we expect our thinkers to meet the crises of the day with pluck, resilience, and practical counsel. Alienation has also, in the last decade, come to designate something purely conceptual and far removed from the sense of vulnerability and exclusion: a doctrine of irrealism that presumes so thoroughgoing an estrangement of language and perception from the world that language cannot be said to correspond even remotely to reality. Such an alienation, when formulated as a principle of literary representation, as it commonly is, amounts to a doctrine of the necessity, and finally the value, of unrelieved artifice and of self-congratulary but undisciplined styles of composition that do not pretend to transcribe reality: the antistory, "surfiction," the "free play of un-grounded discourse," *"jouissance,"* the obliteration of the world for the aggrandizement of the word. It is not the least indecency of such writing that its proselytizers, taking refuge in schadenfreude from the shocks of history and recollection, commonly invoke the Holocaust to illustrate the basic uncertainties of life that justify the "disarticulations" of their writ-ing. Because the world has become unglued, goes the standard apologia, art must follow suit. It is the rescue of alienation from these twin sentimentalities, of exhaustion and schadenfreude, that this book hopes to achieve. Certainly, recent history provides a precedent for practical alienation. At the moment when Jewish writers and their work began to flower in the gardens of American literature, alienation of a particularly gritty sort was the spirit that drove them, and it was neither a counsel of resignation nor a gesture of arrogance but a necessary and radical form of engagement.

II

To speak of beginnings is to presume endings, and to understand births one needs to know something of the deaths that paved the way. The arrival of the Jew on center stage in American literature was not a casual event, a natural percolation of talent and ambition into the upper reaches of art and thought or a simple transfer into secular literature of passions once spent on biblical studies. It was rather a renaissance, a rebirth. While it did partake of the rising fortunes of the Jewish com-munity as a whole and draw upon two millennia of devotion to books and study, it also obeyed its own laws, laws that divided artists and intellectuals sharply from the Jewish mainstream and even placed them in open revolt against it. It is a curious feature of the relation between Jewish intellectuals and the Jewish middle class that they acknowledge different histories, as though their pasts were chosen to suit their ambi-tions rather than immutably given.

And to a degree the past *is* chosen, as every intellectual who has found himself forced to invent his own culture is keenly aware. The Jewish middle class, its ties to the old country irrevocably shattered, nonetheless imagines Jewish history in lines of unbroken continuity from Abraham, Isaac, and Jacob to itself. The collective "we" of Jewish ceremony—*"our fathers were slaves unto Pharoah in Egypt"*—has the effect of compress-ing millennia into moments and bringing present generations in direct touch with biblical ancestors. It is precisely such biblical syncretism, the

folding of the ancient past into the present, that permits the religious
parties in Israel to claim political jurisdiction over the West Bank, Judea
and Samaria, by biblical right. Artist and intellectual, by contrast, are
attuned to the discontinuities of life and define themselves in terms of
whatever in traditional culture and belief, or in their own experiences, is
no longer available to them. "What have I in common with the Jews?"
asked Franz Kafka. "I scarcely have anything in common with myself."
Or note the predicament of Sam Slovoda, the central character in Norman Mailer's early story "The Man Who Studied Yoga."

> Since he quit Party work he has studied a great deal. He can tell you about
> prison camps and the secret police, political murders, the Moscow trials,
> the exploitation of Soviet labor, the privileges of the bureaucracy; it is all
> painful to him. He is straddled between the loss of a country he has never
> seen, and his repudiation of the country in which he lives.[19]

That loss of a country he has never seen, Russia, and the repudiation
of the country in which he lives is one of the great founding themes of
the Jewish renaissance, and if we look beyond Mailer's references and
generalize Sam Slovoda's lost country to all the lands, cultures, movements, and spiritual homesteads that the Jews have forsaken or been
driven out of, we may capture something of the spirit of isolation and
self-reliance in which the Jewish literary renaissance took root. In our
time, art and thought owe more to vertigo than to equilibrium, and the
successful contemporary writer is, as likely as not, one who has seized
upon his disablements as opportunities. When a familiar terrain of ideas
disappears overnight and writers and artists who had stood with both
feet on the terra firma of a known and shared conception of reality
suddenly find themselves groping around in terra incognita, predictably,
talents that had been trained on the old certainties may lose their grip
and begin to slide. Just as predictably, writers with a gift for losing their
bearings may discover orientation as their calling and thrive on the very
conditions that sap others of their spirits. Sam Slovoda may have been
blocked in his writing and his affections, incapable of either love or
work, but Mailer in 1956, when the story appeared, was not: straddling
between worlds was proving to be an opportunity and a release, a belated
release from the threadbare Trotskyism that had made a shambles of his
second novel, *Barbary Shore,* and an opportunity to chart a new course, to
think everything afresh. Out of that dilemma, the impossibility of affirm-
ing anything, would come his perplexed and stunning book *Advertisements for Myself,* whose farrago of interviews, screeds, poems, reviews,

boasts, and assaults would rescue his stymied career by turning it inside out.

or Mailer, the moment when the past was violently shattered and a new self released from the husk of the old came a decade later than it did for many others. Generally, it was the 1940s that proved to be the interlude between affirmations, between the innocent revolutionism of the 1930s and the twice-born boosterism of the 1950s. The decade of the 1940s was the still point in the turning world, the moment of sorrow and new beginnings when the imagination was turned loose from its customary moorings and set adrift among strange currents. Philip Rahv sensed it in 1948: " 'All the beautiful ideologies have burst,' a British poet has lately written. That is true, and it has left a good many of us with the kind of wasteland feeling which in the thirties, in the palmy days of Marxist hope and enthusiasm, we used to ascribe to the 'bourgeois intellectuals' as their exclusive malaise."[20] The malaise of which Rahv complained was indeed the prevailing mood for intellectuals, but it was also the root and ground of their tortured vitality, quite as if the imagination, sensing an opportunity to evade wearisome duties, came alive at just the moment when the political and social will collapsed. A paradoxical effect of the shocks of politics and war was a revitalization of sensibility: at the heart of what was most provocative in American thought and writing in the postwar years were the energies set free within and among the intellectuals by their long retreat from the revolutionary vanguard.

We hardly need reminding that a crisis of major proportions beset American writers during and just after the Second World War, especially those who had come of age during the Depression and had taken it for granted that Western civilization lay at death's door. Such writers looked to the East for consolation and drew courage from the heroic legends of the Russian revolution until they were aroused from the Marxist slumber by the revelations, which came slowly but with great force, of the totalitarian nature of Soviet communism. Whatever remnants of hope for the declining West may have survived such revelations about the redemptive East were dashed by the brutalities of the war, with its death camps, its terror bombings, and its mass exterminations. Hiroshima and Nagasaki brought the cycle of wartime horrors to an unexpected climax: liberal democracy proved as equipped, morally as well as materially, for mass murder as communism and fascism. American intellectuals lived from crisis to crisis without respite: from the Depression and the disintegration of Europe to the war, the Holocaust, the Cold War, the Great American Communist Hunt, and the less tangible metaphysics of exhaustion, which were all the more baffling for being conceptual and emotional rather than economic or political. There would be no New Deal to soften the demoralizing blows of the war and its aftermath, no Marshall Plan to shore up shattered mental economies, no fireside chats to reassure intellectuals that they had nothing to fear but fear itself. "Before what we now know," wrote Lionel Trilling in 1948, "the mind stops; the great psychological fact of our time which we all observe with baffled wonder and shame is that there is no possible way of responding to Belsen and Buchenwald. The activity of mind fails before the incommunicability of man's suffering."[21] Though safely this side of the devastations of war, which they experienced only in the newsreels and in their mind's eyes, the intellectuals at war's end wrote as if they stood among the ruins and were the dispossessed of Europe.

It is little wonder that a certain dissociation of sensibility should have become commonplace among postwar writers and thinkers. Much as the exploitation of the working class by the owners and bankers had dominated the moral imagination of the 1930s, the alienation of the modern man became morally central a decade later. Sociologists set out to explore the headwaters of alienation and map its course; psychiatrists and psychoanalysts had already begun, even before the war, to pronounce upon its implications for what Karen Horney had called "the neurotic personality of our time"; publishers got busy compiling anthologies of alienation to market en masse to the undergraduate; and novelists settled down with the grave new world in which all was robed in shades of existential gray, like Sloan Wilson's man in the flannel suit. Just consider the titles of popular books of the day: Saul Bellow's *Dangling Man* (1944) and *The Victim* (1947), Arthur Miller's *Death of a Salesman* (1949), Robert Linder's *Rebel without a Cause* (1944), David Riesman's *The Lonely Crowd* (1950), William Styron's *Lie Down in Darkness* (1951), Carson McCullers's *The Ballad of the Sad Café* (1951), Robert Lowell's *Lord Weary's Castle* (1946), Randall Jarrell's *Losses* (1948)—litanies all of modern distress and portraits of the American character divorced from nature, from work, and from the wellsprings of vitality within the self. If the effects of the Depression at the foot of the economic ladder preoccupied intellectuals to an exceptional degree in the 1930s, it was the depression at the top that would fascinate them in the next two decades.[22]

Depression was the affliction of choice for those intellectuals who only yesterday had championed the state's withering away. America's economic boom and political hegemony after the war guaranteed their isolation, as the emergence of an unprecedented consumer economy at home and the escalation of the Cold War in Europe cut the ground out from under their dreams of egalitarian socialism and popular front camaraderie. Europe's dramatic recovery, fueled by Marshall Plan dollars, meant new markets for American goods and fresh opportunities for investment abroad, while the shield of American power, codified by the Truman Doctrine and armed by NATO, promised political stability for economic growth in the West and a sound return on the invested dollar. The Great Depression had ended but the depression of the homeless radicals who had yearned for a different world only deepened, becoming all the more poignant for being so wholly out of phase with the new American power. Shadows of defeat fell across a landscape where all should have been bathed in coronas of victory and fulfillment. In the long run, the alternative that appealed to many was to sign on aboard the American ship of state and turn their energies to the vigorous promotion of values as they found them and the new prosperity as *it* began to find *them*. "The leisure of the theory class," as Daniel Bell called it, was not irrelevant to the conversion of the intellectuals in the postwar years, though it was scarcely the world story. For some, the pendulum swing of atonement brought them back to positions of the most pristine orthodoxy, even, indeed, to church and temple. But for most of those who saw themselves as writers and critics, the post-Marxist deconversions were gradual and tortured, and it was not until the *Partisan Review* symposium "Our Country and Our Culture," in 1952, that we find among the disarmed radicals a consensus of opinion favorable to the American century and to those values and institutions that had once been dismissed as "bourgeois democracy."[23] A tolerance for liberal democracy, a steady job, and a reasonable standard of living, even at the price of an economy mobilized for war, had to be nursed into existence through a decade of indecision, during which the mood of disillusionment was almost universal.

It is hardly to be wondered, therefore, that the figures who instructed earlier generations in rationalism or pragmatism or Marxism, and the habits of progressive optimism for which they spoke, were largely discarded for the philosophers of dislocation and the theoreticians of strangeness: Jaspers, Durkheim, Simmel, Kierkegaard, Sartre, Heidegger, and, especially, Kafka and Dostoevsky, whose exquisite disorientations were interpreted as harbingers of the new temper. As this sampling from the new pantheon suggests, the germinal ideas among American intellectuals in the post-Depression years were not of American patent at all, as the ebullient nativism of the 1930s ("Don't mourn for me boys. Organize.") was washed over by waves of gloomy and intricate European thought, skeptical about human nature and destiny ("Hell is other peo-

ple"), drenched in angst, promoting the tragic view of life, and intimat-
ing the existence of higher but frightfully obscure realities upon which
mere reason had no purchase. As industrial capital traversed the Atlantic
from west to east under the Marshall Plan, the bitter European ideas that
came out of the war were sent to America by return ship, sometimes
flying colors of French existentialism. America exported her victory in
the form of investment capital and motion pictures;[24] Europe exported
her experience, her terrible knowledge of devastation, and those attitudes that historian Judith Shklar has called "the romanticism of defeat."[25] For American intellectuals, Sartre and Camus stood for a stream
of experience that ran deeper than sunny native attitudes and cut closer
to the bone of man's ultimate fate. In the 1940s, one could scarcely open
an issue of any of the serious journals that kept a watch on international
letters—*Commentary, Partisan Review*—without stumbling across some
new interpretation of Kafka or imitation of Dostoevsky or lecture on the
crisis of reason or failure of nerve. In reading the literature of the period
or the major documents of sociology and social psychology, one would
be hard put to infer anything like widespread national self-esteem, or
even that we had won the war. Rather than an era of easy credit, social
advancement, increased leisure, the rapid expansion of the suburb and
the supermarket, one would see rather a time of anxiety, guilt, and
disorientation. One would infer, indeed, that we were a defeated nation.
As the lingering signs of the Depression appeared to have been eradi-
cated, at least in the expanding middle class, and as unemployment
decreased to the vanishing point of the structural margin, it was not
comfort, achievement, or pride that came to the fore in the documents
of our self-examination, but alienation; not the unparalleled boom in
sales but the death of the salesman.

In fiction, while naturalist and realist novels, camped on native
grounds and fed upon progressive militancy, did not fade immediately
from the lists, they gradually surrendered their cachet to writing that was
decidedly more European in its views and techniques, as, for example,
Norman Mailer's panoramic war novel *The Naked and The Dead* (1948),
which plundered Melville for American monomania and Dos Passos for
social anger and cinematic montage, was followed by an austere and
claustral *Barbary Shore* (1951), whose "existential" air of confinement
recalled Sartre's *Huis Clos*. Even Richard Wright, author of *Native Son*
(1940) and *Black Boy* (1945), yielded to the continent in the fifties with
The Outsider (1953), whose very title pays homage to Camus's *L'Etranger*.

The new hero of our literature showed little of the American optimism of effort, the pioneer spunk and Yankee know-how that sent Jay

Gatsby out in quest of the green light or the heroes of Odets, Michael Gold, and a hundred one-shot proletarians off to the strike lines, the meeting halls, or Union Square in the 1930s to resuscitate a flagging economy and wrest the future from the clutches of an afflicted capitalism. He was more likely to be impaled upon the past than lured forward by the future and thus was usually beaten before he started, like Arthur Miller's Willie Loman or Bernard Miller of Isaac Rosenfeld's novel *Passage From Home* or such orphans of a vanishing leftism as Lovett and McLeod of Mailer's *Barbary Shore* and the abundant shlemiels and shlemazels of Bernard Malamud's stories in which, in the 1950s, the widespread sense of impotence and resignation was distilled into a convenient symbol of the Jewish condition and therefore, by a logic that Malamud himself endorsed ("all men are Jews"), the very terms of modern existence. Here were Americans who believed in neither the green light nor the red, only in the broken heart that lay on the road to either.

It was from such a sense of crisis and unfocused emergency that the Jewish novel arose. Among the postwar books by Jews to strike the familiar note of isolation and drift were Saul Bellow's first novels, *Dangling Man* (1944) and *The Victim* (1947), Michael Seide's *The Common Thread* (1944), Isaac Rosenfeld's *Passage from Home* (1946) and his short stories, which were collected posthumously in *Alpha and Omega* (1966), Lionel Trilling's *The Middle of the Journey* (1947), Delmore Schwartz's stories in *The World Is a Wedding* (1948), Arthur Miller's *Death of a Salesman* (1949) and *After the Fall* (1964), Paul Goodman's *The Breakup of Our Camp* (1949) and *The Empire City* (published in 1959, it was Goodman's dreary *Gesamtwerk*, some fifteen years in the writing), Norman Mailer's *Barbary Shore* (1951) and *The Deer Park* (1955), Bernard Malamud's *The Natural* (1952) and *The Assistant* (1957), Herbert Gold's *The Man Who Was Not With It* (1954), Wallace Markfield's *To an Early Grave* (1964), and Meyer Liben's *Justice Hunger* (1967). Against such a background, Allen Ginsberg's *Howl* (1956), which is normally taken for a new departure in American poetry, looks like nothing so much as a hallucinated reprise of the Jewish blues that arose in the dark hours of the midforties.

It is easy to see why Jews should have become major importers and wholesalers of crisis and exhaustion after the war. They had more at stake in politics than did other Americans. The Jewish intellectuals, for one thing, had oversubscribed the coming revolution in the 1930s and were deeply shaken by the retrenchments they were obliged to declare afterwards. Morris Dickstein was not mistaken, in his survey of the postwar Zeitgeist, *Gates of Eden*, to read the founding mood of Jewish writing in the 1940s, with its chaste moralism and brooding introspection, as an atonement for Jewish revolutionism, though that view should be tempered by an awareness that the Jewish sense of vulnerability had warrant in catastrophic events, and that the retreat from revolutionism was fueled as much by grief as by guilt.[26] The shock administered by the Holocaust is in itself sufficient explanation of why the Jews, and especially the intellectuals, held themselves apart initially from American good cheer, even if they consistently availed themselves of the opportunities opened by economic expansion. America may have won the war in spectacular fashion, but the Jews had lost a culture and a history, and while as Americans they shared "our" victory, as Jews they were inconsolable in their defeat.

Even the terms of their being in America, which had turned out to be their haven and refuge—the best exile the Jews ever had—were called into question by events in both Europe and Palestine, which forced them to rethink the logic of assimilation that had governed their stance toward American society up through the 1930s. The slaughter of the Jews in Europe and the establishment of a Jewish state in Israel, bringing an end to nearly two millennia of exile, called for nothing less than a reformulation of Jewishness as an historical identity, and even cosmopolitan intellectuals who had either inherited a tradition of secular Jewishness or had personally called it quits with Judaism were not unaffected. Though American Jewish writers were slow to react thematically to those events—most of them did not write about the Holocaust or Israel—they were quick to respond symptomatically. Jewish writers began to symbolize the traumas of death and rebirth long before they began to examine the new realities. Indeed, in some cases, the momentous facts of contemporary Jewish history would not come to consciousness for a generation. Israel played no part in Saul Bellow's writing, for example, until the mid 1970s, when the chapters of *To Jerusalem and Back* began appearing in *The New Yorker*. But conscious or not, the great events had been absorbed and had lodged beneath the skin, to be experienced as a persistent and painful maladjustment.

The immediate postwar era was, then, a time of paradoxes, and the Jews responded paradoxically. Listening in upon this experience from the prospect of our own time, when this outburst of energy-in-anguish has largely exhausted itself, we may hear occasional rhapsodic notes in the elegiac music. The real depression of so many books shades off readily into the theater of despair, as readily as manifesto shades off into performance or *Dangling Man* shades off into *Herzog* or Mailer's *Barbary*

Shore into *Advertisements for Myself*. No one ever celebrated their own bewilderment or held their own tragic condition in higher esteem than did the Jewish intellectuals at the very nadir of their defeat. If some, like Issac Rosenfeld and Delmore Schwartz, eventually succumbed, unfulfilled, to the exhaustion of their powers, others—Goodman, Mailer, Trilling, Kazin, Bellow, Rahv—found the crisis paradoxically bracing. In the 1940s, it seems, one could aspire to be Franz Kafka.

3. The Aftermath of Socialism

TO CONSIDER the fate of those writers and intellectuals who started out in the thirties is to examine those paradigms of experience and belief that gave order to their lives and a collective identity to their generation: their initial embrace of radical ideas and progressive movements and their eventual disillusionment with both during the years roughly between 1936 and 1945, that is, between the first of the show trials in Moscow and the end of the Second World War. We recall such repentent ex-communists, fellow travellers, Trotskyists, and free-lance revolutionists as James Burnham, Irving Kristol, Will Herberg, Granville Hicks, Sidney Hook, Whittaker Chambers, Max Eastman, Max Shachtman, and John Dos Passos, whose headlong flights from revolutionism to reaction exemplified the panic and instability of those years.[1] So common was the experience that it would appear, in retrospect, to be the defining feature of the era's moral history and a living dramatization of Ignazio Silone's prophecy that the final struggle would be between the communists and the ex-communists. By the early 1950s, the class of '39, acting out rituals of atonement for sins both real and imagined, had assumed spokesmanship for the spirit of postwar deconversion that went by the name of Moral Realism or Crisis Theology or Realpolitik or Pluralism or Pragmatism or the End of Ideology. As we are yet reminded by the passions that can still be aroused by talk of the Hiss or Rosenberg trials or by the charges that continued to be traded even into the early 1980s by such veterans of the cultural Cold War as Lillian Hellman, Mary McCarthy, and Diana Trilling, there remain pockets of the intellectual life in America where one's moral credit is still computed from the year, even the month, in which one resigned from the Communist party or walked out of the John Reed Club or League of American Writers or let

32

it be known in the right places that one would no longer turn somersaults for the Soviet Union.[2]

Viewed from far enough away, this experience seems entirely unified, and many of the survivors continue to speak of it as *the* experience of *the* thirties or of *our* generation, as though it were a great collective saga with its own oral tradition—who said what to whom the day Zinoviev confessed—its own stations of the cross, and its own secularized myths of death and resurrection. But as we draw close to individual lives, the appearance of uniformity dissolves. The syndrome of pure and simple reaction was not the universal experience, which rarely traced a flawless arc from Union Square to the American Enterprise Institute. Not all postwar sentiment among retreating radicals Kristolized on the right, and not everyone who had once sworn solidarity with striking miners in Harlan County or subscribed to the Comintern's policy of united front from below or waged bitter factional wars over whether the Soviet Union should be regarded as a degenerated worker's state or a bureaucratic collectivist one later signed up for duty with the *Reader's Digest* or pled the case of the free world and its free markets in the pages of *Time, Life, Fortune, National Review, Reporter, Freeman, The Public Interest, Encounter* or *Commentary.*

More definitive of the prewar Left's fate than its eventual anticommunism was its decompositon. A comprehensive history of the great disillusionment would highlight just how complex and eccentric post-Marxist careers could be. It would point out that residuum of anarcho-pacifists who wrote for Dwight Macdonald's *Politics* in the 1940s and never did get around to supporting America's war effort. It would note the stubborn holdouts for solidarity with the Soviet Union who went underground on command in the 1950s and needed the invasion of Hungary and Krushchev's de-Stalinization speech in 1956 to drive home to them the bitter truth. It would feature Edmund Wilson, who passed through Marxism like a night train through the Finland Station on his way to becoming a Yankee curmudgeon. It would take account of the art critics Harold Rosenberg, Meyer Schapiro, and Clement Greenberg, who found more to sustain them in Klee, Michelangelo, Duchamp, or de Kooning than in the pronouncements of their generation's leading spokesmen. It would highlight the religious converts who genuflected to Earl Browder one day and Fulton Sheen the next. And it would give special attention, as this book shall, to the outpatients of culture who amended their enthusiasm for social progress by embracing Alienation or Psychoanalysis or Gestalt Psychology or Orgonomy or the Tragic

Sense of Life or The Will in Repose or whatever promising schemes for interior revitalization could be shored up against their ruins.

The retreat from radical allegiances fractured the intellectual life of a generation. In the first two postwar decades, no single issue or point of view could command the center of thought as the failures of capitalism had in the 1930s or the Vietnam War would in the 1960s. Even the momentous political trials of Alger Hiss in 1949 and Julius and Ethel Rosenberg in 1950 and 1951 rallied intellectuals into postures of combat only by stirring up their nostalgia for seeing Shelley plain and giving them momentary respite from the ambiguities of post-Marxist politics. Such a complication took place not because the postwar era marked the end of ideology; only Marxism gave signs of being depleted. What it lacked was the ruling idea and sense of common pursuit to give definition to its conflicts. Not even anticommunism, which served as a halfway house for the disenchanted, was ever a comprehensive world view, let alone a sufficient basis for a national politics. It never had a cogent program, save containment abroad and purification at home, and except for purposes of slander and self-advancement, it gave no more guidance to presidents than it did to municipal mayors, since little that matters in the routine operation of electoral politics or government at any level obeys its crude polarities. What are the respective communist and anti-communist (and anti-anticommunist) views on street sanitation, neighborhood redevelopment, nuclear power, sex education in the schools, the death penalty, the Federal Reserve Board, tax reform, nuclear power, water pollution, affirmative action, free trade and protectionism, the Islamic revolution, the PLO? (In Buffalo, where the politics are fiercely patriotic, communism takes a back seat to abortion, crime, utility rates, unemployment, and snow removal as the great bête noire at election time.) That prominent anticommunists these days have strong views on such issues has nothing to do with anticommunism as such. Anticommunism developed in America as a theology without doctrines, a faith without articles, giving it a pragmatic adaptability that positive ideologies invariably lack. That is why a resourceful opportunist like Richard Nixon could rise to power on public fears of domestic subversion and ideological contamination and, once in power, strike Metternichian deals with the Soviet Union, citing for domestic consumption the opportunities for American business, and open relations with China, citing the need for allies against the Soviet menace. Even for intellectuals, who esteem ideologies as sticks with which to beat one another, left anti-Stalinism, which became liberal anticommunism after the war, was a conundrum shot through with compromise, and no one could be surprised at how easily these anticommunists were outflanked and thrown into disarray in the 1950s by the more self-assured and resolutely anti-intellectual assaults upon communism spearheaded by HUAC, Senator Joseph McCarthy, and the campaign of big business to roll back the New Deal. When the liberal anticommunists regained their balance in the 1960s in time to make serious bids for power, it was not strictly as anticommunists at all but as antimodernists and gladiators of culture, taking up arms against the cultural threat they defined as the "adversary culture" or sometimes the "new class" which they, with their special treason-seeking radar, were uniquely equipped to detect.*

But if anticommunism as a world view did not provide post-Marxist intellectuals with a secure base of operations, it was, for two decades, the soil in which social thought invariably took root. "The Cold War," as Alan Trachtenberg has reminded us, "was an inescapable fact of life, implicated as much in the spectacular development of technologies of warfare and of communication and transportation as in the unprece-dented concentration of power in government agencies, especially those concerned with military affairs and with espionage. . . . The picture of a world divided between 'us,' 'free' and democratic, and 'them,' total-itarian and 'godless,' seemed unshakable, as was the corollary of a need for military strength, preparedness, vigilance."[3] What has to be remem-bered about the Cold War mind is its apocalyptic pessimism, the convic-tion that Armageddon is just around the corner, if it hasn't happened already, not with a bang but a whimper. While the United States escaped from World War II virtually unscathed and with unprecedented power and responsibility on the world scene, the immediate postwar years had brought home sharply the burden of that power in a series of shocks that undercut our élan and turned it into doubt, suspicion, and no small degree of self-laceration. The closing of the Soviet noose around Eastern Europe (to be blamed on Yalta), the fall of China to communism (to be blamed on the State Department), the Russian explosion of an atomic bomb in 1949 (to be blamed on espionage), and the palpable threats to

---

*Among those for whom anticommunism *did* become a sufficient politics may be counted a few ex-revolutionists who had tempered their steel in the faction fights of the Marxist Left and had brought with them into the conservative camp the hashmarks of their Realpolitik: an intolerance of complexity, a casual acceptance of "necessary" violence, a taste for abstract justifications of actual outrages, a contempt for liberals (including social democrats, democratic centrists, Mensheviks, libertarians, anarchists, and Amnesty Inter-national types), a flair for personal invective, and a low capacity for self-reflection. The fondness for the sword once evidenced in the defense of the Red Army against the sailors at Kronstadt comes in handy when Argentine torturers and Guatemalan death squads need explaining to uncomprehending liberals. Traversing the political stage from left to right they never wavered in their contempt for liberal qualms or their faith in *raison d'état*. They just changed *états*.

Western interests in Greece, Berlin, and Korea brought the welcome news that not only would our celebration be brief but that our triumph might well have been an apparition, a dream of victory from which we had just awakened to the truth of defeat. Though Americans were no strangers to international power politics before the war, they experienced for the first time the exposure of world leadership and the vulnerability of being the bull's-eye on someone else's coordinates.

The American response to these traumas took two distinct forms that were linked historically but not, it seems, inevitably. One was the garrison state. Unlike the earlier postwar era, America did not demobilize; rather it retooled for the next struggle, putting the American economy on a permanent wartime footing. In diplomatic terms, the new reality took shape behind the Truman Doctrine, which elevated containment into the cardinal principle of American diplomacy, and the NATO and SEATO alliances, which formalized and armed the borders of the "free world." But for the first time in American history, diplomatic warfare took on a distinct ideological coloring, as the potential for ideas as weapons finally sank in and intellectuals in unprecedented numbers were recruited to oversee the new arsenal that was being geared up to meet the ideological challenge of communism. That Jews—to return to our subject—should have figured prominently in this mobilization should surprise no one.

It was internally, however, that the strains of the Cold War first began to show and the term Cold War itself became synonymous with a climate of fear. The blossoming of domestic anticommunism and the emergence of the political bounty hunter as power broker in American politics cut deep into American life, transforming the international state of tension into a domestic state of nerves. The campaigns of the House Committee on Un-American Activities in academia and Hollywood, the wild crusades of Senator McCarthy which culminated in a quixotic assault on the U.S. Army, the jagged ascent of Richard Nixon from Orange County freedom fighter to United States president and "leader of the free world," the trials of Alger Hiss and the Rosenbergs were all symptomatic features of the moral climate in which Americans assaulted other Americans in fearful and often cynical campaigns to gain leverage in domestic power struggles.

II

So pervasive were Cold War assumptions in the first two decades after the war and so great their cultural authority that we are amazed in turning to the literary record of the era to find that the Cold War is not much engaged. Certainly we find nothing comparable to the wholesale radical effusions of the 1920s and 1930s, when writers took up causes as naturally as they took to their typewriters, as though protest were the very charter of the imagination. That the wave of anticommunism that swept America should have left us no major body of imaginative literature to document its passing is one of the curious sidelights of American literary politics. We speak readily of Cold War politics or Cold War scholarship or Cold War rationality, this last a manner of thinking about "the free world" and "the iron curtain countries" in terms of opposing conceptions of human nature, strategies of containment, and deep fears of nuclear annihilation. But where is America's Cold War literature? The fact is that American writers produced nothing that cut as deeply into the popular revulsion against communism or the intellectuals' muted revolt against anticommunism as did their counterparts in Europe, where the experience of political ideas was concrete and immediate and etched into the very grain of political and social life. There is no denying that America produced no political writing to rival Arthur Koestler's *Darkness at Noon,* George Orwell's *Animal Farm* and *1984,* and Aldous Huxley's *Brave New World.* Even Lionel Trilling's *The Middle of the Journey,* in which Whittaker Chambers made his debut in fiction as a symbol of postradical penance before he appeared in public life as Alger Hiss's persecutory conscience, typifies the American climate of reticence in raising the plane of discourse from the political to the metaphysical, arguing, as Trilling would confirm in a belated introduction to the novel in 1975, that the refusal to face up to death, not a weakness for totalitarianism, is the moral failing of the progressive mind. As for other Jewish writers, it is well known, and in some circles much lamented, that the most gifted of them turned away from the great events of Jewish and world history and piled their art in isolation, permitting the historical novel to become the exclusive domain of the book-club middlebrows. In emptying themselves of historical reflection and the data of social experience, the Jewish writers were indistinguishable from other American novelists. In the atmosphere of brooding and withdrawal that came to dominate the 1940s, much of the best fiction gave little suggestion that it was an era of turbulence or that a major reshaping of the globe was under way. "Consider the image of political man with which [John] Dos Passo, [Robert Penn] Warren and [Lionel] Trilling end their novels," Irving Howe was to observe in his book *Politics and the Novel.*

> Ben Compton, a shattered revolutionary, walking the streets of New York, without belief or hope or even self-regard. Jack Burden, asking himself

how he could place his trust in a puny dictator like Willie Stark and wondering, in the total isolation that has overcome him, what is to become of his life. John Laskell, waiting alone in a railroad station to begin the middle of his journey, his pieties and passions behind him, and little before him but spiritual exhaustion and a bleak integrity. The image raised by all these critical scenes is one of isolation, an isolation that a wounded intelligence is trying desperately to transform into the composure of solitude.[4]

The direction taken after the war by The Novel as an historically evolving genre, with its exalted patrimony of a Great Tradition, its overbearing mystique of embodying The Modern Temper, and, in the starstruck aftermath of Hemingway, its promises of money, manhood, and fame, exercised a profound influence on young writers who yearned to be novelists before they knew what, if anything, they had to say. Encouraged by the rapid expansion of an academic criticism that issued claims for the novel as an independent, organic growth with its own laws and values, its own culture and cultus (and thereby subject exclusively to interpretation by the trained acolytes of "English"), writers dreamed of ascent into that empyrean of the written word, The Great Tradition, in order, as T. S. Eliot had promised in a tantalizing formulation, to revise the tradition by their very contribution to The Novel. Such heady visions of power and quasi-ecclesiastical investiture through the mere act of writing a book could only serve to heighten the disparity between the serious novel and the popular, the one oriented toward the history of its own development, and the other toward the contemporary market for daydreams. Though the division between fiction as art and fiction as business has been a feature of the literary landscape since the nineteenth century, there have always been writers, from Dickens to Hemingway and Fitzgerald, who commanded both worlds by some combination of superior imagination and social intelligence. They gratified, in the same gesture, both the vanguard taste for irony and *le mot juste* and the common reader's desire for romance and instruction. But in the immediate postwar decades, without a Hemingway or a Fitzgerald to stoke the popular imagination while keeping critics busy explicating their deeper strategies, the serious novel withdrew from the field of social analysis and polemic carved out by the tradition of American realism after Howells. Only in the popular novel and its mass market shadow, the *Reader's Digest Condensed Book,* did what Trilling disparagingly called "the liberal imagination" live on, and we may learn something about the life cycle of progressive realism by studying the careers of left-wing realists like Irwin Shaw and Howard Fast, who paralyed their youthful educations in militancy and social realism into successful book-club sinecures, or from the radicals who ascended from Brooklyn to Hollywood where, until the great purge, they prospered as contract workers, turning out melodramas by the reel, their indentured status as semiskilled laborers at routine tasks made bearable by their extravagant salaries and lavish dachas in Brentwood. It is in this brief heyday of the left-wing screen-writers and book-club superstars that we have our most vivid illustration of Harold Rosenberg's remark that "collapsed ideologies are not blown away by the winds . . . [but] spread throughout society and take the form of popular culture."[5]

Advanced fiction, by contrast, in failing to address itself with any enthusiasm to the politics of the age, took a back seat to both popular fiction and the literature of fact, especially autobiography. Autobiography was to the post-Marxist turn of mind what documentary journalism had been to the Marxist: the medium that best conveyed its essential drama. In the 1930s, eyewitness testimony and documentary photography gave form and voice to the spirit of national self-inquiry that gripped America. As the title of Margaret Bourke-White and Erskine Caldwell's documentary of the Depression put it baldly, *You Have Seen Their Faces.* Reality was defined in mass terms, and the failure of American institutions was calculated in mass distress. In the forties, when attention shifted away from social conditions toward private motives, a writer's self-inquiry was likely to resolve itself in litanies of regret for his misspent radical youth. At the theological moment when unemployment counted for less than regret, the *fact* ceased to be social and statistical and became instead personal and spiritual: *you have seen our souls.*

As the camera eye yielded authority to the confessional, the era's typical book became the apostate's memoir, the story, formulaic in its redundancy, of how a neophyte in revolt, outraged by social injustice, passionate for striking a blow against the captains of industry, and dismissive of ordinary caveats, was lured into the Communist party by promises of justice, bread, freedom, and twentieth-century Americanism, only to find himself, not a modern-day Tom Paine standing shoulder to shoulder with a phalanx of minutemen, but a party apparatchik, fearfully carrying out orders in an atmosphere thick with suspicion. Or worse, in extreme situations, he found himself a traitor to his country. Disillusioned by some spectacular betrayal, of which the era provided many, he "broke" and sought expiation for his crimes through a lurid public recantation of them. Typical books of the era were Louis Budenz's *This Is My Story* (1947), Granville Hicks's *Where We Came Out* (1954), Elizabeth Bentley's *Out of Bondage* (1952), Whittaker Chambers's *Witness* (1952), and Freda Utley's *Lost Illusions* (1948). Benjamin Gitlow, once head of the CPUSA and twice its candidate for vice-president of the United States, found the exercise of confession so bracing that he did it twice, with *I Confess* (1940) and *The Whole of Their Lives* (1948). If the era's classic text is Richard Crossman's *The God That Failed* (1949), with its depositions by Arthur Koestler, Ignazio Silone, Richard Wright, André Gide, Louis Fischer, and Stephen Spender, its monument is the record of the House Committee on Un-American Activities, an archive of persecution, submission, and remorse so vast that Eric Bentley's digest of it, *Thirty Years of Treason* (1971), is almost a thousand pages long.[6] Throughout the first two postwar decades, such affidavits of deconversion, in which the mythos of sin and redemption was not only the dominant scheme of personal values but the very definition of human nature ("we are all guilty"), were the routine fare of the reading public and were even brutally institutionalized in the doxologies of allegiance that former communists and fellow travellers were compelled to pronounce before HUAC. How was mere fiction to compete with the daily *apologia pro vita sua* in the morning papers, right out of St. Augustine and Cardinal Newman, what with J. Edgar Hoover and the Inquisiton waiting in the wings?*

Philip Rahv would complain in 1952, "The rout of the left-wing movement has depoliticalized literature—which is not necessarily a bad thing in itself if the political motive had been simply not abandoned but creatively displaced by a root-idea of a different order. No such idea having emerged so far, what is to be observed now is a kind of detachment from principle and fragmentation of the literary life."[7] This detachment made itself known at the outset by a chastening of rhetoric, a scaling down of ambitions, a narrowing of the dramatic *mise en scène*, an overvaluation of precious effects and velleities of feeling, a moral austerity, and a stress on the isolated self in crisis and the family in peril.** Despite the hectorings of such critics as Archibald MacLeish, Lewis Mumford, Van Wyck Brooks, Bernard DeVoto, J. Donald Adams, and

*When Louis Budenz, one-time managing editor of *The Daily Worker* and later anticommunism's witness *extraordinaire*, published his memoir, *This Is My Story*, he dedicated the book "To Mary Immaculate: Patroness of Our Beloved Land," as if to announce that henceforth Catholicism was to be twentieth-century Americanism.

**The sober realism of postwar fiction was very much in the temper of a time that found a chastened Granville Hicks confessing, in his book *Where We Came Out*, that he would be "better occupied with jobs close at hand than with grandiose programs for remaking society," and applying his efforts to such hometown projects as improved fire protection, schools, and libraries. The literary counterpart to that spirit was the fiction that preferred whispers to cries, small town or suburban settings to large cities, lives on the domestic scale to those on the heroic.

John Chamberlain, who seized upon wartime fears and postwar uncertainties to denounce the indulgence that had given us modernism *and*
proletarianism (they were twice-beleaguered), writers who had had their
fill of rebellion in the 1930s were largely reluctant to genuflect before
free enterprise or the pioneer spirit of Yankee pluck and know-how or
Brook's version of the "life drive."[8] The Brooks-MacLeish thesis, as it
came to be called, which urged writers to think positively, support the
"life drive," and boost America, had no takers, so far as one can tell,
among creative artists, save possibly MacLeish himself, though the campaign was scarcely helped by Brooks's proposal in the late thirties that
"committees be formed in towns to make house-to-house collections of
objects made in Germany, which might be destroyed in public bonfires"
to show Hitler that "democracy has something to say."[9] Even the well-
orchestrated endeavors of the American Committee for Cultural Freedom in the 1950s to mobilize literary opinion behind the cultural Cold
War left no mark on our fiction comparable to the one it left on our
journalism and criticism.* To be sure, when Saul Bellow's Augie March
announced in 1950, "I am an American, Chicago born," he was embracing a mood of celebration that had been prepared for him by the
breaking of socialism and the waning of alienation, but that hardly
amounted to a belated acquiescence to Brooks-MacLeish. Bellow
marched in nobody's brigade; like Augie March, he was too intent on
going at things as he had taught himself, free-style.

Calling novelists to duty is a favorite sport of critics. A critic of our own
era, Morris Dickstein, taking a liberal stand on the social duties of fiction
while concurring with MacLeish et al. that it *has* such duties, has charged
that after the war "the literary intellectuals, while maintaining the cult of
alienation, simply abandoned politics to pursue private myths and fantasies, to devote their work to the closet intensities of the isolated self or
isolated personal relationships."[10] Though Dickstein conducts his argu-
ments with considerably more skill and ingenuity than did Brooks in
1941—Brooks's latter-day crankiness lacked entirely the tang and concision of his youthful radicalism—and approaches literature from another point on the political compass, his assumptions are wholly in the

---

*This vigorous and widespread campaign to inject a note of celebration into fiction and
poetry can be virtually dismissed since its effects were negligible. The novel after socialism
would have been largely what it was without all the noisy cheerleading from the sidelines.
But as an omen of the crusade for political conformity that descended upon the entertainment industry in the 1950s, where the studio system and heavy capital investment made
artists vulnerable, it was ominous. In entertainment, the assault of *Kulturbolschewismus* was
entirely successful, thanks to the faintheartedness of moguls and investors eager to sacrifice whatever or whoever stood in the way of profits.

spirit of Brooks's charge that "to think of literature as merely literary, as something that is dervied from literature, seems to me utterly frivolous." But there Dickstein parts company with the literary legionnaires and joins in solidarity with Malcolm Cowley, who lamented in *The Literary Situation,* "In these days of investigations run wild, Americans are learning to be timid about expressing their opinions, especially if these are in the least heretical. The result is that we are now reading novels by intellectuals, for intellectuals, about supposedly intellectual or at least well-educated characters, in which not a single intelligent notion is expressed about the world in which we live."[11]

The Cowley-Dickstein thesis has become by now something of a critical standard: after the war, it is widely agreed, writing did indeed shrink from the more strident and ambitious forms of social assertion. But one might add in extenuation that neither guilt nor cowardice need be held entirely responsible for that. Factors native to the imagination were also at work. The imagination is not obedient to conventional reasoning or mindful of universally perceived threats, even when novelists themselves share the common apprehensions. The very refusal of modern art to serve as an accessory to public mobilization is the very charter of its modernity. Moreover, the political content of art and the sources of its passion are not always available in rationally stated or dramatically rendered forms. They may find their expression in images or moods arising from the core of the writer's being, which are suffused throughout the writing as an incandescence of language or a darkening of mood and style. Alfred Kazin speaks of "the marginal suggestiveness which in a great writer always indicates those unspoken reserves, that silent assessment of life, that can be heard below and beyond the slow marshaling of his thought."[12] Whatever else it may be, fiction is not normally a catechism that gives firm answers to direct questions. Ideology usually enters it obliquely, or through modulations of tone and mood, those primal syllogisms of the inner life that imply everything and specify nothing.

The new fiction, which Cowley called "a tidy room in bedlam" and Dickstein characterizes in a fine and pointed phrase as "anguish hemmed in by form," was also, in its circumspection, a fiction of power, propelled by inner dynamisms that were largely hidden from view but capable of effects quite out of proportion to their manifest plots and situations. When the thread of connection between literature and social realism began to wear thin at the end of the thirties, literature set out on a course of self-examination to find out by what means it could fill the void left by the dissolution of a firm social picture. And, being thrown back on its own resources, it became both more introspective and more literary, or as the jargon of our time now puts it, more "intertextual." Postwar writers tended to look less to common social experience for themes and more to other literature, especially to continental writing in which they recognized anticipations of their own disillusionment and indecisiveness. Thus they appropriated the great European moderns, Dostoevsky, Kafka, Proust, Joyce, as well as their own contemporaries, Sartre and Camus in particular. The immediate result of this turn to European models was a heightened sense of craft and a corresponding shrinking of the social panorama, a surrender of scope and social purpose for depth. It was the recovery of modernism, no longer as an adventure but as a tradition—indeed, as a hallowed cannon of texts—that marked postwar fiction. Insofar as the Jewish novel began to gain notice as something new on the horizon by the close of the 1940s, it is largely due to its absorption of modernist ideas and New Critical notions of what fiction ought to be: severe, private, symbolic, brittle. If we are inclined to belabor the new novelists for failing to challenge the political currents of the time, we could characterize their modernization as simply a politics of retreat, a failure of nerve cleverly disguised as a strategy of silence, exile, and cunning. But we do so only at the cost of misconstruing the forces at play about the literature and within the writers. It strikes me as more generous to see this shift in sensibility as a politics, and in a way a poetics, of shock, in which the most pervasive fears and desires of the writers are not abandoned but registered as trauma rather than as proposition.

In fact, if postwar Jewish modernism, in whose earliest guises the new stringencies of form are obeyed, had a consistent aesthetic character at the very outset, it was this self-conscious exhibition of Prufrockian diffidence: it did not dare to eat a peach. Though the best of the Jewish writers would eventually change their minds about this fastidiousness of style and the conspicuous alienation for which it stood, Jewish modernism first comes into view in Saul Bellow's first two novels, *Dangling Man* and *The Victim,* the stories and poems of Delmore Schwartz, and the early stories of Isaac Rosenfeld, Michael Seide, Meyer Liben, and Bernard Malamud as a fiction whose torments are imperfectly sequestered behind a code of reticence. Bellow's Joseph in *Dangling Man* speaks disparagingly of his era as one of hard-boileddom, and though he pretends to break through that code to a more supple and personal form of expression, in the end he proves as hard-boiled as anyone. The stiffness and formality of much of this writing, whose deeper agitations are largely unspoken but perpetually symbolized, constitutes a poetics of stifled fear and rage. Passions, political or otherwise, do not follow ideas into the dustbin of history when decades change and eras come to a close; they go underground where, as Freud said of repressed wishes, they proliferate in the dark. In a fiction of banished terrors, what is most overdetermined is likely to be most understated. In such a writing, it is the repressed that commands attention, and when we try to interpret individual instances of anguish hemmed in by form, it makes a good deal of difference whether we are more attentive to the anguish or more taken by the form.

III

> "In their vulnerable position of exposure and deracination, Jews have frequently proved to be the modernists par excellence, but, at least in some notable instances, they retain a lingering suspicion that the whole dramatic agony of modernity is not worth the candle, that there is something perhaps bogus and certainly futile in the effort to be authentically modern through a heroism of the imagination."
>
> —Robert Alter, *Defenses of the Imagination*

In reviewing the literary record of the first postwar decades, we would automatically single out for special consideration the converts to the inner life, because the artistic by-products of their conversions were particularly rich: much of what was vital in American writing after the war came down in the fertile precipitate of ideas and attitudes released into their thought by the chemistry of socialism on the wane. Yet I call them converts to the inner life advisedly, since such emphasis upon private experience as one finds in the early fiction of Bellow, Rosenfeld, Schwartz, Malamud, and the Norman Mailer of *Barbary Shore* and *The Deer Park* is richly interfused with social consciousness. Turn inward these writers most certainly did; though unlike the symbolists and modernists whom they looked to for lessons in how to charm the unconscious into speech, they did not lock themselves up in Axel's castle. Not for them the oozy synesthesia of *La Nausée* or the Freudian psychodramatics of *Ulysses*. They were unmoved by dissolving perspectives and infinite regresses. They proved to be the most circumspect of modernists. While cheering the rebellious imperatives of the alienated self and adopting the techniques of symbolism and myth that were the formal counterparts of their mood of recoil, they also paid careful attention to the world they anathematized. We can scarcely mistake Bernard Malamud's grocery stores or Saul Bellow's rooming houses or the Brownsville streets of Alfred Kazin's memoirs for the indeterminate or parodic worlds of vanguard fiction. These writers had buckled on the reality principle as securely as one buckles on a seat belt.

In such writing, the harsh world of conditions, exploited with dogmatic fervor by novelists of an earlier decade, is not forsaken for the lush foliage of the dark interior—the flowers of evil—but given an extra degree of resonance. Reality is spiritualized without being dematerialized. It shimmers and becomes, at times, almost intolerably vivid. Such writers pioneered a realism beyond Marx, though not, it seems, beyond Dostoevsky, for even as they flirted with depths beyond what reason alone could countenance, cheering Dostoevsky's underground man and his insistence that two plus two *could* make five if one willed it, they clung fast to a realism that was too deeply rooted to be overthrown by merely literary passions. The postwar Jewish writers favored the self-consciousness of Kafka or Joyce to that of Rimbaud, a self-consciousness haunted by history, not overwrought nerves, whose interior life contained both a social dimension and a political agenda. Saul Bellow's *Dangling Man* and *The Victim,* books so pointedly Russian and dismal, are early instances of a world view that treats the inner life as a theater of *social* drama. Norman Mailer's *Barbary Shore,* with its imaginary rooming houses with real Trotskyists in them, could have been that generation's signature book had it dealt more skillfully with its materials.

The lessons that socialism had taught the Jewish writers about the material foundations of reality, which they absorbed in copious drafts even as they grew skeptical about Marxist calls for a workers' international and socialist appeals for nationalization of productive capital, were appended to the lessons of their own working-class upbringing. They made much of the thick coils of environment and the power of circumstances. Socialism taught them little that childhood poverty had not taught better, that one did not always have choices. Without the shields of money or caste or old boychik connections to defend them against the harsher realities of life, they grew up with a profound respect for the power of property and institutions and a finely tuned receptivity to the weight and solidity of the circumstances in which life is carried on. They never forgot what the Depression taught them: that the irreducible key to life in America was money, and that there was no shame in joining the struggle and battling your way to the top. "What made Sammy run," observes Irving Howe, "was partly that his father and his father's father had been bound hand and foot."[13] The Jewish writers' fathers had fled from pogroms in Galicia and service to the czar in Russia to wind up in

America behind a cart or a counter or a table piled high with piecework. They had exchanged the ghettoes of racial oppression for those of economic necessity. It was a step upward of a sort, though in the early years you had to be a skilled opportunist or a Hegelian (from such misery as this must come the synthesis) to see the lower East Side as a marked improvement in your worldly position. The Jewish writers grew up with the economics of scarcity, the only economics they knew: their first paychecks as writers, in some instances, would come from the WPA's Federal Writers' Project in the late 1930s. The world was very much with them, or against them as the case may be, and the ethic of achievement in which they were steeped as thoroughly as their grandfathers were steeped in Talmud and Torah left no room for aristocratic sighs of *contemptus mundi*. How could they reject the modern world when they had scarcely been uptown to catch a glimpse of it? The world to be savored in all its particularity and strangeness was all the more precious for being available to them largely through books, which served as their port of entry into the exotic realms of American manners and morals.

These sons of peddlers and garment workers found a haven in the library, where the great world, as a vast panorama of books, poured out its secrets to them, and they learned to cherish the intricacy of its manners, the strangeness of its rites, the elegance of its decor. As Alfred Kazin recalls,

> "For almost five years I had worked toward the book [*On Native Grounds*] in the great open reading room, 315, of the New York Public Library, often in great all-day bouts of reading that began when the place opened at nine in the morning and that ended only at ten at night. . . . Year after year I seemed to have nothing more delightful to do than sit much of the day and many an evening at one of those great golden tables acquainting myself with every side of my subject. Whenever I was free to read, the great Library seemed free to receive me."[14]

There it was, in the grand chambers of the public library, amid the chronicles of a world that was hidden from them in fact but revealed to them in spirit, that these Jews discovered life outside the ghetto to be as rich in customs and folkways, in taste and order, as the one within. There a young Alfred Kazin learned to write as confidently of the gilded parlors and panelled boardrooms he had never seen as he would *only later* of the Brownsville streets on which he still lived. Philip Rahv would discover, in the Jackson Square Public Library (which F. W. Dupee referred to as "Rahv's alma mater"), an affinity with Henry James that would prove more durable than his fading passion for Karl Marx, while

Lionel Trilling would discover, in Columbia's Low Library, a mind as intricate and subtle, solid and "Hebraic," as his own: Matthew Arnold. Culture was their romance.

The spirit that animated their writing, fiction and criticism alike, was the spirit of total surrender to canonical texts, as the library replaced the synagogue, Western history displaced biblical lore, and the novel came to do service for the Torah. The word is overdrawn, as if it were holy writ. "There was something about the vibrating empty rooms early in the morning," says Kazin of the Public Library, "light falling through the great tall windows, the sun burning the smooth tops of the golden tables as if they had been freshly painted—that made me restless with the need to grab up every book, press into every single mind right there on the open shelves."[15] Is this library not a temple? Has Kazin not been at prayer? Not for such young men as this the affected languors of the well-bred or the despairs of the sated. Busy as they were absorbing whatever these books could tell them about history and culture, they gave themselves no time to become a lost generation. Lamenting the modern wasteland was strictly a pastime for Ivy League alumni.

How much of this secular transcendence is a residue of the God-intoxicated Hasidism of their grandparents, exalting the splendor of this earth as the handiwork of divinity, is difficult to say, for there are lines of force in this writing that are difficult to trace with any assurance and which the writers themselves may hardly be conscious of. The best one can claim with any assurance is that the Hasidic spirit seems to insinuate itself into the writing of Bellow, Rosenfeld, Kazin, and Fiedler, though it commonly admits indebtedness to Whitman and Emerson rather than the Bal Shem Tov. Bellow's Moses Herzog, in a phrase borrowed from the French philosopher Jean Wahl, speaks of "transcendence down-ward" as his personal aesthetic, and it was an aesthetic that captured many of Bellow's contemporaries who, bereft of all traditional forms of spirituality, could not leave the spirit alone and brought it into the home as a household god. Even Lionel Trilling, that patriot of evanescence and apprentice to Arnold, Freud, and Hegel, acknowledged in two of his most influential essays in *The Liberal Imagination* that class and money were basic to the novel. "[The novel] tells us about the look and feel of things, how things are done and what things are worth and what they cost. . . . Every situation in Dostoevski, no matter how spiritual, starts with a point of social pride and a certain number of rubles."[16] To be sure, Trilling was characterizing the novel in its great nineteenth-century incarnation and not the fiction of his contemporaries, which had less of a taste for class, institutions, and the bric-a-brac of traditional cultures. It was the nineteenth-century novel, with its thickness of social texture and density of moral implication, that Trilling found congenial to his own brand of moral intelligence, in no small measure because the great social drama of the novel, the drama of class conflict and class mobility, bore directly upon the social drama of his generation of Jews: the movement from one social class and cultural milieu to another.

Yet at the very moment Trilling was promulgating such views, to speak of money, class, and social pride was already passé in an atmosphere dominated by the asocial methodologies of the New Criticism. Not only did that smack of the shopworn litanies of the 1930s, but it hearkened back to outmoded patterns of social conflict, like the combat between a prosperous and self-satisfied bourgeois class and the restive young artists who rebel against it in the name of higher values: truth, art, the life of the senses, the uncreated conscience of their race. Not only had middle-class authority over the terms of culture been fatally undermined by a half-century of modernist assault, but the educated portions of the middle class had even gone over the rebellion and come out from behind their masks of power and privilege to recite in unison the last word in alienation: *we are all ill*. Yet it is precisely the *backward* note in Trilling's criticism, his consistent allusion to the material solidity of a life founded upon tradition and property, that is his trademark, as it is that of his generation of Jewish intellectuals. Having imported the corrosive spirits of Kafka, Dostoevsky, Freud, and Marx into American letters, the New York intellectuals maintained an untimely interest in social forms and values that were being undercut by the very writers they championed. Their sense of conflict and revolt belonged to the nineteenth century as did their image of the whole life. It might be said of the Jewish writers that they established their credentials as moderns by grounding them-selves firmly in the last century—in Tolstoy, Chekhov, Arnold, Mill, Twain, Melville—heeding the example, in this as in so much else, of their Yankee paterfamilias, Edmund Wilson. "It was as though he came into being with the steam engine," recalled Mary McCarthy of Philip Rahv. "For him, literature began with Dostoevsky and stopped with Joyce, Proust, and Eliot; politics began with Marx and Engels and stopped with Lenin. He was not interested in Shakespeare, the classics, Greek city states; and he despised most contemporary writing and contemporary political groups. . . ."[17]

In our age of Beckett, Borges, Burroughs, Robbe-Grillet, Nabokov, and the fifty-seven varieties of French critical theory that sanctify the more splendid alienations and boost the "decentered universe" and the *"toujours déjà"* as our birthright, the New York intellectuals by and large are not to be found among the advance men for future shock or the metaphysicians of the void. They constitute an intelligentsia as opposed to an avant-garde, upholding the name of reason in public life above all. "When the intelligentsia turns its attention, or renders homage, to a work of art," observes Renato Poggioli, "it almost always functions in terms of ideological adhesion, that is to say, it attaches itself to content."[18] Or, as Saul Bellow has complained, a bit disingenuously one feels, "Art in the twentieth century is more greatly appreciated if it is directly translatable into intellectual interests, if it stimulates ideas, if it lends itself to discourse. Because intellectuals do not like to suspend themselves in works of the imagination. They prefer to talk."[19] Largely averse to formalism in all its aspects, the Jewish writers in America, none more persistently than Bellow himself, have continued to devote themselves to reason, reality, and discourse, and to produce a fiction and a criticism that brood over questions of social ambition, social justice, moral judgment, sexual conflict, duty, and guilt, as though the avant-garde had not dismissed them as ephemeral or indeterminate or, worst of all, irredeemably bourgeois. Where among any of the *Partisan Review* critics, for all their youthful campaigns for rebellion and modernism, does one find a taste for the Romantic rebel described by Rimbaud as *"le grand malade, le grand criminel, le grand maudit, et le suprême savant"*?[20] They refused to let go of this world and persisted in wrestling with it because, ineluctably, it was there.

IV

The 1940s did produce one notable exception to this rule, though one that confirms the Weltanschauung shared by the rest: Delmore Schwartz, the only poet to penetrate the *Partisan Review* inner circle and the one writer of that generation in whom the waters of modernism ran clear. Unlike the others, he had no tolerance for the drag and friction of daily living, for what E. M. Forster once called "the world of telegrams and anger," though in the end he suffered more telegrams and anger than any of them. He had no politics to speak of, no inherited cultural baggage he would not gladly jettison, and little more than a midsummer night's dream of history. His imagination lacked the specific gravity of experience and locale, and his romance of origins, no less strong than that of his contemporaries, lacked the grit and vitality of a Yiddish past and ghetto childhood; it was entirely a family romance in the Freudian sense, looking no farther back than his own lamentable birth or, as in his famous story, "In Dreams Begin Responsibilities," the dark hour of his parents' courtship. Having thrown over the ballast of all that was solid and circumscribed, he sought to ground himself in poetry alone, which turned out to be a little like touching down on a cloud. He wrote endless epic poems and verse tragedies about himself, their manner as conspicuously Miltonic as their matter was conspicuously neurotic. He even kept a journal in blank verse, as if to remind himself that nothing less than *Paradise Lost* was the model of his own tragic passage through this veil of tears. In the end, his only anchor was the guilt that bore him down entirely, drawing him to the profession of poetry as to a priesthood of the guilty, but giving him neither doctrine nor experience on which to train his agony. He had nothing of Baudelaire's contempt or Joris-Karl Huysmans's voluptuary metaphysics or Proust's genius for reverie or Eliot's scholarship or Joyce's love and hate of Ireland. He declared himself daily for Beauty and Art, but never knew quite how to conjure up either except to invoke Pegasus, broadcast his misery, and wait for the reviewers to anoint him troubadour of misery.

> I am to my own heart merely a serf
> And follow humbly as it glides with autos
> And come attentive when it is too sick,
> In the bad cold of sorrow much too weak,
> To drink some coffee, light a cigarette
> And think of summer beaches, blue and gay.
> I climb the sides of buildings just to get
> Merely a gob of gum, all that is left
> Of its infatuation of last year.
> Being the servant of incredible assumption,
> Being to my own heart merely a serf.[21]

"A poet shouldn't be that unhappy," Auden said of him, but, then, misery was his very charter as a poet, his precise and sole claim to the calling.[22]

A photo of Schwartz in James Atlas's biography shows him in his twenty-fifth year standing by a table piled high with his notebooks, his collected works, one would guess. One hand is draped with studied languor over a small stack of books—presumably *Oedipus, Hamlet,* and *Werther*—the other holds up a plaster bust of Homer for his dreamy contemplation. The young Narcissus is lost in thought: the tragic sense of life is upon him, and his eyes do not meet Homer's blind gaze except perhaps in infinity where, for all we know, blind gazes, like parallel lines, intersect. On the facing page is a photograph whose tortured narcissism is blunter: Delmore staring intently into a mirror at an afflicted Delmore, "the furtive / Fugitive, looking backward . . . his / Ghost in the mirror, his shameful eyes, his mouth diseased."[23] Only the muse of tragedy can give rise to such trouble, for nothing less than the Fall of Man can be the cause of it. As a poet, Schwartz went in for essentials. Impatient with the given rhythm of things, he short-circuited the normal processes of crime and punishment and got right to the guilt without troubling with the sin. His fondness for the iconography of Christ on Calvary reflected his own secularized version of original sin; his guilt, so far as can be learned from his poetry, attached itself to nothing he had actually done. It was too pure, too bound up with the flagging energies of the universe itself, the entropy of the stars, to be reduced to specific crimes.

Schwartz was, the point bears emphasizing, born into an affluent though profoundly unhappy family, and was therefore a generation up on the other *Partisan Review* intellectuals in being middle class and miserable and free to abandon himself to mere neurosis. A haut-bourgeois aristocrat of the spirit, he did not rise by luck and pluck from the ghetto like the rest of them; he had the misfortune of falling from a higher place—Washington Heights to be exact—which, when the poetic fever was upon him, he mistook for paradise. He shared the birthright of the *poète maudit* of every age, a cosseted but turbulent childhood that could be blamed for his ills and abjured daily with fanfare and tears. He had a world to lose and apprenticed himself accordingly to the great Christian practitioners of *contemptus mundi:* Rimbaud, Baudelaire, Proust, Pound, and especially Eliot. He even entertained wishes, common to poets of his day, of becoming a Catholic. Lacking the leaded keel of a traditional culture, he adopted poetry as a surrogate culture that gave sanction to his misery, his narcissism, his guilt, his love of vast and airy things.

> For poetry is like light, and it is light.
> It shines over all, like the blue sky, with the same blue justice.
> For poetry is the sunlight of consciousness:
> It is also the soil of the fruits of knowledge in the orchards of being:
>> *It shows us the pleasures of the city.*
>> *It lights up the structures of reality.*
>> *It is a cause of knowledge and laughter:*
>> *It sharpens the whistles of the witty:*
>> *It is like morning and the flutes of morning, chanting and enchanted.*
>> *It is the birth and rebirth of the first morning forever.*[24]

In view of such an ardent nostalgia for heaven, we may wonder what Alfred Kazin had in mind in declaring that "In Dreams Begin Responsibilities," in which a twenty-one-year-old Schwartz implores his parents in a dream not to marry because the result will be monstrous, "was the greatest fable I was ever to read of 'our experience.' "[25] Their experience? On the face of it, Schwartz's aspiration was to be all that his generation on the whole was not: transcendent, world-historical, an apostolic successor to Homer, Shakespeare, and Goethe. The disparity between his ambition and his achievement tells us something about the limits beyond which a Jewish intellectual of his generation could not venture. He strikes us now as more the admonitory example than the prophet, a reminder of what the void holds in store for those who launch themselves toward the firmament without inertial guidance systems to hold their point in the churning gravitational fields of the psyche. It may be overstating a point to insist that Schwartz's fate might have been less tragic and his poetry more durable had he been more Jewish, but it may not be wide of the mark to think that he suffered from a personal culture too thin to stand up against the vertigo that vision alone can release in the romantic ego that would rather play Hamlet or Byron than find moral examples closer to home. Schwartz immersed himself in poetry, in sharp contrast to the others of his generation—Bellow, Rahv, Fiedler, Trilling, Kazin—who took their cues from the novel, which offered them the balance and skepticism, the grain of salt, that poetry can ill afford, and which, in its realism, its "manners," its attention to social conflict, social aspiration, social mobility, and social snobbery, could be reconciled with the tatters of Jewishness remaining in them and even be made to stand for them.

V

I don't wish to give the impression that a purely aesthetic tension between realism and modernism or bourgeois and bohemian tastes has been the driving force of the Jewish imagination in America. That would be putting the aesthetics before the history, the taste before the circumstances, and in treating of Jewish writers, even those most committed to L'art pour l'art, one begins with the circumstantial. Behind the formal tensions in the writing of Jews is the demiurge of history and the twin demons of the Jewish imagination throughout its years of exile: past and future, the one called Torah or tradition or Yiskor or "remembering thee O Zion," the other, "when the Messiah comes" or "next year in Jerusalem." What Jewish book of importance, from the Bible to The Interpretation of Dreams, has not been a quarrel between memory and desire, between melancholy recollection and prophetic longing, between Mr. Sammler's prison and Mr. Sammler's planet?

From this dual venture of breaking free of the Jewish past while standing firm against the full impact of modern life has emerged a sensibility divided against itself, at once conservative in its nostalgia and radical in its disconnection from nearly every remnant of Jewish history save its most tragic moments. Yet, despite their detachment from Jewish history, the Jewish intellectuals remained, in their relation to Jewish life at large, something less than aliens. They were subsidized rebels, taking flight from their culture with its tacit blessing for the dormitories of parentally approved alienation, where the naked lunch looked gratefully like a tongue sandwich and every path out of Bohemia was a turnpike to *Commentary.* They did not make a clean break with their social base. They uprooted themselves from the middle class only to return to it for moral reinforcement and even inspiration—sometimes just for lunch. The revolts they affected in their youths came to seem, later on, bar mitzvahs, demonstrations that, contrary to Thomas Wolfe, you *could* go home again. You had to. Your lotkes were getting cold. There was little besides the passion for writing and an instinct for rebellion to bind them to the young men of 1919, who returned from the Great War to New York, "to the homeland of the uprooted," as Malcolm Cowley called it in *Exile's Return,* "where everyone you met came from another town and tried to forget it; where nobody seemed to have parents, or a past more distant than last night's swell party, or a future beyond the swell party this evening and the disillusioned book he would write tomorrow."[26] Trilling, Mailer, Kazin, Howe, among others, didn't migrate halfway across America to find Greenwich Village or Columbia; they just got on the bus or the IRT. Leslie Fiedler took the Holland Tunnel from Newark; Allen Ginsberg, a decade later, hitchhiked in from Paterson. Even Bellow and Rosenfeld, who came from a Chicago neighborhood that was little more than Williamsburg writ small, uprooted themselves in the spirit of homecoming. The small towns they forsook in their pursuit of the great world were a far cry from Winesburg, Ohio; the shtetl of Brooklyn was itself something of an international enclave with its own restless and exploratory spirit, its own candy store cosmopolitanism. William Barrett recalls his astonishment in the thirties to find, in visiting the homes of his Jewish schoolmates, "that they could bring into the midst of their family, and as noisily as they liked, their own radical ideas on the intellectual themes of the classroom."[27] The rich vein of sentimentality one finds in some of Bellow's heroes, which the wife of one nastily dismisses as his *nostalgie de la boue,* is more than an indulgence of memory; it is a living bridge of family ties and street corner connections that keeps him mindful of his origins, no matter how high he may rise.

In an autobiographical sketch written in 1946, Irving Howe recalls the painful attendance of the young intellectual, himself, at a family Seder at which he self-consciously keeps watch on himself, "he whose head may have been buzzing a few hours back with Kafka or Existentialism or the theory of permanent revolution or Chagall's technique, and he wonders: where does he fit in now?"[28] In 1946, Howe's point would have been the deep chasm that had opened up between the young rebel's adopted values and the dwindling ceremonial life of the Jewish people, which troubles him with recollections of warmth and ease he no longer can share. "The words of the prayer, which he does not understand, and the melodies of the chants, which touch some subterranean sources of kinship, stir in him a feeling of continuity that conflicts with his rejection of the ceremony." But from another point of view, one informed by the knowledge of Howe's subsequent career as the celebrant and historian of Yiddish culture, the striking fact is not that the young man is a stranger at the Seder but *that he is there anyway* and that his very being is saturated in the ceremonies from which he feels alien.

Howe, whose voracious studies of modernism, communism, American fiction, and Yiddish culture typify the ambition, restlessness, and fractured sensibility of the second-generation intellectual, has coined the phrase "tradition as discontinuity" to characterize the heritage of the American Jew, whose fundamental experience of the historical life of his people is the loss of it. True enough, and yet, if one takes a long enough view of these discontinuities they begin to look like traditions. That the agitated young apprentice to Kafka and Trotsky should mature into the anthologist of Aleichem and Peretz should not surprise us; it is perfectly natural.* "The longest way round," James Joyce has his Leopold Bloom observe, "is the shortest way home," and Joyce, we recall, gave a lifetime of exile from Ireland to recreate the history and moral geography of his people.[29]

The cycle of exile and return, rebellion and reconciliation that marks

---

*We may go a step farther and say that there is no discrepency at all, that Marx and Trotsky, Sholom Aleichem and Peretz, are witnesses to the same historic disruptions of Jewish life that followed upon its encounter with the modern world. But where the first two confront these disruptions as international proletarians, the second two do so from within Jewish culture, if not exactly Judaic tradition. The Yiddish of Peretz and Aleichem, to see this in another way, was also the first language of Jewish socialism and of the Jews who entered the CPUSA in 1919, when the bulk of the party's membership was in its foreign language divisions. At a certain point in the history of Jewish self-modernization, to write in Yiddish was to be progressive, if not downright insurrectionary.

the lives of contemporary Jewish intellectuals gives us a double perspective on such books as Kazin's lyrical memoirs, *A Walker in the City, Starting Out in the Thirties,* and *New York Jew,* Howe's own refulgent history of the immigrant generation, *World of Our Fathers,* and those portions of Bellow's *Herzog* or Doctorow's *Ragtime* that throw such rainbows of love on the lower East Side or Montreal's Napoleon Street. On the one hand we see them as instances of the past honored as it only can be by men who are cut off from its customs and values: freshened up and put on display as exhibit and myth. Delancey Street or Napoleon Street or Rockaway Avenue now constitute a romance of the irretrievable, as colorful and mysterious in their gritty way as Easter Island or Macchu Picchu.* But here is an alienation crossed by longing: these exhibitions of conspicuous nostalgia are fashioned out of love. This is how, one begins to think, culture renews itself, through the exiles' return, and it may not be too far-fetched to suggest that a culture's surest guarantee of staying power is the vitality and success of its rebels.

The Jewish intellectuals who ventured forth into America did not return empty-handed from the other world, but brought back with them souvenirs of travel, among whom was the wife, the shikse, who put the stamp of authenticity upon their dreams of the American heartland. They also returned with new histories, new interpretations of *their* past which, on the face of them, had bearing upon historical Judaism. It is a striking feature of their generation's labors that the Jewish intellectuals' most thoroughgoing efforts to be reconciled with the past were not their aureate memoirs of Williamsburg or scholarly reconstruction of Jewish socialism or theater but their devoted investigations *of other people's traditions,* traditions at once more progressive than Ashkenazic Judaism and, in their own right, grounded in history and bound up in elaborate codes of manners and morals. Lionel Trilling steeped himself in Matthew Arnold, E. M. Forster, John Stuart Mill, and the tenets of English liberal humanism; Philip Rahv improvised a concordat between Dostoevsky

---

*The nineteenth-century German science of Judaism, the *Wissenschaft des Judentums,* returns with a vengeance in the modern Jewish Studies program, with its compulsive ethnography, its nostalgia for the souvenirs of vanished folk life, and its guided tours of Williamsburg in search of live Hasidim. This has to be done; there is no cultural continuity or renewal in the modern world without a curator to recall us to what has been forgotten. Cultures are discarded so swiftly that we need textbooks and museums to tell us how our parents lived and cassettes to bring us the language our grandparents spoke. None of this quite adds up to a total vision of life to match those metaphysical longings for complete immersion that nothing short of a religious revival can satisfy. But in a secular world, where rituals are carried out largely "for the kids," the textbook and the museum are sounder guides to tradition than the family.

and Henry James; Alfred Kazin compiled the annals of American realism; Leslie Fiedler discovered the mythos of homosexuality and miscegenation at the heart of the American novel; Irving Howe, after his
eclectic fashion, apprenticed himself in turn to Karl Marx, Leon Trotsky,
Sherwood Anderson, William Faulkner, and Thomas Hardy, all the
while reading Sholom Aleichem on the sly. Allen Ginsberg became
America's only Buddhist to look, sound, and behave exactly like a
Hasidic rebbe. Here is no Torah, no Talmud, no recitation of the *shema*,
but the next best thing for a Jew in the labors of casting off the shackles
of the rabbinic tradition but anxious not to become too up-to-date all at
once: the guidance of highly moralized literatures and instruction in
principles of conduct from cultures with more experience than his own
in bootstrap morality.

Lionel Trilling's example is telling here. Trilling had no nostalgia for
his Jewish origins and went so far as to announce that efforts made by
Jewish-American writers of his generation to reclaim their roots were of
no avail to their writing.[30] Though he had begun publishing in 1925 in
Elliot Cohen and Henry Hurwitz's *Menorah Journal*, the monthly publication of the Menorah Society, whose broad purpose was to form a nonsec-
tarian, humanist, and progressive Jewish consciousness in America, he
readily deserted that enterprise and its efforts at cosmopolitan Jewishness in 1930 for the riptides of the intellectual mainstream, which
meant largely the *Nation* and the *New Republic*, but included a brief and
gingerly debut as a leftist in V. F. Calverton's *Modern Quarterly/Modern
Monthly*. In 1944, reflecting on the depth and import of his Jewishness,
he refused to waste any sentiment on his youthful torments over his
Jewish identity, with which the better part of his *Menorah Journal* stories
and essays were concerned, or to recognize any redeeming grace in the
parochialism of organized Jewish life. "As the Jewish community now
exists," he observed, "it can give no sustenance to the American artist or
intellectual who is born a Jew. And so far as I am aware, it has not done
so in the past. I know of writers who have used their Jewish experience as
the subject of excellent work: I know of no writer in English who has
added a micromillimetre to his stature by 'realizing his Jewishness,'
although I know of some who have curtailed their promise by trying to
heighten their Jewish consciousness." Subsequently, he declined Elliot
Cohen's invitation to join the editorial board of *Commentary* when it was
being formed.

Trilling's break with the Jewish past, then, was more thoroughgoing
and irreversible than that of other Jewish intellectuals. He was no self-
conscious rebel like Irving Howe, taking flight from his father's world in

youth only to bow to its authority—now become its charm—in middle age. Nor was he an accomplished funambulist like Alfred Kazin, making an original synthesis out of Winesburg and Williamsburg by draping his American dreams in folds of Baltic melancholy. Trilling resisted the appeal of cultural blends and combinations and shunned the exotic possibilities of the hyphenated identity. He was a refiner, whose sensibility was established upon dissociation, upon cutting away parts of the self and suppressing the past. Jewishness was transformed and heightened, refined practically out of existence. Old associations were kept at bay, the unconscious squelched, "authenticity" taken to task, and a curriculum of reading taken on as a surrogate identity. The simulated English bearing was not just a literary taste or professorial affectation; it was an identity.

The strain of anglophilia that was particularly intense in Trilling was latent in the very schooling of his generation; in more attenuated form it left its mark on Kazin, Bellow, and Schwartz, and became particularly visible in the hundreds of Jewish academics who flocked into "English" after the war and quickly became leading authorities on Shakespeare, Joyce, *Paradise Lost,* and *The Faerie Queene.* And yet, though the gap between British and traditional Jewish culture would seem to be vast, there are points of moral contact that make the transfer of loyalties relatively convenient. It is not difficult for a Jew who has been indoctrinated at home in habits of responsibility, prudence, thrift, study, achievement, and other moral austerities of the "Protestant ethic" to lend sympathy to a literature so saturated with a concern for individual conduct as the British, and especially the Victorian, with its stress on faith, discipline, stoic forebearance and self-improvement—all that is implied by stiffening the upper lip and biting the bullet. It was the appeal of one culture grounded upon ethical precept for another.

Trilling's anglophilia was wholly consistent with his rabbinism, its fulfillment rather than its contradiction, and he became more the Jew by becoming more the Victorian. The catalyst for this daring gambit was Matthew Arnold, Trilling's guide to the nineteenth century and his ideal Hebraist, his master in strictness of conscience. Like Arnold, he extrapolated from life to art, from society to fiction, preferring in art as in life all that was problematic, thick, and morally ambiguous. Like the rabbis, he distrusted art, a distrust especially marked in his suspicion of modernism. Trilling's brand of anglophilia, one suspects, was a back door Judaism after all, with the novel its Torah and criticism its commentary.

4. From Socialism to Therapy, I
Sigmund Freud

I

IT WAS IN this postwar climate of disorientation and regrouping that a few disheartened radicals turned toward psychoanalysis as an alternative to their shattered Marxism. One-time partisans of the workers' vanguard or the popular front against fascism quietly lay aside their copies of *State and Revolution* to comb through *The Psychopathology of Everyday Life* or *The Function of the Orgasm* for clues to the universal affliction that Karen Horney had called "the neurotic personality of our time." For such disheartened revolutionists, who despaired at last of mobilizing the toiling masses and turned instead to questions of the afflicted self, the exchange of a historic dialectic for a mental or bioenergetic one was not so complicated a maneuver. Marxism had served their generation as an institute for grand theory, and its ambitious habits of mind were readily transferrable to schools of thought that, like the Marxist, promised their disciples a basic interpretation of events and an integrated picture of the world. Like the materialist dialectic that found in every instance of culture the same laws of social development, the Freudian aptitude for spotting in a story, a philosophy, or an entire civilization the very infantile drives it found in dreams and neuroses gathered the world into a fundamental unity, whose every part was joined to every other by a determinism of mind as strict as the Marxist determinism of matter.[1]

If Marxism was a school of determinism, it was a veritable institute of dialectics, which prepared the minds of a generation to cope with the complex and grandiose dialectics of Freudian hermeneutics, in which what is manifest both expresses and contradicts what is latent and authentic, precisely as the social or aesthetic superstructure reveals, as through a glass darkly, the economic base. Both systems foster a profound distrust of appearances, regarding them as masks for deeper and more basic forces. Freud's dynamic unconscious, whose implacable will is the hidden demiurge of consciousness and culture, bears patent similarities to Marx's "objective" reality of productive relations and class interests, while the defensive acrobatics of the dreamwork resemble the clever distortions of ideology. [Ideology has been called the collective rationalization of a group, rationalization the private ideology of the individual.] Both systems disclose the grim truth about noble sentiments and uplifting ideas, to which they counterpose the tragic but "scientific" facts about life: the class struggles being waged beneath the placid surfaces of bourgeois culture and the incestuous and parricidal yearnings beneath the veneer of bourgeois love. Both proffer a history, or etiology, which describes the fall into neurosis or alienation or slavery: the son's struggle with the father, the division of labor. Both prescribe the application of reason and will for the undoing of the fall. For both, progress is possible only through the shedding of illusions and a grappling with the hidden, controlling forces. And both, being moral disciplines as well as sciences of·the hidden life of culture, offer codes of value and didactic aids to conduct: revolution in one case, relentless self-interrogation in the other. Is it in any way surprising, then, that when Marxism collapsed for so many American radicals in the late 1930s, a fair proportion would find in psychoanalysis the consolations of a system which appeared to be more precise in its findings than Marxism while gratefully less exacting in its moral prescriptions?

For in point of personal freedom, the differences could not be greater. Psychoanalysis *as a therapeutic* grounds its moral calculus in the dynamics of the will rather than the equations of economic necessity and is therefore a dialectic of options rather than of forces. It denies the instruments of redemption to the emergent class and places them at the disposal of the individual. Its doctrine of psychic determinism, which holds that there can be no accidents in the mind, nonetheless leaves ample room for a free will that, by the very discipline of bracing itself against the surge of irrational forces from below, factors itself into the equations of behavior.*

---

*Marx's own estimate of the Enlightenment's faith in self-reformation through self-knowledge was itself ambiguous, but he gave short shrift to any social claims put forward on behalf of interiority and held out small hope that the human condition might be ameliorated by so frail an instrument as self-reflection. As he observed in *The German Ideology:* "All forms and products of consciousness cannot be dissolved by mental criticism, by resolution into 'self-consciousness' or tránsformation into 'apparitions,' 'spectres,' 'fancies,' etc., *but only by the practical overthrow of the actual social relations which gave rise to this idealistic humbug . . .*" (italics mine). Karl Marx and Friedrich Engels, *The German Ideology,* ed. R. Pascal (New York: International Publishers, 1947), 28–29.

It was this democratic blend of freedom and structure, the availability of free choice within an orderly system, that made psychoanalysis so appealing to the renegade leftists who clustered about *Partisan Review,* and, briefly, Dwight Macdonald's *Politics,* in the 1940s. By the war's end, a fair proportion of them had turned to assumptions of therapeutic origin as guides to the perplexed—themselves—and as instruments of literary and social analysis. Lionel Trilling adopted Freud as a guide to the variousness and possibility wanting in the liberal imagination. Issac Rosenfeld submitted himself to Reichian therapy for personal deliverance and aesthetic counsel, as did his friend from Chicago, Saul Bellow. Arthur Miller would write play after play in homage to the return of the repressed. Paul Goodman cooked up his own psychology, Gestalt, and fashioned a libertarian-anarchist program upon his own findings about the mind in the modern world. Leslie Fiedler, peering into the cauldron from the distant prospect of Missoula, Montana, an outpost of *Partisan Review* as remote and improbable as the moon, became a Jungian and tracked the spoor of the archetypal unconscious into the myth-bearing American wilderness. Delmore Schwartz pored over Freud's collected works and grew ill. Felix Morrow, a leading Trotskyist in the thirties and author of *Revolution and Counter-Revolution in Spain,* would take a long detour through psychoanalysis on his route to Gurdjieff, the mystic arts, and soft-core erotica.[2] A decade later, in the 1950s, Bellow would base two of his liveliest novels, *Seize the Day* and *Henderson the Rain King,* upon points of therapeutic lore, while Norman Mailer and Allen Ginsberg would turn their bitter flights from the middle class into strident Reichian programs for personal salvation through sexual liberation and make a stir by conducting their treatments in public. If it can be charged against some of these that their regrouping of energies around the embattled self signalled a retreat from political struggle in favor of purely private gestures of revolt, it needs also to be added that it expressed the seriousness of their inquiries into the terms of human existence and a more sober estimate of the prospects for progressive politics and the eradication of social evils by purely social measures. Certainly none of them followed the lead of Arthur Koestler, who, in his novel *Arrival and Departure,* cavalierly called upon psychoanalysis to pronounce upon the pathology of revolutionism, conveniently forgetting that if we are all ill then filial piety is no less pathological than parricide.

In the atmosphere of diffuse alarm that marked the 1940s, the Freudian picture of mind as a center of perpetual crisis appealed to intellectuals as a sanction for their own beleaguered spirits. Jewish intellectuals especially, badly shaken in their optimism by the more gruesome revelations of the war, had need of a psychology that not only accounted for the brutalities they had witnessed but would explain their own flagging spirits and guilt-ridden consciences. Psychoanalysis jettisoned the utilitarian psychology shared by Marxism and the American work ethic for a dialectical psychology that identified doubt, conflict, repression, and guilt as the very agencies of thought, rather than as moral indulgences or "bourgeois metaphysics." The unconscious mind, it taught, was always in a state of upheaval, and the normal function of the ego in its relation to the panic below was to mask it and keep up the fiction that everything is under control. Psychoanalysis, citing the ego's inauthentic relation to the repressed, called into question all claims of moral authority and epistemological certainty by demonstrating the fundamental defensiveness, even panic, underlying all organized brands of self-assurance. Especially for Jews, psychoanalysis gave license to self-doubt and ambivalence, and as so much postwar fiction testifies, to be ambivalent was the very best way to confront the modern crisis. The best, all agreed with Yeats, lack all conviction. Under the sanction of psychoanalysis, disorientation began to look like a form of heroism, a code of resistance that singled out the neurotic as the exemplary individual who evaded moral compromises and debilitating commitments by keeping himself chronically off balance. His disturbance was his freedom, and so long as he could not pursue a course or make a pledge or affirm too stringent a value he was a freedom fighter for the unfettered spirit: the goldbricker become rebel without a cause.

Even Lionel Trilling concurred on this point in praising Dostoevsky's underground man,* that paragon of masochism who haunts the imagination of the 1940s: "He has arranged his own misery—arranged it in the interests of his dignity, which is to say, of his freedom."[3] In a similar spirit, if not so spectacular a fashion, John Laskell, the reconstructed liberal of Trilling's *The Middle of the Journey,* demonstrates his newly found maturity and moral realism by declining to take a stand on anything but his own negative capability. And Joseph, the neurasthenic ex-socialist of Bellow's *Dangling Man,* negotiates his way through a thicket of competing claims by refusing to be deterred by any of them: by being, as a matter of right, *irresponsible.* In even so recent a novel as Philip Roth's *The Ghost Writer,* set in 1956, a phrase from Henry James'

---

*That Trilling would not, in *Sincerity and Authenticity,* extend his approbation of the underground man to R. D. Laing and the cult of the psychotic as secular saint is worth pondering, since his appeal on behalf of the neurotic who gains freedom through perversity entitled him to take the next step. But, then, taking the next step is precisely what Trilling was famed for refusing to do.

The Middle Years is heralded as the anthem of an era's brash muddlement. "We work in the dark—we do what we can—we give what we have. Our doubt is our passion and our passion is our task. The rest is the madness of art."[4] At a historical juncture when the disintegrated consciousness of modern life appeared to have gained not only victory among the intellectuals but their esteem as well, psychoanalysis won favor as both justification and cure. It was fastened upon as the key to health by those who embraced balance, sanity, responsibility, and work [*Lieben und Arbeiten,* the principle standards of Freud himself] *and* invoked as the authorization of illness by rebels against the conventional life, who scorned mere sanity as the ideology of the suburb.

It would be mistaken, then, to see the quest for spiritual redemption or just plain relief from symptoms as the sole attraction of psychoanalysis for postwar writers and intellectuals, just as it would have been in error to hold the prospect for revolution as the sole attraction of Marxism a decade earlier. Psychotherapy, in all its variants, was also a literary idea that appealed to writers as writers. This was as true for the critics, Trilling, Fiedler, and Kazin, as it was for novelists, dramatists, and poets: Bellow, Rosenfeld, Miller, Mailer, and Ginsberg. Psychoanalysis was a climate of thought to be exploited as much for its metaphors and allusions as for its curative benefits. Though many writers did seek out psychoanalytic treatment of one brand or another, they could not fail to observe how their recourse to therapy validated their reading, bringing them into personal relation with literary history. The wish to be cured of history, or the wish to succumb in protest, are very literary wishes, after all, which put one in touch with writers of prior generations who secured a privileged relation to their ages by taking to their beds in defiance. "The hard-boiled are compensated for their silence," observes Saul Bellow's Joseph, at the very beginning of *Dangling Man* in 1944, adding, more in self-congratulation than in distress, "They fly planes or fight bulls or catch tarpon, whereas I rarely leave my room."[5] Such a declaration brings to mind not only Hemingway and his cultic swordfish but the great romantic connoisseurs of defeat for whom history was a nightmare and their own illnesses the *via regia* to insight into it: Kafka, with his parables of self-affliction; Eliot, his tender nerves thrown in patterns on a screen; Baudelaire, dressed in black in celebration of all that is being buried; Proust, prowling the hidden corners of his own past from the protected confines of his cork-lined bedroom; Mann's Hans Castorp, suffering the decline of the West on his magic mountain; Huysmans's Des Esseintes, composing tunes on his palate with his organ of liqueurs; Valery's M. Teste, purged of activity, cultivating his ruminations, his insomnia, his migraines.

II

But psychoanalysis made its contribution to *social* philosophy on grounds that had little to do with the cachet of disorientation, and to appraise its social function after the war we must observe a clear distinction between psychoanalysis as a therapeutic, with its generous estimate of the human capacity for self-reflection and self-correction, and Freud's social philosophy which, after *Beyond the Pleasure Principle* in 1920, was grounded in serious reservations about the curative optimism of the early psychoanalysts, reservations that have remained a challenge to psychoanalysis ever since. Much of the furor of schism and contention that has marked the psychoanalytic movement since Freud arises out of questions of freedom and determinism that Freud first posed and left unresolved. Psychoanalylsis never has possessed a consistent social philosophy, though it has been charged with being just about everything from a counsel of adjustment to an ideology of grievance. The ambiguities of freedom and determinism that run through its conception of mind reflect Freud's own fluctuating estimate of the scope of reason in human affairs. Two distinct and opposed attitudes marked his thought: one, affirmative and liberal, the other disconsolate and conservative, and it is hardly surprising that social thinkers of every stripe, from sexual romantics like Wilhelm Reich and Norman O. Brown to Christian theologians like Reinhold Niebuhr and born-again conservatives like Max Eastman should have found sponsorship for their beliefs in elements of Freud's system. Initially, psychoanalysis was a child of Enlightenment rationalism, pressing the claim for self-knowledge and self-regulation and adopting the Socratic principle of *know thyself* as a realizable, if strenuous, goal of psychotherapy. "Turn your eyes inward, look into your own depths, learn first to know yourself. Then you will understand why you were bound to fall ill; and perhaps, you will avoid falling ill in the future."[6] The doctrine of psychic determinism was initially nothing more than the axiom that the mind is orderly and law abiding and that every mental event exists in a determinate relation to others and takes its meaning from those relations. Such a determinism was the sine qua non of analysis and therapy; without it the mind was a thicket of unreason. Yet it was fully consistent with the principles of free will and moral responsibility; it stressed the obligation of the conscious will—the ego—to make choices by placing it in a competitive relation to other psychic factors: unconscious wishes, infantile appetites, the reality principle, the habits of a lifetime. The ego's struggles to master the impediments thrown up by the other agencies of the mind was the essential drama of therapy, and if psychoanalysis did not exactly promise a universal reprieve from neurosis, it did propose that the knowledge to be gained in analysis was a distinct advantage in taking command of one's own life. "Where id was there ego shall be" was a bold statement of confidence in the powers of human reason.

But as that account suggests, psychoanalysis is a theory of mental forces in precarious balance, and one sees Freud, even at his most buoyant, wrestling with determinisms: with the phylogenetic inheritance of man in the form of biological endowments, with the primal crime that every generation must expiate in its own way, and with the deterministic features of childhood. "His mother's tenderness was fateful for him," he wrote of Leonardo in 1910, "it determined his destiny and the privations that were in store for him."[7] As Freud's outlook darkened, only minor adjustments in the alignment of forces were needed to turn the hopefulness of psychoanalysis into a Hobbesian revulsion at human nature. The addition of two new premises in the 1920s was enough to tip the scales against the therapeutic in psychoanalysis; the universal death instinct in man and the mental structure that fractured the mind into three implacably hostile centers of interest: an id, an ego, and a superego.[8] It is difficult not to see through these developments to the world war that had made a heartbreak house of Europe and to the anti-Semitism that had arisen in its wake and brought to Jews of Europe a consciousness of vulnerability and peril. In 1930, the year Freud published *Civilization and Its Discontents*, the Nazis in Germany made spectacular gains in the Reichstag by winning 107 seats where they had previously held just 12, becoming thereby the second most powerful party in Germany. The danger signs for Jews, especially in the German-speaking countries, were plentiful, and it would not have been lost on Freud that it was in his beloved Vienna that a young Adolf Hitler had first tasted the thrill and observed the political advantage—in Karl Lueger's election as mayor in 1895—of publicly reviling the Jews. The books of Freud's later years are documents of their place and time, Central Europe between two wars, and are marked by Freud's awareness of the new, brutal equations of power that had broken through the mask of bourgeois civility and loosed upon Europe forces for which neither reason nor liberalism could serve as antidotes.[9]

Freud's books after *Beyond the Pleasure Principle* were endeavors to amend his theory of mind to account for this brutality in human affairs, as though it were a mental fact first and foremost to which the psychology of the unconscious held the key. The revised blueprint of id, ego, and superego cast the mind in a far more factious mold than anything psychoanalysis had yet countenanced, and replaced the affirmative psychology of freedom within conditions with a savage geometry of forces. Strict necessities took the place of *Wissen macht frei,* which was not only the moral basis of psychotherapy but also the slogan of Austrian liberalism. Under siege from below by an infantile and clamorous id and from above by an intransigent superego, the ego enjoyed fewer degrees of freedom than ever before. Freud no longer spoke of the pleasure and reality principles reaching modi vivendi in "compromise formations"; he spoke of eros and death fighting it out; of a basic aggressiveness in humanity that was biological and immitigable; of a fire raging in the heart of every man that could be quenched only by his neighbor's death. "Anyone who calls to mind the atrocities committed during the racial migrations or the invasion of the Huns," Freud wrote in *Civilization and Its Discontents,* "or by the people known as Mongols under Jenghis Kahn and Tamerlane, or at the capture of Jerusalem by the pious crusaders, or even, indeed the horrors of the recent World War—anyone who calls these things to mind will have to bow humbly before the truth of this view."[10] The revised Freudian picture of man made him appear as helpless before inner forces as ever he had been, in liberal and Marxist thought, before material ones. As the struggle between eros and death became, for Freud, more overbearing and determinate, the freedom of the individual will receded toward the vanishing point and the death instinct began to look more and more like the old discarded determinisms, Marxist and Christian alike, revived as biological commandments. The formulation of the death instinct, indeed, was the crucial step in the transformation of psychoanalysis's hopeful science into a tragic theology that gave original sin a new lease on life as an organic imperative.

With the transformation of psychoanalysis in the twenties, Freud in effect stole his own creation away from liberalism and made it available to conservatism, putting subsequent liberals and leftists, desirous of a theory of mind to authorize their social beliefs, in the position of either repudiating it in favor of more hopeful theories of mind or patching it with escape clauses in an effort to salvage the optimism that had given psychoanalysis its original, progressive coloration.* In some cases, however, it is hard to tell their successes from grudging capitulations. Even

---

*One such effort was Erich Fromm's formula for destructiveness: *"the outcome of unlived life,"* which left the door open for a mitigation of violence through an expansion of "life," provided the means could be found to achieve that. In practice, it was a formula for saving Marxism as a humane science without ruling out the therapeutic alternatives. Once the *Verfremdungskritik* has identified unused biological potential as the root cause of our woe, we needed only a Paul Goodman or a Fritz Perls or a Leo Buscaglia to make it operational.

so devoted a progressive humanist as Erich Fromm, who sought to purge psychoanalysis of its instinctual necessitarianism, resorted in his most influential book, *Escape from Freedom* [1941], to a quasi-instinctual defect in human nature, the intolerance for loneliness, to explain the triumph of facism in Germany.[11] Since the "alienation" on which Fromm based his argument was a constant human potential that had been released into history by the steady decomposition of the European social fabric since the Renaissance, the disasters it had called forth seemed no less inevitable than they did under the sign of the death instinct. Indeed, to accept Fromm's account of fascism—as a desperate and infantile effort to heal the fractured experience of modern man—was to conclude that liberal democracy hadn't a leg to stand on and that fascism, through its appeal to the most infantile layers of the psyche, was certain to sweep the West. In 1941, when the book was published, such gloom seemed justified by events. The "tragic sense of life," which found its warrant in cues from Freud and even some reluctant neo-Freudians, was a world view ideally suited for a generation whose initial postwar task was to find a use for its rage and guilt.

If the Freud whose authority was cited as sponsoring the libidinal hedonism of the 1920s was the Freud of the early explorations and case studies—*Interpretation of Dreams, The Psychopathology of Everyday Life, Three Contributions to a Theory of Sexuality*—the Freud who brooded over later decades was a very different figure: the author of *Beyond the Pleasure Principle* and *Civilization and Its Discontents,* the stern philosopher of the difficult and the tragic. Indeed, Freud was popularly read in the twenties as a handmaiden to Marx, a witness in the realms of the mind to the same hypocrises of bourgeois society that Marx had identified through a study of class relations. Psychoanalysis, as seen in the twenties from the special vantage point of Greenwich Village, had only clarified the picture of modern alienation by giving it firmer intellectual credentials, whereas in later decades it was offered in evidence of the shallowness of Marx's social thought. Thus Max Eastman, who as a young radical had championed the Freud-Marx synthesis but survived to play gray eminence to neoconservatism, grounded his ultimate rejection of Marxism on new evidence about the nature of man drawn from authorities as diverse as Freud, Konrad Lorenz, Robert Ardrey, and Mark Twain, who knew all along that "the hereditary nature [of man] is still that of the tribal savage; and that it contains, among other things, a taste for fighting and that tendency to bow down to others or boss them which makes group solidarity in gregarious animals spontaneous."[12] Lionel Trilling, following a similar line of reasoning, would intone darkly in 1948, "Now . . .

the old margin [of optimism] no longer exists; the facade is down; society's resistance to the discovery of depravity has ceased; now everyone knows that Thackeray was wrong, Swift right."[13] Arthur Schlesinger, a founding member of Americans for Democratic Action (ADA) and one who, like Trilling, took it upon himself to renovate liberalism in light of new revelations, would announce in his doctrinal book *The Vital Center,* "As the child of eighteenth-century rationalism and nineteenth century romanticism, progressivism was committed to an unwarranted optimism about man."[14] Citing the views of Dostoevsky, Sorel, Kierkegaard, Nietzsche, and Freud, the great anti-Romantic precursors of modern pessimism, Schlesinger argued that no liberalism that had not assimilated the tragic view of human potential had anything to say to contemporary politics.* "No," thundered James Burnham in his summary indictment of liberalism, *Suicide of the West,* "we must repeat: if human nature is scored by innate defects, if the optimistic account of man is unjustified, then is all the liberal faith vain."[15]

III

But every realism breeds its own sentimentality, and the ease with which this new clarity could be converted into a metaphysics is suggested by Arthur Miller's Freudian melodrama, *After the Fall* [1964], in which political guilt (lying for the party, betraying old comrades, naming names), sexual guilt (the usual), and survivor's guilt are pressed together into a single, immitigable feature of human nature that is no more amenable to therapeutic repair than it is to social correction.[16] Staged in the shadow of the death camps—a gun tower is the only recognizable prop on the stage—*After the Fall* is a play about the original nature of man as revealed by the romance of communism, the Holocaust, and, of all things, divorce. "A life, after all, is evidence," cries Miller's hero, Quentin, the man of marital sorrows, "and I have two divorces in my safe-deposit box." Under the sign of original sin, any crime is the prototype of all crimes, and Quentin complains of his marriages as though their inner meaning—betrayal—had been layed bare by the Final Solution. Quentin is a lawyer with a history of fellow-travelling, whose closest friend and client, Lou, and law partner, Mickey, have been called before

---

*Indeed, to think of Trilling in the light of Schlesinger is to suggest an answer to the question of what Trilling's politics were in the 1940s. *The Vital Center* (1949) and *The Liberal Imagination* (1950), read together as companion volumes, suggest the conclusion that Trilling's politics in the 1940s were essentially those of the ADA, transposed into a different key and given a cultural twist.

the committee to answer questions. Lou has vowed to stonewall, Mickey to make a clean breast of it, to name names, including Lou's. Lou takes his life by leaping into the path of a subway train the very night Quentin is to discuss his case with the firm but, his attentions being elsewhere, misses the meeting. The implication of this is that Lou, sensing Quentin's betrayal, has no choice but to destroy himself. Quentin is scarcely luckier with wives than he is with comrades. The first, Louise, has steamed and fretted her way through a dry marriage, and by the time she is liberated by psychoanalysis, is a mass of resentments and asperities. Maggie, who promises Quentin life, turns out to have little to spare for herself and finally dies of an overdose of barbiturates because, it seems, his love was small compensation for that long disease, her life. At the end, Holga is waiting in the wings, and Quentin dares not hope for much. "I loved them all, all!" he protests, ". . . and gave them willingly to failure and to death that I might live." After the fall, which for Miller is an omnibus psychological, political, and evolutionary-genetic darkening of the human spirit, every embrace, every act of love is a Judas kiss. "What is the cure?" he cries, turning dramatically toward the tower "as toward a terrible God."

> Who can be innocent on this mountain of skulls? I tell you what I know! My brothers died here—but my brothers built this place; our hearts have cut these stones!

My brothers? one wants to ask. *Our* hearts? The old popular front of the innocent, it appears, has given way to the rank and file of the guilty. Taking the bestiality of the human heart in deadly earnest, Miller does everything but declare that we are all guilty of the Holocaust, though plainly that is both his meaning and Quentin's ultimate alibi. Quentin, however, a collector of self accusations, is hardly cheered by the invitation to take himself off the hook. All of history is implicated in his crises, which are magnified to world-historical dimensions by the brooding companionship of the tower. *Man* plotted the extermination of the Jews; *Man* fell for the Soviet myth and lied in its defense, *Man* named names and *Man* deserted his friends at their moment of trial. *Man* divorces and *Man* remarries. After the fall, *Man* lives in perpetual bad faith. Such a metaphysics of universal guilt raises questions about Quentin's breast-beating that he is ill equipped to answer, for if *we* are all guilty then what can *he* be held to account for? For that matter, what guilt can be ascribed to Lou, Mickey, Louise, or Maggie, who are only acting out their fallen natures? Their hearts having been darkened by conditions beyond their control, are they free to be better than they are? After such a fall what redemption? Naming names? Entering analysis? Slitting one's wrists? *After the Fall* does not address such questions, but it is clear that a theology of impersonal and ineluctable guilt that provides neither the leavening of grace nor a weekly confessional leaves scant room for individual freedom or individual responsibility. There is even a taste of inverted liberalism to such an instinctual stringency, a sociology of conditions driven inward to become a determinism of nature that is no more receptive to the possibilities of freedom and responsibility than the determinism it has replaced. None of the characters is presented as capable of volition; they are no less victims of conditions than the characters in the agitprop theater of thirty years before.

In light of such premises, one is struck dumb by Quentin's strange envoy, a testament to "what burning cities taught her [Holga] and the death of love taught me: that we are very dangerous. *And that, that's why I wake each morning like a boy—even now, even now! I swear to you, I could love the world again!*" (italics mine). Little wonder that the play sank beneath the weight of its own contradictions. Seeking remission of Quentin's injured feelings, it failed to capitalize on his experiences and his ideas about Man and permit him the one and only credible resolution to his conflicts: conversion to neoconservatism. In less agonized hands, the secular reconstruction of original sin as original damage—the Greek *hamartia* updated by science and universalized—or original aggression—the Christian pride revamped as bestiality but still going before a fall—did not issue normally in mea culpas but in mobilizations. It is the very root and ground of neoconservatism. If man is basically a dog, counsels neoconservatism, then surely it is better to be top dog than bottom dog, and no damned nonsense about loving the world again. That *After the Fall* concludes with Quentin's, and presumably Miller's, hopes intact without giving them a shred of evidence on which to build a case is the play's fatal flaw, for it prevents Quentin's ordeal from achieving the stature of experience and rules out anything so dramatic as a conversion. Quentin learns nothing. Had he emerged from his trials a Buckleyite or a Cold War liberal or just a man of cooler and more self-protective instincts, *After the Fall* might well have been a dramatic sensation, a parable of generational disillusionment and a portrait of its age rather than, as it was, a sentimental souvenir of harried progressivism and a flop.

Yet, despite its shortcomings as drama or dramatized philosophy, *After the Fall* has historical interest for bringing together in a single play the two faces of the Freudian ethos as the postwar imagination construed it:

the clinical-analytic and the cultural-pessimistic. The exposure of Quentin's inner torment through a series of dissolving hallucinations—the return of the repressed dramatized as a play of spectral voices—is conventional Freudian dramaturgy, as are Quentin's free associations around the theme of guilt and betrayal, his feverish ransacking of the past for causes and motives, the play's condensation of scattered fragments of a life into a psychic unity, its picture of a moral universe infected with bad faith, and its general ambience of neurosis and complaint. The play is formed along the lines of Quentin's neurotic guilt, which is limitless and ceaselessly on the prowl for crimes to make it appear warranted. That was nothing less, after all, than the strategy of James Joyce in the nighttown episode of *Ulysses,* in which Bloom's guilt releases a wild phantasmagoria of imagined crimes and penances. But whereas Joyce did not believe in Bloom's guilt but only in the comedy of guilt, Miller not only believed in Quentin's, he suffered along with it. Bloom's *Walpurgisnacht,* consequently, is a rich comedy of imaginary afflictions, while Quentin's *Walpurgistag* is in the main just the regurgitation of undigested miseries.

It was bound to happen that a conception of human nature which first gained praise as a form of realism and prudence and a curb to the sentimentalities of human perfectability would, in the hands of writers with a taste for grand and simple explanations, become a countersentimentality, a theology of human wickedness that did little more than modulate the myths of progressive sociology into a more somber key, turning them into myths of perpetual and irredeemable guilt. If one were to construct a triptych of representative plays to illustrate the drift in social mythologies over thirty years, one could do worse than select Clifford Odets's *Awake and Sing* (1935) and two of Miller's plays, *Death of a Salesman* (1949) and *After the Fall* (1964), for one's exemplary panels, and caption them, respectively, Progress through Teamwork, Man Alone, and We Are All Ill.

5. Psychoanalysis and Liberalism
The Case of Lionel Trilling

"AS CHARLES PÉGUY SAID," wrote Lionel Trilling in the preface to *The Liberal Imagination* in 1950, " '*Tout commence en mystique et finit en politique*' —everything begins in sentiment and assumption and finds its issue in political action and institutions. The converse is also true: just as sentiments become ideas, ideas eventually establish themselves as sentiments."[1] It was precisely in this crossroads of ideas and sentiments, of *politique* and *mystique,* that Trilling staked out his own ground after the war, challenging the mystiques of progressive liberalism and speaking for the more timely mystiques of disorientation: ambivalence, variousness and possibility, ideas in modulation, moral realism (the acceptance of "good and evil"), and the tragic view of life. He emerged in the forties as a pivotal figure among the New York intellectuals, and though he quickly became a *primus inter pares*, a silhouette of his career would trace a familiar profile. He was a Jew, and as a Jew had been schooled in the revolutionary Marxism of the 1930s, whose programmatic raptures and denunciations he was quick to forsake for the more difficult teachings of Arnold, James, Forster, Mill, Freud, and Hegel. Like most New York intellectuals, he fancied himself a modern, although he distrusted the extremity of literary modernism and was more at home with the modulations and dense moral fabrics of the Victorian age. He shared with his contemporaries, the New York intellectuals of his generation, the view of literature as the expression of history, politics, class, and the zeitgeist and made a practice of keeping watch over the trends and excesses of what his circle called "the culture" (and he sometimes just called "we")—the opinions, tastes, and social habits of the Eastern liberal intelligentsia. And, after his fashion, he entered the postwar era suffering from the same virus of alienation and withdrawal that infected so many ex-leftists of his generation. He didn't celebrate alienation as such, nor did he ever exploit the rhetorical authority that the doxologies of depression acquired after the war. He was, after all, a professor at Columbia, not a streetwise alumnus of the Federal Writers' Project. But in the forties one could despair of civilization even on Morningside Heights, and the prevailing mood of Trilling's postwar essays, as well as of his novel *The Middle of the Journey,* was that of loss and uncertainty.[2]

Though we do not commonly think of Trilling as the historian of his own emotions, we can read the progression of moods he documented and the positions he championed as contributions to a Romantic autobiography of the sort that in the nineteenth century fairly defined the progress of the modern spirit: youthful precocity, mid life emotional crisis, conversion, and revival. *The Middle of the Journey,* in its diffident way, is a chronicle of spiritual death and rebirth not unlike Mill's *Autobiography,* Wordsworth's *The Prelude,* Carlyle's *Sartor Resartus,* and Tennyson's *In Memoriam.* But the metaphors of death and resurrection that lie at the heart of *The Middle of the Journey* are etched deeply into the larger movement of Trilling's writing, as they were into the work and lives of so many of his contemporaries, though the healing powers of Tennyson's faith, Carlyle's gospel of work, and Wordsworth's powerful emotions recollected in tranquillity were located by Trilling in psychoanalysis and modern literature. Trilling was aware of the precedents; psychoanalysis, as he understood it, was a codification of the great surge of self-discovery and self-healing that marked the literature of the nineteenth century, and Mill in particular appealed to him as a model of interior regeneration, not only in his *Autobiography* but in the essays on Bentham and Coleridge, which stood behind the lessons on politics and the emotional life that Trilling himself delivered to his own generation in *The Liberal Imagination.*

Trilling's case against the liberal imagination needs no review here; his estimate of its shallowness of mind is part of our intellectual patrimony nowadays, even if the recoil from large ideas that liberalism's failings once seemed to justify is no longer cheered as the last word in political maturity. But what still needs to be examined is the role of psychoanalysis in Trilling's efforts at renovating liberalism, for the dominant themes of Trilling's political and cultural thought in the forties grew in tandem with his involvement in psychoanalysis, and it is plain that his encounter with Freud prompted those attitudes toward the progressive culture that are the polemical heart of *The Liberal Imagination.*

The logical place to begin is to note that Freud's conception of mind, if not therapy itself, was to be prescribed for the intellectual culture at large, together with medicinal potions of literature, as an elixir for fatigued emotions and an antidote to a progressivism that, in its instrumental view of reality and rough behaviorist psychology, "drifts toward a denial of the emotions and the imagination."[3] Freudian man was a step upwards from liberal man—even his contrary—in complication and mystery. He harbored unconscious desires that were not always in accord with either his conscious will or his class interests; he entertained contradictory ideas and emotions and tormented himself with his own ambiguities; he fell into irrational fits of brooding or guilt and performed unexplained rites of expiation for crimes he had not committed, and he had a fondness for self-defeat that made his failures seem more genuine expressions of purpose than his successes.[4] How unlike the utilitarian man of liberalism who maximizes pleasure and knows where his interests lie, and how much closer to the neurotic hero of contemporary fiction, who confirms the modern character that Hegel called the "disintegrated consciousness." For Trilling, the literary prototype of psychological man was Rameau's nephew, Diderot's creature of desires and deceits in whom he saw an epitome of the modern crisis and a preview of the therapeutic man: willful, insatiable, and contradictory.[5] Psychoanalysis and contemporary fiction agree on the alienation of consciousness from both society and the body and the readiness of the self to go it alone in an absurd universe, leaving both culture and biology behind. For Trilling, the sufficient measure of liberalism's bankruptcy was its failure to admit this wound, and, accordingly, to capture the imagination of any of the important modern writers. Denying any alienations but those of class, liberalism failed the tests of both psychoanalysis and fiction.[6]

Though Trilling assailed liberalism for its shallow apprehensions of mind, nowhere did he venture an estimate of its social ideas or programs comparable to his assessment of its imagination. A writer who was so widely regarded as a political intellectual, Trilling provides surprisingly little concrete political direction. He departed from the example of his English mentors—Coleridge, Mill, and Arnold—in volunteering no social ideas of his own, only sentiments and aesthetic choices that did not add up to an alternative liberalism or, for that matter, and alternative conservatism. (Arnold's outspokenness on the Governor Eyre case, for example, is scarcely mentioned in Trilling's *Matthew Arnold.*[7] The Arnold who was deeply involved in the events of his day is not the Arnold that engaged him.) His revitalized versions of the liberal imagination could never be put to political tests, only aesthetic ones, for only in relation to literature and literary styles of representation had they any chance at validation. By finessing all talk of politics, power, and institutions, except by way of sentiment and mystique, Trilling could chastise liberalism for its shallow grasp of reality without having to confront the conditions to which the liberals responded. The author of *The Liberal Imagination* was no Edmund Wilson, whose cross-country surveys of American life and labor in *The American Jitters* (later revised as *The American Earthquake*) lent a sense of immediacy to his politics.[8] For what Trilling normally meant by politics were ideologies, those large ideas of broad currency that frame reality, justify action, set the agendas of intellectual culture, and regulate the lives of intellectuals. But his version of ideology was not what a sociologist might see, a system of belief serving to legitimate power or action, but what a critic of literature might see, a personal aesthetics of vision. Trilling read liberalism through its tastes rather than its platforms, and, in effect, left the dissection of liberal politics to others.* The context of his ideas in the forties, after all, was the dismemberment of the Popular Front from all quarters, when everyone, especially the old Trotskyists, demanded a piece of the corpse.

This deflection of attention from power and its uses to the intellectuals and their perceptions was Trilling's method for detaching himself from the liberal mainstream to become its critic. His finest essays were candid snapshots of contemporary intellectuals in the act of defining reality. His essays in *The Liberal Imagination* on Dreiser ("Reality in America") and the Kinsey Report are superb analyses of American and liberal styles of social understanding, and if one learns little from them about the details of social reality in America, one learns a great deal about the principles of social vision in a society founded upon rationalized optimism. One also learns from Trilling something about the tonal qualities of ideas and programs, their harmonies and vibrations, their general sense of life. What he would recall most vividly of the thirties was the dreariness of its politics. In his introduction to Tess Slesinger's novel of life among the New York intellectuals in their fellow-travelling days, *The Unpossessed*, he recalled coldly "the dryness and deadness that lay at the heart of [the intellectuals'] drama," noting their proclivity for a "peculiarly American

---

*See, for comparison, Arthur Schlesinger's *The Vital Center* (Boston: Houghton Mifflin, 1949), which was, like *The Liberal Imagination* and *The Middle of the Journey*, a plea for liberalism to cast off its illusions about the nature of man, about the inexorable progress of history and the benignity of Soviet communism. Its detailed analyses of the history, organization, and tactics of the American progressive movement make it a useful companion volume to Trilling's two books, for it throws into precise relief the details that Trilling's more remote point of view will not resolve.

dessication of temperament."[9] Yet such sensitivity to the dominion of ideas over character, based as it was upon a belief in their power to transform life, was bought at a price. Here, as elsewhere, Trilling suppressed those dimensions of reality boosted by insurgent realism: the depression, the hunger, the evictions, the bloody labor wars, the advances of fascism in Europe—in short, the general desperation. It was as though the world of dustbowls and breadlines were only a liberal delusion, a phantom of the proletarian aesthetic that could be exorcized through a simple adjustment of vision. What comes into view when the camera dissolves from Harlan County to rural Connecticut in *The Middle of the Journey* is a movie of the 1930s featuring the self-deceived and self-destroying intellectuals themselves, and consequently dominated by ideas rather than the circumstances that had brought them into play.

II

> 'To be resigned, as one passes one's life in the midst of false and unjust men'—that was the sage's program. And he was right. The most solid goodness is that which is based on perfect ennui, on the clear realization that everything in this world is frivolous and without real foundation.
>
> —Renan on Marcus Aurelius

The potentials and limitations of Trilling's approach to the politics of culture are on display in *The Middle of the Journey,* his most ambitious effort to gain a political point by purely literary means. The novel was an attempt to bring to the politics of contemporary culture a Victorian sensibility Trilling had concocted for himself, an impasto of attitudes synthesized out of Mill, Arnold, Forster, Freud, and Keats, that would highlight, from a great distance, the follies of liberalism, by arguing the stultifying effect of its unremitting cheerfulness upon the human heart. In later years, Trilling recalled that he had intended *The Middle of the Journey* to be a book about death and the refusal of intellectuals schooled in the liberal tradition to countenance it because it threatened the factitious optimism of their progressive fantasies.[10] John Laskell, his somewhat retiring spokesman in *The Middle of the Journey,* has recently lost the woman he loved to a sudden illness and has himself just recovered from a dangerous attack of scarlet fever. In his convalescence he visits the rustic Connecticut home of Arthur and Nancy Croom, sunny, robotic progressives who, armored by their idealism, can scarcely pronounce the word death let alone draw tragic lessons from the arrival of this walking *memento mori* into their midst. Laskell, however, needing to talk about his brush with death and to examine its meaning, finds himself isolated from his friends, for he has looked into the abyss and seen the end of ideology. His experience has taught him the lesson of perspective, that in the long run we're all dead, and he is a convert to long views. He is joined at the Crooms's by another apostate from the left, Gifford Maxim, a repentant Communist, indeed, secret agent for the Comintern, whose political views have swung radically to the right without surrendering an ounce of their millenarian zeal. No matter whom he serves, he is a terrorist at heart. Laskell thinks of him as "the man of the far future, the bloody, moral apocalyptic future that was sure to come."[11] As we now know, Maxim is modelled upon Whittaker Chambers, whose transformation from minor-league spy to witness against Alger Hiss won him a starring role in the World Series of anticommunism in the early fifties.

Maxim, Laskell, and the Crooms are sharply drawn, representative figures who stand for political positions and processes that engaged, and ruined, so many intellectuals in the thirties. But *The Middle of the Journey* is first of all about the social imagination under the impact of political ideas and especially about that region of mind that is given neither to pure will nor pure idea, where the return of the repressed invades the historical sense and *mystique* takes shape as *politique*. The politics of *The Middle of the Journey* is largely a politics of character; the book's historical dimension is drastically foreshortened, and the background of actual events and circumstances is too generalized to exert any pressure on the story. The reader can scarcely fix the moment; only fleeting references to Spain and the Moscow trials locate the moment as somewhere in the neighborhood of 1936. Yet it is the spirit of an era rather than its events that Trilling wished to document, the still point of the turning world that produced the American intellectual class as it came to consciousness of itself after the tragic events of the thirties. *The Middle of the Journey* is a testament of a generation's disillusionment and conversion, which brought forth the chastened politics and subdued aesthetics of the post-war era. *The Middle of the Journey* reflects not only the triumph of the will in repose over the will in action, of ideas in modulation over the logic of the next step, but of modernism over realism and sensibility over agit prop. It is, then, very much a book about what Trilling would call "the self in crisis." This bears emphasizing. Most commentators on the book have taken its central figure, John Laskell, to be a stand-in for Trilling, as no doubt he largely is. They have also taken him and his spokesmanship for Erasmian humanism for a moral standard by which Maxim and the

Crooms may be judged, failing to observe that he too is subject to judgment as a distinctively modern character type. For the "disintegrated consciousness" that Trilling, following Hegel, would later attribute to the modern character (in *Sincerity and Authenticity*) is apparent in the delineation of Laskell, though in a subdued and benign form. He is a dangling man, having neither parents nor family nor anything that can be deemed a past. A bachelor at thirty-three, he is currently unattached; he has no children and no apparent future, and is in recoil anyway from the very assumptions of futurity. Did Beckett, did Dostoevsky, did Isaac Rosenfeld ever create a figure more alienated than this? He even looks upon himself as "a French poet of a man, sourly regarding his wasted, vanished youth, slack, with a body that felt gray and heavy, bitter of his fallen youth. *'J'ai perdu ma force et ma vie.'* "[12] No firebrand of revolutionism now, if ever he had been one, he is a figure of Romantic languor. His chief possessions are ideas, which he holds gingerly, with no great conviction. As an intellectual, he is supposed to be a hero of maturity and moderation, but as a man, he is bleak and unappealing and more chaste than his mere resistance to dangerous ideologies will explain. Though the political moment in *The Middle of the Journey* is the late thirties, the book otherwise is a typical product of the mid forties. It is very much to the point that Laskell has been ill and is presently convalescing, for though we are told that he has been laid low by scarlet fever, we know that he has really been stricken with history and is recuperating from the past. We know that the hot and molten Maxim and the cool Laskell, apparent antagonists, are really secret sharers, comparable American lives in search of second acts. Each is trying to recuperate in his own way from the same disease—scarlet fever, or an overdose of red—but where Maxim, racked by the more virulent strain, is riding the pendulum of atonement, Laskell just wants to take it easy, like Renan's Marcus Aurelius, basing his goodness on a perfect ennui. Maxim's politics are those of penance—reversal and undoing—while Laskell's are those of recovery (that Rooseveltian word)—abstinence and moderation.*

Yet for all its apparent concern with the self, *The Middle of the Journey* lacks the interiority of the true psychological novel. Except for Laskell's, and Trilling's, appreciation for ambivalence as nobility of character—

---

*Readers who are looking for a down-to-earth message in *The Middle of the Journey* may not be amiss in finding a retrospective vote for Roosevelt and the politics of the New Deal. In 1948, Laskell, could he have roused himself to get to the polls, would have voted for Truman, the Crooms for Henry Wallace, Maxim for Dewey.

that is, as a form of moral realism—and the mystique of easeful death, for which Keats is as much to blame as Freud, there is scarcely a Freudian idea in the book or a fictional technique whose provenance might be traced to the climate of modern introspection. *The Middle of the Journey* is very much about the dilemmas of the *conscious* mind; the forces in contest are ideas, not instincts, and the inner dynamics of character are simple and shallow. It is also a conventional novel, deliberately un-fashionable in its ideas and technical strategies, which derive mainly from the line of philosophical humanism that runs from Austen and George Eliot to Forster and James. Against the claims of the more ideological brands of naturalism and realism that held sway in the thirties, it poses not the radical subjectivity of Joyce or Proust but the sensibility of the Victorian novel of manners.

The Middle of the Journey's link to psychoanalysis, then, lies neither in its ideas nor in its aesthetic strategies but in the deeper rhythm of experi-ence that plots its moral curve; the rhythm of illness and recovery that sets us to talking about ideological movements and revolutions in the language of disease and health. Laskell, Maxim, and the Crooms all suffer from ideas—they are literally sick with modern thought. In the grim postwar years, history could scarcely seem anything other than a disease, nor recovery anything less than the most pressing business at hand. The "Wasteland outlook," now so much derided by the neoconser-vatives, came naturally to an age that had seen the collapse of Europe. In the aftermath of the war and the Holocaust, Trilling was not alone in pondering the ubiquity of neurosis and the cultural import of the Freud-ian maxim "We are all ill." "Now," he observed in his gloomy essay "Art and Fortune," "the old margin [for doubt] no longer exists; the facade is down; society's resistance to the discovery of depravity has ceased; now everyone knows that Thackeray was wrong, Swift right."

> The novel is a kind of summary and paradigm of our cultural life, which is perhaps why we speak sooner of its death than of the death of any other form of thought. It has been of all literary forms the most devoted to the celebration and investigation of the human will; and the will of our society is dying of its own excess. The religious will, the political will, the sexual will, the artisic will—each is dying of its own excess.[13]

Tinker with the language, and this might be Erich Fromm or Paul Goodman, or, for that matter, Isaac Rosenfeld or Norman Mailer. Even announcing *the* death of *the* sexual will was scarcely unique. Where Trilling's voice could be distinguished amid the general clamor was not in its bleak diagnosis but in his prescriptions for relief. He distinguished himself from both the Reichians, for whom the sexual will was also distressed, the liberals, and the unreconstructed Marxists in his vote for psychoanalysis and the novel as co-remedies. It was not exactly relief that Trilling was after, not in the sense of either release from the imperatives of the superego or the structures of culture, but a flexible détente with the dilemma. Freudian that he was, he did not court a remission of symptoms so much as a set of rules for constructing a modern self, a resilient ego that would be equal to the demands of the age, and he attempted the transformation by plunging into literature and attaching himself to the monuments of unaging intellect. He undertook to *become* the writers he cherished. Though that was a personal mission, Trilling habitually treated it as the project of his generation through the neat rhetorical gambit of turning the ambivalent "I" into a discriminating "we," disguising the personal stakes involved and playing up the shared dimensions of the crisis. Trilling had no difficulty regarding himself a representative case, thereby turning the education of his own feelings through the exploration of inner conflict and the cultivation of sensibility into a program: to reform the imagination of the prevailing liberal culture, or "to recall liberalism to its first essential, [the] imagination of variousness and possibility, which implies the awareness of complexity and difficulty."[14] What gave Trilling's own version of the crisis of feeling its pedagogical edge was his adherence to the example of Mill, thinking the crisis through and drawing the connections between his own troubles and the historical dilemmas of his generation. The essays in *The Liberal Imagination* can be read as chapters in a modern *Pilgrim's Progress* and *tableaux vivants* of the civilized ego in the agony of self-renovation.

It seems quixotic to seek revival for oneself, let alone for one's entire culture, through the ministry of, of all things, the novel. Given the depth of the crisis, one would have thought such remedy beyond the powers of mere literature. But for Trilling literature was never *mere,* possessing as he did so high an estimation of the novel's capacity for social intelligence, and crediting it, above all other products of human imagination, with representing the mind in its rarest and most civilized operations. For Trilling, the modern crisis was not primarily one of circumstances, however awful they might be, but of feeling and imagination; it was to the impoverished inner life that the lessons in *The Liberal Imagination* were addressed. And it was in the novel, especially the great novels of the nineteenth century, that Trilling saw the modern social imagination playing in its highest registers. Flaubert, Stendahl, Austen, James, Forster, and Tolstoy were for him not only great novelists but monuments of civilized intelligence in full bloom: symbols of that flowering of Western social consciousness that began in the Enlightenment and reached its apogee in the age of Queen Victoria.

But Trilling was almost always studying himself, and the essay in which he made his most exalted claims for the novel, "Art and Fortune," is also a spiritual autobiography in miniature, done according to the Romantic paradigm. Ostensibly a meditation on the death of the novel, it is really about the death and rebirth of "the will," and there can hardly be any doubt about whose will is at issue. But, in claiming for the novel the power to renovate the will, Trilling apparently had in mind not only his own intimate communion with literature but the example of Mill, whose youthful depression was cured by the reading of Marmontel's *Memoires* and whose convalescence and emotional reintegration were abetted by medicinal helpings of Wordsworth. To put the matter simply, the imagination heals what politics has injured. To reflect back on *The Middle of the Journey* with such a lesson in mind is to recognize Trilling's central failure in motivating John Laskell, in allowing his character to speak for his convictions without the benefit of Trilling's vital experiences, that is to say, his years spent in the library. Laskell's recovery from liberalism, unmediated by anything but a bedside rose upon which he meditates by the hour, rather than by something more substantial, like a romantic novel or a Victorian tract, is never credible.* By contrast, Gifford Maxim's conversion to muscular Christianity, set into motion by a hard-earned attack of remorse, is so much more convincing than Laskell's conversion to modulation and sensibility, which seems both unmotivated and intellectually flimsy. Laskell displays the sort of character that might be formed under the aegis of Henry James or T. S. Eliot; he is the Prufrock of post-Marxism. His convictions, lacking intellectual support, are scarcely to be distinguished from his manners.

Indeed, Laskell's abstractness goes to the heart of the book. By removing the action from natural arenas of conflict to a world apart in rural Connecticut, Trilling enabled himself to write a moral eclogue peopled with representative abstractions. Laskell in Connecticut is like Rasselas in Abyssinia, learning that you don't have to number the streaks of the tulip so long as you get the general drift. Gone are the cotton field, the assembly line, the picket line, and the meeting hall, but gone too are all social institutions and specific locales—the town, the family, or the university—in which cultural or political issues can be examined within a

---

*Even at his most bookish and prescient, however, Laskell could not have had the advantage of Whittaker Chambers's *Witness* to steer him toward a new sensibility, for that book would not be published for another sixteen years, in 1952.

firm network of social relations. Connecticut is not a metaphor for the world but for the seminar room, and the ranks of the possessed and the unpossessed who gather at the Crooms' have nothing to work out but ideas. To throw the emphasis of dramatic action upon the collision of ideas in isolation, or in Connecticut, which is pretty much the same thing, may argue the importance of ideas to history, but it tells us nothing about the pressure of history upon ideas.

III

> In time it may become apparent that Freud and his doctrine have undergone an inexorable disciplining by the culture, and that the exemplary cast of Freud's mind and character is more enduring than the particulars of his doctrine. In culture it is always the example that survives; the person is the immortal idea. Psychoanalysis was the perfect vehicle for Freud's intellectual character.
>
> —Philip Rieff, The Triumph of the Therapeutic

Finding the imaginative life of Western culture at bay, Trilling leapt to the defense of art wherever he saw it threatened, whether by the ideological demands of the political Left, the pedagogical reductions of the New Criticism, or by psychoanalysis, in its claims that the pleasures of art were "substitute gratifications," that poetry was a continuation of daydreaming, and that art was neurosis by other means. Thus he was passionate in defending art against Edmund Wilson's claim, in *The Wound and the Bow,* that it issues from injury and that, citing the myth of Philoctetes, the bow of creativity is drawn by a "wound." For if literature should remain under the cloud of neurosis, as a mere symptom sublimated upward, then it is unfit to heal what politics has injured, and the moral point of appealing to the novel as a tonic for the social will "dying of its own excess" is foolish. The cornerstone of Trilling's moral system was the essential balance and health of art, and Trilling portrayed those writers whom he favored as object lessons in psychic composure. He endorsed Lamb's dictum that true genius is sane, that "the true poet dreams being awake. He is not possessed by his subject but has dominion over it."[15] Laboring under the shadow of universal illness, the artist is exemplary in managing his conflicts and putting them to aesthetic use. "He is what he is by virtue of his successful objectification of his neurosis, by his shaping it and making it available to others in a way which has its effect upon their own egos in struggle."[16] Regardless of the conflicts and neuroses that may underlie his writing, what is healthy in the artist is his power "to conceive, to plan, to work, and to bring his work to a conclusion."

What invariably captured Trilling's attention was the pedagogical example, and his books are little pantheons of exemplary minds whose ways of balancing pressures and reconciling tensions shine forth as instructive for us all. James, Keats, Austen, Forster, Arnold, Mill, Orwell, and, especially, Freud are heroes of thought whose heroism lay in a judicious management of claims, a skeptical peace with the cultural donnée, and a qualified détente with the conditioned nature of social existence. They are, in a phrase, wise adversaries of culture. Trilling was a believer in chastened and mature rebellions that combined radical criticism of the existing order with tragic resignation, and he exalted the career of Sigmund Freud as the very paradigm of such a rebellion. Psychoanalysis entered such a system as a guide to judgment rather than a tool of investigation—an ethical posture and a statement, in the idiom of a science, of the moral life of Sigmund Freud. "The figure of Freud," notes Steven Marcus, "was for him something very close to a moral ideal, or to an ideal of personal character and conduct. Freud's fierceness, boldness, honesty and independence, his sense of tragedy and stoical resistance all served or figured as models for him, models that he reaffirmed in his own person and tried to fulfill in his own existence."[17]

As Trilling understood, psychoanalysis *is* a moral psychology whose values are embodied in the character of Freud himself, with his skepticism, his intellectual restlessness, his militant rationalism, and his subjection of his own motives and dreams, as well as those of his patients, to rigorous interrogation. Its very object is the character of the patient, the composition of habits and manners, experiences and ideas that constitutes his identity, and it was the most radical and enduring of Freud's discoveries that his neurotic patients were suffering from ideas rather than from neurological disorders and that treatment properly began with an examination of those ideas. The features of mind that are the hallmarks of the psychoanalytic view: repression, the dynamic unconscious, and the contrast between "manifest" and "latent" mental events are moral concepts that locate truth in the unconscious mind. And yet in view of Trilling's declarations of indebtedness to Freud, nothing is so characteristic of him as the discrepancy between his zeal for Freud and his application of him. While many of Trilling's essays may be read as applied Freud, they are largely applications of his character and his outlook rather than his methodologies of interpretation. Trilling's relation to psychoanalysis was dominated by his shyness about its explanatory conventions and his penchant for leavening his insights with large helpings of rhetorical tact.

In part, this reflected Trilling's fidelity to modulation, the conviction that too strenuous a pursuit of radical ideas violated the delicate textures of thought and betrayed the ambiguities of social or literary situations. Trilling's exposure to Marxist criticism, in which what passed for engagement and precision was often just bullying and ignorance, turned him against all efforts to regiment the play of thought. Though he, like other disenchanted left intellectuals in the 1940s, turned to Freud and cultivated innerness out of a disaffection from progressive dogmas, his very style of embracing psychoanalysis reflected his habits of circumspection. Nowhere in his criticism do we find the nerveless joy of dissection that marks the scientific attitude: no relentless scurrying after latent meanings, no boastful disclosures of infantile wishes and irrational drives that "explain" Orwell or Babel or Austen. He followed Freud himself in proclaiming the helplessness of the psychoanalyst before the mysteries of the creative gift and joined his mentor in disparaging the application of coarse clinical language to art. He did not believe that psychoanalysis had anything to say about the artist's "unconscious intention as it exists apart from the work itself."[18]

If Trilling neglected to apply psychoanalysis with rigor and zeal, then, it is because he lacked enthusiasm for the diagnostic reduction of complex feelings and perceptions. As a partisan of literature he was distressed by the psychoanalytic practice of analyzing downward toward the infantile, the sexual, the irrational, and the unconscious. Anyone who has read Trilling on Freud carefully and observed his Freudianism in operation is bound to be puzzled by Saul Bellow's claim that "Professor Trilling wishes to leave the surface of life with its stories and descend into the depths of the unconscious in search of truth and maturity, becoming, if he can think hard and face the unconscious fearlessly, one of Aristotle's Great Souled Men. Thus Professor Trilling seems to agree . . . that there is no such thing as a grown-up person."[19] Surely, this is as far from the spirit of Trilling's practice as it is possible to get. If the basic theorem of psychoanalysis is that the mind of every adult harbors a baby literally crying for immediate gratification, then Trilling stood opposed to the basic theorem, preferring to look in every great writer for the adult battling his way toward equilibrium, reality, and self-acceptance—toward being grown-up.

There is considerable wisdom in this. Distant though this practice may appear from the deep-analytic strategies of psychoanalytic interpretation as it is commonly employed, Trilling was adapting to criticism the ethics of the therapist, who allies himself with the adult element of the patient's psyche in its war against the infantile. The therapeutic proposition, "Where id was, there ego shall be," became in Trilling's hands a principle of critical aid. Determined not to be one of Max Weber's specialists without heart, he championed the beleaguered ego in its battles to sustain itself between a demanding and insatiable id and a repressive superego.

But to commend Trilling's partisanship of reason and adulthood raises the question of whether his style of befriending art by refusing to set down in the imagination's more turbulent waters and by keeping his distance from patently troubled or demonic writers—from, in short, romantics—did not weaken the claims of art. Observing rhetorical etiquette is not the same thing as defending complex and subtle ideas against reduction, and what passes in Trilling for balance or modulation or negative capability or a full and judicious view of situations is sometimes just a blanket of decorum that, denying the demonic in order to affirm the rational, denies art the full range of its power and the artist his courage.

This reticence about the explanatory powers of psychoanalysis in the face of literature may explain why Trilling neglected the early analytical books in Freud's canon in favor of the later, speculative books in which Freud turned his attention to cultural, social, and metaphysical questions and produced such adventures in analysis-at-a-distance as *Beyond the Pleasure Principle*, *Group Psychology and the Analysis of the Ego*, *The Future of an Illusion*, and *Civilization and Its Discontents*. We might even regard Trilling's psychoanalysis as largely a habit of dialectical thought that had been purged of its specific theses and sublimed into a phenomenology of the mind. Consider what is not to be found in it. Guilt is conspicuously absent, though Trilling never tired of adverting to the special insight into human depravity that psychoanalysis shares with modern fiction. The dynamic unconscious is missing entirely and with it the characteristic rhythm of repression and the return of the repressed that for Freud was the very pulse of dreams, myths, and neuroses. Dreams themselves were apparently ruled out, along with the fantasy life of the artist, and with them went not only the distinction between manifest and latent meanings but the whole inventory of formal transformations that Freud called dreamwork. We find only rare, and somewhat embarrassed, mention of infantile sexuality and its bodily stages and derivative passions and practices, though sex, even of the conventional, adult varieties, had little place in Trilling's reformed liberalism. Of what he might have gathered from the psychology of jokes or that of the errors and self-betrayals of daily life, Trilling makes no mention.

What he kept was largely the structural or dialectical model of the mind and the intrapsychic dynamism of ego, id, and superego—"the Wagnerian theory of warring instincts" as Frederick Crews calls it—that brings conflict, indecision, and self-torment to the forefront of our view of the emotions.[20] He kept the biologism, which he employed in a late essay, "Freud: Within and Beyond Culture," as a rebuke to the social Freudians who had given, he would claim, too much authority to culture and had robbed the individual of a degree of freedom that his biology, existing apart from culture, afforded him.[21] He also adopted the cultural dialectic of *Civilization and Its Discontents,* the struggle of the ego to claim a niche for itself between instinct and culture. He admired those attitudes and personal traits that bespoke Freud's concern for shoring up the distressed ego: his commitment to secular rationalism and his opposition to the delusions of mythic and religious thinking, his wary approval of culture, his refusal to allow disappointment, opposition, and pain to weaken his convictions or hinder his work, and his very definition of mental health as the capacity for love and work. But, above all, Trilling prized Freud's stoicism and the idea of the self, as Steven Marcus has put it, "affirmed in self-denial, of the idea that life is nothing if not sacrificial."[22] But such an endorsement identifies Trilling's Freud as the Freud of *outlook,* not the Freud of *insight,* and indicates that his admiration has been won at the cost of favoring his "philosophy" over his diagnostic psychology.

This taste for the shadows in Freud shows up in Trilling's thought as something distinct from psychoanalysis, and Trilling sometimes followed it to conclusions that look less like reasoned assessments than tragic postures. The death instinct, for instance, was valued for its reflection of Freud's character and as a moral touchstone for modern man's self-evaluation, rather than for its philosopical cogency or empirical plausibility. In a review of the third volume of Ernest Jones's biography of Freud, Trilling offered the observation that the death instinct "may be understood as the intellectual expression of Freud's pride, of his passion for autonomy."

> The theory certainly would seem to be in the interests of human autonomy—if we accept it, we must see that it is no more absurd to say that a man wills to die than to say that he wills to eat or to copulate.[23]

We may justly suspect the reasoning, since any idea we accept ceases instantly to be absurd, and we may be suspicious as well of the detachment of a portion of Freud's metapsychology from the findings that support it and the consequences of its application and its attachment to the character of the scientist. The empirical validity and explanatory sufficiency of the death instinct are dispensed with in favor of its philosophical elegance and moral elevation, its grandeur, and its resistance to those influences in modern culture that incline toward making life "weightless."[24]

> Hence [Freud's] celebration of what he called the "energizing pessimism" of the Greeks in their great day, hence his passionate recommendation of *amor fati,* which might be translated by a phrase of Marx's, "the appropriation of human reality" which includes, Marx said, human suffering, "for suffering humanly considered is an enjoyment of the self for man."

In other words, if the death instinct can't be entirely believed, its tonic effect on the afflicted will "dying of its own excess" may nonetheless be honored. For with Freud as it had been with Arnold, it is the value of the myth, not the demonstrability of the fact, that is the object of devotion, for it is the myth rather than the fact that shapes behavior and determines the values and the destiny of culture.

IV

Just once did Trilling indulge his psychoanalytic curiosity and permit himself the freedom of its insights. That was in "The Poet as Hero: Keats in His Letters" (in *The Opposing Self*), in which he invoked the authority of Freudian ideas to argue for Keat's geniality, his passion, and his courage.[25] Not incidentally, the Keats essay is Trilling's most devoted study, after the Arnold and Forster books, of a single author and his work. Certainly it is central to any appraisal of how Trilling employed psychoanalysis, not just because it features the one straightforward demonstration of analytic reasoning in all his writing, but also because it advances psychoanalytic interpretation in the spirit of Freudian rectitude. As a critic primed by psychoanalysis was bound to see, Keats is the most voluptuous of the English poets, vigorous in his appetites and open in his eroticism, a man for whom "the sensory, the sensuous, and the sensual were all one. He is possibly unique among poets in the extent of his reference to eating and drinking and to its pleasurable and distasteful sensations." But, having admitted that, Trilling obligingly entered the caveat that to characterize Keats as an"oral" character, as the diagnostic side of psychoanalysis would recommend, would imply an unseemly passivity, a submission to appetites that should have been subordinated to more "manly" concerns, and a lingering emotional dependence upon a mother whose importance is everywhere implied but nowhere acknowledged in her son's letters. Yet, as those letters testify, this writer who could celebrate the cool gush of a nectarine sliding down his throat and call out, in his great "Ode to a Nightingale," for "a beaker of the warm South,/ . . . With beaded bubbles winking at the brim" was no aging infant or emotional invalid whose genius was founded upon arrested development but an independent, sensible, spirited, intelligent man, whom both Freud and Trilling would agree to call an adult. Trilling's dilemma, then, was twofold: to reconcile the indulgence of the poetry with the spirited intelligence of the letters and to account for the ample eroticism and happy gluttony in the poetry of someone whose mother has seemingly been banished from his memory, though his speech is thick with such metaphors as "the heart is the teat from which the mind or intelligence sucks identity."

These ambiguities may have bothered the moralist in Trilling but not the dialectician. Of the mother, little could be said; her apparent absence from her son's thought, even in intimate letters to his brothers and sister, brought forth the estimation that "there was much, it would seem, to be forgotten." And yet, if the son's vigor and self-acceptance are to be understood and brother George's praise for her taken into account, "There would seem to be no reason to question, there is indeed, reason to suppose, her affectionate and indulgent nature—what we may call a biological generosity." Clearly, such a line of investigation—the reconstruction of Mrs. Keats—is a dead end. But not so the conjunction of indulgence and maturity, of childishness and heroism in Keats. This fusion of opposites is built into the very evolution of the passions, and, in fact, by the age of five we already have evidence of the militant young Keats. "We read of the violent child of five who armed himself with a sword and brandished it on guard at the door and refused to let his mother leave the house; the story in this form is given by Haydon, who is not reliable, though usually apt, in the stories he tells; another version of the story is that Keats used the sword to keep anyone from entering his mother's room when she was ill." Such Oepidal sergeant-at-armsmanship is prelude to the next stage of the emotions, a gateway to fortitude, energy, and even negative capability. "It is possible to say of Keats that the indulgence of his childhood goes far toward explaining the remarkable *firmness of his character,* which I have spoken of as *his heroic quality*" (italics mine). The discrepant elements in Keats, then, are just phases of a natural growth in which the things of childhood were not put aside but assimilated, the man becoming the sum of all his biological potentials.

The figure thus drawn is the most familiar of Trilling heroes, the divided self, though in this instance the divisions are happily resolved in the interests of energy and self-acceptance. Still, despite the tidy resolution, the exercise is edged in discomfort, and the ingenious developmental argument reads as though it was brought into play not just to save the critic from contradiction but to deliver the artist from the subversive charges of psychoanalysis itself. Trilling's labored defense of Keats's maturity is a bid to save him from the Romantic view that he was a languid spokesman for sleep and poetry and a frail victim of the world's cruelties, who died, not of tuberculosis, but of reviews. Psychoanalysis endorses that view by treating the creative imaginative as akin to daydreaming and child's play and by showing a solicitude for evidence of weakness, debility, and dependence in its relentless search for pathology. Little wonder, then, that Trilling deploys the evolutionary dialectics of psychoanalysis here in an effort to get beyond its moral bias, which is to uncover the wellsprings of imagination in regressed emotions and to find meaning in the poet's *unconscious* symbolism. The Keats essay registers the strain between the subversiveness of psychoanalysis as a diagnostic and the balance and poise of the Freudian ethic. Henceforth, in Trilling's writing, psychoanalysis would take a back seat to Freud, and the dynamics of creativity to the parameters of the "modern self" in the modern world.

This absorption in Keats's letters rather than his poetry, was, like the elevation of Freud's Weltanschauung over his methods, a shying away from the asocial element in poetry itself. If Keats's letters to his brother George are taken to be more reliable guides to the cast of his mind than "Ode to Indolence," then his spiritedness may be praised without extenuation. But to rescue Keats from the distortions of the Romantic agony is also to isolate him neatly from the driven and vulnerable parts of his own personality and thus from the very pressures and fears that sparked his imagination and brought forth such a body of great poetry before his death at twenty-five. Lionel Trilling may have been a friend to literature but he was no lover of poetry, and the Keats essay demonstrates amply why the novel, with its hum and buzz of social implication, gratified him far better than did poetry, with its taste for the self in isolation and its traffic in those portions of the emotional life that lie below "character," that is, below scruples, judgment, values, reason, and the social instincts. In this, Trilling reflects the general suspicion of poetry that characterizes

Enlightenment rationalism, which takes instruction to be the proper function of art and is nervous about its emotional and irrational appeals.

After the Keats essay, not only were there no more ventures into applied psychoanalysis but not more encounters with poetry. That side of the self engaged by poetry and psychoanalysis alike was not the side that Trilling cared to pursue, and as James and Austen bulked larger in his thoughts, poetry underwent a diminution. We hear nothing about the nineteenth century's poets, even such relatively social poets as Scott, Byron, Browning, or Tennyson, let alone the dithyrambic poets like Shelley and Swinburne. The century shapes up in Trilling's portrait as the exclusive domain of its great novelists.

Here, then, was a circumspect partisanship of the depths, a rhetoric of the depths, really, which extolled the inner life without giving it too much actual play. Trilling was captivated by the *idea* of the inner life, much as he was by the idea of politics or the idea of death; he Hegelianized psychoanalysis for the same reasons he Platonized politics: to refine out the cruder elements and isolate the essential ideas. Morris Dickstein has characterized Trilling as a Tory radical, a useful way to conceptualize his ambiguities provided we keep in mind that the radical element was largely a genius for deploying ideas and imagining ever more subtle essences rather than a passion for uncovering irreducible roots and motives.[26] If radical thought in its customary modern forms is the paring away of "superstructures" (or "bourgeois illusions") to lay bare the brute facts of biological need or infantile experience or class interest behind an idea or ideology, then Trilling's brand of radicalism was something decidedly unfamiliar: an upward distillation of the vapors of thought into their rarest and most abstract expressions.

A good deal can be said in favor of such an unfashionable, high-minded radicalism that reduces to general ideas rather than to prior conditions, for it is, like all radical styles, a way of precipitating essentials out of their solution of incidentals. But Trilling's high-mindedness was compromised by his fastidiousness, which made his brand of negative capability sound occasionally like squeamishness and his dialectics like mere ceremonies of fussiness. One often feels that Trilling is holding too much at bay, as though his first consideration were to deny extremes. Certainly the habits of balance, skepticism, and irony that stood him in good stead during a decade of dogma and intellectual vulgarity also served to cut short reasonable lines of intellectual inquiry. Too fine a judiciousness may cut off the avenues of adventure. What passes from one point of view for negative capability may look like protective irony from another.

Trilling, then, is elusive, especially when one is concerned to pin down his ambiguities and link up his "positions" with the historical situation and to what he would call "the will." What is not ambiguous is his role in the postwar redefinition of liberalism, for he must be counted among the intellectuals who altered the prevailing rhetoric of liberalism from one of social progress and justice to one of sensibility and depth, all the while tidying up the depths by purging them of whatever was embarrassing, childish, or undignified. For the intellectuals, Trilling pointed the way from Henry Wallace to Adlai Stevenson and from a politics of quantities that spoke of masses and dreamed of the greatest good for the greatest number to one of qualities, that counselled self-development and self-restraint. Trilling's brands of modulation and synthesis were a boon to his criticism; the range of voices and the purchase on ideas they brought gave him a grasp and flexibility matched by few of his contemporaries. But such intellectual syntheses as he could effect, including the blending of psychoanalysis and liberalism, were achieved at great cost to the radical features of the original ideas. Thus psychoanalysis was asked to surrender its critical bite and liberalism its progressive expectations. Consequently, such upgrading, deepening, and enrichment as Trilling brought to liberalism also deflected it from its historical mission: to ameliorate the conditions of life. And without a program of reform, liberalism found itself in the 1950s on the sidelines, armed only with irony which, as Adlai Stevenson demonstrated so well, fell short of being a sufficient politics. Disenchanted with economics, disillusioned with "reality in America," ready at long last to endorse the basic premises of American society, and only casually interested in those elements of the self that can least tolerate the constraints of culture, liberalism set the conditions for its own demise in the 1960s, when its ideas in modulation would be shaken by the tremors of an unmodulated world.

6. From Socialism to Therapy, II
Wilhelm Reich

> The politics of the prewar Marxist parties has no future. Just as the concept of the sexual energy perished within the psychoanalytic organization and arose anew, young and vigorous, from the discovery of the orgone, so did the concept of the international worker perish in the Marxist party doings and arise anew in the framework of sex-economic sociology.
> —Wilhelm Reich, *The Function of the Orgasm*

> To get laid is actually socially constructive and useful, an act of citizenship.
> —Moses Herzog, in Bellow, *Herzog*

> I suggest to her that fucking was a philosophical act of considerable importance.
> —Daniel Isaacson, in Doctorow, *The Book of Daniel*

THE MOST AFFIRMATIVE of the doctrines to make headway among writers during and after the war were those of Wilhelm Reich, whose system of character analysis (or vegetotherapy or, as it grew metaphysical, orgonomy) pinpointed the source of recent political disaster in the armored character of Western Man and prescribed an arduous program of action therapy as the key to individual salvation and social renewal. Reich's theories of sex economy and character armoring plausibly accounted for certain observed universals of political behavior: the weakness for authoritarianism in the democratic nations and the rule of what political philosopher Robert Michels had called the "iron law of

oligarchy" in political systems everywhere, including the most revolutionary and "democratic" parties.[1] Unlike Freud, whose politics were
tinged with skepticism, Reich was nothing if not righteous and impas-
sioned, and his political credentials were, on the face of them, impecca-
bly radical. He fancied himself a democrat and a feminist and
propounded something he called "work democracy," which he defined
in terms reminiscent of the young, "humanist" Karl Marx as the "sum
total of all naturally developed and developing life functions which
organically govern rational human relationships."[2] Fascism, then, which
Reich abominated, was the political expression of an organic maladjustment, the epidemic severence of men from their life functions, rendering them susceptible to demagogic promises of fulfillment through
submission to authority and explosive outbursts of violence. (Some of his
followers, however, including Norman Mailer and Paul Goodman,
would regard such outbursts as tonic.) And despite an early affection for
Marxism and membership in the German Communist party, from which
he was expelled, Reich was, by the postwar era, bitterly opposed to
Stalinism. He called it "red fascism" and "Modju"* and saw it as a retreat
from the ideals of Marx, Engels, and Lenin toward dictatorship, a retreat
abetted, not incidentally, by the Russian masses themselves. Substitute
Stalinism for fascism in the following typical explanation of the latter in
The Mass Psychology of Fascism, and you have Reich's essential explanation
of it.

> My medical experience with individuals from all kinds of social strata,
> races, nationalities and religions showed me that "fascism" is only the
> politically organized expression of the average human character structure,
> a character structure which has nothing to do with this or that race, nation
> or party but which is general and international. In this characterological
> sense, *"fascism" is the basic emotional attitude of man in authoritarian society, with
> its machine civilization and its mechanistic-mystical view of life.*[3]

Such views are consistent with those of Freud, who also took politics
for an expression of the universals in the character of man, and with
those of Erich Fromm, who read in fascism the human desire to escape
from freedom and submit to the mass and the dictates of authority.
But where Reich distinguished himself from Freud and the neo-
Freudians was in exalting the sexual principle as the key determinant of
the social will. "In brief, the goal of sexual suppression," he urged in

---

*"Modju" was a term Reich constructed from the initial letters of Mocenigo, the man
who denounced Giordano Bruno, and Dzhugashvili, Stalin's original, Georgian name.

Mass Psychology, "is that of producing an individual who is adjusted to the authoritarian order and who will submit to it in spite of all misery and degradation."

> At first, the child has to adjust to the structure of the authoritarian miniature state, the family; this makes it capable of later subordination to the general authoritarian system. *The formation of the authoritarian structure takes place through the anchoring of sexual inhibition and sexual anxiety.*[4]

Neither the death instinct nor the superego nor the innate aggression of the species nor alienation but "the social suppression of genital love" is the bacillus of totalitarianism. But like a bacillus and unlike a genetic defect, it is susceptible to countermeasures. In narrowing down the problem of alienation to the sexual sphere, Reich rescued political psychology from tragic biology and delivered it into the hands of medicine—not, to be sure, conventional medicine, as the American Medical Association and the Federal Drug Administration understood it, but medicine as premodern naturalists imagined it, as a branch of moral philosophy. Notwithstanding the bold sweep of his analyses, Reich was the most resolutely biologistic of Freud's renegade disciples, and there is ample reason to look upon his system as a political neurobiology and *not* as a psychology.

Reich's attraction for intellectuals in the 1940s lay partly in his reduction of the field of battle from society to the body, where gains might be more easily registered, and partly in his gospel of the orgasm as the sine qua non of psychological and social hygiene. In part also it lay in his putative ability to account for the failures of the Russian revolution and of leftism everywhere by fastening upon the sexual sphere as the missing variable in prior revolutionary calculations, and therefore, in effect, keeping revolutionary hopes alive. Sex, for Reich, *was* politics, and the contentious language of his manifestoes, with its military metaphors of blocks and breakthroughs, made his system sound less like a retreat from the blows of history than a regrouping for a war of liberation against the residual puritanism and production-oriented austerities of American life. His rejection of adjustment in favor of revolutionary assault upon all superegos, personal and social, and his clinical methods for relaxing muscular rigidity, dissolving psychic resistance, and storming the barricades of sexual pleasure appealed to stymied radicals as adjustments downward of the campaign against Wall Street that more conventional strategies had failed to carry through.

"In the gloom of the Cold War years," Frederick Crews has observed, "intellectuals whose historicism had been shaken faced the choice of either accommodating themselves to a prosperous anti-Communist society or taking a stand directly on what Mailer, citing Reich, called 'the rebellious imperatives of the self.'"[5] Crews poses the alternatives perhaps too starkly. One could be Dwight Macdonald and cling to an undefined anarcho-pacifism, risking the isolation and impotence of anarcho-pacifists everywhere. Still, Crews rightly points out that Reich's ideas had a special cachet for revolutionists without a revolution, for whom the field of battle had dwindled to the self. It was as a sanction for individual desublimation that Reich's orgonomy rendered its appeal as an insurrectionary code, as hostile to the fetishes of party and doctrine in Russia as it was to those of achievement and production in America. Paul Goodman, in touting the political superiority of Reich's psychology in the 1940s, spoke contemptuously of the counterrevolutionary social adjustments demanded by the New Deal and Stalinism alike.[6] Such a cavalier linking of Roosevelt and Stalin seems sheer madness to us now that the nature of the Soviet state is so plain and so appalling (though it was anything but a secret in 1945), though it seemed perfectly plausible to some radicals after the war who saw little more in the struggle between East and West than shadowboxing between Gog and Magog, variants on the same predatory imperialism. Some, like Goodman and Dwight Macdonald, were anarchists; others, certainly Norman Mailer in the forties, were lingering Leninists who still smarted, ten years after the fact, from the Comintern's scuttling of all-out class warfare for a meliorist "people's front" in 1935. But anarchists and class warriors alike, they held fast to their old dreams of striking deep, disclosing the basic laws of human conduct, and drawing up blueprints for the liberation of man wherever he was oppressed, in Russia or America.

In fact, once the question of Russia was settled for all but a handful of popular front loyalists, America became the great conundrum. For homeless radicals of the 1940s, some of whom found a home in Dwight Macdonald's *Politics* during its brief existence, Moscow and Levittown enjoyed a certain parity as centers of the emotional plague. America's wartime alliance with Russia was either the lull before Armageddon or a treacherous reconciliation of opposites into a repressive global imperium—the end of history by bang or by whimper. "It is a war fought by two different exploitative systems," instructs McLeod, Norman Mailer's spokesman for the Trotskyist analysis in his novel *Barbary Shore*, "a system vigorous in the fever of death, and another monstrous in the swelling of anemia. One doesn't predict the time precisely, but regardless of the temporary flux of the military situation, it is a war which ends as a conflict between two virtually identical forms of exploitation."[7] The prospect of peace between the new superpowers was scarcely more cheering than the threat of war. For the work of liberating mankind, hands across the sea loomed as ominous as guns along the shore. The state of tension, even were it not to erupt into shooting, could only strengthen the machinery of domination in both societies, fostering permanent garrison states in which the regimentation of populaces, sustained by their citizens' anxious flights from freedom, would effectively destroy all social distinctions between the two. Indeed, the advent of McCarthyism would be taken by some as proof positive of the Stalinization of America. And yet, while Trotskyists and anarchists alike might concur on such theses as these, few had any heart for spirited calls to arms. To whom would they be issued? To the rank and file of America's "proletarians," employed as never before in a dynamic, expanding economy and organized into labor unions that were skilled at converting surly impulses into wage and hour demands? To the restive petite bourgeoisie who were so busy turning their candy stores into supermarkets that calls to revolution never got past their answering services? To the legions of white negros (and some black ones too) gathering nightly at the San Remo or the White Horse in anticipation of the Great Revolt or a fistfight between rival poets? To the comic armies of the night that, two decades later, would endeavor to levitate the Pentagon by mantra power alone? Who were the toiling masses anyway?

It was altogether reasonable, then, that stymied intellectuals, drugged by the daily crisis, downcast over their isolation, and weary of signing up for Cold War conferences sponsored by Moscow or Washington, would respond to a political biology that appealed to their most anarchic appetites while promising comprehensive social benefits from their indulgence. "Unrepressed people," declared Paul Goodman in the pages of *Politics* in 1945, citing Reich, "will provide for themselves a society that is peaceable and orderly enough."[8] Saul Bellow's Moses Herzog says it more bluntly later on, musing that "to get laid is actually socially constructive and useful, an act of citizenship." Would that Reich had Herzog's concision, for the latter's aphorism speaks tedious volumes. Reich could be as literal-minded about sex and salvation as any bachelor on the loose and just as monotonous. Dispensing with the tedium of organization and theory, of party caucuses and Marxist study groups, he envisioned a revolutionary spirit disburdened of wearisome politics. The revolution could be forwarded at home, in bed, in the revolutionist's spare time, saving him the agonies of canvassing and cajoling, factional rivalries and power struggles, conflicting doctrines and hairsplitting interpretations, and, most gratefully, painful appeals to a working class that was fundamentally hostile to revolutionism. In the Reichian utopia, the party would be abolished and the new revolutionary movement organized along the lines of the clinic or research institute. (Indeed, as social redemption became a function of personal prophylaxis, doctrine took a back seat to counselling.) Man's compulsive escape from freedom would now reverse itself spontaneously as his treatment took effect.

The flow of consciousness envisioned by Reich was spontaneous and ineluctable, carrying the analysand from private desublimation to public vigilance. The lineaments of gratified desire had the curious feature of bringing to life one's social dissatisfactions. The "little man" made whole and sexually vital would not stand for a corrupt, armored, or fascist world. As he gained harmony with his own nature, his militancy would spread in ripples from the body to the body politic, which Reich imagined in almost Platonic terms as the individual writ large. Man and state, microcosm and macrocosm, were joined by the life force itself, and whatever impinged upon the one would quickly be registered upon the other.

Of itself that vision hardly distinguished Reich from Marx; after all, a metaphysic of correspondences is not very different in its working details from a dialectic of man and society. What distinguished Reich is the literalness with which he imagined the metaphor of the body politic and the vectors of revolutionary potential. Reich's revolutionary equations always began with the private, sexual self and flowed outward toward the public, political self. (Late in his career, his erotics of redemption stretched all the way from the genitals to the heavens.) Such a metaphysics of bodily revolt ("the gonad theory of revolution," sneered C. Wright Mills)[9] not only played down questions of institutional, impersonal power, it happily cancelled the tragic conflict of self and civilization that Freud took to be irreducible. At its most extreme, orgonomy turned against the Freudian virtues of sublimation, strength of character, and self-knowledge, abominating them as toxic substances, literally carcinogens. In his later years, Reich would complain—or was it a boast?— that *Civilizations and Its Discontents* was written in response to one of his, Reich's, lectures in Freud's home in 1929: "I was the one who was 'unbehaglich in der Kultur.'"[10] Not only were the tragic vistas of the later Freud washed over by the orgonomic streams of Eros, so was the sole ground of optimism on which a younger Freud had established his own therapeutic discipline: the potential for self-correction through self-awareness. Under the Reichian dispensation, self-inquiry became just another layer of suppressive armor, a clinically fashionable way of blocking the flow of natural vegetative juices. If the hero of Freud's old age was Moses, that of Reich's was the segmented earthworm.[11] The modern therapeutic offshoots of the Reichian ethos such as est have maintained this hostility to reasoned self-interrogation which, according to them, merely reinforces the inhibitions that afflict the neurotic. Viewing modern man as Hamlet, they see the native hue of resolution everywhere sicklied o'er with the pale cast of thought.

How American this sounds, and how profitable it has become to Reich's spiritual heirs, from Fritz Perls and Ida Rolf to Arthur Janov and Werner Erhard, who recognized the growth potential of spiritual relief and were wary enough not to rouse the Federal Drug Administration on the way to the bank. And thus how strange it is to ponder the FDA's persecution of Reich for so naive a contraption as the orgone accumulator, which posed neither a political nor a sexual challenge to American society and was so transparently useless that the taste for it would shortly have proven as perishable as the rage for T'ai Ch'i or the Last Chance Diet had not the FDA confirmed Reich's paranoia by tacking an earthly martyrdom onto his intergalactic trials.[12] That too, Reich's final episode of arrogant hucksterism—which he conducted, naturally, as a crusade—was American to the core. The orgone accumulator was as harmless as Hadacol and as innocent as snake oil. Reich's bioenergetic revivalism, despite its origin in German dialectics and the thought-tormented arena of Jewish modernity, was surprisingly in tune with the upbeat mood of postwar suburbia. Its promises of psychic rebirth, moral reawakening, and a magical reintegration of the alienated self had an American zest to them. Reich didn't put the ailing into analysis; he sent them into training, and there is a quality in his demeanor—the crackpot boosterism—and a note in his voice—a boozy collegiate vivacity—that recalls not Freud or Marx or Trotsky but Woody Hayes. Had the FDA not prosecuted him as a cancer quack and banned the sale of his orgone accumulators—those upright plywood coffins, their walls packed with rockwool and steelwool to catch and focus the fluxions of eternity—they would surely have found their way into dens and rumpus rooms all over America, alongside the barbells and the exercycle, to become bioenergetic supplements to aerobic dancing and tantric yoga. In the orgone box, as on the exercycle, one enjoys the grateful illusion of moving forward without having to leave the house.

Reich was a revivalist for the post-Bible belt, and what he offered was nothing so much as a secular, erotic baptism into a life beyond conflict and neurosis. Such an appeal, the appeal of ecstatic rebirth, had implications far beyond the intellectual circles in which they initially took root.

When one peels away the layers of militancy that were properties of Reich's own abrasive character but not necessarily of his therapy, one discovers a revolutionism for the depressed suburbanite, fearful of conforming and just as fearful of taking any drastic step that might expose his imaginary independence. We see him on bike paths everywhere as the man in the gray flannel warm-ups, jogging away the blues, lonely as a long-distance runner in the evening, solid as a Rotarian from nine to five. Holding the therapies of "adjustment" in contempt, Reichianism and its spin-offs from Gestalt to est have cleared a path to social adjustment by inducing regular, convulsive fits of rage in the therapeutic session, creating a purely synaptic equilibrium and permitting the troubled individual to get on with the loathesome job at hand. In orgonomy, Freud's reflex arc becomes Reich's guide to the perplexed.

Even among intellectuals, who are less inclined to equipoise and appreciate the use of imbalance, it does seem to be the case that they, in their Reichian phases, while striking anti-American postures were always profoundly patriotic in their deeper intuitions. "America," announced Allen Ginsberg in a famous early poem, "I'm putting my queer shoulder to the wheel."[13] Certainly, the self-reliant brand of radicalism they advanced appealed to the same American love of tinkering and weekend projects that spawned the do-it-yourself craze in home improvement and auto repair. Reichianism was pragmatic and self-applied, and like capitalism it envisioned the transformation of private labors into public benefits. Yet it was not just the convenience of mounting a revolution by simply mounting a friend or the authorization of the orgasm as a blow against repression or even the opportunity to join erotic forces with the hedonists of Peyton Place that made the appeal to intellectuals so seductive. Another factor was bound to register with artists and writers: the promise that sexual desublimation would also free the imagination. Artists and writers, after all, are patrons of the unconscious and know better than anyone how painful the daily solicitation can be. The deeper life on which the artist must draw is not always on tap, and artists are always on the lookout for ways to allure it, stalk it, beguile and tame it. Philip Reiff charges in *The Triumph of the Therapeutic* that artists in the forties and fifties found the Reichian doctrine that identifies the artists with the "genital character" flattering and therefore flocked to it from a grateful sense of being the erotic elect. Yet common sense and some available evidence urge a different view: that it was misery, not self-congratulation, that drew artists and writers to orgonomy, the misery of not being able to strike deep at will. Orgonomy promised baptism in the waters of the imagination as they raced through the canyons of the mind.[14]

And yet, one wants also to observe the degree to which Reichianism *did* elevate the free-lance intellectual into the role of moral and cultural leader who could exercise a salubrious influence on the culture by the example of transcending it. As Paul Goodman, as Norman Mailer, as Allen Ginsberg all understood in the sixties, it was not only their ideas that elevated them to positions of moral eminence but their examples, the lives of free eroticism they *seemed* to be living. Goodman, chagrined by the prospect of sainthood before death, endeavored mightily to keep all that was raw and tormented in his character on show. It did little good, as the cachet attached to his spokesmanship for desublimation overshadowed the more unsavory aspects of his compulsive cruising. Reichianism is indeed, as Rieff has complained, an antipolitics, though a more precise term might be counterpolitics, since it seeks to revolutionize the social order by transforming the individual, rather than organizing and deploying power. In Reichian thought—and the politics of Goodman's Gestalt were essentially Reichian—personal culture, rather than being a superstructure, is the very engine of the social order and therefore the key to social change. It is the magnetic field that binds the politics of the body to the body politic and the crucible in which the liberated intellectual, not the politician or the minister or even the soldier, is the indispensable catalyst of change. Yet, in a counterpolitics as in any other, the rebel has his eye on power; he simply approaches it in new ways and looks for new windows of vulnerability. The hero of a counterpolitics confronts power without a sword, armed only with the moral example of his being, an example which the isolate, the martyr, and the poet are best equipped to furnish. In a counterpolitics, the only slingshot David permits himself is his superior moral character. Where Gandhi, modern history's outstanding counterpolitician, took that superiority from an exemplary abstinence, Reich supposed it to derive from an exemplary indulgence. If Freud, then, was the social philosopher for intellectuals who saw in the agony of Europe a picture of man's fate, Reich supplied the program for those who saw in America—an eroticised, Whitmanized America to be sure—a picture of man's hope.

Thus it was Reich more than Freud who captured the imagination of a handful of stranded ex-Trotskyists in the 1940s and provided the program that, for a brief moment, was the implicit script for efforts to confirm a new literary radicalism. Jew, exile, and finally martyr, he was the Trotsky of mental revolutionism, a romantic hero for homeless radicals in search of a rallying point during and just after the war. Like revolutionary Marxism, Reichianism was an ideology of liberation with uncompromising values, a world-integrative view of reality that armed its adherents with basic interpretations, and rigid internal dialects that pointed the way to freedom through submission to a stern agenda of treatment. It was both a dogma and a discipline. Among the literary Reichians, Isaac Rosenfeld recast his entire life into a bioenergetic mold, becoming for his contemporaries the spirit of Greenwich Village incarnate as he conducted his life with the aim of breaking through to his "animal nature."[15] His fiction and literary essays incorporated major elements of Reich's moralized energetics, and they can still be read as illustrations of the power and the limits of a moral criticism that portrays life as a flux of vital substances. Saul Bellow absorbed the Reichian system intact into his own scheme of character analysis in two novels, *Seize the Day* and *Henderson the Rain King,* and two plays, "The Last Analysis" and "The Wrecker." But in all this writing Bellow's typically ironic handling of ideas makes it hard to tell where he is appealing to their explanatory powers and where exploiting their amusement value. Paul Goodman, the only therapist among the New York intellectuals, fashioned his own system of Gestalt therapy on a Reichian base and would later become the most influential spokesman for Reich's ideas. And Norman Mailer would, in his *Village Voice* columns and *Advertisements for Myself,* conduct a stunning public demonstration of therapy that would eventually make him famous and rich.

Conversions affected under such auspices were not so much changes of mind as upheavals of *will,* violent purges of all that was routine and stagnant in existence. Sometimes the violence was physical. In the therapeutic session the patient was urged to smash his character armor with spontaneous screams or "clonisms," involuntary spasms of the "orgasm reflex" that replicated, as Reich believed, the lusty thrashings of the segmented earthworm. Outside the clinic, he could look forward to the apocalyptic orgasm, the party to end all parties, the fistfight, even the stabbing. In the fifties, a certain romance of violence affected writers who were up on the latest calisthenics of self-renewal and denounced composure as not only self-destroying but counterrevolutionary. The artist entered therapy to shake loose the mind-forged manacles of surplus culture and disburden himself of craft, of caution, of history, of tradition, of guilt, of the superego—of the Jew in himself. The superego, that Nobodaddy of the mind to which Freud had assigned the task of keeping the instincts in line, was now assigned the role in the morality play of revolution formerly held by the bourgeoisie. Bellow, in recalling the temper of revolt in which he wrote *The Adventures of Augie March,* would reflect years later:

A writer should be able to express himself easily, naturally, copiously in a form which frees his mind, his energies. Why should he hobble himself with formalities? With a borrowed sensibility? With the desire to be "correct"? Why should I force myself to write like an Englishman or a contributor to *The New Yorker?*[16]

Mailer, in a more violent idiom, would speak in *Advertisements for Myself* of "blowing up the logjam of accumulated timidities and restraints" and of becoming "a psychic outlaw." Allen Ginsberg would howl to Carl Solomon, "I'm with you in Rockland / Where you're madder than I am," and Philip Roth, roughly a decade later, would agitate for putting the id back into Yid. All courted exposure—even sought humiliation—in order to reclaim their spontaneity and their genius. Propelled by an energy of self-rejection, such conversions were normally convulsive, reckless, and a little hysterical.

It was in the writing of Goodman, Mailer, and Allen Ginsberg in the 1950s that Reich's revivalism was most faithfully recorded and the ideology of the redemptive orgasm most consistently promoted as a comprehensive plan of social renewal. These three were the most political of the literary Reichians and, not surprisingly, the most influential in an intensely political decade. It was they who made the romantic ferment of the late 1940s available to the counterculture of the 1960s, who joined hands between kindred decades across the great divide of the fifties. They were the conduits for that current of revivalism that looked to the body as the redeeming agent in a corrupt world. They were the instructors in breaking through.

7. Preserving the Hunger
Isaac Rosenfeld

I

Consider that the intellectual Bohemian or proletarian has turned into a marginal figure nowadays, reminding us in his rather quixotic
aloneness of the ardors and truancies of the
past.
—Philip Rahv

The hunger must be preserved at all costs.
—Isaac Rosenfeld

IN THE dust-jacket photo for the posthumous collection of his essays, *An Age of Enormity*, Isaac Rosenfeld turns a precocious face to the camera. He is approaching thirty, it appears, but the lower half of his face, the full mouth and softly rounded cheeks, is mischievous and boyish. The upper half—the eyeglasses, the emotional eyes, the high temples, from which the hair is brushed back severely in the continental manner— suggests a European intellectual. A cigarette smolders in one hand, while another hand relaxes forgetfully around a pen. He appears to have been writing or talking or both under serious clouds of smoke. His lips are pursed and his lower lip is full and heavy, like the worsted suit that drapes him as loosely as a fur, and he sits back as if to engage the photographer in intellectual banter or to toss off confident observations about the Fate of Civilization in the West. It is a deceptive pose that belies what we know of Rosenfeld, for here is a young man who wears his knowledge as casually as he wears his suit.

There was nothing casual about Isaac Rosenfeld. Intensely and pain- fully intellectual and beset by a demanding conscience that was ever laboring to reconcile hedonism with responsibility, he was always on guard for signs in himself of moral laxity. He was a fierce moralist of pleasure, eager to explore the avenues of sensation, even in the face of the guilt, the shame, the conviction of failure that attended each break-through. *Post coitum animal triste* was his melancholy slogan, and he shared with his patron saint, Dostoevsky's underground man, the conviction that the state of secular grace called gratified desire was propaganda and that pleasure naturally resolved itself only in shame and expression. Like that expert in humiliation, he took shame to be the bedrock of consciousness and therefore a principle, a truth. He wrote in his journal: "I hold the conviction—it amounts to something of a theory—that embarrassment represents the true state of affairs, & the sooner we strike shame, the sooner we draw blood." But of guilt and self-repression he vowed: "I shall struggle against it with all my might, all my courage & cowardice, every part of me: I shan't give in. We have enough of guilt, a sickening overload of it."[1] The force that drove him through his crusades of self-renovation was his passion to free his spirit from the dead hand of guilt, whose precise claims upon him he never fathomed.

Unlike most other Jewish intellectuals of his generation, Rosenfeld never made his peace with the American dream. Rather, he followed a discipline of conduct that looked like unswerving downward mobility, recoiling from the icy touch of success that lurked everywhere around him in the late 1940s. In 1949, after a dispiriting visit to the offices of *Commentary,* where his work was no longer esteemed and where, as he saw it, his contemporaries Nathan Glazer, Irving Kristol, and Robert Warshow had already taken fatal vows of accommodation, he lamented, "Alas, alas. Youth is fleeting. The young men locked in offices, locked in stale marriages & growing quietly, desperately ill."

For Rosenfeld, who trusted only latent contents, what lay beneath the American dream of individual fulfillment was its true meaning—the life of quiet desperation—and he set his face implacably against it, abominating it in his Reichian way as the emotional plague. In the struggle between civilization and instinct, he declared for instinct and struck out for remote inner landscapes where the beleaguered ego, exhausted from fending off attacks on every front, might repose among the foliage of the instincts in a state of grace. He bet everything on the chances for self-renewal, on breaking through to the vein of life pulsing deep within. Under a self-imposed injunction to simplify in order to purify, he jettisoned the excess baggage of the conventional life: steady work, a profession, and, in the long run, even his family and his fiction.

Lest that make Rosenfeld sound too much the Village Sybarite, let me add that he was the most cautious of sexologues and paid richly in guilt for whatever he achieved in pleasure. "Now I know what Eliot means by 'the greater torment of love satisfied,'" he wrote in one of his later journals. "If one could only find some other consecration for love than the guilt-ridden act. Perhaps religion is born post coitum triste." Pleasure, it seems, was permissible only so long as it was a duty, and in time the search for other sacraments overcame the sensuality and his resolute Bohemianism resolved itself in asceticism, as he took up forms of marginal existence that bore the imprint of the ghetto. Long before the 1960s made a sacrament of elective poverty, Rosenfeld became a Luftmensch by design. "He did not follow the fat gods," Saul Bellow said of him after his death. "I think he liked the miserable failures in the Village better than the miserable successes Uptown, but I believe he understood that the failures had not failed enough but were fairly well satisfied with the mild form of social revolt which their incomplete ruin represented."[2] Maybe, like Kafka's hunger artist, Rosenfeld just never found a food he liked. Certainly, like the hunger artist, he succumbed to the perverse dialectics of self-denial, the pride in self-abnegation that makes each stage of mortification seem another step toward beatitude. The experience must be something like what scuba divers know as the rapture of the depths, an ectasy of deprivation that warns of impending blackout.

The literary legacy of all this terrible yearning is small: one novel, *Passage from Home,* a posthumous collection of stories, *Alpha and Omega,* and one of essays, *An Age of Enormity,* these last two assembled by Rosenfeld's friends and admirers after his death.[3] We've lost contact with Isaac Rosenfeld as a writer. He remains alive for us only in the memoirs of his contemporaries, Alfred Kazin and Irving Howe most recently, in which he figures as a brilliant episode in Village history, an embodied moment of hope and adventure.[4] When struck down by a heart attack in 1956, Rosenfeld was thirty-eight, and for fifteen of those years he had been a presence, though sometimes an elusive one, in the eastern intellectual establishment. He was even, for an instant, a master of ceremonies for those young writers and intellectuals who gathered in Greenwich Village during the 1940s, before the migration uptown shattered their brief bohemian/Luftmensch soirée. He had broken in as a poet and fiction writer with the *New Republic* in 1941, at the age of twenty-four, and by the end of the war was a regular contributor to the *New Republic, Partisan Review, Commentary, New Leader,* and the *Nation.* If one totals up all the briefest reviews, Rosenfeld in those years seems a marvel of output, though most of his achievements were unpremeditated triumphs of occasion, book reviews drawn out into proclamations. He published little in the way of fiction, however: one novel and a clutch of stories, four of them, astonishingly, in Yiddish. He is best remem-bered now as a reviewer—of books that for the most part, dropped from sight moments after publication.[5]

Rosenfeld's career *was* a minor one, whose lasting value is less to be sought in the weight of his achievements than in its peculiar definition, its difficult angles and sudden epiphanies. For though he did things in a small way, Rosenfeld did them with all his might. He held nothing back. A Jew and a writer who came to consciousness of himself during an age of horrors, he responded passionately, with his whole being. Though he swam in the company of writers given to masks and postures, he stood out in the clear, guileless, naked, and dangerously unarmed. An artist himself, he distrusted art, preferring the artless, the plain-spoken, the direct. "Where feelings are not dealt with directly," he wrote in his journal, "where they are not expressed or released in the prose, where they are dammed up, they tend to explode in the form of strong, striking images. Conversely, where the flow & release of feelings is steady, where feeling is in large part the subject matter, images tend to disappear, figures of speech even drop out or are met with rarely. Thus Tolstoy, in whom such imagery is low." Dedicating himself to that flow and release of feelings, Rosenfeld produced a charged and poignant critical writing. *An Age of Enormity*, the selection of his essays and reviews published by Theodore Solotaroff in 1962, is a workbook in the rhetoric of literary criticism; its briefest reviews are studies in directness, economy, and clarity.

But that clarity was dearly bought, and Rosenfeld's failure to command it in his fiction disappointed him bitterly. "*The Enemy* bores me," he complained typically. "How I've ruined it with this nonsense [i.e., his psychoanalytic allegorizing]. I want in Pathfinder a person, not a case-history. A *character* by God!" As the decade of the forties drew to a close, it became plain to Rosenfeld that he was blocked and that if he were to continue to write, he would first have to free his voice and restore its flow. His contact with Wilhelm Reich's theories convinced him that his writer's block was a token of sexual inhibition, and he spent much of the late forties waging war upon his own emotions. The emotional plague from which he suffered was everywhere, and he studied himself, and everyone else, with the cold eye of the moral clinician, sparing nobody the grim diagnosis. "I shall rid myself, systematically, of my unconscious mind," he pledged to himself. "Then clean out the ego. Away with this rubbish. I want to find myself. *Me!*"

The fever with which Rosenfeld took up Reich in the 1940s seems a lingering remnant of his boyhood revolutionism. As a teenager in Chicago, growing up in the contentious atmosphere of free-thinking Russian Jews who were saturated in rebellion and socialism, Rosenfeld had been active, along with Bellow, in the Trotskyist movement through the Spartacus Youth League and the Young People's Socialist League during its Trotskyist phase, when, after the Fourth (Trotskyist) International had taken it over, it was popularly known as "YPSL Fourth." Rosenfeld's socialism, however, was evidently a socialism of atmosphere such as young Jewish intellectuals of his generation might be afflicted with, a mystique without a method, a metaphor for Jewish dissent, and by the time he began writing, that metaphor was played out. Of all his contemporaries, Rosenfeld seems to have been the least discomposed by the eclipse of Marxism. Not that he scorned the world of conditions—quite the reverse—but purely economic problems did not nourish his outrage, and even his short story about an experience on the application line for the WPA Writer's Project, "The Hand That Fed Me," has nothing in it of the social animus that socialism commonly feeds on.[6] His 1947 story "The Party" is about a political party that collapses when its members grow bored; it is yawned to death by a caucus of younger comrades—the Ennui Club—who grow drowsy during the national chairman's speeches.[7] The Worker's Party and its chairman, Max Shachtman, are clearly the targets of Rosenfeld's broad satire. Surely there is no nostalgia here for the meeting hall, which has been happily dispensed with for other arenas of engagement.

Rosenfeld has to be counted among those who, in the 1940s, imported psychology into the territory vacated by a retreating American radicalism. His essays and reviews were persuasive demonstrations of how psychoanalysis, largely Wilhelm Reich's insurrectionary renditions of it, might be employed as a general criticism of life. Historically, the deemphasis of social change in favor of self-adjustment may have been a requirement of Rosenfeld's era, much as it has been a feature of our own, but his adoption of psychoanalysis was no modish recycling of world views during a moment of historical shock nor a retreat from analytic intelligence and moral expectation. In a review of Jo Sinclair's novel *Wasteland*, a "drab but profitable little poem in celebration of the beatitudes of psychiatric social work" he complained of the easy complacency of postwar psychiatric rationality, declaring that "the transformation of 'change the world' into 'adjust yourself to it' has had the effect of abolishing concern with the kind of society that is worthy of our adjustment, and of removing the discussion of social problems from a historical context."[8] Rosenfeld was resistant to the strains of social utopianism and adjustment psychiatry in the culture of the therapeutic, and, despite his yearning for détente with his own feelings, was skeptical of designs for general uplift and promises of personal contentment. Rather, it was the critical edge of psychoanalysis, its genius for unmasking motives and debunking pieties, that he found congenial, and accordingly it was the most radical, antinomian outgrowth of the psychoanalytic revolution that he cultivated.

Thus he prevented his treatment from interfering with his alienation, his constitutional disaffection from the world. The Jewish writer, he declared with himself in mind, "is a specialist in alienation (the one international banking system the Jews actually control)."[9] This alienation is both a handicap and an endowment, conferring upon the Jewish writer the gift of insight into his historical being: "[It] puts him in touch with his own past traditions, the history of the Diaspora; with the present predicament of almost all intellectuals and, for all one knows, with the future conditions of civilized humanity." Writing about Abraham Cahan's *The Rise of David Levinsky,* Rosenfeld identified alienation as the clue to Jewish assimilation in America, a core of Jewish loneliness that spoke to the loneliness in the American heart and permitted the Jewish achievement, by a simple exchange of alienations, of "a virtually flawless Americanization."[10]

Alienation was Rosenfeld's personal leitmotif. He held it to be the irreducible condition of the emotions and the first principle of any defensible psychology or literature. And while an awareness of his own conflicts precluded the naive embrace of any systematic politics or social philosophy, it did allow him to frame an aesthetic, for in the judgment of art he could take a stand on his own uncertainties and insist upon a literature grounded in conflict, alienation, and neurosis. He looked in every modern writer for the man divided against himself and read every book as a communiqué from a hidden battlefront. Accordingly, the novel was a lesson in character and a blueprint for emotional management and subject to interpretation, therefore, as a successful, or failed, self-encounter. Literature that pretended to be above the struggle earned Rosenfeld's dismissal as minor, and he accused nearly all contemporary writing of lacking psychological validity. His criticism of the contemporary short story was typical. In two wartime reviews of Martha Foley collections, he chastised story writers for their surrender to conventional formulas that short-circuited imagination and distanced them from inner pressures. "The present [1943] collection offers very little evidence that these ideas symbolize crisis in perception, moral anxieties, themes or fantasies deep in an artist's life: they lack the obsession of the personal." The vast majority of short stories, he complained, are paste-ups, assembled from creative writing kits, their characters, like their plots, only tidy contrivances, "receptacles for the flow of narrative and they never overflow, nor do they receive their fill."[11]

Rosenfeld returned time and again to the sins of the minor writer, the writer incapable, as he saw it, of bringing a sense of life to art. He is not deficient in talent; he may even be burdened with a surplus of it, but he is also addicted to style, with which he distracts himself from his own deeper meanings. The minor writer is a self-entertainer who cannot confront the passions without embarrassment or mannerism. Thus the effect of his technical mastery is to deny his emotions and therefore his own meanings. "This is an old trap of the language bound: where words come first, they can never point beyond words—which is what communication means."[12] The minor writer's domination of commercial markets, moreover, is his reward for successful evasion: the entire literary world, readers included, constitutes a conspiracy of the repressed.

This call for an art that is true to the inner life and its torments is applied Reich. It was Reich whom Rosenfeld drew upon in turning a native self-estrangement into a morality, a morality, moreover, that licensed the book review to be a comprehensive social criticism, for Reich's character analysis contained a theory of culture and his taxonomy of character types—the genital character, the hysterical, the compulsive, the masochistic, the phallic-narcissistic. Under the Reichian gaze, the novel becomes a document of the writer's commerce with his instincts and the writer a stand-in for his culture's favorite devices of instinctual containment. Fiction is treated as a little Globe upon which an entire civilization struts and frets its hour upon the stage, acting out its basic neuroses in stylized commedia dell'arte dress. Accordingly, Rosenfeld's reviews measured fiction against a therapeutic standard, full genitality, and appropriated Reich's bioenergetic dualisms to gauge imaginative success: organism versus mechanism, potency versus rigidity, flow versus blockage, release versus restraint.

Style, for a Reichian, belongs to the ego and therefore to the surfaces of the personality. Style *is* resistance. In diagnosing the minor sensibility in action, whose conflicts are expressed as mannerisms and whose "art" is laid over emotion or thrown up as a screen against it, Rosenfeld found in character analysis—that is, the 1945 edition of Wilhelm Reich's *Character Analysis*—a ready handbook of literary style.[13] Even André Gide, scarcely a minor writer, shows evidence of blockage: "We get the deliberate pressure and the deliberate withholding, but not the natural ease. In place of ease stands embarrassment."[14] Other writers stand accused of unblocking only the narrower channels, like Nancy Hale in whose stories "the surface tension mounts, as in a glass, reaches its climax, breaks, spills over—but at no point is it more than water,"[15] and Ivy Compton-Burnett, whose "manner comes naturally to her in a steady trickle."[16] Christopher Isherwood, by contrast, gets high marks for *Prater Violet,* where the portrayal of Friedrich Bergmann "is a work of joy, and the result of sheer overflow."[17]

However much he deplored the steady trickle, Rosenfeld saved his harshest words for the simulators of the torrent, writers whose vaunted frankness turned out upon examination to be mere attitudinizing. He dealt harshly with Ernest Hemingway, Kenneth Patchen, Henry Miller, and John O'Hara for failing to live up to their self-advertisements. Rosenfeld charged Patchen with treating psychoanalysis, in *Journal of Albion Moonlight* and *Memoirs of a Shy Pornographer,* as a grab bag of titilations to be reached into only for Gothic decor, lurid confirmations of human bestiality.[18] He dismissed Henry Miller as a gifted poseur who, in *The Air-Conditioned Nightmare,* palmed off as revelations commonplaces about American society that are already stocks-in-trade of *Life* magazine.[19] And John O'Hara's sketches in *Pipe Night* of the authentic life of our times as recorded in buses, trains, gin mills, and nightclubs are too obedient to the rules of literature, which happen also to be the rules of the marketplace, to do the job of social analysis.[20] O'Hara, Rosenfeld charged, builds his images of America upon the wholly literary premise of the bittersweet—the premise that beneath every cold exterior there beats a warm heart—thereby protecting his readers and himself from enlightening doses of reality. O'Hara's "realism" is just real enough for a public that is disposed to look upon poverty in the light of romance.

The full weight of Rosenfeld's scorn fell upon Irwin Shaw, the "left-wing middlebrow" novelist whose formula for commercial success: Hemingwayesque sophistication, Jewish issues, and *New Yorker* taste, yielded great book-club profits just after the war.[21] The failures of Patchen, Miller, and O'Hara to produce convincing fiction were primarily their own, whereas Shaw's shortcoming were those of his generation, and his writing was a profitable defense of its prevailing values: an unexamined patriotism, a smug liberalism, and a hard-boiled *savoir faire*—the boosterish values, in short, of a literary culture that looked to the Dow-Jones, rather than to Aristotle, for its lessons in pity and terror. It was not such values per se that Rosenfeld found offensive, for, after all, liberalism, patriotism, and know-how are not such indecencies, even to a consecrated Luftmensch, but the unbuttoned style that made them popular commodities, one that devalued emotion and conflict while pretending to a "guts and dry martini image of life." "He knows everything; that is to say, sex and liquor. He has had all these commodities, not without enjoyment, of course, but nevertheless with just that properly arch touch of weariness, lest anyone think him naive." What Shaw pioneered so successfully was a literature that appeared to grapple with issues while being really shy of moral struggle, for the *New Yorker* sophistication of that era put all struggles behind it.

Where mental conflict is boiled down to a metaphysical scrimmage between the liquid and solid elements in human nature, as it is in orgonomy, psychoanalysis is being invoked through its most vulgar metaphors, and it is the danger of applying Reich that one's characterizations may come to resemble an Elizabethan pharmacopia of humors. But Rosenfeld's criticism was always more than applied Reich, for where Reich was all hydraulics and therefore mechanical, Rosenfeld's first premises were always literary and cultural, to which the tide pools of the libido lent occasional biological confirmations or convenient "as if" metaphors. And while it is sometimes hard to tell where Rosenfeld was invoking orgonomy as a moral science and where just as a repository of metaphors, it is clear that he never fully subordinated his exquisite discriminations to Reich's clumsy diagnostic machinery. Though in facing his own repressions Rosenfeld availed himself of the benefits, whatever they may have been, of Reichian therapy and the orgone accumulator, as a critic he had no need of biological or cosmic potentialities; he possessed a far more complicated and tragic view of the heart, starting with his own, than could ever be registered on a libidinal dynamometer. His criticism no more resembles Reichian character psychology than imagination resembles pressure or prose style resembles the steel plates of character armor. His wish to recover the body for literary criticism may have attached itself to a concept of emotional hygiene that promised a release of power, but at no point did it confuse thought, sensation, and imagination with the stages of tension reduction. Aesthetics enlarges science, Rosenfeld believed, "for the strength of a theory of art lies not in its structural underpinning, but in the directness with which it allows values to come into their own."[22]

Directness was Rosenfeld's law of style. A superior practitioner of English prose, he cultivated its resources of syntax and rhythm until he had composed, in his criticism, a cleaner and more compact style than any of his contemporaries. It is an artfully transparent style, cutting and bright—though lacking the pugnacity of a Rahv or a Macdonald—supple and dense—though lacking the ponderous liquidities of a Trilling—which bears no obvious signature of his genius save its subtlety and its economy. He shrank from demonstrations of virtuosity. "The more I read his letters the harder I find it to trust Saul," he said of Bellow. "There is a figure of speech in every sentence." Yet, like many other second-generation Jewish intellectuals, he was alive to the splendors of English and sought dominion over it as an act of assimilation. Jewish-American intellectuals manifested a strong attraction toward anglophilia as a normal by-product of their Americanization and their romance with the English language, but Rosenfeld never indulged that romance in the manner of Trilling or Delmore Schwartz. Rather, he collaborated with Bellow, Rahv, and Kazin in fashioning an American voice out of Twain's English and Dostoevsky's gloom, marrying American incisiveness to Russian melancholy and producing in the process a tautness of style that distinguished both the fiction and criticism of their generation.

II

Inevitably, the contrast between Rosenfeld's clarity in criticism and his turgidity in fiction raises questions about his own relation to the aesthetic he so incisively applied to others. By his own definitions he was a minor writer, being unable to create both art and life at the same time. His intention was to write a fiction of alienation, but few of his stories stir his conflicts into life; most do little more than announce them. In the main, the stories are cold tableaux of isolation and failure, peopled by passionate and lonely characters who are cut off from their energies and denied, by circumstance or will, the comforts of human companionship. These impotent heroes include an ownerless baseball team that plays out a losing season for lack of anything better to do;* a brigadier of a nameless army in a nameless war, whose passion to understand the enemy leads him to torture his captives but yields him no intelligence; a railroad traffic controller self-exiled in lonely cabooses; a political party whose motto is "Ends Never Meet"; a scholar of the dance who dies of paralysis; a Greenwich Village raconteur who fears contact with the woman he desires. The stories themselves run to the surreal and Kafkaesque; their emotional underpinnings are bleak indeed. But with some exceptions, this bleakness is precious and operatic; it announces its alienation but

---

*The story, "The Misfortunes of the Flapjacks," would appear to have given Philip Roth the kernel of his baseball novel, *The Great American Novel.* The resemblances are too striking to be accidental; in each a ragged squad of Luftmenschen disguised as players enacts a parable of Jewish exile disguised as a season.

gives us "literature," and in the process casts a paradoxical light on Rosenfeld's standards for fiction.

That discrepancy brings Rosenfeld's criticism into focus as self-exhortation. The essays and stories seem to constitute a dialogue in which Rosenfeld's potentialities are thrown into relief by his difficulties and the deeply personal nature of his principles made plain by his failure to realize them. That dialogue discloses the barriers to feeling behind the pleas for clarity and the doubt within the call for joy. Rosenfeld wrote most freely when his personal investment was most easily masked. In fiction, where his themes were painfully personal, he offered up manner in lieu of directness, showing, in effect, just how literary neurotic conflict could be. "I sit down at the typewriter," he wrote in his journal. "Whom shall I imitate today?" One suspects from the manners he cultivated as well as from the writers he embraced—Kafka, Hesse, Tolstoy, Dostoevsky, Y. L. Peretz, Sholom Aleichem—that he fancied being a writer in translation, a European who had been only haltingly rendered into English. He did enjoy greater ease in criticism, as if in illustration of his own observation that "the self is naturally on guard, and to force down its guard is to violate its natural posture. But the imagination betrays the man; the more objective its work and the more distant from the personality, the smaller the suspicion with which it must contend and the greater the personal revelation."

Having committed himself to a championship of the plain and direct, however, Rosenfeld left himself no grounds on which to admire stylistic innovation. The radical in him strong-armed the aesthete, and he seems to have chosen his subjects for review as though his aesthetic sense were under quarantine. Wherever style occupied the foreground, the ego always stood accused of mismanaging its fund of instinct. Thus Rosenfeld had little to say about writing in which artifice, indirection, and even concealment were aesthetic virtues. An aesthetic that served him well in his campaigns against defensive stylists like Hemingway or Irwin Shaw gave him no purchase on the great modernist masters of obliquity, ambiguity, and complication. He kept his distance from modernism, was silent on Joyce, Pound, and Proust, saw in Eliot only the neurasthenic, not the poet, and had praise for Lawrence only as an ideologue of the orgasm. Gide he approached through the journals only, which he read as a case study in the transmutation of neurosis into art. And, in league with most of his generation of Jewish intellectuals, save Schwartz, Rosenfeld shunned poetry. For virtually all of them, the novel alone and the realist tradition were the touchstones of culture and politics, manners and morals, while poetry, lacking explicit social content and gaining its effects through the pure deployment of language, was baffling and alien. Rosenfeld set himself up as an opponent of modernism, seeing it as did Ortega as the dehumanization of art. Clearly, he and most other New York intellectuals after the war held philosophic realism to be the central and abiding tradition of the novel in virtue of its capacity for moral education.

The defining feature of Rosenfeld's modernity was his revulsion against the modern world and his refusal to collaborate with it. In the 1940s, he was indistinguishable from his contemporaries in his conspicuous alienation, the Jewish intellectuals' shorthand for their exclusion from and disdain for the main currents of American life. Alienation was the mark of their exile and their caste. In the 1950s, when universities, fellowships, and publishing opportunities opened up to them, their alienation lost its rhetorical credit, and their militant aloofness crumbled before their opportunities. Notes from underground do not customarily issue from high places. Yet Rosenfeld stood apart from the new order and applied himself to needs that could not be met by position, comfort, and respectability. His experience of alienation cut deeper than the shared rhetoric of his generation, for it issued from his struggles with himself rather than his quarrels with the world. A representative figure in the 1940s, an itinerant intellectual with only a Weltanschauung to call home, he drifted in the 1950s from the center of the intellectual culture to the periphery, allowing the caravan to pass without him. "No matter where he was or what job he had," observes Solotaroff, "he kept himself in the clear, taking risks of instability and independence, of uncertainty, sterility, and failure."[23] The meaning of all this is ambiguous, for what looks like paralysis from one quarter may appear to be heroism from another. After Rosenfeld's death, Saul Bellow praised him for turning his back on the fat gods and praised his refusal to welcome the new order of things as a victory of the spirit. And so it may have been, though Rosenfeld himself understood well enough that his heroic abstinence was a token of trouble.

Disdaining the fat gods, he followed a path of austerity, whose justifying admonitions seemed to come from both psychoanalysis and Jewishness. The latter was not a received identity: it had nothing in it of easy piety or simple acceptance. Nor was it even very clearly understood; suffused throughout his being it nonetheless eluded him, and one sees him in his essays and journals grappling with it, revising it, and imagining it as if, like the personality under therapy, one were free to invent it anew. What emerged from these struggles was a severely literary Jewishness, pieced together out of folklore, myth, and fiction, especially out of Franz Kafka, Sholom Aleichem, Y. L. Peretz, Abraham Cahan, Isaac Babel, and even Simone Weil. Nowhere was Rosenfeld's impulse toward merger with the objects of his contemplation more evident or more touching than in his writing on Jews. In a story of his boyhood, "The World of the Ceiling," he recalled the intensity of his early literary fantasies, his pleasures in imagining himself a revolutionary in czarist Russia, hiding out from Cossack patrols and hopelessly in love with the dark-eyed Yevgenia Borisovna, the darling of the organization, who is unfortunately "as cold as she is beautiful and knows only one love—of terror and reckless action."[24] But normally there was little of such romance to his Jewishness, though the distant beauty of the Yevgenia Borisovnas remained, transformed from an image of unrequited passion into a measure of inner distances; his fiction and criticism alike are haunted by phantom mothers, vanishing or untouchable women, and vacancies of the heart or the mouth or the gut.

His reflections on Jewishness called forth this emptiness. An essay on Abraham Cahan's *The Rise of David Levinsky* and another on Jewish dietary obsessions, "Adam and Eve on Delancey Street," were diagnoses of that empty center, the insatiable hunger to which Rosenfeld had traced the roots of his alienation.[25] A dialectician of diet and despair, Rosenfeld pondered the connection, suggested by psychoanalysis, between hunger and culture, loneliness and success. The kosher laws, he proposed, are symbolic sexual taboos, and the ritual prohibiting eating meat with milk was at bottom an apprenticeship in the commandment against exogamy: Thou Shalt Not Mix! Similarly, the Jewish fetish of a healthy appetite is a "hunger that is not a hunger," a facsimile of hunger that can never be satisfied but must nonetheless be appeased by generous sacrifices of food. The esssay on *David Levinsky* struck the more complicated and sombre version of that note. The hunger is not only insatiable, Rosenfeld claimed there, but is itself the object of desire.

> Thus Levinsky is a man who cannot feel at home with his desires. Because hunger is so strong in him, he must always strive to relieve it; but precisely because it is strong, it has to be preserved. It owes its strength to the fact that for so many years everything that influenced Levinsky most deeply—say, piety and mother love—was inseparable from it. For hunger, in this broader, rather metaphysical sense of the term that I have been using, is not only the state of tension out of which the desires for relief and betterment spring; precisely because the desires are formed under its sign, they become assimilated to it, and convert it into the prime source of all value, so that the man, in his pursuit of whatever he considers pleasurable and good, seeks to return to his yearning as much as he does to escape it.

Or, in a phrase, "The hunger must be preserved at all cost," for it is the man himself.

Where emptiness and depression are the nightmare, fullness and vitality are the dream, and Rosenfeld knew one as intimately as the other. It was the manic in him and its great power over those around him that emerges from the testimony of his friends: Saul Bellow's account of a precocious schoolboy holding forth in knee pants before the Tuley High School debating club on the subject of Schopenhauer; Howe and Kazin recalling the spell of those exciting soirées in his flat on Barrow Street in the Village. Through most of the 1940s the expansive Rosenfeld drew sustenance from Reich, whose concept of character was more or less that of a balloon, swelled by Eros from within and held taut by resistance at the outer boundaries. But by the end of the decade, orgonomy had given way to Hasidism as the justifying myth of his vitalism. Indeed, as Solotaroff has suggested, Rosenfeld's vitalism was an expression of his Jewishness, a latent Hasidism. One of his important reviews in 1949 was of Maurice Samuel's *Prince of the Ghetto,* a retelling of the stories of Y. L. Peretz, the Warsaw social worker and intellectual whose tales and parables of Jewish life were popular around the turn of the century.[26] Though Peretz's social views were those of a progressive, Europeanized intellectual, he had devoted his literary career to telling Hasidic tales of rabbinical wonders. Such a double vision appealed to Rosenfeld as all mental balancing acts did; as a steadfast irresolution quite like his own, "balanced between the sacred and the secular, radical and conservative . . . between the religio-mystic and the sociological." Not a Hasid himself, Peretz nevertheless cherished the Hasidic enthusiasm above "the bourgeois spirit" and embraced a naturalist vitality which "took the hasidic ecstasies not as ultimate things, visions in the midst of appearances, that disclose the noumenal world's unity in love, but rather as immediate phenomena in a radiance of this world."

If Rosenfeld had a rabbinical strain in him it was of this sort, the secular-ecstatic, teaching, like Peretz, "joy in this world," that brand of electric naturalism that Bellow, who shared Rosenfeld's cycle of enthusiasms, would exploit vividly in some of his novels.* It is hardly surprising that Rosenfeld, in extolling Peretz, turned to religion for the language of

---

*The language of the urban erotic in *The Adventures of Augie March* is Chicago Hasidism, and is indistinguishable at this level from practical Reich or applied Nietzsche. The logic of this effervescence, its potential for epiphany, is developed further in the closet transcendentalism of *Herzog,* where the noumenal world peeps out shyly from behind Chicago's phenomenal skirts, and in *Humboldt's Gift,* where it blossoms into a full-blown Platonism. See Chapter 8.

secular vitalism, for the elation he courted was at bottom a religious longing, a desire to make the world reveal God's face. "The vision is strictly of appearances in actual historical time, but they are seen under a holy light." In Peretz, Hasidism and liberal pragmatism meet in the "power of love, drawn from the eros of Hasidism, and fulfilling for him the function of attracting the nations into brotherhood."

This cantor of euphoria and ecumenism was the expansive Rosenfeld, buoyed upon visions of divinity, and yet it was the same alienated Rosenfeld who was so haunted by loneliness and hunger. The vital and the desolate were the same man, just as the Baal Shem Tov and Franz Kafka are moods of a single Jewishness, the manic and depressive voices of the same stormy culture. Rosenfeld was given to wild swings of mood—from exaltation to despair or terror—from which middle terms were cancelled out. This instability was sublimated into principles as Rosenfeld became for a while an extremist of the emotions and an enemy of the calls for modulation—for the "variousness and possibility" of the new liberal imagination—that were in the air. In 1948 and 1949, his contemplation of the Holocaust and new revelations about labor camps in the Soviet Union brought the polarizing tendency of his imagination to the surface in the form of a proposal for a new Nietzschean standard of ethics. In a review of Jacob Pat's *Ashes and Fire,* he argued that knowledge of the Holocaust was sufficient reason to scrap "the wilderness of good and evil, of ethics and morality, of reason, science, method, history, sympathy and mercy, the whole human world, or what was, until now, human."[27] The whole symbolic structure of civilization now lay in shambles, impotent to explain, or mitigate, the terror of the zero moment when all had failed. The only choice for the survivors was to face and accept this new reality and reach beyond obsolete emotions and consolations to the only good that is adequate to such a reality: joy. "How shall we, living in comfort, we American Jews and Gentiles, with brotherhood and interfaith meetings—and in an election year!—understand that there are only two principles?—terror and joy." Rosenfeld, suddenly confronted by upwellings of the terror within himself recoiled by becoming, briefly, a Nietzschean spokesman for "terror beyond evil and joy beyond good," declaring that "that is all there is to work with, whether we are to understand what has happened, or to begin all over again."

In a subsequent *Partisan Review* essay, "The Meaning of Terror," Rosenfeld stepped out from behind the reviewer's desk, announced the end of alienation, and declared the millennium.[28] "Our joy will be in love and restoration, in the sensing of humanity as the concrete thing, the datum of our cultural existence. It will lie in the creation of a new capacity, proof against terror, to experience our natural life to the full." There was something amiss here, a note of dithyrambic fever that spoiled the whole exercise. Too much terror was being denied and too much abstract, hypothetical joy affirmed; the terror was real enough but the joy was little more than an aphoristic vehicle, unreal, Whitmanesque, and impersonal. Needless to add, this invalidation of all traditional ethics and the posing of a new morality in a mere thousand words was an exercise in rope dancing that not even this expert in concision could bring off. The renewal of western man was not within the book reviewer's scope; Rosenfeld was always on firmer ground when he scaled his vision to human proportions, even, as the case may be, canine proportions. The kernal of these Nietzschean declamations lay behind Rosenfeld's one extended exercise in Yiddish, a fable entitled "Dos Meser" (The Knife), which appeared in the Yiddish review *Getseltn* in 1946.[29]

In "Dos Meser," a fable of the Holocaust, the bourgeois and postbourgeois spirits are embodied in the characters of two caged dogs, awaiting in their kennels some gruesome fate in a research laboratory. One is a genteel, highborn spaniel who favors "a moderate approach to the subject of freedom," the other a vicious beast named Red Wolf who hurls himself against the bars of this cage in defiance—an Arnoldian lapdog, in short, and a Nietzschean wolfdog. Both perish in the end, for neither biting the hand that feeds you nor licking it is of any benefit when death is assured, yet it is plain that Rosenfeld valued the rage and insolence of Red Wolf to the modulated reckonings of the spaniel, who meets his death like a liberal: bemused, hurt, perplexed, silent, forgiving.

Thus it was that George Orwell earned Rosenfeld's praise for his accomplishment in writing *1984,* when, at the door of death, he confronted the full horror of totalitarianism and snatched a grace beyond the reach of English decency.[30] What was achieved in *1984* was the double revelation to Winston Smith in the extremity of torture that "the objective of power is power" and that he, at the end, "loved big brother." For Rosenfeld, that last realization was the secret of totalitarianism, its power to invade the minds of its victims and command their obedience from within. Orwell's comprehension of that reality and his horror at it had been checked, in earlier books, by habits of good sense and optimism. Elsewhere his anger did not rise about the note of "You don't do such things!" Only in the final extremity, his tuberculosis unquestionably terminal, could he break free of lifelong habits of restraint to summon up the terror. "Life being what it is in our world, the onset of death is often the first taste a man gets of freedom," the freedom not only to grasp the terrible secret of modern politics, that "the objective of power is power," but also to torment himself for a lifetime of denials. Through his own sickness Orwell penetrated to the heart of the world's sickness and released a flood of truth.

> All that matters is the force of the passion with which the man, who began as a writer in a small way, at the last came through. The force with which he ended is the one with which greatness begins. This force, it will be observed, was enough to kill a man.

One is stopped by so funereal a cadenza, which calls to mind Rosenfeld's own eventual isolation and death. Rosenfeld's last years were bitter ones, marked by stubborn self-denial and gradual self-defeat. After 1951, he wrote less, or perhaps wrote only for himself. He started a book on Tolstoy which he did not complete and one on the Chicago Fire, which was completed after his death by Chicago journalist Robert Cromie.[31] His second novel, *The Enemy,* a Kafkaesque allegory of guilt and suffering, turned out to be unpublishable, and those excerpts that have appeared, with their monotonous allegorical plots, explain why.[32] There were fewer reviews. His marriage broke up, and he drifted from New York to Minneapolis, where he taught briefly at the University of Minnesota, and then back to Chicago. Like Bernard Miller, the youthful hero of *Passage from Home,* Rosenfeld had left his father's house in order to find it, only to discover upon his return, not the tears of joyful reconciliation but a confirmation of his exile. He was apparently planning to leave Chicago again just before he died.

Rosenfeld spent the 1950s in drift and dishevelment amid small, dingy rooms. Yet there was a principle of perverse monasticism in this life, a disorder, as Bellow observed, that had become a discipline. We ought not be surprised; the therapeutic radicalism of Rosenfeld's youth was built upon a deep strain of Puritanism, and it is not hard to see how a disciple of energy might in time wind up mortifying the senses in squalor and purifying the emotions in abstinence, exchanging, in effect, Reich for Gandhi or Simone Weil. Rosenfeld was not the first to walk the path of hedonism to the gates of the monastery.

Rosenfeld half wanted, I think, to be a saint. The demands he placed upon himself—to seek joy through terror and to purge the heart in isolation—could have only sainthood as their object. He denied the world's nurturance and substituted for the sustaining relationships of an ordinary life rites of purification. He set out to cleanse his style, his

courage, his passions, his sensibilities. In time, each failure to achieve
beatitude or to write a page of living prose only brought a redoubling of
the effort and a deepening of the alienation. He played double or
nothing with life. Rosenfeld's premature death of a heart attack was the
fulfillment of the impossible logic of these crisis years, a death, one
might think, of a broken heart. Rosenfeld knew something of what that
logic entailed. In writing of Simone Weil, another virtuoso of abstinence,
he refused to sentimentalize her self-neglect, which sadly recalled familiar symptoms. "How can our world speak of Simone Weil without using
its own language, in which the words, severe and unforgiving though
they may be, are, by definition, *hysteria, masochism,* etc.?[33] Weil's abstinence and eventual starvation may have defined a personal sanctity but it
lacked sharable meaning. "For all her firsthand knowledge of politics,
exile, and universal doubt, she made her way out of our world and
ceased to represent it." Rosenfeld was speaking here out of his own
experience of private beatitude and public irrelevance, for, as his own
conflicts deepened, his solutions grew increasingly private and his writing more hermetic. The problem with *The Enemy* is that it was written in
too private a code; it called not for readers but initiates.

There are signs that in the final months Rosenfeld experienced a
breakthrough of sorts or at very least a remission of conflict that showed
up in his writing as a relaxed and genial manner, a mellow adagio in his
rhythms. One of his best stories, "King Solomon," was written during
this period as was the draft of an essay, "Life in Chicago."[34] Rosenfeld's
King Solomon is a foppish old Jew, an overweight, cigar-smoking, pi-
nochle-playing monarch who can barely recall his former wisdom but is
still beloved by young girls who come from all over Judea—or is it
Flatbush?—to lie beside him and place their hands upon his breast. At
the age of sixty he is courted fiercely by an overblown, bejeweled Queen
of Sheba, a reformed Jewish princess who has let herself go a little and
who, for all her wiles, cannot arouse him from his pinochle. But there is
little tension in this: Solomon's pain is only a wistful, geriatric melancholy. This king is the Emmett Kelly of patriarchs. As for Rosenfeld's
Chicago, it too is a typical creation. Janus-faced, it has a dry and land-
locked midwestern side and a wet, lake-lined eastern one—a schizoid
Chicago such as a Rosenfeld would discover. Yet, while the themes are
familiar, the agitation is gone. "King Solomon" is only ironic, and the
Chicago essay is cool, urban sociology. We cannot say from the writing
alone what sort of change we're seeing or what brought it about or what
engines of creativity were set throbbing by the new mood, though this
writing gives evidence that Rosenfeld's lyric gifts were very much intact.

The last entry in his journal, written, perhaps, within days of his death, is poignantly affirmative, a call to life.

> This is what I have forgotten about the creative process, & am only now beginning to remember—that time spent is time fixed. One creates a work to outlive one—only art does this—& the source of creativity is the desire to reach over one's own death. Maybe now, if I want to create again, I want once more to live; & before I wanted, I suppose, to die.

Rosenfeld's heart attack cut short this affirmation and froze his career into its final shape—the brutal, downward curve of depression.

So devoted a quest for subterranean fires is rare and calls attention to itself. That the visible return was small was in keeping with the venture itself, to distill and burnish a life, not to construct an oeuvre. The labor of renunciation that eventually subdued him was an entirely Jewish rite, a graft of guilt and mourning upon native high spirits in homage to what he took to be the spirit of the ghetto. Rosenfeld's essays and stories were bulletins from some withering shtetl of the soul where cabalists in white silk gabardines pondered the secrets of the Torah in the dark shuls of exile, robed in their scholarship, their disputation, their passion for justice, as if the very breath of God had blown the commandment into their hearts. Possessed of the vision and the sense of unbearable loss in which it took root, Rosenfeld fashioned himself into the last ghetto Jew and pledged solidarity with the ranks of his own dead, who in an age of enormity, bore silent witness to the delinquencies of the living.

8. Down in the Mouth with Saul Bellow

I. Psychological Novelist

CONSIDERATION OF psychology's impact upon contemporary fiction normally calls to mind the "psychological novel," that museum piece of literary modernity whose subject is consciousness itself and whose strategies of exposition are authorized by prevailing theories of mind, which in our century have been largely those of Freud or Jung or Bergson. We think of James Joyce's interior monologues and hallucinatory dramatics, his calculated confusions and multilingual word salads; of Faulkner's spasmodic narratives and his famous tale told by an idiot; of Virginia Woolf's gardens of reverie; and of the *nouveau roman*'s corridors of ambiguity. But such vanguard writing is far from being the only brand of psychologically authorized fiction, for there is an older and more conventional psychological fiction whose aesthetics are more conservative and whose appropriations from psychology are to be found not in the deformations of narrative or decompositions of thought—not, that is, in the dark continents of the interior—but in the study of character in society and all that that implies about social bearing and social behavior, about manners, morals, and the novel. This fiction of character far antedates Freudian psychology and antedates, even, the novel itself. It arises on the Elizabethan stage—in Shakespeare's temperamental heroes, Ben Jonson's humors, and the outpourings of rage and pathology in Jacobean drama—and flowers in the novels of Fielding and Dickens. Its origins, indeed, go back to Galen and Greek medicine. Though convention-bound, it is a tradition more closely aligned with realism in its basic aesthetic charter and more resolutely moral and moralizing than the "psychological novel," for while it may entertain a curiosity about mental causes, its lessons are always drawn from social behavior—in a word, from conduct.

When Saul Bellow discovered Wilhelm Reich in the late forties, he found ready to hand a modern psychology of humors whose cameos of extravagance and monomania resembled nothing so much as a cast of Jonsonian characters or the grotesquery of commedia dell'arte. Reich's psychology, as it appeared just after the war, before his sexology had given way to rainmaking, cancer biopathy, and isotope experiments, was a psychology of conduct, complete with preferred and anathematized character types and theories of behavior that, like the psychology of humors, imagined human behavior as an expression of liquid substances coursing through the body like liquors in a distillery, causing mischief. *The Function of the Orgasm,* published in 1942, was a handbook for satirists, with its vivid nosology of character types, its physician's guide to physical aberrations, and its erudite and novelistic rendering of "armored" bearing and behavior. Though Reich was never a stylist of Freud's stature, he did have an artist's intuition—a cartoonist's intuition, really—for the look and feel of pathology, the syncopations in the bodily cadence that signalled a block in the energetic flux or a resistance to natural outpourings. Just as the Freudian analyst trains himself to attend to language with the "third ear," the Reichian trains his eye to the syntax of the body: the choreography of gesture and gait, the formal lines of posture. Unlike psychoanalysis, which is a psychology of language, Reichian orgonomy is a psychology of gesture. "Many people have a mask-like facial expression," notes Reich in a typical diagnosis. "The chin is pushed forward and looks broad; the neck below the chin is 'lifeless.' The lateral neck muscles which go to the breastbone stand out as thick cords; the muscles under the chin are tense. Such patients often suffer from nausea. Their voice is usually low, monotonous, 'thin.'"[1] The eye of the therapist here is that of a novelist, taking note of collisions deep within the psyche as they are registered in the lifeless neck and the tense muscles of the chin.

What Reich provided the postwar writer, Bellow and Mailer in particular, was a modern version of a medieval craft, physiognomy, the craft of reading the character of the man from the features of the body. Reich put the writer in possession of a typology of character based on a theory of force and restraint whose intricate calculus can be read upon the body, making appearance an index to the whole moral life. He even drew elaborate charts of psychic disturbances and their somatic representations, presenting moral equivalents to hypertension, rheumatism, constipation, hemorrhoids, obesity, and cancer, conveniently locating the moral life at certain neurological pressure points where energy was imprisoned and from which it begged release. Clinician and novelist alike are bound to be drawn to wherever the moral life is concentrated and visible, and Bellow is an acute observer of necks, throats, chests, mouths, teeth, and the inflected corners of the eyes, tiny fortresses in which the defenses of the entire system may be read.

Bellow, then, may be thought of as a diagnostic novelist specializing in the diseases of civilization and the distortions of the emotional life that underlie them. And though the terms of the diagnosis vary, the Reichian have been the most durable. In book after book, especially from *The Victim* through *Herzog*, we find repression standing opposed to liberation, boredom to ecstatic energy, blockage to breakthrough, tension to grace, and character armor to healthy genitality. Bellow has acknowledged his debts to Reich over the years, though he's been understandably reserved about the details. In part, that is because his Reichianism threw him in the fifties into the company of Paul Goodman, Allen Ginsberg, Norman Mailer, and Jack Kerouac, with whom he had little in common save a passion for therapeutic self-development. He was a Reichian with a difference. While Mailer was touting the White Negro, while Kerouac and Ginsberg were lionizing Neil Cassady, and while Paul Goodman instructing youth in his own brand of anarchism, compounded of equal parts pansexuality and urban planning, Bellow was exploring more guarded versions of the therapeutic, resisting entirely the political dimensions of Reich's bioenergetic program. The others took Reich as the Luther of a new, erotic Reformation that would liberate and pacify Western civilization, but Bellow was too ironic for such visions, perferring a more modest revolutionism that, like charity, began at home. And even that was normally rendered as comedy. The Reich we meet in his books is a vaudevillian physician out of an old Smith and Dale routine, Dr. Kronkheit. He is a Dahfu, a Henderson, a Tamkin, a Bummidge malpracticing without a license, punctuating his lectures with pratfalls and dialect routines, and dispensing fake remedies in real hospitals. Or, at least, he makes them sound like fake remedies even when, it seems, he has made the right diagnoses, for Bellow's comedy is an overlay upon a quest, and his irony is only a transparent film over a powerful idea that is held with great passion: *that a man must live,* even though it may cost him everything else. *"Grun-tu-molani,"* Eugene Henderson learns in Africa, "Man want to live." Through all the variety, complexity, and imposing urbanity of Bellow's books this idea is repeated in endless variaton: "Man want to live." But what a fearful job living turns out to be and how much of man's self has to be conquered or cut loose before it becomes possible! From book to book we discover characters who either are unable to feel or who feel only rage where there should be love, or rush to atone for uncommitted crimes, or sabotage their lives in order to promote their failures, or, more rarely, tackle their repressions and fight their way toward joy and self-realization. All are haunted by the unlived quality of their lives and yet terrified by the possibility of having to affirm life.

Thus Bellow's books are far from being therapeutic tracts, for in the main his great theme has been the pain of achieving emotional clarity: Joseph *(Dangling Man)* and Tommy Wilhelm *(Seize the Day)* fail at it; Augie March is too busy for it; Asa Leventhal *(The Victim)* settles for his modest fund of shallow emotion; Philip Bummidge *(The Last Analysis)* is reborn, but from a clothes hamper and on television; Eugene Henderson takes a dubious allegorical cure; and Moses Herzog's deliverance is little more than a sudden disinclination to write imaginary letters, not a fully realized state of mind. Charles Citrine *(Humboldt's Gift)* stands on his head to no useful purpose. Only Arthur Sammler (Mr. Sammler's Planet) and Albert Corde *(The Dean's December)* have scuttled the mission of self-regeneration entirely.

Therapeutic moralities are treacherous for fiction because they lend themselves too easily to mystagogy or mass-produced versions of transcendence. Sooner or later the doctors are exposed as madmen and their patients declared sane. Too, the turbulent dialectics of repression are invariably more interesting than inner peace, harmony with the body, and clarity of purpose, and books that plan to inspire us with tales of self-realization risk being boring or smug. With one exception, Moses Herzog, Bellow's characters are typically most endearing when they are sunk in troubles and least believable when they appear to be working things out, like Eugene Henderson and Phillip Bummidge. It is easy enough, under the sway of any scheme of redemption, to be a zealot and a bore, and one finds in some of Bellow's alter egos—Augie March, Charles Citrine, and Albert Corde—a ferocious tediousness. Even to talk about the search for peace while demonstrating its pitfalls can be risky, and Bellow at his best makes certain that when we must be lectured on how to live Dr. Kronkheit delivers the lines.

II. Chicago Dostoevskian

> You keep your spirit under lock and key. That's the way you're brought up. You make it your business assistant, and it's safe and tame and never leads you toward anything risky. Nothing dangerous and nothing glorious. Nothing ever tempts you to dissolve yourself.
>
> —Kirby Allbee, in Bellow,
> *The Victim*

Bellow began his career as a post-Marxist writer in 1944 with *Dangling Man*, a book premised on the Fall. Not only is Joseph, the hero of *Dangling Man*, a survivor of the Marxist wars, but the very tone of his being, his astringent inward music, is a sonata upon the God That Failed. This seems only a recessive note to the contemporary undergraduate, whose only hint of it is Joseph's encounter in a Manhattan cafeteria with a former comrade who will not acknowledge him, but in 1944 any reader in tune with circumstances would have recognized immediately that *Dangling Man* was a post-Marxist *roman à thèse*. "This is the experience of the generation that has come to maturity during the depression," wrote Delmore Schwartz in 1944, "the sanguine period of the New Deal, the days of the Popular Front and the days of Munich and the slow, loud, ticking imminence of a new war."[2] Resemblances between Joseph and Trilling's John Laskell are by no means accidental, for both are strategically passive, demonstrating by the atrophy of their emotions that they have put aside activism to court illness. Joseph, like Laskell, is moody, irritable, and none too well, another patient of history etherized upon a table. Joseph is the first of Bellow's moody philosophers, a morose Dostoevskian preoccupied with his grievances and affecting a bitter composure that takes the place of opinions. Suspended between the civilian life and the military as he anticipates his draft call, for this is winter 1942–43, he retreats from his feelings and relationships and sullenly abides his destiny. Though he throws the burden of his dissatisfaction upon the times, depression seems to suit him; like later Bellow heroes who suffer through the boom years, Joseph is firm in his irritability. This inner shrinking is the problem that later books have to solve: Joseph is the basic Bellow equation, and every book that follows *Dangling Man* takes a stand either for or against him.

The consistency of Joseph's depression and its air of principle have opened *Dangling Man* up to the charge of being essentially a dramatized idea, which it is to the degree that Joseph's bleakness has as much to do with the stoic realism of European thought during the years of fascist domination as it does with Bellow's disposition. Irving Howe has called this depressiveness Bellow's "Russian" manner, though one imagines it also to be a French manner, for there is as much ennui in Joseph's indisposition as there is despair.[3] *Dangling Man* is as dogmatically somber as the later *Adventures of Augie March* is dogmatically affirmative. Indeed, *Dangling Man* and *Augie March*, read together as a '40s book and a '50s book, or books about alienation and "our country and our culture," respectively, illustrate the difficulties inherent in a fiction of fashionable sentiments. The central problem with such a fiction is that the characters are not free to alter the basic terms of their lives. They are fixed by the climate of feeling in which the author lives. Fortunately, *Dangling Man,* like much of Bellow's work, survives this fixity through the spiritedness of its impressions. It is Bellow's minutiae that count for so much; the momentary gesture, the flash of characterization, and the spontaneous pulse of a fugitive thought frequently overpower his metaphysics. If *Dangling Man* and the later books *The Victim* (1947) and *Seize the Day* (1956) overcome the aridity of their themes, it is because Bellow's senses are on the prowl and his prose responsive to the most reclusive details. What Bellow gets from the modernist writers, Joyce in particular, is an eye for shabbiness, and his best writing can be positively lyrical about the debased, the seamy, and the discarded. He brings energy to despair.

> In the upper light there were small fair heads of cloud turning. The streets, in contrast, looked burnt out; the chimneys pointed heavenward in openmouthed exhaustion. The turf, intersected by sidewalk, was bedraggled with the whole winter's deposit of deadwood, match cards, cigarettes, dogmire, rubble. The grass behind the palings and wrought-iron frills was still yellow, although in many places the sun had already succeeded in shaking it into livelier green.

This Chicago winterscape from *Dangling Man* is vintage Bellow: the blasted urban scene and the sharp details in which the symptoms of cultural decline are sublimed into local color or spiritual portent. Bellow's gift for sluicing out the sensuous or the comic from what appears to be dead is a bedrock aesthetic that comes before ideas in his best books. It analyzes depressive aggregates into vivid particulars and shows how the wreckage of the modern city may appeal to the inner eye as potential vitality. This is a classic depressive's aesthetic, shared alike by the great melancholics from Robert Burton to Dostoevsky and Eliot, and to read Bellow at such haggard moments is to understand how depression came to be the Cadillac of the emotions. "The Wasteland" is one of the liveliest poems of this century.

The passage also shows us how landscape may be a metaphor for character, for it is Joseph who is burnt out, exhausted, and bedraggled, and Joseph who harbors a subterranean pulse. Prick this world and it will bleed. Though *Dangling Man* precedes the therapeutic novels, we can nonetheless begin to see in it what Bellow is seeking: the molten core that will burst like a geyser through the frozen exterior, and sooner or later every one of his characters will enter the tempest of fire and ice.

When Bellow revised Dostoevsky's novella *The Eternal Husband* for his second novel, *The Victim,* he found ready to hand a situation—a man's struggles with his persecutory double—and a mood—the "poetical strangeness" of St. Petersburg, as Philip Rahv once called it. But missing from Dostoevsky's novella were a usable character and a history. Dostoevsky's Velchaninov is only a pencil sketch; his dilemma, his confrontation with a man he had once wronged, intrigued Dostoevsky more than Velchaninov himself. As for his double, Pavel Pavlovitch Trusotsky, the "eternal husband," we know little except that he is a born cuckold and a waster with a craving for pity and alchohol. For history, Bellow simply chose his own moment and for situation a vague ambience of persecution and guilt. The Holocaust is background to *The Victim* in much the same way Marxism is backgound to *Dangling Man,* deeply buried yet tightly woven into the fabric of the narrative, rarely explicit but always there, like a symptom. For character, Bellow drew cautiously upon Wilhelm Reich's characterology, which was still, in 1945, when he began work on *The Victim,* a fresh item on the market. Reich's *The Function of the Orgasm* was published in English translation in 1942, the second edition of *Character Analysis* in 1945, and both books had created a stir in the small circle of intellectuals who were attuned to whatever *"commence en mystique et finit en politique."*

Dostoevsky's Velchaninov is a man of failing powers, nervous and valetudinarian, but of impressive stature and a degree of charm, nevertheless. He was altogether too vigorous, then, for Bellow, who needed a Jew and had a conception of the Jew he wanted: a victim, a "little man" and a human boiler, ice and fire. From Reich's physiognomy, Bellow drew a distinctive characterology, a gallery of expressions and postures illustrating the deforming power of tension. Asa Leventhal is a model of self-restraint. "[His eyes] seemed to disclose an intelligence not greatly interested in its own powers, as if preferring not to be bothered by them, indifferent. . . . He did not look sullen but rather unaccommodating, impassive." He smiles only with the greatest of effort, with a line of strain about his mouth.

The situation in which Leventhal finds himself is one of those minor impasses that in Dostoevsky, as in Chekhov and Joyce, explodes into a major conflict. Leventhal's wife is away, and he finds himself being mysteriously watched and finally hounded by one Kirby Allbee, a marginal acquaintance of some years back who has returned to haunt him with a crime he may or may not have committed.

Allbee is a type who has long been a standby of Jewish fiction: the hard-living, hard-drinking goy who is in touch with his appetites and does not fear the consequences of his intemperance. What he tells Leventhal about himself can be taken for Bellow's estimation of Jewish character armor. "You keep your spirit under lock and key. That's the way you're brought up. You make it your business assistant, and it's safe and tame and never leads you toward anything risky. Nothing dangerous and nothing glorious. Nothing ever tempts you to dissolve yourself." Leventhal *is* tempted but the temptation is so far beneath the threshold of consciousness that all we see are the consequences of its containment: his hair-trigger temper and his sullen demeanor. The departure of Leventhal's wife has opened up erotic possibilities which he is determined to deny. He leaves the double, Allbee, to act out his desires, which Allbee does by bringing a woman into Leventhal's apartment. "It gave you a bang to put your whore where I sleep," says Leventhal, and he shoves Allbee violently down the stairs, drawing blood. His violence here is diagnostic; his annoyance, fueled by sexual tension, makes him touchy and dangerous. This tremulous potential for violence pops up in most of Bellow's heroes, though in the main, their aggression is nothing worse than a petty rudeness or a minor unsociability, though they can be violent. In *Dangling Man*, Joseph spontaneously assaults his landlord one frigid Sunday when the heat is suddenly turned off. "This was not 'like me,' " he protests afterwards, "It was an early symptom." Moses Herzog comes close to crossing the line from distemper to homicide when he sets out to shoot Madeleine and Valentine Gersbach. Artur Sammler, who has globalized his aggressions and wishes the world no good, confesses that "my impatience sometimes borders on rage. It is clinical." Only he among them has actually killed, a wartime murder which he had found satisfying.

It would appear, then, that with *The Victim* Bellow had scrapped his existentialism for a more dynamic, psychological view of alienation. Where *Dangling Man* was roughly a book about "the human condition," *The Victim* is much more a book about "our time." Not only is it anchored in specific domestic arrangements, but it trades in the spirit of conditions, which are larger than life, for that of situations, which are of human scale. Conditions affect man in the mass, while each man confronts his situation alone. If economics and sociology describe the laws of conditions, psychology describes those of situations. To pursue this a little farther, character is irrelevant to conditions; one must either submit, or join up, or rally in opposition, and Joseph, in *Dangling Man*, finally joins up. But character is the very fulcrum of situations. Asa Leventhal's character, his job, his marriage, and his family obligations are arrayed against an eruption of dangerous emotions, and the tension in the story reflects the uncertainty of his control. Allbee drops into his life like a dream or a symptom; he is the return of the repressed or a return of the missing half of the riven self, a half that is, however, no closer to the truth of life than Leventhal himself. Between the two of them, Leventhal and Allbee divide up the pathology.

III. Coming Through

> Whatever thy hand findeth to do, do it with thy might.
> —Epigraph to Bellow's
> "Looking for Mr. Green"

> Nobody takes that seriously any more, the dance of conduct. There're other steps that have been crowding our legs. We're more and more in the open of our natures, nearer and nearer to the original personal quality in people. . . . The old props, manners . . . unless you want to die at the last post, a gentleman, *homme raffiné*, and a heroic sacrifice to a good opinion of people and respect for your fellows against all evidence. Okay, if you do. But the next conduct will have to come from the heart, from attachment to life despite the worst it has shown us, and it has shown us just about everything.
> —Weyl, in Bellow's
> "The Trip to Galena"

Presumably this immersion in the gloomy, the perverse, and the irrational—the Petersburgian mode—was to be continued by a longer effort in that line, a novel to be entitled *The Crab and the Butterfly,* on which Bellow set to work after completing *The Victim.* It was, one guesses, to round out the Petersburg phase of his writing and be a summa of Chicago Dostoevskianism, a *Poetics* of the lower depths. It was never completed, and all we have of it is a chapter published in *Partisan Review* in 1950 as "The Trip to Galena."[4] The story is the unhinged monologue of Weyl, a patient in a mental hospital, whose tale of a disastrous trip to Galena with his sister slowly effervesces into a ramble, spinning off a froth of metaphysics: wild speculations on shoes and garters, murder and mass murder, conduct and the depths of life. Weyl is a manic-depressive who bursts out of his iron lethargy while telling his story to a fellow patient, Scampi, and sinks in again once he is finished. His ramblings, bewildering but not thoughtless, sound like rehearsals for von Humboldt Fleisher's torrents of speech in *Humboldt's Gift,* while the campaign for deeper meanings is straight out of Rosenfeld, and it is conceivable that Weyl was meant to be a pastiche of Rosenfeld and

Delmore Schwartz. Indeed, some of his speeches sound like virtual paraphrases of Rosenfeld's essay on terror and joy.

> You heard me tell my old aunt a while back when she asked me what I wanted, that I didn't want to be sad any more. I meant it to the letter. That being sad is being disfigured, and the first reply I feel like making to it is a good fast kick in the wind. As far as I'm concerned it's a platitude and an indecency. You damn well, in that condition, go on eating and drinking, minding your lines and even cementing your social position, but it's done as though you had gone over the knowledge of the world and sounded out everything and had found out about everything but joy. Ah, nobody knows that much. That's not knowledge, that's sophistication.

On the whole the story is wintry in the manner of the earlier novels, as if some commandment of decorum had laid a hand on whatever was unruly in Bellow's imagination and ordered, "Thou shalt not." Yet the method runs against the grain of Weyl's message, a rousing, Nietzschean "Thou shalt." The Dostoevskian manner, then, was the wrong vehicle for the Nietzschean message, except, perhaps, in a mental ward, and Bellow needed a new framework that would permit him to take the call for joy off the wards and release it into the streets. *Augie March* is not just a departure, it is a "breakthrough," a shattering of forms, and if the book should now seem strained in its exuberance and shrill in its composition, it was so for personal, expressive reasons. Bellow was announcing that he was through with the old props. The new imperative is get it all said, quite as if the book's frightful talkers and theoreticians—Einhorn, Simon March, Mintouchian, Basteshaw—were merely objective correlatives of a state of mind, symbols of a violent mental shudder. The book is explicitly therapeutic; its careening adventurism departs sharply from the leaden stasis of the earlier novels as if to say, "Look, I've come through." Coming through is Bellow's great theme, and *Augie March* makes it seem easy, a matter of forsaking the dance of conduct and entering the charged circuits of life, signing up with the life force itself.

There is a politics to such conversions. In the forties, Van Wyck Brooks had attempted to politicize the "life-drive" by dividing up literature into "primary" and "coterie" writing and anathematizing all of modernism, including Joyce and Eliot, as mere "coterie" literature. There was a patriotic note to Brooks's position; his famed essay was a wartime effusion, and its detractors, fretting over the prospect of Zhdanovite ukases from the Library of Congress, read it in light of Archibald MacLeish's more baldly jingoistic attacks on the modernists, "The Irresponsibles."[5] Indeed, if Brooks, toward the end of his career, could have designed an American novel to embody his sense of the life drive, it would have shared features with *The Adventures of Augie March,* certainly the linkage of patriotism with sweat. For if Bellow's first two novels are ploddingly "Russian" in their rhythms, *Augie March* is rousingly American. It is hard to miss the national theme, though Bellow sometimes treats it as a regional theme, the larky Chicago spirit he would sometimes affect as if the life force were domiciled somewhere between Hyde Park and the stockyards. But there is no mistaking the book's turn toward America in its Whitmanizing of life: its embrace of contradiction and ambivalence, its salute to possibility, its Yankee yawp, its cult of experience.

But Bellow didn't need Brooks and MacLeish to instruct his emotions. He had Wilhelm Reich and the entire college of positive thinkers whom the new optimism brought in its train, from Emerson and Whitman to Horatio Alger, Elbert Hubbard, Carl Sandburg, and the French psychotherapist Emile Coué ("Every day in every way I am getting better and better"). The theoreticians among whom Augie falls, from the paralyzed entrepreneur Einhorn to the mad psycho-biophysicist Basteshaw, are all effort-optimists, ministers of "I can, I must, I shall." For a choir he had the *Partisan Review* symposium "Our Country and Our Culture," which was inadvertently a hallelujah chorus for such a novel as *Augie March.* Like Weyl and Augie, the intellectuals didn't want to be sad anymore. The therapeutic blueprint, every day in every way getting better and better, then, was also a political posture, and the implicit postulate is hard to mistake: becoming American is a remedy for the blues.

Though the national theme is played fortissimo in *Augie March,* the therapeutic is pianissimo. In *Augie March,* as in the two earlier books, *Dangling Man* and *The Victim,* the therapeutic is not present as doctrine but as music. *The Victim's* leaden largos give way to *Augie March's* robust allegros (or, to borrow Augie's language, dirges give way to rhumbas) in ways that suggest breakthrough, health, vivacity. The sourpuss is transformed into a cheerleader. The depths of life that Joseph and Asa Leventhal cannot sound wash over Augie March like water over a fall. In *The Adventures of Augie March,* the therapeutic is the music of catalogues, breathlessness, outpouring, moxie, get-up-and-go.

IV. The Noble Savage

The reader who takes Bellow's novels in the order of their composition might well observe in the flux of mood from one book to the next a pattern akin to the boom and bust cycle in the American economy. "Art fosters Fortune; Fortune fosters Art," Lionel Trilling quoted Agathon in a famous formulation, and no artist in recent times has been more observant of fortune and its vicissitudes than Bellow.[6] In *Augie March,* the ebb and flow of mood follows closely the ebb and flow of fortune. Augie's model and mentor, Einhorn, when flush with fortune in the 1920s, steeps himself in the philosophers of self-enhancement: Coué, Hubbard, Teddy Roosevelt, and Reverend Beecher ("Ye are as Gods, you are crystalline, your faces are radiant"). After the crash, however, the crystalline loses its fascination for him, and the reader would be forgiven for wondering if this were not a clinical indicator, a reader's guide to the manic-depressive cycle. For the mind itself, in a Bellow novel, behaves like a commodity on some biorhythmic stock exchange, suffering mysterious bulls and bears as if subject to the same laws of fluctuation that govern the market.

The most striking instance of this is not to be found *in* any of Bellow's books but *between* them, each book coming in reply to the earlier one with a regular systolic wheeze and diastolic thump: now riotous, now gloomy, now bright, now umbral, now Nietzschean, now Dostoevskian. You could almost follow it with an oscilloscope. Thus the noisy *Augie March,* which came into being as a corrective to the laconic *Dangling Man* and *The Victim,* was followed by *Seize the Day,* whose dwindlings are balanced directly against the earlier book's swellings. *Seize the Day,* published in 1956, three years after *Augie March,* might well have been titled *The Downside of Tommy Wilhelm,* since the deterioration of Tommy Wilhelm's character so closely follows the decline in his fortunes and appears to be a part of it. Character fosters fortune, fortune fosters character. The commodities exchange, Tommy Wilhelm's plummeting lard futures, the dishevelled economy, and the cash nexus that divides Tommy from his father and turns a bad poet, Tamkin, into a cunning swindler are the neurotic fallout of a world in which only the most reactionary emotions—jealousy, rage, greed—are deeply felt. Tommy Wilhelm loses as he does because it is his nature to lose; he is dead set on being gulled. His long career of mistakes, he believes, "expressed the very purpose of his life and the essence of his being here." With his massive aggressions, his secret guilt, his will to failure, his nervous feet and constricted chest, he is a walking nosology, a compendium of symptoms from Reich's *Character Analysis.* Tommy is a clinical set piece, a hysteric whose rigid character has been mobilized against his unconscious wishes, mainly his murderous rage againt his father. That rage has been uneasily repressed and redirected against Tommy himself, tightening his chest, thickening his breath, and congealing his speech into a stammer. His guilt takes the form of respiratory difficulties. Though he is light years from Augie March, as a victim and a clinical type he bears ballpark affinities to Joseph and Leventhal.

Tamkin, his guru and investment counselor, is one of Bellow's great inventions, a shyster Fritz Perls who dabbles cunningly in verses and values, commodities and the spirit, quite as if one man could be rabbi, consultant, therapist, and thief, all in one. He is Kirby Allbee with a lifetime's training at being a pest, who takes Tommy for his last seven hundred dollars while making the plunge into lard seems a cure, even a blessing. Tamkin is a champion of Gestalt "here and now" therapy, which he perverts into "Trust me here and now." Yet his advice to Tommy is not just a swindle; his counsel to live in the present and come to grips with the "real" world is orthodox psychiatric piety, rooted in the popular texts of the day and ratified by Tamkin's own suffering. "You see," he counsels Tommy, "I understand what it is when the lonely person begins to feel like an animal. When the night comes and he feels like howling from his window like a wolf." And he knows too, from reading *Gestalt Therapy* by Paul Goodman, Fritz Perls, and Ralph Hefferline, that actually howling from the window would do a spot of good.* A fellow sufferer, Tamkin is a shrewd diagnostician, and Tommy signs over power of attorney to him in the spirit of payment for services rendered. Like many another sufferer in the commercial wilderness, Tamkin has parlayed his misery into a business. Pain is his grubstake, his venture capital, his shtick.

But Tommy is in no position to enter the here and now, since his reality is an actual hell, not just a mental one, and to seize the day could only mean to seize his father, or Tamkin, by the throat and beat him silly. A release of passions would be a release of violence, and Tommy is not prepared, any more than is Bellow, for blood. The only breakthrough Tommy is permitted is a shower of tears for an anonymous corpse, a stranger into whose funeral he has been swept by a crowd. *Seize the Day* ends with Bellow's famous paragraph of oceanic dissolution, as Tommy weeps before the body of the unknown father.

> The flowers and lights fused ecstatically in Wilhelm's blind, wet eyes; the heavy sea-like music came up to his ears. It poured into him where he had hidden himself in the center of a crowd, by the great and happy oblivion of

---

*The scheme that sends Tommy's father, Dr. Adler, into gales of laughter, Tamkin's device to awaken drowsy truck drivers with a shock when they grow drowsy at the wheel, is actually proposed by Perls on page 19 of *Gestalt Therapy*.[7]

tears. He heard it and sank deeper than sorrow, through torn sobs and cries toward the consummation of his heart's ultimate need.

Here, it seems, in the most meticulously plotted of Bellow's novels, a resolution is effected through music rather than action. While Tommy's outburst of tears ties up some symbolic currents in the book—severing his knot of emotions and bringing all the water music to a grand finale—it does nothing for his real problems: finding Tamkin, paying child support and rent, and discovering the emotional resources to carry on. Trouble is resolved in a cadenza of sobs. As such, it is a typical Bellow conclusion, a symbolic resolution to a real crisis, getting the novel off the hook but leaving its hero at the funeral. For Tommy's putative break-through into feeling is set apart as a momentary swoon that has no consequences. The difficulty lies not in Bellow's craft, which is at its height in *Seize the Day,* but in a conception of human nature that defies the conventions of plotting. The metaphysics of release are not dra-matic; they do not require a resolved conflict with another person. The self simply bursts into song. Tommy's burst of tears occurs significantly away from his father, his wife Margaret, and Tamkin. It is, in the Reichian lexicon, a vegetative streaming whose benefits for Tommy have yet to be tested in a relationship. It is also unclear what Tommy has learned, for the therapeutic doesn't traffic in education but contents itself with epiphanies, sudden emotional blossomings that may come, as they often do in treatment, bare of insights. The epiphany of sorrow at the end of *Seize the Day* is a powerful coda to a wretched life, and is entirely convincing so long as one does not demand too precise an accounting of what it means.

It was with the unfinished business of *Seize the Day* in mind, then, that Bellow started to work on *Henderson the Rain King* in 1956, the book that would show the therapeutic at work bringing an afflicted character through the dark night of the soul into the light of common day. It was also in 1956, however, that Wilhelm Reich died in a federal prison, convicted of medical fraud, his life's work largely discredited as a result of his latter day confusion of himself with Faust. A writer more timid than Bellow would have concluded that the time was ripe to drop the subject and move on to other things, while a more credulous one would have damned the torpedoes and written the therapeutic epic. Being neither timid nor credulous, Bellow chose to take up the unfinished business of *Seize the Day* in the ambiguous form of a comic romance, a form rich in possibility, which permits ideas to be tried out and indulged without being promoted. *Henderson* is Bellow's comic farewell to Reich, a lighthearted valedictory that takes Reich's ideas in the spirit of Bellow's own grateful amusement. That spirit proved to be a happy one; *Henderson the Rain King* is one of Bellow's most charming and friendly books, akin in its high spirits to *The Adventures of Augie March* but lacking that book's edge of mandatory liveliness. In Eugene Henderson, a wealthy pig farmer from upstate New York who has shipped out to Africa in answer to an inner voice that demands, "I want, I want," Bellow created a character primed for adventure and capable of any combination of folly and heroism: making rain, blowing up wells, precipitating frog-storms, roaring with lions, wrestling with mother figures, taking instruction from witch doctors. In Dahfu, the therapist-king, he invented a board-certified shaman who speaks a most erudite brand of pidgin, a compound of big words and open syntax that reminds one a little of Tamkin speaking through a handkerchief. Bellow's friend Richard Stern calls the argot "Bellafrikanisch."[8] The book is a celebration of what the imagination can do when freed from the necessity of making points and permitted to indulge the comedy of point-making itself.

Like Tommy Wilhelm, Eugene Henderson is an avoider with a propensity for flight, especially from women. He had left his wife Lily once before, when she casually bared her breasts one afternoon when he wasn't feeling up to the challenge. This time he is set off on his quest by the death of Miss Lenox, a spinster from across the road. He enters her cottage to find it choked with the debris of a squandered life. Henderson, who shares upper respiratory maladies with Tommy, is made so claustrophobic that he foresees his own death in the choked cabin: "The last little room of dirt is waiting," he fears. "Without windows."

There is a splendid realism to the early pages of *Henderson*, but once our man gets in Africa that realism gives way to romance and all its gimmickry, including portentous symbolic action. What actually goes on in the heart of Henderson's Africa is vague and allegorical, as ill-defined as the desires that drive him there. The inner voice calls its tireless, Blakean "I want, I want," without ever specifying what. In search of the remotest locale on the map—the deepest unconscious—Henderson winds up in a symbolic wasteland where the trouble seems to be the usual affliction of post-Eliotic wastelands: drought. But it was Reich, not Eliot, who gave Bellow the metaphor, having pursued his bioenergetic researches in the forties into rainmaking with his cloud-buster experiments, practicing, as it were, orgonomy on the parched earth.

It is among the Wariri, a people as dry and unfortunate as himself, that Henderson stops wanting and starts getting. He brings on rain by lifting and carrying the massive goddess of the rain, Mummah, from one place to another, not only satisfying his need for useful work—getting him into his "real depth"—but raising his stock among the suddenly sopping Wariri, who anoint him their rain king for his inadvertent cloud-busting. Is Reich being spoofed or honored by such high jinks? Both, one guesses, for this entire Bob Hope routine is superimposed upon Henderson's quest for deep feeling and "reality," and it is the Wariri king, Dahfu, who gives him his first lessons in living. Dahfu is an American-educated witch doctor/analyst whose pidgin occasionally lapses into an odd German-Jewish lingo. Dahfu is, one wants to say, a cross between the noble savage and Dr. Kronkheit, though he is an honest practitioner as well, Tamkin unspoiled by capitalism. Despite his own enormous royal aggravations, Dahfu accepts Henderson without a referral and treats him to lessons on living, lessons that bring Henderson face to face with one Atti, a sweetheart of a lioness whom Dahfu houses beneath the palace as a pet and a teacher's aid.

Atti is reality. "First," instructs Dahfu, "she is unavoidable. Test it, and you will find she is unavoidable. And this is what you need, as you are an avoider." As for the here and now, "She will force the present moment upon you." Second, she incarnates all that is ecstatic and graceful in the body. No clumsy intellectual at war with her own flesh, she is at home with her limbs, her breath, her stride.

> "Contemplate her. How does she stride, how does she saunter, how does she lie and gaze or rest or breathe? I stress the respiratory part. . . . She do not breathe shallow. This freedom of the intercostal muscles and her abdominal flexibility . . . gives the vital continuity between her parts. It brings those brown jewel eyes their hotness."

Bellow had toyed with symbology of this sort once before, in *Augie March*, where Thea Fenchel's eagle Caligula, was supposed to be a lesson to Augie in courage and spontaneity. But Caligula turned out to be a dud at hunting, and Augie himself proved too urban to profit from the lessons of the wild. Atti's feline simplicity, by contrast, is prophylactic for the uptight Henderson. Down there in the cave with Dahfu and Atti, Henderson learns to snarl, to bellow, and to strike out with his paws. "For the moment," Dahfu commands, "be it utterly," and Henderson, struggling mightily against his native sense of the ironic, roars. After just a few days of primal roar therapy, Henderson sends off an ecstatic letter to his forsaken Lily, in which he claims to be bursting with life, with reality, with prose, and with the resolve to get home, sell the pigs, and, at fifty-five, enter med school.

Despite the vaudeville, Bellow does little to disguise the doctrine in *Henderson*. Here we are, in the middle of Africa, remembering Conrad and awaiting some awful bulletins about the human heart, and we get, in lieu of the horror, the treatment. For this deep forest is not the Congo of the heart but the Esalen Institute, where deep release and consultation mean more than empire and brutishness. At the far end of his journey and his muddle, after months and pages of diffuse monologues about the intractability of the emotions and the mysterious ways of the heart, Henderson learns that what the heart of darkness offers mankind are the techniques of self-restoration.

It may be noted that these lessons amount to pure neural engineering; they do not follow upon any analysis of Henderson's difficulties. It is the trademark of Reichianism that the production of high spirits by massaging the psychic apparatus is divorced from the Freudian goals of interpretation and self-definition. "The living organism," says Reich, "functions autonomously, beyond the sphere of language, intellect and volition."[9] Language belongs to the affliction, and the more verbal one is, the more armored. The Reichian novel, indeed, is a contradiction in terms, since language intrudes upon man's basic nature rather than being its highest expression. Bellow, apparently in sympathy with a psychology that ricochets past analysis on its way to euphoria, is coy about what Henderson's trouble really is and what his cure represents, and it is no wonder that the conclusion to *Henderson* is as inconclusive as that of *Seize the Day*. Henderson returns home with a lion cub in tow and while on the plane from Europe befriends an orphaned boy who is flying alone to America. When the plane stops at Gander to refuel, the ecstatic Henderson leaps out into the snows of Newfoundland with the boy and proceeds to caper around the plane like a leaping Hasid. This Ode to Joy simply happens, and while Henderson tries out his newfound plasma mobility the reader can only marvel at the fact of it: that a little roaring goes a long way. But that is precisely the distinguishing feature of Reichian therapy, which short-circuits the accustomed rhythms of a life to install new ones. As such, it lends itself poorly to the novel as opposed to the fairy tale, where ugly ducklings turn into handsome swans and frogs regularly become princes. The Reichian universe is alive with magic.

In fact, *Henderson* deals as much in magic and metaphysic as it does in psychology, and there are movements in it that look beyond the achievement of a good gestalt. A glimpse at Dahfu before he dies at the paws of a lion (the FDA?) reveals a shimmer of genuine beatitude about him.

> The king had thrown off his hat; it would have got in his way; and about
> his tight-grown hair, which rose barely an eighth of an inch above his scalp,
> the blue of the atmosphere seemed to condense, as when you light a few
> sticks in the woods and about these black sticks the blue begins to wrinkle.

There is no mistaking this blue corona. This Dahfu is not only at one
with his body but with the aurora borealis as well.

After *Henderson*, this energism drops out of Bellow's novels and for
good reason, since whatever wisdom it may proffer is hard to make
dramatically credible. The idea, or even the fact, that a man can redeem
himself by releasing the energy locked in the intercostal muscles of his
chest is alien to the spirit of the novel, which looks to social relationships
for redemptions and to the failures of character for dramatic interest.
Character, in contemporary fiction, is a particular style of incapacity, and
the characters who create obstacles to their own fulfillment are the ones
who must typically capture our interest. Tommy Wilhelm the neurotic is
more interesting, more fun, than Augie March the American.

V. Last Analyses

> Where family and nation once stood, or Church
> and Party, there will be hospital and theatre too,
> the normative institutions of the next culture.
> —Philip Rieff, *The Triumph
> of Therapeutic.*

> Why so vivid within, so dead outside?
> —Bummidge, in Bellow,
> *The Last Analysis*

> And what you really want is to get rid of every-
> body, to tune out and be a law unto yourself.
> Just you and your misunderstood heart,
> Charlie.
> —Denise, in Bellow,
> *Humboldt's Gift*

If *Henderson* was an affectionate farewell to Reich, *The Last Analysis* is
something of an ironic hello to Freud. It is commonly taken for a satire
on psychoanalysis, though the bulk of its aggression falls upon the
characters in the play rather than upon psychoanalysis, which, though
treated ambiguously, emerges finally as an affirmative moral doctrine.
While therapy is treated as spectacle and farce, its efficacy is never in
question. A successful treatment takes place on stage, and despite all the

antics that attend it, we're never given to doubt that the play's hero, Philip Bummidge, has benefited from it. Bummidge is a sixty-year-old comedian-turned-self-analyst suffering from "Humanitis," an ailment brought about by an overexposure to the human condition. Seeking both relief as a patient and applause as a performer he takes his treatment in public, acting out pivotal moments in his life, even his death and resurrection, on closed-circuit television. He is yet another of Bellow's energy cultists, his vitalism established upon a therapeutic discipline called *Existenz*-Action self analysis, a brand of self-induced regression therapy that mobilizes ancient grievances and purges them through dramatic reenactment.

Act I is a sequence of preliminaries consisting mainly of Bummidge's trial by family and acquaintances (he has no friends) who have put the touch on him, demanding a piece of his career and earnings. To them, his self-analysis is just a routine, a class act, a shtick for the highbrows. Act II is Bummidge's closed-circuit follies, featuring his greatest traumatic moments. Enlisting the aid of his squabbling entourage (a cousin, an estranged wife, a sister, a son, a paramour, a tailor, an agent, and several walk-ons), Bummidge dramatizes the moment of his conception (the primal scene), his birth, his first lesson in reality (the loss of the breast), the struggle within him between Eros and Thanatos, and some fifty years of history, concluding with his death (apparently of stale routines), and rebirth. "Come forth, Lazarus," he cries from his makeshift coffin in the wardrobe basket, and as we await the punchline Bummidge is delivered with nary a wisecrack. Reborn, renewed, and professionally redeemed—his *Existenz*-Action blackouts have been a smash hit—he gains the enlightenment that has previously eluded him: that his entire entourage, especially the family, is a pain in the neck and must be dumped.

The Last Analysis flopped on Broadway in 1964 and did but slightly better in a 1971 off-Broadway revival.[10] The demands of the lead role aside, which are formidable, *The Last Analysis* is unpleasant. Shrill in its relentless rehearsal of crisis, bristling with complaint, and dominated by a character whose demands upon others are imperious, the play assaults and wearies its audience. For all its conspicuous virtuosity, *The Last Analysis* is a ferociously cold performance, and even Bummidge's rebirth is a rebirth to irritation and recoil. Acting out the Christ myth on stage, Bummidge is crucified by the Jews—his family—and is resurrected as a saint of rejection. "Please—please don't crowd," he entreats to the end. "Oh, don't touch! It makes me cold in the bowels. I feel you breathing on me. See how my skin is wincing." He expresses his beatitude, in short, by declaring the world infectious and drawing a *cordon sanitaire* about his person. "Noli me tangere," he declaims, to which one is prompted to add, "for I am Bellow's."

The triumph of the therapeutic here is the release of narcissism, not joy, as in *Henderson*. Bummidge's rebirth removes him from the money culture in the name of higher values and exacts revenge upon all those nagging, grasping sons, wives, sisters, and lovers, quite as if *Seize the Day* had been rewritten in solicitude for harried fathers and the final, nasty truth could be told at last: a noisy, impecunious son *is* a pest.

A sequel to *Henderson*, then, and another fable of regeneration, *The Last Analysis* is far different in spirit, dyspeptic where the novel is effervescent. Twenty years after *Dangling Man,* it would appear that Bellow had returned to square one with a hero whose tortuous recycling of the self had turned him into a character as touchy and aloof as Joseph. But true to Marx's law, the first time as tragedy, the second time as farce, Joseph's Weltschmerz is now Bummidge's slapstick and the Chicago Dostoevskian now a clown, a little dishevelled, a little *tsedrayt*, a little off his rocker, but the only man on the Eastern Seaboard with a definitely higher purpose. Joseph, after all, suffered on behalf of a world brought to its knees; the full weight of Europe's tragedy lay behind his testiness. Bummidge, like Moses Herzog, with whom he shares grievances and a publication date, is simply put upon.

As for Bellow's attitude toward psychoanalysis and the therapeutic, it is difficult to fathom at this point, and he would appear to be using it for the leverage it can provide him against his assailants while at the same time hedging his bets, making an ambiguous statement, a lament within a farce. Years later, in an interview, Bellow would complain of the schematic properties of Freudian ideas that begged the question of the unconscious while pretending to answer it, and *The Last Analysis* most certainly *is* a comedy of the schematic, Bummidge suffering the whole syllabus of authorized traumas from The Birth Trauma and The Primal Scene to The Death Wish. But really suffering them. "Madge," he lectures his sister, "you have no idea what human beings really are: the stages of the psyche—polymorphous, oral, anal, narcissistic. It's fantastic, intricate, complicated, hidden." And, he neglects to add, absolutely routine.

With *Herzog,* Bellow made his bid to write the great American novel, and a just claim can be made for his having succeeded in his effort. For after the claims of *Moby Dick, Huck Finn, The Scarlet Letter,* and *The Sun Also Rises* are weighed, one can't suppress the feeling that the first two are romances for adolescents (top of the line romances, to be sure) and the latter two chapbooks for narrow moral imaginations: puritans and sportsmen, respectively. For nuance and an adults' view of life, only Henry James bears comparison to Bellow, and James's recoil before the nastier facts of existence and his thin relation to the passions are finally no less narrowing than Hawthorne's obsession with sin and Hemingway's fetishes of violence and fishing.

Herzog too suffers limitations. It develops no great theme, unless divorce is now granted the high moral seriousness once reserved for mortal sin or social ambition or the invasion of Russia. It is a wholly mental performance, a pastiche of reveries and imaginings in which action is only a backdrop to the drama of a mind at bay. Nowhere else in American literature do we find so rich an example of Herzog's particular brand of secular religion: the quest for salvation through ideas. Herzog is possessed by tag lines from Heidegger, Nietzsche, Spengler, and Teilhard de Chardin—his imaginary correspondents—as though the key to self-knowledge lay in an aphoristic relation to modern thought. "What America needs is a good five-cent synthesis." For all that, *Herzog* throbs with a life rare in American fiction. Boisterous and brooding, erotic and philosophical, brightly colored and buffeted by strange emotional weathers, it is a noisy, turbulent, thrilling book.

Herzog was published in October, 1964, eight days after the first performance of *The Last Analysis,* and while it is the more accomplished piece of writing, it has broad thematic correspondences with the play. Both star beleaguered heroes who are assailed by nothing more deadly than domestic vexations, which they globalize into litmus tests of "the human condition." (Typical of the literature of affluence, they confuse marriage with crucifixion and presume a Via Dolorosa running from the bedroom to the divorce court.) Both are animated by an energy of rejection. Both are fables of trial and regeneration, and both seek restoration in the primitive regions of the self, through, to use the Freudian term for it, regression. Bummidge's *Existenz* analysis is more or less what Herzog applies to himself or has applied to him by his "reality instructors." But where *The Last Analysis* is openly doctrinal, *Herzog* shrewdly buries the doctrine, embodying it in Herzog's trials. In the language of the therapeutic, Herzog is a "working through" of trauma.

The events in *Herzog* flow from very primitive feelings and experiences: a betrayal, a separation, Herzog's exposure to a woman who had murdered her child, his fears for his daughter and confusion of himself with her, and his search for rescue in the maternal embraces of Ramona Donsell. Bellow makes a temple of these agonies, beating raw emotions into arabesques of lamentation. In *Herzog,* Bellow seems to have understood the chief aesthetic legacy of the Freudian revolution: that the way to the depths lies in a close attention to the surfaces, for the unconscious is invested everywhere in language and in decor. The old nostrum about the novel of manners, "trust the furniture," takes on a new value in the modern psychological novel. For if the dream is the *via regia* to the unconscious, furniture is the freeway. Bellow's most painstaking bid to write a novel of manners is also his most impressive psychological novel as well, a book both decorous and penetrating. Notice how he anoints his characters' most vulnerable moments with his most elegant writing, as if every blow were a benediction. Note how he stages Madeleine Herzog's announcement that the marriage is over!

> All this happened on a bright, keen fall day. He had been in the back yard putting in the storm windows. The first frost had already caught the tomatoes. The grass was dense and soft, with the peculiar beauty it gains when the cold days come and the gossamers lie on it in the morning; the dew is thick and lasting. The tomato vines had blackened and the red globes had burst.

How vivid a backdrop for Herzog's fall! It is always thus with Bellow: the disasters of his Josephs, Leventhals, Wilhelms, Herzogs, and Sammlers are his occasions to descant upon his own gifts.

> In the window on glass shelves there stood an ornamental collection of small glass bottles, Venetian and Swedish. They came with the house. The sun now caught them. They were pierced with the light. Herzog saw the waves, the threads of color, the spectral intersecting bars, and especially a great blot of flaming white on the center of the wall above Madeleine. She was saying, "We can't live together any more."

What was she saying? Herzog is so transfixed by the play of color and we by the meditation on optics that we all nearly missed the punchline, for these are sensational bottles. In a Victorian novel of manners we would know immediately how to read them. They would frame Madeleine amid the accoutrements of her own bourgeois taste and fix her in their refracted light as a tasteful, expensive, and cold object. But furniture in *Herzog* doesn't belong simply to the social order; it belongs to the psychological as well, and those bottles express Moses even as they judge Madeleine, for despite his protestations to the contrary, this is a moment of great vividness for him. Though he protests that he loves Madeleine still, his joy at being set free is bursting upon him like so many ripe tomatoes, or phrases.

This is where the vitalism has come to rest. These dazzling sets enter the mental dramas of Bellow's heroes as insignias of the hidden life—secret passions projected upon the world. Moses Herzog is only glum in principle; in fact he floats upon a swell of joy that presses lightly at the borders of a happy psychosis. He wants to go entirely mad, to break through the front wall of his body and escape his incessant, eager impulses. "If I am out of my mind, it's all right with me," he boasts, and his out-of-mindness touches everything with fire, even New Jersey.

> The cold fall sun flamed over the New Jersey mills. Volcanic shapes of slag, rushes, dumps, refineries, ghostly torches, and presently the fields and woods. The short oaks bristled like metal. The fields turned blue. Each radio spire was like a needle's eye with a drop of blood in it. The dull bricks of Elizabeth fell behind. At dusk Trenton approached like the heart of a coal fire. Herzog read the municipal sign—TRENTON MAKES, THE WORLD TAKES.

Here is precisely where Tamkin, Dahfu, and Bummidge have been leading us—to a here and now in which Chicago's Congress Street or Trenton tremble like a plasma and even Elizabeth spins in the joyous cosmology. The quest for essentials leads beyond experience to the beachheads of mystery. This New Jersey landscape is the bright garment of a higher reality; these are inhabited details.

This flirtation with mystery leads not only upward but, as in *The Last Analysis,* backward as well. Herzog's epiphanies are possible only on the condition that he provisionally suspend his maturity and descend into primal seas. His separation from Madeleine is an occasion to recall other separations and other, more primitive terrors. While waiting for his lawyer-friend Simkin, Herzog sits through two emblematic trials that confront him with sexual aberration and failure: of a German medical student who had made a pass at a policeman in a public toilet and of a bisexual prostitute who had held up a drygoods store with a toy pistol. Herzog feels his body erupt in protest at this exposure to the freakish edge of things and he flees the courtroom, for primitive scenes are being enacted there that mobilize within him archaic and bitter recollections. A toxic reaction seizes his chest as though he had swallowed a mouthful of poison. "How long can I stand such inner beating? The front wall of this body will go down. My whole life beating against its boundaries, and the force of balked longings coming back as stinging poison." This bursting of the soul brings forth a surge of memories; he recalls his mother's death and her selflessness during those final days when, at the door of death, her only thought had been for *his* comfort. But he had been a "bookish, callow boy" and could not cry at the funeral.

Herzog returns to the courtroom to hear the case of a woman from Trenton who had beaten her child to death in a seedy hotel room while her lover looked on from the bed. The details of the case are hideous, reawakening the terror in Herzog until the gall rises in his throat and his lungs scald with fire. He has been reading Spengler's *The Decline of the West,* and here is its symbol, naked and horrible. He has also been brooding over his mother and his failures as a son—his selfish withholding of affection—and it is as a son, a bookish, callow boy in a man's straw hat and striped jacket, that he hears the testimony of the child's fatal beating. He identifies fiercely with the child, and his body erupts in protest.

What action there is in *Herzog* is provoked by this experience, for Moses had taken to imagining, upon the flimsiest of evidence, that Madeleine and Valentine Gersbach had been abusing his daughter, Junie. The horror of the trial moves Herzog to action for the only time; he collects his father's old pistol and flies to Chicago to murder Madeleine and Gersbach. As a man and injured husband he had never acted to defend himself. It is as a battered child, however, and in the name of his daughter, that he resolves to take revenge upon his wife and her lover for the crimes of the woman from Trenton. This identification with children is of a piece with both Herzog's frenzy of letter writing and his adoration of landscapes, for he has broken through the veil of adult sensibility and emerged with the animate universe of childhood, where all is alive and filled with portent.

We may be certain that this manchild in sport's clothing will harbor a killer's rage but not a killer's resolve. Prowling at the rear of Madeleine's apartment, he observes through the bathroom window a gentle, domesticated Gersbach bathing Junie with fatherly solicitude and is overwhelmed with shame at his self-delusion. He flees and quickly atones for his impulsiveness the following day with a car accident during a visitation with Junie. Maneuvering a rented car onto Outer Drive, in his clumsy manner he hits his brakes too abruptly and is rammed from the rear by a small German truck that butts him into a utility pole. He is, of course, not hurt, only deflated and momentarily knocked out. Had this been a dream, the symbolism of remorse would have been embarrassingly plain. How else do we read a collision that resembles a spanking? As fiction, it is one more example of Herzog's comic superego at work, contriving his defeat in order to instruct, amuse, and humiliate him. Moses spanks himself.

The novel's denouement, which begins in the police station where Herzog confronts Madeleine, brings him back with a thump from the higher worlds of his contemplation. This is Herzog's nth fall into the quotidian, a region in which reality comes not in visions but in blows. Courtroom, precinct station, ex-wife, ex-friend, shell-shocked daughter, and chagrined older brothers are his stations of the domestic cross. Reality, as no lapsed Marxist ever forgets, is this grim bourgeois life, though now the cash nexus of the marketplace counts for less than the erotic nexus of the marriage bed. If there is to be any transcendence in such a life, a man must supply his own; this world, this social order will not lift a finger in his behalf. Bellow and Herzog, however, do manage their own transcendence, through visions, through art, and through language. And, it seems, through fresh supplies of women. (Albert Corde, in *The Dean's December,* confirms the connection of women to transcendence through a wonderful gambit: he marries an astronomer.) When last seen, Herzog is alone in a hammock in Ludeyville, anticipating dinner with Ramona.

Moses Herzog succeeds in doing what every other Bellow hero needs to do—to go slightly berserk in the name of all those impulses crowding up through his nature. Of course, expressive victories are not artistic achievements: Herzog's accomplishment in seizing the day—he seizes a week, in fact—could have produced an artless novel in the bargain. But what Bellow accomplished in *Herzog* was to create a condition of mind that for once justified his animated style and made it seem neither pumped in nor ideologically contrived. For elsewhere, in *Augie March, Henderson,* and *Sammler,* when Bellow's impulse to pile up detail runs against the grain of a mood or a situation, it sounds like a tic, which, rather than communicating his hero's capacity for life, reads like Bellow's own compulsion to name. But given a manic hero, a philosopher-cuckold who is at the edge of sanity and stoked by great surges of adrenalin, Bellow's compulsion becomes Herzog's performance and the high-wire act is breathtaking to watch.

VI. The Long Retreat

> He might look down his conscious nose at sensual delight, but with her, when their clothes were off, he knew what it was. No amount of sublimation could replace the erotic happiness, that knowledge.
>
> —Bellow, *Herzog*

> [He saw] . . . the right to be uninhibited, spontaneous, urinating, defecating, belching, coupling in all positions, tripling, quadrupling,

polymorphous, noble in being natural, primitive, combining the leisure and luxurious in-
ventiveness of Versailles with the hibiscus-
covered erotic ease of Samoa.
—Bellow, *Mr. Sammler's Planet*

Artur Sammler, casting a cold eye on life, on death, from the far shore
of the prudent '70s—this century's '70s as well as his own—deplores all
this vitality as "attempting to make interest," a Jewish-Polish-Oxonian
locution, one gathers, for trying to make life interesting. "Madness," he
scornfully observes, "is the attempted liberty of people who feel themselves overwhelmed by giant forces of organized control. Seeking the
magic of extremes. Madness is a base form of the religious life." Sammler
is particularly vain about having stubbornly kept his sanity in a world
that tempts those around him into modish forms of lunacy. Everyone
else, excepting his nephew, Dr. Arnold (Elya) Gruner, and the Indian
lunar expert, Govinda Lal, is quite batty, obliging Sammler to be *their*
reality instructor. His daughter, Shula, is a blissed out schizophrenic who
wears cheap wigs, converses with flowers, collects trash, and steals a
manuscript from Dr. Lal, imagining that her father might have a use for
it. Her ex-husband, Eisen, is a contemporary muscular Jew and a sculp-
tor whose medium is fool's gold, out of which he casts Star-of-David and
Sherman tank medallions. Then there is Gruner's son, Wallace, another
Tommy Wilhelm whose cracked schemes to promote himself always
shatter. His sister, Angela, is a nymphomaniac with "fucked out eyes," as
her father says. And there are others: the entrepreneur Feffer, who puts
together mad business deals all over the world; the fetishist Bruch, who
adores women's arms and casually masturbates against the support posts
on the IRT, and Sammler's niece Margot, who is hooked on liberal
nostrums and quotes Hannah Arendt on the human condition. And
finally there is the *soigné* black pickpocket who prowls the West Side
busses in a camel's hair coat and Dior shades and, in a moment of cold
assertion, silently backs Sammler against a wall and displays his cock.

This is a full Dickensian crew, and there is reason to regard *Mr.
Sammler's Planet,* with its wealth of humors, its sober moralism, its tedious
philosophical digressions—Herzog's scribblings become interior monologues—and its harsh verdict upon modern life, as Bellow's attempt to
write an English social novel after the manner of Dickens or Wells or
Disraeli. But unlike anything of Dickens, this novel lacks a heart; its
sympathies are about as open as a cul de sac. The patron saint of *Sammler*
is not Dickens but Ben Jonson, for these humors are malicious. An artist
may seek to pay off scores by fixing his enemies for all eternity as

caricatures, but he must at least love his creations and charge them with life, as Bellow himself did with Madeleine and Gersbach, whom he made the most vital characters in *Herzog*. But no affection is lavished on the characters in *Sammler*. They are poor monsters at best. Like Jonson's sharpers and gulls, they are interchangeable symptoms of an unbalanced age—the age of runaway desublimation—and essentially indistinguishable. Grotesques take over, but they are no longer baroque images of the self, like Lucas Asphalter of *Herzog*, whose efforts to save his tubercular monkey by mouth-to-mouth resuscitation contain a tincture of Herzog's own strangeness. They are invaders and barbarians, costumed and eroticised masses, improvising an elaborate and vulgar theater of self-assertion. Their nympho-, klepto-, and megalomanias (Sammler is the only -phobic in this crowd of -philics) are equivalent vanities of the therapeutic era, an era in which "acting out" has replaced performing one's duty as a cultural ideal. The one good man is Sammler's nephew, Elya Gruner, who has selflessly maintained Sammler and Shula from the moment of rescuing them from a DP camp, and whose death from a stroke brings the book to a close. Yet he barely exists as a character at all and is portrayed as little more than an emblem of duty.

Only Sammler himself is spared the jiffy diagnosis, and yet what we learn of him hardly amounts to a full picture of humanity. He has none of Moses Herzog's élan or complexity and lacks even the sullen ambiguities of a Leventhal or a Wilhelm. If those around him are Jonsonian humors, he himself is a kind of Jonson, at least as Edmund Wilson has characterized him: anal and morose.[11] Like Tommy Wilhelm, he is a mountain of symptoms, his repressions being, if anything, more rigid than Leventhal's or Wilhelm's and his character armor more tightly fastened because founded upon principle. His life sanctifies his armor; he had been captured by the Nazis in Poland during the war and left for dead in a mass grave, reason enough to live out one's span divorced from all joy. But the significant question is not why Sammler is the man he is but why Bellow should have created him at this time and summoned the Holocaust in defense of his choice. For the Holocaust here is not seriously confronted, only flaunted as Sammler's moral pedigree. It is a gimmick and a weapon, employed here as a prop to Sammler's opinions and an explanation of his character.* That character represents a retreat

---

*Whether Sammler can be said to have a character at all is open to question. Character is revealed in action, and Sammler refrains almost entirely from action. His life consists of being beset by others and holding disgruntled opinions. These opinions are presented *as if* they might define a man by negatives: by his disapprovals shall ye know him.

from a long and difficult line of emotional improvisation and looks oddly like Bellow's attempt to bring his career full circle. Artur Sammler harkens back to Bummidge and Joseph: he is Joseph in his eighth decade, more erudite but more ill-tempered and ultimately less appealing. He rallies behind Joseph's praise of regular hours, regimentation, and supervision of the spirit, but at his own stubborn Polonian pace.

The harshness of his judgments casts an odd light upon his genealogy within Bellow's canon. His strictures on modernity encompass some of Bellow's earlier heroes and, in the case of Augie March, Henderson, and Herzog, their heroic vitalism. His animadversions on the Enlightenment and the debasement of individualism in modern life are not only assaults upon Reichian orgonomy but upon the entire Romantic cult of the self, which Sammler understands to be a cult of "limitless demand—insatiability, refusal of the doomed creature . . . to go away from this earth unsatisfied. A full bill of demand and complaint was therefore presented by each individual. Non-negotiable. Recognizing no scarcity of supply in any human department." Augie March's bounce and strut, Henderson's "man want to live," and Herzog's tormented hedonism are all under indictment. Sammler is the Jeremiah of those near at hand. *Mr. Sammler's Planet* is not only an attack on the political culture of the 1960s, it is Bellow's plan of personal reorganization, a palinode, if you like, to *Augie March* and *Henderson,* the "Il Pensoroso" to their "L'Allegro." Sometime between the completion of *Herzog* and the writing of *Sammler* the exquisite balance that Bellow had maintained for himself between restraint and remission collapsed, calling up the old rage for order in a particularly virulent form. This call is issued under the guise of a cultural manifesto, but it is not difficult to see that Sammler's judgments are a front for Bellow's worries. Bellow has spent much of his career courting the transcendent and the Dionysian, often with happy consequences for his writing, and Moses Herzog is most charming when his control is most in doubt, when messages are piling up so fast that his answering machine is deluged and blown. Artur Sammler represents a protest against the Herzogian frenzy and the Humboltian ecstasy; his indignation is positively Swiftian. *Sammler* is the superego's book.

If "Our Country and Our Culture" is a gloss on *The Adventures of Augie March,* then possibly Lionel Trilling's *Sincerity and Authenticity,* which warns against the fashionable '60s sentiment for hailing insanity as an authentic mode of human existence, is a guide to *Mr. Sammler's Planet.* For the latter is a book about the 1960s, a decade in which therapy took to the streets in an effort to break into history. Segments of the Movement promoted cryptomedical remedies for social ills, finding in the corruptions of the system the virus of the bourgeois character. As the idea of cure took on a millenarian cast, the field of radical politics that had previously been held by social theory, organization, and struggle gave way to ad hoc rites of personal liberation, dedicated to the production of good feelings and good karma. For those who, like Bellow, had grown skeptical of a Reichian metaphysic that had not delivered on all its promises, this degeneration of a therapy into a spectacle was reason enough to finally veto it. But it appears that Bellow, in putting distance between himself and an old romance that had gone sour, simply denied therapeutic vitalism altogether and, along with it, some of his best insights and steadiest resources. Bellow's fiction has been liveliest where he has pushed his characters to the edge of sanity and lent an ear to other voices murmuring restlessly in other rooms. It springs to life wherever the mad entrepreneurs of the spirit—the Einhorns and Mintouchians, the Weyls, Tamkins, Dahfus, Herzogs, and von Humboldt Fleishers—hold center stage. In their absence, Bellow's fiction dwindles into pure polemic. *Sammler* suffers from too much opinion, opinion that places Artur Sammler at too great a distance from life to know what he is talking about.

VII. Recorso

> Last of all—remember: we are not natural beings but supernatural beings. Lovingly, Humboldt.
>
> —von Humboldt Fleisher, *Humboldt's Gift*

If the sine-wave model of Bellow's career has predictive power, it predicts that the book after *Mr. Sammler's Planet* will return to the urgent, vivid style of *Augie March, Henderson,* and *Herzog* and that the book after *that* will inherit the sullen atmospherics of *Dangling Man, The Victim,* and *Mr. Sammler's Planet.* It predicts with considerable accuracy *Humboldt's Gift* and *The Dean's December.* The litany of annoyances in *Sammler* is not Bellow's final word on human vitality after all, just a purgation in the service of the spleen and a breather between major efforts in forming a higher self. In a word, *Sammler* is a potboiler. Bellow is a little like Sisyphus, sometimes letting go of his rock in order to get up steam for the next push. *Humboldt's Gift* returns to the main line of Bellow's vitalism and makes manifest the religious dimension that has been latent in it all along. The instructor now is Rudolf Steiner (d. 1925) who stands in the same relation to *Humboldt's Gift* that Wilhelm Reich did to *Henderson.*

Indeed, Steiner is an immediate successor to Reich as Bellow's champion of the biological/spiritual life as against the commercial/practical. Not, this time, in the name of thrust and discharge, but in the name of spiritual wakefulness and the immortal soul bicycling among the stars.

The central character and Bellow's stand-in in *Humboldt's Gift* is a dreary piece of goods named Charles Citrine, playwright, philosopher, amateur amorist, and professional fall guy, whose divorce trials and run-ins with disorganized crime stamp him as the most typical of all Bellow heroes: "He-Who-Is-Put-Upon." But the figure who dominates the book is Citrine's fallen comrade-in-books, von Humboldt Fleisher, the martyred poet who succumbs to the effects of being an American and an insomniac. ("He said that history was a nightmare during which he was trying to get a good night's rest.") His appeal to Citrine, as well as to us, is the appeal of genius, of manic-depressive power in full cycle.

> From [J. Edgar Hoover] Humboldt turned to Roosevelt's sex life. Then from Roosevelt and J. Edgar Hoover to Lenin and Dzerzhinsky of the GPU. Then back to Sejanus and the origins of secret police in the Roman Empire. Then he spoke of Trotsky's literary theories and how heavy a load great art made in the baggage train of the Revolution. Then he went back to Ike and the peacetime life of the professional soldiers in the Thirties. The drinking habits of the military. Churchill and the bottle.

A bill is paid for this terrible energy, first in sleeplessness, then in depression, and finally in collapse. A life that begins with wild hopes and brilliant achievements ends in flophouses and straitjackets. But in youth, under a full head of steam, Humboldt is a creature of energy and light. His conversation is a breathless recital of arcana, and the awestruck Citrine can scarcely keep up with the sweep and flow of his subjects: Calvinism, Grace and Depravity, Henry Adams, Tocqueville, Horatio Alger, baseball, Blake, Milton, Plato's *Timaeus*, Lenin, Hegel. Later, as Citrine himself achieves fame as a journalist and playwright and Humboldt deliquesces in alcohol, pills, and despair, the two rarely meet. Citrine last glimpses Humboldt on West 46th Street, eating a pretzel and floundering in a too-large gray suit, the gray of death already on his face. Citrine takes cover behind parked cars and flees, only to be haunted for years after by the panic of that moment. For to have ducked and fled on that day, when the webbing of the grave lay in Humboldt's hair like the tent caterpillar's cocoon, was to have betrayed him, and Citrine's later obsession for contacting the dead is also a search for atonement, a plea broadcast into the void for a token of forgiveness. Which he is granted in the form of film royalties worth some $80,000.

Humboldt is a lightly fictionalized portrait of Delmore Schwartz, and his failure, in the novel as in life, is the failure of precocious and unpremeditated transcendence. Citrine calls him the "Mozart of conversation," and he gives all the appearance in youth of being an Amadeus. But he is an unstrung, distracted Amadeus, in whom the voice of God comes not in melodies but in discords. Humboldt is a higher self of the wrong kind, a hyperactive Übermensch whose synapses fire off at unnatural rates, making him a menace to himself and an emotional gangster toward others.

The ideal of life at full tilt, then, which Dahfu and Tamkin preached and Augie March, Eugene Henderson, and Moses Herzog tried to practice, has grown problematic, not simply because a dyspeptic Sammler or Albert Corde (of *The Dean's December*) condemn it as a symptom of runaway individualism and evidence of the decline of the West, but because it remains an ideal even as the costs mount up. Sammler's manifestoes of duty must somehow be reconciled with King Dahfu's cult of force and the whole project brought through to a picture of a full life. In *Humboldt's Gift* the characters with force—Humboldt, Rinaldo Cantabile, Renata—are superior beings, though their superiority is no guarantor of peace or happiness; all suffer and spread misery, but for all that they are more alive than those around them, including Citrine himself. It is little wonder that *Humboldt's Gift* is so long, digressive, and unhinged a book! What to deny and what to affirm are now more difficult than ever.

Rudolf Steiner's anthroposophy, then, serves Bellow as the one last desperate striving after an ideal construction that could supply transcendence without harmful side-effects. Reichianism, after all, comes fully equipped with risks and side-effects, from the risks involved in placing too high a premium upon sexuality to the side effects of smashing one's own habitual defenses. Anthroposophy is comparatively risk-free. It is private, wholly inward, and does not require testing upon another person. One need simply tune out the world and switch in the visionary circuits—a little like switching from noisy AM to placid FM—when the situation demands. It takes discipline, but the benefits would seem to be simple and immediate: clarity, a sense of individual well-being in a fallen world, and sensations of high endeavor when among low characters. Charles Citrine's capture by Rinaldo Cantabile is a case in point.

Citrine is being shaken down by Cantabile for some $450 the latter has won in a card game, which Citrine has refused to pay because the game, he believes, was rigged. The shakedown begins with Cantabile's battering Citrine's sleek Mercedes with a baseball bat one night, convincing Citrine that it is time to settle. The settlement, a day of choreographed torments by Cantabile and improvised atonements by Citrine, begins at the Russian Bath on Division Street, where Cantabile, a novice at violence, loses control of his bowels and drags Citrine with him into a toilet stall to stand in embarrassment and contemplate "the human condition overall" while Cantabile eases his bowels and settles his composure.

> Perhaps fantasies of savagery and monstrosity, of beating my brains out, had loosened his bowels. Humankind is full of nervous invention of this type, and I started to think (to distract myself) of all the volumes of ape behavior I had read in my time, of Kohler and Yerkes and Zuckerman, of Marais on baboons and Schaller on gorillas, and of the rich repertory of visceral-emotional sensitivities in the anthropoid branch.

In this wonderful scene, Citrine dramatizes a truth about the tactics of transcendence. No amount of distraction will deliver him from the stall, but with ample high-mindedness he may be able to drown his humiliation in seas of thought. An autodidact, he treats himself to a lesson in the consolations of philosophy.

I've said elsewhere that one element of Bellow's staying power is a marked degree of worldliness—a respect for the biologically given and the inertia of things as they are—and a stout resistance to easy despair. He has more affection for the terrain of daily life than any other writer of his generation. Yet he is not without his cup of world-hatred. We are bound to observe that the note of rejection that is heard in *The Last Analysis* echoes through *Herzog, Mr. Sammler's Planet, Humboldt's Gift,* and *The Dean's December.* Rudolf Steiner may well have uttered great truths, as Citrine and Bellow believe, but what commands our attention in *Humboldt's Gift* is not Citrine anointing himself with stardust but the exasperation with which he does it. "What you really want," accuses Citrine's wife, Denise, "is to get rid of everybody, to tune out and be a law unto yourself. Just you and your misunderstood heart, Charlie." Chalk that up though we may to Denise's resentment, she has plainly drawn a proper bead on her husband. "There's nobody good enough for you." Citrine's spiritualizing, like Bummidge's action-*Existenz* analysis and Sammler's code of homely virtues, is meant to harden the *cordon sanitaire* he has drawn about himself, through which he permits only selected voluptuous women. Wives need not apply.

Even these exceptions are provisional and may be revoked at any time. Renata in *Humboldt's Gift,* like Ramona in *Herzog,* does indeed provide the animal comforts that a divorced man needs, but unlike Ramona she is a woman of bad character, which she demonstrates in the end by abandoning a cash-poor Citrine for her wealthy undertaker friend, Flonzaley. An honest sexuality is no guarantee of a loyal character; sex and character belong to decidedly different spheres. Whereas it was possible for Moses Herzog to speculate that to get laid is an act of citizenship, such thoughts are alien to Charles Citrine, who has discovered in Eros yet another veil of illusion. Sex has its pleasures and its rewards, but it is no longer a distinct moral force.

The sort of discipline that Citrine practices does a double take on life, pressing him more completely into the natural world while withdrawing him from the social. Clouds, flowers, sunlight, trees grow more vivid, while people grow, if not dim, then sentimental and implausible. Citrine spends a good deal of his time standing on his head or meditating, tuning out the static of existence and learning to tolerate the unending raids upon his money, for, as in *The Last Analysis* and *Herzog,* everyone is going through the hero's pockets. If reality, as Moses Herzog says, is nastiness in the transcendent position, then *Humboldt's Gift* is a *Hammond's World Atlas* of the real.

But the double focus that can zoom in like a microscope on details as fine as an eyelash can also pan back to the human condition overall. Citrine can lose himself, for pages, in asides on immortality, spiritual sleep and storms of clarity, the life to come, ontogeny and phylogeny, the bobbing of the earth in waves of light. The effort to write a comprehensive moral geography in *Humboldt* proceeds as it were from bottom to top, from microcosm to macrocosm, from the bed to the beyond. Musing upon Baudelaire's *Intimate Journals,* which he had read on a plane, Citrine reflects:

> In Baudelaire I had found the following piece of curious advice: Whenever you receive a letter from a creditor write fifty lines upon some extraterrestrial subject and you will be saved. What this implied was that the *vie quotidienne* drove you from the globe, but the deeper implication was that real life flowed between *here* and *there*. Real life was a relationship between *here* and *there*.

Citrine wonders if he has not stumbled upon the moral geography of his own experience: Cantabile, he observes, is so totally *here*, while Humboldt was irredeemably *there*. One is tempted to think too that this conception of reality as a flowing of life between here and there takes us close to a comprehensive formula for Bellow's writing throughout. Elsewhere I've tried to sum up the sensibility of the contemporary

Jewish writer, taking Bellow, Philip Roth, and Norman Mailer as cases, as "psychological realism" in recognition of its odd and fertile blend of social documentary and psychological penetration. Toss metaphysical longing into the mixture and the conclusion would apply with particular point to Bellow's writing.

> The impurity of its origins and the indeterminacy of its allegiances . . . constitutes its strength; it is ideally suited to the expression of extremes of thought as well as extremes of doubt, that is, to modern states of informed confusion. Psychologically, this sensibility stands at the boundary between outer and inner worlds, just as it seems, stylistically, to accommodate both realism and interior monologue, as though in acknowledgement that to be both Jewish and modern—in America, at any rate—is to be a bridge between worlds and to be required, above all else, to keep the traffic flowing.[12]

VIII. Postscript: The Dean's December

The Dean's December is a distinctly minor production of Bellow's, and it is also one, like *Mr. Sammler's Planet,* in which the transformation of the self is not a point at issue. These two facts have, I suspect, some bearing upon each other, though which derives from which I couldn't say. Both books appear also to be potboilers, bread cast upon the waters of publishing in the hope that a school of readers might be swimming by. (The sign of the potboiler in Bellow is simple: the prose. Normally a writer of the most compact and treasure-laden prose to be found anywhere in American writing, Bellow allows his language to grow slack in the potboilers. A page from the middle of *Sammler* or *The Dean's December* read side-by-side with one from *Herzog* or *Humboldt* should satisfy practically any reader about which books are written out of love and which out of necessity.) Every writer has his potboilers, and there is no reason to take alarm at Bellow's.

One may note, however, that they seem to form a distinct thematic subgenre within his work, one that denies, even repudiates so much of the rest of it. In the potboilers, Bellow departs entirely from the labor of autorehabilitation and simply assumes, for the purposes of his social polemic, the basic integrity of his central character. The man has his integrity throughout, while the world lies shattered. Indeed, the one character in *The Dean's December* who has enlisted in the wars of self-restoration, Dewey Spangler, Dean Albert Corde's childhood companion, is treated by Bellow with no little bit of scorn, the special scorn reserved by Bellow for his Chicago-born tough guys and others whose stock-in-trade is knowing the score. A boy aesthete and reader of Swinburne, Wilde, Nietzsche, and Whitman, Spangler has grown up to be a journalist of Irving Kristol-like renown and a twice-born power intellectual, having been "recycled on the couch" to think better of geopolitics. Bellow treats these therapeutic upgradings as indulgences and worse, as contemptible undertakings that lack the steady integrity of Dean Albert Corde, Bellow's *porte-parole* for his new Hebraism. The fate of sex in such a climate is predictable: we've seen it already in *Sammler*. No longer an agent of wakefulness, or even of ordinary pleasure, it is now a regrettable relic of Albert Corde's past and the dirty little secret of dishonorable men, the pulse behind their nastiness. Corde admits to a history of erotic instability, and even boasts to himself a record approaching Don Giovanni's 1,003 seductions. But that zone of indulgence is never recalled in any of its specifics or with any joy but rather as a disease that has been successfully treated, like alcoholism or drug abuse. Corde has put himself on something like moral methadone, and all his thoughts on sex in the book are leering or accusatory. He has settled down, while others continue to spray the world with their sexual juices.

Prominent among those is Corde's own cousin, Max Detillion, a lawyer and a gonif with a perpetual hard-on, who brings to Corde's mind "Balzac's sex monsters in *Cousine Bette*, and the pitiable Baron Hulot, a feeble ancient man making passes at the woman who was nursing his dying wife." Another of Bellow/Corde's touchstones for the new bestiality that has taken over in such cities as Chicago is Spofford Mitchell, a rapist killer who had kept a woman in the trunk of his car for sexual pleasure until finally killing her. As Corde imagines their last moments: "One is staring at the other with terror, and the man is filled with a staggering passion to *break through*, in the only way he can conceive of breaking through—a sexual crash into release." Corde has taken the Reichian language of breakthrough and release and filled it with dread. Bellow is still trading, backhandedly, in Reichian views, in a world in which the triumph of the plague is definitive. The passion for release, now, is seen in its criminal, rather than its therapeutic, aspects.

Bellow, then, remains a sexologue but a negative one. He is now a spelunker of the darker impulses, like Freud himself in his later years. Spangler, though one of *The Dean's December*'s more odious villains, nevertheless speaks directly for Bellow in his discourse upon "bestial venery, feral wanderings, incest, and the dead left unburied," adding, as if to emphasize the sexual basis of such moral monstrosity, the example of Jonestown, where, before the mass suicide, "they put on public displays of racially mixed cunnilingus as a declaration of equality." Spangler's very name underscores the book's pessimism, putting us in mind of Oswald Spengler, whose *The Decline of the West* appears to be the inspiration for this novel. *The Dean's December* is a monograph on that decline: into totalitarianism in the countries under Soviet domination and into chaos in the West proper, if, that is, Chicago be permitted to stand for all that is rank under democracy. For Bellow, it is plain, now goes in for worst-case analyses.

The Dean's December is set in two locales: Bucharest, Rumania, where Corde has gone with his wife, Minna, to sit at the deathbed of her mother, and Chicago, where Corde is Dean of something at the College of Something and has gotten involved in the trial of a young black man accused of killing a student. The rest of his dean's duties are left blank, for what counts simply is a vision of contrasting cities, one rigid in bureaucracy, the other terrible in chaos: an Orwellian hell and a Hobbesian one. Bellow's Bucharest is a vision of life as organized by the politics of suspicion and the economics of depletion: its watchwords are surveillance and scarcity. An eastern outpost of the Roman Empire and the Catholic Church, it now boasts its own version of the Holy Trinity: the rulers, the ruled, and the secret police. The jackboot is not in evidence, however, just the whisper. Every concierge, every driver, every phone operator is an eavesdropper. The walls have ears. Dossiers are longer than breadlines. The effects of this may be read on the bodies and spirits of the administered, for everyone in this Rumania seems smaller than life: hemmed in, shrunken, a trifle less human for the daily scheming, the bribing, the wariness, the whispering.

Chicago, despite obvious differences, produces similar effects upon people, dwindling their humanity and disfiguring their spirits. Instead of secret police, its agents of soul murder are the muggers, the dopers, the dealers, and the sex criminals, a vast, largely black, demimonde that is overseen and tolerated by the mayors, the aldermen, the slumlords, the contractors, the kickback artists, and the brothers-in-law—all the short-sellers of spiritual goods who make a killing on mass despair. This corner of the "free world," innocent of official terror, is rife with freelance terror, a regional manifestation, you might say, of the universal Zeitgeist, the universal degeneration.

Bellow shows a proper instinct for what the age demands in turning to public themes and the great issues that send a shiver through modern life; a writer can't soar forever on the wings of merely personal aggravation. But the question for the critic is not whether the writer's conception of life is timely but whether it is in tune with the deepest levels of his imagination and is capable of releasing his talent. On that score, the judgment would seem to be in. The grand themes of war and peace, communism and capitalism, the death camp and the gulag, the fate of man, etc., have no particular purchase on Bellow's imagination. He has never found the metaphor to bring those issues into focus at any level beyond the purely polemical. I can't help but see, in this book, the emergence of a side of Bellow that has long been reclusive, so long, at least, as he was courting affirmations: the Trotskyist. The spirit of *The Dean's December* reminds us of nothing so much as the Malaquaian analysis we used to see in Norman Mailer, which holds Stalinism and capitalism to be equally exploitive, equally degenerate systems, bent on divvying up the world into spheres of domination. Bellow probably hasn't dipped into his Marxist texts since leaving the Spartacus Youth League in the '30s, yet there is something reminiscent of the old Trotskyist mentality in Bellow/Corde's balanced condemnation, even if his actual vantage point seems closer to the orbit of Jupiter than to any of the broadsides with which Trotsky peppered the world in his lifetime. (It is not for nothing that Corde's wife is an astronomer.) The spirit that unhinges this book might be called transcendental Trotskyism, a diffuse, global outrage at modern life that takes on all comers and is notably weak on distinctions. It also remains disturbingly personal, confusing the deceits of Mason Zaehner (yet another relative of Corde's), Max Detillion, and Dewey Spangler with the catastrophes of our century, quite as if the human condition overall still were, as psychoanalysis once hoped, the case history writ large.

We would be mistaken to try to sum up in any easy formulation so rich and varied and open-ended a career as Bellow's. At seventy (as of 1985) Bellow should have yet another book in him, if not another *Herzog* or *Seize the Day*, then surely not another *Dean's December* either. It should be a more buoyant performance, suffused with the optimism and vitality that weave through some of his books like bright threads through a dark tapestry. More than any other writer of our time, Bellow has taken up in his fiction the job Lionel Trilling set down for criticism, "the imagination of variousness and possibility" in a career that has produced novels so unlike each other as *Dangling Man, Henderson the Rain King*, and *Humboldt's Gift*. Elusive as a "drumlin woodchuck" a phrase Mark Harris has applied to him in an attempted biography, Bellow has refused to be pinned down or to pin himself down, ideologically or stylistically. There is a Bellow voice, I think—knowing, allusive, urban, sophisticated, crackling with wit and erudition. But it never quite hardens into a routine or a manner. Even at its most indelicate, as it is in much of *The Dean's December,* that voice is alert and full of surprises.

Still, for all of Bellow's variousness and possibility, there are identifiable rhythms to his work which stamp it with the indelible mark of his personality: a rhythm of depression and ecstasy and one of transcendence and worldliness, which is occasionally resolved in transcendence downward. Those rhythms are not simply grace notes to Bellow's writing, drifting in and out of it as melodies drift in and out of the mind. They are the very pump of his art, the force that has propelled it through all its fantastic gyrations since *Dangling Man* in 1944. The writing arises, it would appear, in response to those moods, in order to express them, contain them, and give them image, form, and stories to tell. What that moodiness suggests, finally, is a mind that has not entirely settled in with life, accepted the given, or been beguiled by its own solutions. Rather, it is a voice that continues to say, like the voice within Eugene Henderson, "I want, I want," and continues to wait for an answer to its want the way some Jews wait for the Messiah.

9. Memoirs of a Revolutionist
Norman Mailer in the '50s

I

WERE WE TO SELECT one book to symbolize this movement, it would likely be Norman Mailer's *Advertisements for Myself*, and if we were to narrow our selection down even further, we'd be bound to settle on "The White Negro," the essay that was the *fons et origo* of all that Mailer was later to become. *Advertisements for Myself* was the book that shattered the mold for Mailer, transubstantiating him from a novelist of conventional aspirations if unsteady lights into a provocateur and a guerrilla against "the totalitarianism of the totally pleasant personality," while "The White Negro" was the formal launching of the automythology of the hipster that has sustained him ever since. We can trace a vector of myth from "The White Negro" through *The Executioner's Song* right into Mailer's life. The stabbing of his wife Adele in 1960 and his unfortunate championship of Jack Henry Abbott in 1981 are myth-driven events, which find Mailer acting out in the real world the imperatives of an insurrectionary dream. *The Naked and the Dead* may yet be the book by which literary history will remember Mailer, but *Advertisements for Myself* will remain the one through which contemporary culture will understand him, for it was there that he first disclosed his ambition to revolutionize the consciousness of his time and proposed a conception of character suited to those ambitions.

But Mailer always took himself for a revolutionary; all three of his early novels, *The Naked and the Dead*, *Barbary Shore*, and *The Deer Park*, were propelled by mutinous impulses toward an American society that possessed all the salient features of totalitarianism. Until *Advertisements*, however, those impulses were not articulated precisely, because Mailer lacked a name for the froth of emotions bubbling up within him and

159

mistook his sexual frustrations, his social irritations, and his Faustian ambitions for signs that he was a Marxist, bred in the bone. The varieties of political ideology he would improvise for nine years after *The Naked and the Dead* were instances of a fever in search of a form.

Mailer initially launched himself as a conventional, if somewhat dated, revolutionary type. For an instant in 1948 he joined forces with what remained of the Popular Front, the Progressive party, barnstorming for former Vice-President Henry Wallace on a platform that called for the United States to unilaterally cease its provocations against the Soviet Union. Conducted under the shadow of the Czech coup and the Berlin blockade, the Wallace campaign attracted only hardened russophiles and sentimentalists of wartime collaboration and had no significant impact on that year's election. But even as he toured for Wallace, Mailer was falling under the spell of Jean Malaquais, Marxist theoretician, novelist, and anti-Stalinist intellectual, whom he had met the previous year in Paris. Under Malaquais's tutelage, Mailer broke with the Popular Front in 1949 and armed himself with a quasi-Trotskyist vision of the global situation, an Olympian revolutionary standard that beheld no major difference between the United States and the Soviet Union as evolving social systems. To the penetrating eye of the economic determinist, they were Gog and Magog.

There are two statements from this period that capture the essence of Mailer's tortured politics. One is an impromptu confession made at the "Cultural and Scientific Conference for World Peace" held at the Waldorf Astoria Hotel in March, 1949; the other, the statement in "Our Country and Our Culture" in 1952. The Cultural and Scientific Conference, or Waldorf conference as it was popularly known, was the second such conference sponsored by the Soviet Union and its Western sympathizers, influential party members and fellow travellers.[1] It was to be the cutting edge of the Soviet Union's postwar cultural offensive, a demonstration that culture in the Soviet Union was vital, progressive, and free. Since, in fact, the last years of Stalin's regime were years of savage cultural reaction during which many artists and intellectuals lost their livelihoods or even their lives, the Waldorf conference and the previous year's Congress of Intellectuals in Wroclaw, Poland failed dismally to have the intended effect. If anything, they generated potent reactions: Western cultural legions marshaled their forces against the Communist offensive, including the Congress for Cultural Freedom, founded in 1950, and the American Committee for Cultural Freedom, established in 1951. The Waldorf conference boasted a list of some five hundred sponsors, including Aaron Copeland, W. E. B. Dubois, Albert Einstein, Howard Fast,

F. O. Matthiessen, Arthur Miller, Clifford Odets, I. F. Stone, Paul Sweezy, and other writers and artists who continued to float like empty lifeboats in the Wallace oil slick.

As one might guess, no *Partisan Review* writers were invited to be delegates, though several, including Dwight Macdonald, Mary McCarthy, and Sidney Hook, organized a protest group, Americans for Intellectual Freedom, whose mission was to ask pointed questions of the Soviet participants from the floor. Mailer, on the strength of his support for Wallace, was invited to participate on the writing and publishing panel along with the likes of Fast, DuBois, Agnes Smedley, Ira Wolfert, Dmitri Shostakovich, and A. A. Fadayev, secretary of the Union of Soviet Writers, a minor novelist who was also, in his capacity as a Soviet functionary, a commissar of ideas. Mailer's contribution to the proceedings, halting and uncertain as it was, was not at all what his sponsors had counted on. Calling himself a Trojan horse, Mailer announced that "so long as there is capitalism, there is going to be war. Until you have a decent, equitable socialism, you can't have peace."

> But you can't have socialism until the mass of workers are organized into a revolutionary party. And as I look about me here, I see few who believe in revolutions and many who believe in resolutions. . . . I am going to make myself even more unpopular. I am afraid that both the United States and the Soviet Union are moving toward state capitalism. There is no future in that. I see the peoples of *both* America and Russia—neither of them want war—caught in a mechanism which is steadily grinding on to produce war. The two systems approach each other constantly.

What one is bound to notice, beyond the language of yesterday's catechism, is the programmatic symmetry, the tidy equation of the US and USSR as "state capitalist" empires. All apparent differences are only, as an older Marxist language would say it, "superstructure," and while Mailer was too self-conscious a writer to use a word like that, the concept is built into his rhetoric. This symmetry, mandated by the iron laws of economics, is the clockwork of Armageddon, driving these rival empires willy-nilly toward mutual annihilation, like matter and antimatter. Based on a dogmatic cryptoscience of history, this vision betrays an almost geometrical neatness, and it is not beside the point to recall that Mailer's undergraduate years at Harvard were spent studying engineering. There is much about his later thinking, even as a sexologue and a hipster, that suggests an engineer's training in schematics. Not that the quasi-Trotskyist analysis of the world order was entirely mistaken about the peril of mighty arsenals or the permanent war economy that commands vast resources and orders national priorities in both countries, but like prophetic systems everywhere that profess to know the timetable of oblivion, the system supplied its own evidence.

It was during this period, the spring of 1949, that Mailer was laboring joylessly over *Barbary Shore*. That novel, published in 1951, was a murky concoction of fleabag existentialism and bedroom dialectics, in which the world-historical questions of a previous generation are worked out agonistically between sinister tenants. Its dramatic climax is a long address to the assembled housemates by a character steeped in Trotsky-cum-Malaquais lore on the collision of state-capitalist empires; it shudders with intransigent phrases like "historical imperative," "proper analysis," "monopoly capitalism," and "those backward areas of the globe so necessary to monopoly cannot be lost." The book's sustained dreariness, its revolutionary pathos, "the febrile and despairing utopianism of lost causes," as Marvin Murdick has called it,[2] symbolized better than Mailer knew his state of mind at the moment, for to transpose the metaphysics of empire and apocalypse into a rooming house allegory was to write a *Kapital* of his own faltering mental economy. A cheerless revolutionary tract and an aria of inhibition, *Barbary Shore* was a prophecy, couched in cryptic Marxian terms, of a coming explosion.

It was also, for all its allegorical vagueness, a starkly honest book, a cry of dismay by a young writer caught between worlds, out of phase with the times, out of touch with his own thoughts, and withal passionate to mount a revolution, if only he could find a revolution to mount. For if *Barbary Shore* is doctrinally a broadside on state and revolution, it is tonally a book of nightmare sexuality, of frozen encounters and rigid copulations that are either unexplained or chalked up to the dialectics of production. But having no calculus for charting these connections and no formula for bringing his grand theses to life in a rooming house, Mailer quickly fell into his worst posture, the pamphleteer, as if uncertain whether his mission were to write fiction or commit sociology. As an incomplete and tormented book, however, *Barbary Shore* highlighted the pressures that were driving Mailer to write even as they were undermining his fiction, for it is a desperate performance whose conflicts cannot be contained by the formal limits of the well-made novel to which Mailer had bound his talents.

By 1952, in "Our Country and Our Culture," the ideological bands had begun to loosen, and while Mailer was still pontificating about the "crisis of world capitalism" and "the disappearance of the world market" there was more free form and vigor to his anathemas.

A symposium of this sort I find shocking. One expects a J. Donald Adams to initiate it, a John Chamberlain to bristle with editorials in its support, a Bernard De Voto to flex his muscles. This period smacks of healthy manifestoes. Everywhere the American writer is being dunned to become healthy, to grow up, to accept the American reality, to integrate himself, to eschew disease, to revalue institutions. Is there nothing to remind us that the writer does not need to be integrated into his society, and often works best in opposition to it? I would propose that the artist feels most alienated when he loses the sharp sense of what he is alienated from.

A touch of the old polemical color was back, though edged with sectarian slang. In 1952, Mailer was not quite prepared to "choose the west" along with the other participants, along, indeed, with Dwight Macdonald, who shared Mailer's resistance to affirmations but had decided at last that there was more to the world situation than the contest of lethal empires.[3]

II

While "Our Country and Our Culture" heralded a new beginning for New York intellectual culture at large, it closed the book on an old dispensation for Mailer; it was the last shudder of Marxism before the fizz of sex-pol that was beginning to bubble up in *The Deer Park* and the stories "The Man Who Studied Yoga" and "The Time of Her Time." *The Deer Park* is generally conceded to be a transition book for Mailer, begun in one era and one frame of mind and concluded in another. Mailer first sat down to it in the spring of 1952, as the Korean War continued amid fruitless peace talks, Senator Joseph McCarthy's anti-Communist crusade was in full tilt, Alger Hiss was in prison for perjury, the Rosenbergs were on death row, and, in Russia, Joseph Stalin's reign was reaching its brutal climax. By the time Mailer had slogged his way through the final rewrite in August 1955, however, global and national tensions had abated. Stalin had died and been succeeded first by a tractable Georgi Malenkov and then by a shoe-pounding but cautious Nikita Khrushchev. The Korean War had ended, not in Armageddon, but in a standoff, as both the United States and the Soviet Union learned lessons about the limits of power and showed an unexpected tolerance for ambiguous endings. At home, Senator McCarthy's stranglehold on domestic politics had been broken by his televised investigation of the army in 1954, which turned up no subversives but exposed his cruelty to a national audience and turned public opinion decisively against him.

His censure by his colleagues in the Senate the following year effectively erased him from the American political landscape.

By fall 1955, the world seemed a far less menacing place than it had just three years before. Fears of nuclear annihilation had subsided; international tensions had decreased, and domestic anticommunism was on hold, as the Cold War entered a new phase, one of economic competition. When Khrushchev boasted, "We will bury you," he made it plain that he meant economically. As historian Eric Goldman has noted, "With the signing of the Indochinese truce on July 20, 1954, no shooting war existed anywhere on the globe for the first time since the Japanese invaded Manchuria twenty-three years before."[4]

Mailer had begun *The Deer Park* in 1952 as a Cold War novel, setting it in a Hollywood that had become the symbol of Cold War hysteria on the domestic scene. The purge of the studios launched by the House Committee on Un-American Activities in 1947, the wholesale blacklisting of writers, directors, and actors, and the imprisonment of the Hollywood Ten in 1950 had lent credibility to the warnings of Mailer, Macdonald, and others that a permanent war economy could only be maintained at the cost of domestic liberties. If one were out to demonstrate that the Moscow trials had found their American counterpart and that totalitarianism was just around the corner, the ravaging of Hollywood would seem to offer confirmation.[5]

Hollywood has long fascinated writers as the place where money, politics, and art collide, to the ostensible detriment of art. It is the classic intersection of America's commercial life and its dream life and the place where immigrant producers aspired to manufacture ersatz American dreams much as their cousins in New York manufactured authentic American clothing: by piecework, mass production, and a keen eye to the drift of fashion. It is little wonder that so many of the novelists who flocked to Hollywood to cash in on its promises of a quick score and a larger public than the novel could ever produce would find in the witch's brew of fantasy, business, politics, and power an irresistible subject for the rueful novels of disillusionment they would eventually write. Scott Fitzgerald's unfinished novel, *The Last Tycoon,* Nathaniel West's *The Day of the Locust,* Christopher Isherwood's *Prater Violet,* Budd Schulberg's *What Makes Sammy Run?* are only the better known of dozens of novels to come out of the Hollywood experience, most of them bitter portraits of the moguls, the studio system, and the production schedules that had more in common with the routines of the sweatshop than with the conviviality of the theater or the lonely intensities of solitary writing.

Mailer was conscious of a portion of the tradition—certainly of West, who used Hollywood as a sound stage for his vision of the apocalypse: the burning of Los Angeles. Mailer too was possessed by apocalyptic visions; when he began working on *The Deer Park* his mind was still saturated with fears of the global endgame, of which the McCarthyite frenzy and Stalin's final paroxysms were last-minute preparations. In Hollywood—indeed, in Palm Springs (the model for the book's Desert D'Or), a desert watering hole of the movie colony—Mailer saw written boldly against the diorama of the surrounding mountains nothing less than the decline of the West, "that gorge of innocence and virtue in which were engulfed so many victims who when they returned to society brought with them depravity, debauchery and all the vices they naturally acquired from the infamous officials of such a place."[6]

The Deer Park was Mailer's valedictory to Popular Front liberalism, though in some way or other he had been bidding farewell to liberalism right along: the killing of Lieutenant Hearn in *The Naked and the Dead* was a gesture in that direction, and the collapse of Charles Eitel would be another. But whereas Hearn is destroyed by more cunning and battlewise forces—he never really has a chance—Eitel, we are to believe, collaborates in his own destruction. Hearn is a victim, Eitel a failure.

A figure of his time, a blacklisted director with a vaguely progressive political past, Eitel has all the credentials of a Popular Front martyr. Never a party member—Mailer seems to imply that he lacks the full courage of his convictions—he has fellow-travelled through the usual committees and done the obligatory tour with the Abraham Lincoln Brigade in the Spanish Civil War. He is at best a minor talent with a knack for atmosphere, and his name is synonymous with the higher reaches of B-grade. But he has illusions and takes himself for an artist who has taken temporary leave of his gifts. Since his blacklisting he has been revamping, with enormous pain, an old screenplay that he imagines to be a great original but sounds in fact like a parody of Nathaniel West's *Miss Lonelyhearts,* in a bid to reclaim his buried creative talents. The profile of Eitel is not entirely a savory one, and for a character in whom Mailer was to invest so much of his political and sexual fears, he stands decidedly outside the glow of Mailer's sympathy. Character is destiny, and Eitel possesses the character, and suffers the destiny, of the liberal.

Mailer subjects Eitel to two complementary ordeals: an ordeal of politics and one of sex. Eitel has been blacklisted for refusing to name names, and his career has been placed in escrow by the Committee, in collusion with Supreme Pictures, which is for all intents and purposes synonymous with its head, Herman Teppis. We know at the outset that

Eitel will crack as his savings run low, for if Mailer's parading of his weaknesses were not enough, there is his morality-play name, "I tell."

Eitel's political ordeal is complemented by a sexual one—his affair with Elena Esposito, whose Latin sensuality (Mailer calls her Italian and gives her a Spanish name) at first overwhelms him, arouses him from a sort of biological slumber—which is related in some unexplained way to his drowsy politics—and charges him with an erotic potential he had never known before. But it is only a matter of time before the charge dissipates and he begins faking his emotions and cruising for assignations. By the time he says "yes" to the Committee he has long since said "no" to Elena, though in a strange way, by pleading with her to marry him, and we are invited to draw the inference that his collapse before the Committee and his failure to be forthright with Elena are, at bottom, the same liberal failure of nerve.

The picture I've drawn here is schematic at best, and *The Deer Park* on the whole is a more penetrating novel than these simple schematics of collapse would suggest. It stands up, thirty years later, as Mailer's most painfully conceived book of fiction, despite its simple thesis, which is scarcely more than a trim little parabola of failure laid out upon axes of cowardice and courage. The fall of Eitel is a simple sex-pol morality play, and there is something decidedly unfair, not to say ahistorical, about a political-sexual equation that explains the progressive mind as a mere absence of balls. Yet, by the time Mailer was in the throes of writing *The Deer Park,* that metaphor had become virtually literal for him. As the old class-bound divisions of the world faded into oblivion, Mailer divided it anew into those who had balls and those who did not.

Accordingly, Eitel's politics get short shrift; we learn virtually nothing of his history, save Spain, or his politics. We know nothing of who he is preparing to name, what options he is considering, what motives of vengeance or loyalty still possess him. Possibly, Mailer feared that to risk giving Eitel a leftist past was to resurrect a voice like that of McLeod in *Barbary Shore,* and he was not going to open that Pandora's box again. But more plausibly, I think, Mailer had simply exhausted his feuilletonism in the earlier novel and had nothing more to say on the great issues. Whatever the case, the overwhelming effect in *The Deer Park* is one of impatience with politics and a consequent vagueness about it.

The novel draws its authority, rather, from a ripeness of social portraiture, from the brisk little cameos that Mailer was learning to compose for the first time in *The Deer Park,* and which would become the mainstay of his journalism in years to come. There was none of this in *Barbary Shore* and only the crude "Time Machine" flashbacks in *The Naked and the*

Dead. In *The Deer Park,* however, these portraits replace social ideas, as though Mailer had abandoned ideology for portraiture or had learned to observe how social organization was embodied in character and how character, consequently, could be employed as an index to society. Culture and power are installed within the individual as manners, and Mailer was learning that he need not launch tirades on the contradictions of capitalism or the disappearance of the world market; he need only draw the contradictions of Eitel or Herman Teppis or Collie Munshin or Lulu Meyers, figures in whom the antinomies of society are inscribed as distortions of the ego—as injuries. If, as Dwight Macdonald would proclaim, the root is man, then the novelist is closer to the root and possesses the more radical vision than the sociologist or the ideologue.

Herman Teppis embodies vividly the book's contradictions. Avuncular and ruthless, a sentimentalist and a commissar, a corporate paterfamilias and child of the bottom line, a real toad in an imaginary garden, he is the Stalin of the studios, and if he doesn't strew the lots with corpses he does the next best thing: litter them with dead reputations. He is a sexual hypocrite, weeping openly over the joys of marriage while keeping a string of starlets at his "thumb of power" for casual recreation. "I haven't slept with a woman in ten years," he boasts, and he is probably not lying since "sleeping with" them is not his modus operandi. It was the scene in which Bobby, a part-time prostitute, gives Teppis a blow job in his office that caused Rinehart to renege on his contract with Mailer and send him off on a cruise to six timid publishers before he found a safe harbor at Putnam. Mailer would later claim in *Advertisements for Myself* that he could not excise the scene, however cunningly he might cloud the language, because the offending lines were "the moral center of the novel." For it is in that scene that Mailer's new vision of power found its image; everyone in the film industry sooner or later must take an oath of loyalty while sucking at the thumb of power.

Taking a page from Reich, Mailer read the politics and the aesthetics of Hollywood as being of a piece with its sexuality: exaggerated, obsessive, tangled. In Hollywood, the plague had reached epidemic proportions: the hearings and the blacklists, the narcissism and the bed hopping, the romance and the kitsch, the tyranny of the committee and the despotism of the studio, the false tinsel over the real tinsel all spring from the same illness. Herman Teppis's boast of not sleeping with women, including, presumably, his wife, is the symbol of all that is haywire in Hollywood.

In some instances, the sexual disorientation is apparent. Teddy Pope, a minor actor whom Teppis wants Lulu Meyers to marry for publicity reasons, is a homosexual; Marion Faye, a proto-hipster who prefigures the White Negro of *Advertisements,* is a pimp; Martin Pelley, husband of a fading actress, is impotent most of the time.* In other instances, it is simply implied, a background to character. Lulu Meyers's narcissism and fickleness, Herman Teppis's megalomania, Collie Munshin's wheedling and conniving, Eitel's writer's block and despair are symbols of a common malaise. *The Deer Park* is a bestiary of the armored and the stricken. This conception of character as a sexual distortion will become basic to Mailer's writing and perhaps explains why the one male figure in *The Deer Park* whom Mailer guards from the taint of disfigurement, Sergius O'Shaughnessy, is the book's least interesting character.** Through three complete writings, Mailer was at a loss for what to do with Sergius, and his Reichian characterology explains why. If neurosis is a private theater with an actor and an audience of one and Sergius O'Shaugnessy has no need of theatrics, then how does the author give him a vivid profile? To be healthy is to be a nullity.

Were its gallery of misfits and case histories all *The Deer Park* had to offer, it would be, at best, a comic novel of a Dickensian sort, which it does resemble in places. The shennanigans of Herman Teppis, in their mixture of vanity and ruthlessness, recall the charades of Charlie Chaplin and Jack Oakie as Hitler and Mussolini in *The Great Dictator.* But though the book occasionally gravitates toward caricature, it is pulled back by the affair between Eitel and Elena, in which Mailer risked, for the only time in his career, a trial of love and vulnerability and probed with care the blossoming and souring of a love affair. The explosive opening up of Eitel to Elena and the slow, painful closing of the doors features some of the tenderest writing Mailer ever produced, before or since. It is generally thought that Mailer, in framing that relationship, was drawing on his own with Adele Morales, celebrating its intensities while anticipating its end. Perhaps. But if so, then the contribution of that relationship was to wean him momentarily from ideology and grant him an intermission between certainties: the dialectical inevitabilities of Marxism and the libidinal bluff of hipsterism. Love, politics, and power were suddenly mysteries again, and Mailer declined to strike poses in a world already plagued by postures. (The Reichian plague is not offered as an explanation of all the failures in the book. It is merely a storm in

---

*Even Sergius, who trots around Desert D'Or unscathed by the wreckage, has a brief history of impotence—a transient war injury, we are told, which fades along with his memories of the Korean War.

**For a more detailed description of the Reichian characterology as a novelistic device, see pp. 121–23.

which everyone is drenched.) Fragile, sentimental, full of the pathos of defeat, *The Deer Park* was Mailer's *A Farewell to Arms.*

Despite its reticence in announcing its principles, *The Deer Park* has the ambition of a daring sociology—to map the equations between politics, sex, and money—to which it adds the ambition of the novelist—to project himself into these equations by putting his experience to the test of his ideas. The conventional view of *The Deer Park* is that it is the book in which Mailer's political critique of America became a sexual one—that erotics, in effect, replaced economics as the key to personal destiny. Something like that does happen, but in an additive rather than in substitutive fashion. Sex is added to what Mailer already understood about money, power, and society, giving power a face, a voice, a locale, a taste, and a thumb. The system that gave us the Popular Front in one generation and the blacklists in the next, it suggests, also gave us the American film industry and the sexual paralysis of the *beau monde*, and whether that assessment is true or not, Mailer managed to shape it into a curious myth of power in America.

The Deer Park finds Mailer suspended between Eitel and Sergius: yesterday's liberal and tomorrow's matador. That Mailer would later cast his lot with the Sergius in himself and reject utterly his own Eitelism was a blow to his fiction, and he would never again write a novel that displayed any sympathy for common human dilemmas. The rejection of Eitel may have been the rejection of liberalism, but it was also a rejection of the entire agenda of predicaments and frailties that had made Eitel recognizably human. The Sergiuses who were to follow: Stephen Rojack *(An American Dream)*, DJ *(Why Are We in Vietnam?)*, Gary Gilmore *(The Executioner's Song)*, and Tim Madden *(Tough Guys Don't Dance)* were up from liberalism but down from humanity.

Much of the strange brew of straight-from-the-gut naiveté—the Hemingway cocktail of macho and innocence—that distinguishes Mailer's writing since *The Deer Park* derives from his inability to face up one more time, without posturing and gimmickry, to those mysteries of sexual and emotional failure that he had begun to explore in *The Deer Park.* Indeed, it is the very fascination with success and the denial of the more modest, the more compromised, the more compassionate dimensions of life that sets Mailer apart from other Jewish writers (making him presumably more "American") and have prevented him from developing some of his own early intuitions about the deeper ironies of the American dream.

These judgments are retrospective, thirty years after the fact and in full knowledge of Mailer's subsequent career. In 1955, however, shadowed by *The Naked and the Dead*, *The Deer Park* seemed less striking a performance. The reviews, though not so scornful as those of *Barbary Shore*, were mixed, and sales figures were correspondingly ambiguous. *The Deer Park* didn't head straight for the remainder bin, but neither did it make a sensation; even the censors, whose power was not broken until the sixties, left it alone. The novel's reception did nothing to restore Mailer's reputation as the rising star of American letters and did further damage to whatever remained of his confidence.

The Deer Park was a harrowing book to write. Mailer's account in *Advertisements for Myself* of the trials of finding a publisher are no less chilling than those of finding a voice, even finding himself. Between 1952 and 1955, when Putnam agreed to publish *The Deer Park*, the book had been written at least twice over, against terrific resistance, some of which is reflected within the novel in Eitel's labors to wrestle a redemptive screenplay out of his sluggish imagination.

> No matter how he tried, and there were days when he drove himself into exhaustion, sitting before his desk twelve and fourteen hours, the work would always turn into something shoddy or something contrived, into something false. . . . Certain nights with his desire to understand himself, he would draw even more deeply from his depleted energy, he would gamble for knowledge by taking several cups of coffee and drugging them with sleeping pills, until like a cave explorer he would be able to wander into himself, the thread of his escape a bottle of whisky, for with the liquor he could always return when what he learned about himself became too large, too complex, too directly dangerous.

That, plainly, was Mailer's advertisement for himself as a blocked writer, trying mightily to will a book into existence against the silent protests of his unconscious. Predictably, Mailer was unimpressed by the results. Threatening as the muted sexuality of *The Deer Park* would be to publishers, it disappointed Mailer himself, who would look back on *The Deer Park* a few years later as "a timid, inhibited book."[7] While the book was in progress, he had married Adele, discovered marijuana and the whole pharmacopia of psychoactive drugs, performed a self-analysis, and had an erotic awakening, all of which had opened the doors of perception and given him a new vision of what it meant to be a man and a writer. The book now appeared to him as precious and contrived, "too self-consciously attractive and formal."

Tame though the thumb of power scene was, Rinehart, Mailer's publisher for his first two books, kicked up a fuss and eventually broke its contract with Mailer three months before publication, sending him from door to publisher's door: Random House, Knopf, Simon and Schuster, Harper's, Scribner's, Harcourt, Brace, and, finally, Putnam. Mailer has given a blow by blow account of that dreary business in *Advertisements* and there is no point in retelling it here. What needs to be stressed is the catalytic effect of these blows upon Mailer's ego and his transfiguration as a result of them from a pin-striped revolutionist into a "psychic outlaw." The trials of publishing *The Deer Park* only served to push him farther in the direction of sexual revolutionism, as he was learning that the zone of affliction was not to be sought in the precincts of production and labor but in those of sex and manliness. If the equation of liberalism with moral and sexual cowardice needed confirmation, Mailer found it in the ugly retreats of the publishers, who "murder their writers," as he would put it in *Advertisements*, "and then decorate their graves."[8] Looking for a courageous publisher, he turned up a brigade of Charles Eitels and Herman Teppises, prominent among them Bennett Cerf, who not only turned *The Deer Park* down for Random House but waged a campaign to prevent anyone from publishing it.[9] In *Barbary Shore*, he could publish whatever revolutionary claptrap he wanted, denouncing America, prophesying world war, making sexual innuendos about the FBI—it didn't matter. He couldn't even get a rise out of HUAC.* But as soon as he put mouth to cock, the liberal publishing world came down on him. By the time G. P. Putnam and Sons rescued the book, something had caught fire in Mailer and he had begun to fancy himself an outlaw.

> I turned within my psyche I can almost believe, for I felt something shift to murder in me. I finally had the simple sense to understand that if I wanted my work to travel further than others, the life of my talent depended on fighting a little more, and looking for help a little less. But I deny the sequence in putting it this way, for it took me years to come to this fine point. All I felt then was that I was an outlaw, a psychic outlaw, and I liked it, I liked it a good sight better than trying to be a gentleman and with a set of emotions accelerating one on the other. I mined down deep into the murderous message of marijuana, the smoke of the assassins, and for the first time in my life I knew what it was to make your kicks.

Alive at least to his own rage, Mailer insisted on rewriting *The Deer Park* one more time in order to roughen its texture and disrupt its closely milled surfaces—to make a more muscular book of it. But whatever torments he had endured in first writing the book were compounded as he slogged through it one more time, plagued by fears about his powers,

---

*Which is not to say that Mailer was left entirely alone, for the Civil Service Commission did make a half-hearted attempt in 1952 to have his father, Barney Mailer, dismissed from his job as an accountant for the Army because of his "close association" with a "concealed communist"—his son. After a protest by Mailer and his lawyer-cousin Charles "Cy" Rembar, the commission backed off.[10]

questions about his manhood, and resistances of uncertain origin. Driving himself to the brink of illness, he flogged his brain with marijuana to coax images out of his unconscious and with amphetamines to speed up production. He admits to finishing the final paragraphs with a boost from mescaline, and there is indeed an oceanic swoon to them, with their stammerings about Sex and Time and "the connection of new circuits," suggesting a mind that has gone surfing on psychedelic shores. The process took him close to collapse, and when he was done it was clear that the path he had been following, the one marked "serious American novelist-intellectual," was a cul de sac. The costs were too great and the rewards too small. He would have to survey the terrain one more time and regroup his forces.

III. Non Serviam

If *Barbary Shore* and *The Deer Park* are portents—easy enough to see with the infallibility of hindsight—*Advertisements for Myself* is the fulfillment. If they are the rumblings, it is the blast. A carnival of stories, broadsides, assaults, and self-promotions, it was a daring gambit, all-or-nothing, a challenge to conventional sensibility, an affront to taste, and a test of the limits of public utterance. It was a driven book, a portrait of the artist as a middle-aged desperado betting everything on one last chance to redeem his failures by staging a sensational raid on the literary market. Should it fail, Mailer would have no place to go except back to the novel, about which he had already broadcast his frustrations, or into the encyclopedia of one-book wonders, another American life without a second act. It would be either a badge of recovery or a certificate of burnout, a baptism or a burial. Disorderly, blustery, accusatory, self-doubting, and self-celebrating, it shattered the novelist's mask and brought the man center stage, singing the song of himself, chanting the body electric, saluting the phallus erect.

After the solemnities of *Barbary Shore* and *The Deer Park*, which were radical in mission but technically conservative, *Advertisements for Myself* was an audacious performance. Unbuttoning the hairshirt of received literary culture, Mailer took leave of the novel itself and those conventions that had brought him such grief: plot, character, exposition, unity of action, and consecutive reasoning. The great tradition, Mailer had concluded, was also a great straitjacket, and marching in lockstep from one novel to the next was a form of self-immolation. His restless personality demanded more direct forms of expression, and when

Mailer at last uttered his *non serviam,* it was not only the times and the powers, the publishers and the state capitalist empires that he would no longer serve but the tradition of the novel as well.*

Advertisements for Myself was an exceptional book for its time—audacious, fresh, and compelling, a challenge to Eisenhowerism, to publishing, to mass sensibility, to, most of all, himself to make a clean break with all that was stifling in society and cowardly in himself. Structurally it was a hodgepodge of manifestoes, juvenilia, interviews, fragments of never-to-be-written novels, reckless *Village Voice* editorials, and instant poems lassoed together by filaments of personal narrative, his feisty "advertisements." It made a racket, as converts' testimonials often do. But at the bottom of this bouillabaisse was an economy of moral design. The apparent clutter was the exuberance of self-emancipation, of having outfoxed the super-ego and conquered writer's block in a single blow. It is as if Mailer had turned himself inside out and converted latent content into manifest form. In *The Deer Park,* Eitel's bewilderments and Mailer's own turbulence are cast into a "porcelain of a false style"—Mailer's phrase—while in *Advertisements for Myself,* every transient impulse is shipped instantly to the surface, giving it a certain playful unpredictability but leaving the inner design lucid and simple: "The shits are killing us." In the reading, one's initial impression of the book's scatter quickly gives way to an appreciation of its unity.

It is not difficult to spot the therapeutic agenda behind such a performance. Like Freud, Mailer had done an analysis of himself without any aid save that of drugs (Freud had his cocaine) and had come away with a burning awareness of his own needs, ambitions, and terrors. As with Freud, the self-analysis was prelude to a burst of creativity and a new direction. And while the precise revelations that set them on their new courses have never been disclosed, we can, in Mailer's case, reconstruct their major themes with confidence, since they have dominated his writing ever since: courage, manliness, combat, God, and sex. Indeed, after Freud's own fashion, Mailer came away from his revelations with a renewed belief in the urgency of sex, to become a sexologue and a

---

*That Mailer never did entirely forsake the novel, however, is testimony to its continuing power and the magnetic aura of Hemingway. A writer in America can win many honors doing other things, but the novel remains the great prize. In later attempts, Mailer would try every means to outflank the well-made novel. *An American Dream,* first serialized in *Esquire* in 1964, was an experiment in spontaneity and a joust with deadlines. *Why Are We in Vietnam?* in 1967 would hide its ambitions behind a mask of insouciant verbal pyrotechnics. It was not until 1979, twenty-four years after *The Deer Park,* when Mailer gathered Lawrence Schiller's tapes and notes into *The Executioner's Song,* that he would again attempt anything of the scope and ambition of a major novel.

barnstormer for the erotic. But the similarity ends there. The conventional aim of Freudian analysis is to bring life under control, to rescue it from the dictatorship of guilt and place it under the firm stewardship of reason, for though its ultimate destination is pleasure and freedom, it navigates by way of prudence and rational calculation. Though what Mailer had put himself through shared the emancipatory aims of Freudian psychoanalysis, he had little patience with the prudential Freudian ethic and would chart his own immoderate course to *Lieben und Arbeiten:* the road of excess, taking the hipster for his trail guide.[11]

The insignia piece of *Advertisements* is the essay "The White Negro." First published in *Dissent* magazine in 1957, it is the program behind the performance and a profile of the character that might stand as the antidote to contemporary conformism, the hipster.[12] Assigning him the role of "American existentialist," Mailer identified his precursors and partial selves as the Negro, the jazz musician, the psychopath, and the mystic. Like the Negro, whose experience of life as combat freed him from the constraints of conscience, the hipster derived a special degree of freedom from new factors in the psychic economy of the West: the normalization of terror and the quantum leap in human powers of devastation. A product of the atomic age and *l'univers concentrationnaire*, he had given civilization the slip and "set out on that uncharted journey with the rebellious imperatives of the self." Part psychopath, part juvenile delinquent, part ghetto mystic and curbside warrior, part phallic narcissist, part "frontiersman of the wild west of the American night life" and "wise primitive in a giant jungle," part social datum, and part self-projection, he was the incarnation of a vitalist myth, an icon of appetite. Innoculated against pain, he cultivated a morality of pleasure: "The only Hip morality . . . is to do what one feels whenever and wherever it is possible, and—this is how the war of the Hip and the Square begins—to be engaged in one primal battle: to open the limits of the possible for oneself, for oneself alone, because that is one's need."

We could cite Nietzsche's Übermensch as the hipster's prototype, but that would cost us a view of how contemporary a figure he cut in 1957. He was a vade mecum of popular revolt, cribbed in roughly equal parts from current fiction, cinema, jazz, rock 'n' roll, and popular social science. Behind him stand Wilhelm Reich, Robert Lindner *(Rebel without a Cause)*, David Riesman *(The Lonely Crowd)*, Ernest Hemingway (grace under pressure), James Dean, Marlon Brando, and the king of the white Negroes, Elvis Presley. One facet of his character was taken from Riesman, who had divided the social universe into inner- and other-directed characters and made a clear moral distinction between the two.

The dominant moralities of the era, he held, were other-directed. Contemporary man takes his cues from the family or the firm or the party or the society; he is bound by chains of shame to the institutions in which he lives. In Mailer's countermyth, the Negro and the psychopath, being pariahs, are invulnerable to social demands and are inner-directed, driven solely by their appetites rather than their fears or their obligations.

Riesman's contribution to the script was minor, however, compared to that of Robert Lindner, the Baltimore psychoanalyst with whom Mailer became friendly in the early fifties, at a time when Mailer's ideas were in flux. When Lindner died in 1956, Mailer eulogized him in one of his *Village Voice* columns; he would later quote from *Rebel without a Cause* in "The White Negro." Lindner was unique in being a social critic at a time when psychoanalysis as a whole was busy consolidating its gains behind the shield of American medicine and purging the record of its roots in the German youth movement and European socialism.[13] A psychiatrist in the federal prison system during World War II, he had extensive experience with psychopathic personalities, and his best-known books, *Rebel without a Cause* and *The Fifty-Minute Hour,* are detailed profiles of cases that passed through his care in prison and private practice, several of them criminal psychopaths.[14] The feature of Lindner's case histories that made them popular texts of their time is the writing; his prose is swift and poised and thick with detail—closer to fiction than to the dessicated pseudoscientism of the conventional case history. Lindner was also an independent progressive and a foe of Eisenhowerism and communism alike, the latter of which he interpreted as a collective neurosis that relieved its partisans of the strain of maintaining their own symptoms.[15] The combination of social dissent, literary agility, and anticommunism struck a sympathetic chord in Mailer, who cultivated a friendship with Lindner and may well have collaborated on some of his writing.[16] Lindner's main contribution to Mailer's thought was his designation of the psychopath as a contemporary moral type, whose sudden flowering on the world scene as mass man and totalitarian dictator was "a world-wide disorder, affecting huge segments of the population of the globe, and spreading like some malignant growth within the body of human society."[17] The psychopath impressed Lindner and Mailer alike as the new wave of human development, and there are indeed passages in *Must You Conform?* and "The White Negro" that are virtually interchangeable.

Where Mailer departed from Lindner was in his romantic identification with the psychopath, which the latter, with his prison experience, could not indulge. For Lindner, the psychopath was an unambiguous menace, a "carrier of a plague of wars, revolutions, and convulsions of social unrest," and the harbinger of our downfall.[18] Mailer, less troubled by the downfall of civilization, took him for an evolutionary hero, a rebel against the bourgeois order who, nerve endings aglow, was "trying to create a new nervous system" for himself.[19] Someone, in brief, not unlike himself.

But if Riesman and Lindner wrote portions of the script, it was Reich who provided the crucial sexual element that allowed the orgasm to become the keynote of human advancement. Lindner's criticism, for all its anathemas of modern society, skirted gingerly around the subject of sex, and one can scan the whole of *Must You Conform?* without finding a single reference to it. For that, Mailer invoked Reich and the "orgasm reflex." "At bottom, the drama of the psychopath is that he seeks love. Not love as the search for a mate, but love as the search for an orgasm more apocalyptic than the one which preceded it. Orgasm is his therapy—he knows at the seed of his being that good orgasm opens his possibilities and bad orgasm imprisons him." Note, then, the ingredients for hipsterism: inner-direction, psychopathy, and orgasm, around which are woven grace notes of jazz ("the music of orgasm"), Negro experience, and Greenwich Village night life. One would gather that the findings of Mailer's self-analysis were the nostrums of the dissenting academy. He had searched his heart and found sociology there.

That is only slightly exaggerated. It seems to be the case that Mailer's grasp of experience, even at its most feverish, was sluiced through channels of theory and that "The White Negro" was a crossroads of experience and theory. The hipster is, at bottom, the agent of an ambitious dialectical system—an antithesis—and it was not beyond Mailer to call for "a neo-Marxism calculus aimed at comprehending every circuit and process of society from ukase to kiss as the communications of human energy—a calculus capable of translating the economic relations of man into his psychological relations and then back again." Some of Mailer's critics, including Malaquais, would observe that the white Negro was a libidinized variant on Marx's proletarian, a demiurge of history aroused from his middle-class slumber by the violence of the times.[20] But it was culture rather than economics that produced him, and with his hair-trigger sexuality and ready violence he had something about him of the alienated intellectual returned from the tents of exile as a warrior. Sired by Hegel out of the streets of New York, he was as much the antiworker as he was the antibourgeois, the anti-Jew, anti-intellectual, and antiliberal. He was the new Adam, the wrath and scourge of the libido come to cleanse the earth of the accumulated grime of repression, his body his only scripture, his penis his only sword.

How theatrical a conception he was, this Baudelaire of the back streets, this *poète maudit* in a zoot suit! How cinematic! It can hardly escape our attention that Mailer's previous novel was about the film industry and that he would go on in the sixties to make three films of his own. If Robert Lindner's *Rebel without a Cause* would provide Mailer with the white Negro's social script, James Dean, in the film that had virtually nothing to do with the study, would lend him the tragic image. This rough beast, its hour come 'round at last, was slouching toward Hollywood to be born.

If the white Negro was a figure of unmediated id, then, he was also a marketing device for Mailer, "who knows," as Richard Gilman has said of him, "that prophecy, like any other commodity, has to be sold and that ideas are bought today mainly in conjunction with personality."[21] Or, we might add, in conjunction with an image or a trend, for Mailer, it seems, had hitched his wagon to a trend that was going his way. There is irony in his having chosen a fashion with its own pinched and inexpressive argot—which he praises extravagantly in "The White Negro"—as his remedy for conformism, and Malaquais would point this out in calling the white Negro a "conformist in reverse," who had, in effect, pawned his gray flannels for black leathers. In appending his own liberationist passions to an existing subculture with its own strict codes of dress, speech, and manners, Mailer was taking the first step toward radical chic. What began as one Jewish intellectual's romance of black culture in 1957 would reach its absurd culmination twelve years later in Leonard Bernstein's black tie soirée for the Black Panther Party.

It is plausible, then, to see Mailer's career as social theater, as a strategic sequence of public exhibitions calculated to put him on the cultural map as a customer to be reckoned with. But if it is theater, then it is a theater of a sort we are becoming familiar with in contemporary literature: a theater of convalescence, with each book marking a new stage in the battle against the plague. The litmus test of progress is spontaneity, the ability to call forth from the margins of the imagination a voice vibrant with clean energies, free of cant and jargon, formula and redundancy. It was for reasons of summoning this voice and training himself in spontaneity that Mailer briefly took on in 1956 the discipline of a weekly column in the *Village Voice* where, primed with marijuana and amphetamines, he committed to the page whatever utterances came to mind, goading himself into feats of spontaneity in order to vanquish the timidities and restraints that were holding his imagination at bay. Those columns, for all their folly and bluster, were proving grounds for *Advertisements*, spasmodic rehearsals of the voice he was grooming for his new vocation of self-promoter. But, if *Advertisements* was a promotion it was also a necessity: out of all that dread, self-loathing, blockage, and self-rejection had to come either an outburst or a collapse. Out of fear and cunning combined, Mailer was reinventing Mailer.

IV

Wilhelm Reich died in federal prison in 1956, and "The White Negro" now seems both a eulogy to him and an epitaph. (Robert Lindner also died in 1956, and "The White Negro" was surely meant as a tribute to both men.) Through the forties and early fifties, Reich had been prophet to a small population of radical therapists and Greenwich Village cognoscenti, and it would be Mailer, as much as anyone, who would bring him the wider public that had eluded him in life. Mailer wouldn't be alone in taking up the sex-pol banner—Paul Goodman had been waving it for two decades—but by giving it a literary form in his stories and by investing it with a polemical vigor that eluded Goodman, he would become the most notorious.

Rather than submit to any organized form of analysis or treatment, Mailer, enacting the myth of self-reliance, conducted his own self-analysis, guided by images from Lindner and concepts from Reich, and reprogrammed himself according to home-made definitions. In staging his own death and resurrection, he created his own myth, embodied it, and became its chief advocate, while discreetly burying those elements of the old life that were no longer of service to the new myth: the Harvard boy, the leftist, the progressive, the novelist, the Jew.

For Mailer, the enabling myth was the hipster or white Negro, and throughout this essay I've employed the terms interchangeably, following Mailer's own practice. But a distinction can be made, and it is one that casts light on Mailer's method. The hipster, however Mailer may have imagined him and used him for his own purposes, is a social datum. There were and are real hipsters, aborigines of the urban night whom Mailer would naturally encounter in the bars and jazz clubs of Manhattan in the 1950s. The white Negro, by contrast, is Mailer's invention, the Platonic hipster whom Mailer invested with the world-historical power to redeem America's erotic destiny. The hipster is a fact, the white Negro a dream, a projection of Mailer's apocalyptic imagination, and it is the counterpointing of fact and dream that makes "the White Negro" so challenging a document. If the white Negro lacks firm contours, it was because Mailer was not interested in drawing them. He was out to create a myth and to proclaim its advent, and it was enough to trace out a vague character of an urban Übermensch, a deadly antibourgeois. The myth is a mixture of keen observation and wild delusion, a tantalizing confusion of sociology and wish fulfillment. It is this blending of reality and myth in Mailer's romance with the hipster that has given his writing its eerie power, even over Mailer himself, for in later years it would bring the myth crashing down upon his head in the person of Jack Henry Abbott, an actual psychopath who shed actual blood and redeemed no one at all, neither his victim nor his patron nor himself. Lindner was right. When Abbott came along to hold out the tantalizing promise that the psychopath might also be a genius and the hipster also a writer, he held a demonic mirror up to Mailer himself, a bait that Mailer was bound to strike.

The hipster was as close as Mailer ever came to defining a hero to embody the subterranean energies he had found beneath the surface of American life, and Mailer was at his most authoritative in speaking for the stifled powers held in check by the reactionary climate of the times. He was at his worst in finding embodiments for the hipster's surplus libido—like Jack Kennedy or Gary Gilmore or Jack Henry Abbott. As soon as he tried to apply his visions to real situations—to discover living incarnations of his Nietzschean categories—the project disintegrated. The white Negro's power is that of a negative myth, a challenge to the American mind, which makes no room for sex as anything other than a titilation or a commodity. As a positive myth, to be embodied and acted on, however, the white Negro was a dead end.

The passage from Marxist revolutionism is marked by such odd turnings as this. Mailer's case is noteworthy because its inner dimensions were so readily visible, because the release of energy was so explosive, and because it prefigured a mass social movement. *Advertisements for Myself* stands at the verge of a decade of conversions, when to be a psychic outlaw was one sure way of keeping abreast of the times, and to release your anger, your sexuality, and your primitive impulses was the key to growing up absurd with your generation.

10. Allen Ginsberg
The Poetics of Power

I. The Enlightenment

LIVING IN AN AGE of ornamental poetry in which the essential obligation of the poet is to produce allegories of his own sensitivity, we are likely to find ourselves out of touch with the audacious last line of Shelley's "A Defense of Poetry": "Poets are the unacknowledged legislators of the world." What possible relation, we are bound to wonder, does our poetry have to legislation, to politics, to power? And if we could locate those elements in poetry that might bear some plausible connection to power, how would it be possible, in an age that neither honors nor even reads poetry, for a poet to become the legislator of the world, even an unacknowledged one?

Of course, Shelley's conception of poetry was a far cry from what we find when we open our Eliot, our Lowell, our Ashbery . . . whomever. His defense was rooted in the great dramatic and epic poets: Shakespeare, Sophocles, Plato (whom Shelley deemed a poet of ideas), Homer, Virgil, Dante, and Milton. In the epic, the relation of poetry to the objects of this world is not a product of sensibility—the light cast by private intelligence upon a world of minor objects and tender emotions—but of a priestlike power to divine the spirit of the age from its great events and myths: war and peace, death and judgment, sin and salvation. Shelley's poet is the agent of vast invisible powers and, as such, a rival to those who hold the reigns of visible power. "It is impossible," he wrote, "to read the compositions of the most celebrated writers of the present day without being startled with the electric life which burns within their words."

> They measure the circumference and sound the depths of human nature with a comprehensive and all-penetrating spirit, and they are themselves perhaps the most sincerely astonished at its manifestations; for it is less

their spirit than the spirit of the age. Poets are the hierophants of an unapprehended inspiration; the mirrors of the gigantic shadows which futurity casts upon the present; the words which express what they understand not; the trumpets which sing to battle and feel not what they inspire; the influence which is moved not, but moves.

This a heroic conception of the poet's calling and power, and we can scarcely survey the contemporary literary or artistic terrain and find such scope and ambition in anything but debased or parodic forms: the commercial hierophancy of rock stardom or the cinematic sublimities of the special effects workshop. No one undertakes serious epics these days; no one has the audacity to speak for the spirit of the age or to suppose that the power of words has anything but a subsidiary and ornamental relation to the power of armies or states.

Allen Ginsberg is the lone protester against the surrender of public poetry, having been, these thirty years since the publication of *Howl* in 1956, America's leading and perhaps only example of a power poet: a poet for whom the word is not only a medium of emotional power but a claimant to other forms of power as well. If his achievements have not rivalled his world-transforming ambitions, neither have they been self-deluding. Neither the Milton nor the Blake of our age, he has nonetheless, more than any other American writer since the war, crossed the border from sensibility to power and left his mark upon the events of his time.

My own initial experience of that power dates back to the events of Vietnam Day in Berkeley, California, in 1965. It was on November 20, 1965, that the first massive demonstration against the Vietnam War was mobilized in the San Francisco Bay Area. It was widely feared at the time that the Alameda County authorities (among whom was Edwin Meese, then an assistant district attorney) had deputized the Hell's Angels motorcycle gang to disrupt the march in order to disband and discredit it and had given the Angels carte blanche to do as they pleased without police interference. Ginsberg's role in the organization of that event was that of spiritual monitor: ordaining the spirit of the march, lowering its temperature, and above all, negotiating safe passage for the marchers into the Hell's Angels territory—Oakland—which he did at a public gathering by reading a poem, "To the Hell's Angels."[1] The effect was precisely as Ginsberg had intended. Not only was the march not attacked by either police or Hell's Angels, several Angels joined it. A great social barrier was breached and a fragile synthesis of political rebels and social outlaws was effected that would last for four years until the organizers of the rock festival at Altamont employed Hell's Angels as security guards and were rewarded for their folly by violence, murder, and the symbolic death of the spirit of the sixties.

"To the Hell's Angels" and an introductory manifesto, "How to Make a March/Spectacle," were published in the *Berkeley Barb* and distributed throughout the Bay Area as part of Ginsberg's campaign to secure a peaceful march by sweetening its mood, defusing public anxiety, and arousing media interest, and it was evident at the time that Ginsberg was the only person around with the moral credentials to do anything like that. On all sides, even among Alameda County officials, Ginsberg's authority to pronounce on matters of public conduct was unquestioned. For a moment, Ginsberg stood forth not only as the guru of the peace movement but as the unanointed priest and the unacknowledged legislator of San Francisco.

"How to Make a March/Spectacle" was a brilliant gesture toward transforming the culture of politics from one of conflict and confrontation to one of playfulness and innocence. It was a twenty-point call for the infusion of imagination and play into politics and a lesson in how to prevent an explosion by relaxing one's own reflexes and defusing one's own inclination to violence. It also demonstrated a shrewd grasp of the value of public relations and image making in the formation of a political movement. Seen in the context of the Marxist political culture in which Ginsberg was raised, it was conspicuous in its opposition to agitprop, seeking as it did to create a political spirit through a theater of relaxation rather than of agitation.

> If imaginative, pragmatic, fun, gay, happy, *secure* Propaganda is issued to mass media in advance (and pragmatic leaflets handed out days in advance giving marchers instructions)
> The parade can be made into an exemplary spectacle on how to handle situations of anxiety and fear/threat (such as Spectre of Hells Angels or Spectre of communism)
> To manifest by concrete example, namely the parade itself, how to change war psychology and surpass, go over, the habit-image-reaction of fear/violence.

Calling for masks, costumes, toys, candy bars (to be given to Hell's Angels and police), flowers, mothers, children, grandparents, and musical instruments, it was a prescription for a gathering of the innocents and a showdown with fear and intimidation. The poem too, a rough piece of occasional verse at best, was a plea against violence and an invitation to the Angels to join the spiritual revolution.

To take the heat off, you've got
    to take the heat off
        INSIDE YOURSELVES—
    Find Peace means stop hating yourself
stop hating people who hate you
stop reflecting HEAT
        THERE ARE PEOPLE WHO ARE NOT HEAT
        THE MOST OF PEACE MARCHERS ARE NOT HEAT
They want you to join them to relieve
    the heat on you & on all of us.

Among the recollections I continue to treasure of those times this one stands out: that of Allen Ginsberg as the impresario of that moment when 100,000 people marched through the Bay Area guided by his spirit of play and his rules of peaceable conduct. At that moment, no one else in the Bay Area, maybe not in America, politician or priest, commanded the moral authority of this balding, bearded, libertine, homosexual, Jewish poet.

It goes without saying that to speak of Ginsberg this way is to speak of the man apart from his poetry, and it is true that while poetry has been the vehicle for Ginsberg's spiritual power, the power is something apart from the poetry and vastly more provocative. It is not beyond noticing that Ginsberg's reputation as a cultural figure over the years has exceeded his esteem as a poet, and it is apparently the case that the figure of the poet-shaman looms larger in the public imagination than the poetry. We can count in Ginsberg's collected works a handful of great poems—certainly *Howl* and *Kaddish* rank as great modern poems—and perhaps a dozen others that reward rereading. But by and large the *Collected Poems, 1947–1980* is less the record of sustained creative achievement than a hectic *tsimmes* of landscapes, dreams, jeremiads, exorcisms, anathemas, and prophecies, some of them violent and electric, many of them excruciatingly dull.[2] Despite Ginsberg's conscious effort to be the Whitman of his time—bard, visionary, and prophet of adhesive love—*Collected Poems* is no *Leaves of Grass*; it lacks the discipline and sustained power. In Ginsberg's case, it is the example of the life, and the myth that surrounds it, that is destined to last, while the greater part of the poetry is likely to retain only documentary interest. More so than with any other contemporary writer, even Mailer, Ginsberg's writing is a background to the man, evidence of his moral character, rather than an object of primary interest.

II. The Convert as Culture Hero

Ginsberg's has been a mythic life, not only as he has lived it but as he has imagined it. He is a convert, who, by his own account, has experienced a moment of enlightenment and has devoted his subsequent life to recreating and justifying that moment. Not unlike Mailer, though in more profound fashion, Ginsberg has cast off the given terms of his being and recycled himself as a higher brand of being. He is the legendary man who escaped the initial ground rules of his life and created himself as a visionary figure. Born into a middle-class Jewish family in Paterson, New Jersey, his father a poet and schoolteacher, his mother insane and institutionalized while he was still young, his own emotions askew and his sexual identity in tatters, Ginsberg was handed an unpromising life script. As his letters, journals, and early poetry all suggest, he was cut out to be an emotional cripple, a victim of injuries so vast that only the most resolute of wills was likely to overcome them.[3] Ginsberg's youth was an apprenticeship in failure, and yet he altered the deadly prognosis: by way of Blake and Buddhism he became that mythic American, the self-made man. More bookish, more resolutely literary than any of the other beat writers, he rescued himself through books. What else shall we make of the Blake vision that set into motion his career as a poet but this—that here was a man on his way down who was saved by poetry? Little wonder that he is honored these days in the academy, to whose basic values—dispassionate toil, restraint, objectivity—he is seemingly so anathema, for he is a living defense of the literary vocation.

Ginsberg's myth of himself, then, is one of self-transcendence and transfiguration; he is the man who by vision, by will, by discipline brought himself back from limbo and converted his frailties into powers, his hallucinations into visions, his alienations into prophecies, his wounds into bows. "The story of Ginsberg's development," observes George Dennison, "is the story of a great leap. I do not mean from one stage of mastery to another, but a leap of *being* which transforms life itself into a hazardous, yet brilliantly exciting, field of values."[4]

The key to this transcendence is the famous Blake vision, of which we have perhaps a half dozen accounts, the fullest of which was in the 1966 *Paris Review* interview.[5] In 1948, the twenty-two-year-old Ginsberg was lying on his bed in his apartment in Harlem, having just masturbated, looking out the window at the sky and the cornices of Harlem. Isolated, depressed, lonely, his pants open and a Blake book on his lap, he heard a voice reciting the lines of "Ah, Sunflower." "Suddenly it seemed that I

saw into the depths of the universe, by looking simply into the ancient
sky."

> The sky suddenly seemed very *ancient.* And this was the very ancient place
> that he was talking about, the sweet golden clime, I suddenly realized that
> *this* existence was *it!* And, that I was born in order to experience up to this
> very moment that I was having this experience, to realize what this was all
> about—in other words that this was the moment that I was born for. This
> initiation. Or this vision or this consciousness, of being alive unto myself,
> alive myself unto the Creator. As the son of the Creator—who loved me, I
> realized, or who responded to my desire, say. It was the same desire both
> ways.

This was a moment of initiation, when a life of longing, isolation, and
loneliness was suddenly redeemed by the trembling of the veil.

In an instant the meaning of Ginsberg's life was turned inside out:
absolute purposelessness became divine purpose, the emptiness of daily
life became the fullness of spirit, the despair of masturbation became the
threshold of vision (and, by extension, sex of any form became a visionary threshold), tedium became exaltation, lovelessness (his abandonment
by Neal Cassady) became divine love, poetry became prophecy, the son
of Louis and Naomi Ginsberg became the son of the Creator. It is not
difficult to take a cynical view of such a vision, to see it patently as wish
fulfillment, a desperate longing for love, direction, and purpose mag-
ically answered by the voice of William Blake in one's own room. To read
Blake at such moments—in the depths of spiritual agony and open to
ultimate realities—is to be susceptible to such epiphanies.

What elevates the vision from wish fulfillment into something more
serious is the discipline it inaugurates: the renovation of oneself to affirm
the vision and to fulfill the prophecy inherent in it. That is what distinguishes a conversion from an awakening: the vision is taken for a
calling and life becomes a devotion to powers greater than oneself. In
recompense for such subordination, one dons the mantle and assumes
the powers of the devotional object. One begins as an acolyte and
becomes a priest.

III. The Discipline

In our time it is sometimes hard to distinguish a discipline of the spirit
from a surrender to the flesh, especially where the discipline is one that
attributes spiritual benefits to sexual indulgences: Reichianism, for ex-

ample, or some of the Buddhist sects that have taken up residence in the transcendental corners of the United States: Colorado or Oregon. In Ginsberg's case, the alloy of ascetic practices and orgiastic surrenders makes it difficult to know where he has been putting his spirit to school and where just indulging his appetites, though to a Blakean the appetites are just handmaidens to the spirit anyway. But if a simple sensuality *is* to be one's discipline, why also bother to become a Buddhist? Why not just go out and get laid? Aren't there simpler ways to cultivate one's hedonism?

That is not answerable except by Ginsberg himself, and most of his own accounts of his spiritual odyssey are so opaque that it is virtually impossible to divine clear purposes from them.[6] It seems that Ginsberg has been in pursuit of perhaps as many as three distinct disciplines which, though they appear integrated in him do not necessarily belong together: a discipline of the flesh, whose aim is pleasure and an intimacy with the passions; a vision quest, which seeks mystical knowledge; and a discipline of inner peace, which seeks to quell the inner riot, master the arts of harmony, balance, and calm, and marshall the scattered powers of the mind. The hedonism and the vision quest, with their Blakean sanction, are central to Ginsberg's life and writing up through the early 1960s. The spiritual tours to North Africa, India, and Southeast Asia in search of spiritual guidance and to Mexico and Peru in quest of more powerful hallucinogens, the ecstatic cross-country trips "to find out if I had a vision or you had a vision or he had a vision to find out eternity," all represent the same hectic rush for epiphany. But none of it suggests discipline, except insofar as the quest itself is one's discipline.

The Indian trip of 1962–63 was a watershed for Ginsberg. He went to India as a free-lance visionary, a seeker after grand spiritual truths in the American fashion, by luck and by pluck, and returned with the makings of a systematic culture of the spirit—at least the terminology and the mantras if not always the rigor. He was not a Gary Snyder, who could dedicate himself methodically to the rigors of Zen. More restless and eclectic, more passionate and turbulent than Snyder, Ginsberg could never submit himself entirely to any discipline of renunciation. The best he could do was surround old appetites with new meanings and obey the counsel of Swami Shivananda, which he is fond of quoting: "Your own heart is the Guru," a doctrine that, in effect, anoints the path you happen to be walking as the path of enlightenment.[7]

The practical effect of such a counsel would be to reinforce the Blakean dictum about the road of excess leading to the palace of wisdom. This identity of excess and wisdom is a sustaining principle of

Ginsberg's sense of himself as well as of his public identity as the man who has plumbed the depths of experience and surfaced with his innocence intact and with fresh insights into the human heart and its troubles. Surely that helps us understand why the extraliterary paraphernalia of Ginsberg's life—the letters, journals, table talk, and lectures—should matter as much to the public image as his poetry and occupy a special place in our literature.[8] It is the documentation of a saint's life, recording in minute and often tedious detail the steps from innocence to experience, from beatness to beatitude, from weakness to power. Ginsberg is a hero for the therapeutic age, a saint of indulgence who has publicly subjected his heart to whatever it can bear and survived his ordeals not jaded but eager for more experience.

It has done no damage to the myth that Ginsberg has viewed his life in a didactic and missionary light and has sought opportunities to publicize himself through readings, lectures, rallies, and public appearances. More than any other writer of our time except Paul Goodman—and for reasons similar to Goodman's—Ginsberg has a special affinity for the young and regularly tours the colleges and prep schools with his harmonium and his entourage playing Blake songs, singing mantras, casting spells and charms, and reciting agitational poems about love and sex, war, and the fall of America. Ginsberg's fetishes by now have congealed into a curriculum, and his association with the Naropa Institute and the Jack Kerouac School of Disembodied Poetics in Boulder, Colorado, has given him an institutional setting in which to pursue his calling as a teacher and his lifelong avocation of student. Perhaps in those contexts the teachings have the structure and formal unity of a discipline, but as seen through the writings they are scattered and unsystematic and, when examined closely, not so simple as they may sound. The Ginsberg curriculum is an impasto of antimilitarism, anti-authoritarianism (though there are some exceptions that bear examining), political anarchism, libidinal liberation, homosexuality, spiritual adventure, and *carpe diem.*

Though Ginsberg is not a Reichian through any formal allegiance, he nonetheless can be taken for an incarnation of Reich's sexually improved man, the genital character, who, by virtue of his unarmored erotic nature, will not tolerate a politics that is not consistent with his sexuality: open, democratic, communitarian. It does seem that for Ginsberg sex ordains a politics: that the polymorphousness of his sexual instincts demands a tolerant politics, not only because the political realm should draw lessons from the sexual but because such natures as his own can thrive only under conditions of maximum political toleration, conditions that obtain only in liberal democracies. For all Ginsberg's anathemas of

American society, he understands that he thrives in America far better than he ever could in the "socialist" countries, two of which, Cuba and Czechoslovakia, saw fit in the 1960s to have him deported. Then, in the sixties, Ginsberg consistently represented his bad experiences in the socialist countries as simple reflections of his experiences under capitalism. Thus in "Kraj Majales," his poem about being expelled from Czechoslovakia in 1965 after being crowned King of May (Kraj Majales) by Czech students, he wrote:

> And the Communists have nothing to offer but fat cheeks and eyeglasses
>   and lying policemen
> and the Capitalists proffer Napalm and money in green suitcases to the
>   Naked,
> and the Communists create heavy industry but the heart is also heavy
> and the beautiful engineers are all dead, the secret technicians conspire for
>   their own glamour
> in the Future, but now drink vodka and lament the Security Forces
> and the Capitalists drink gin and whiskey on airplanes but let Indian
>   brown millions starve
> and when Communist and Capitalist assholes tangle the Just man is ar-
>   rested or robbed or had [sic] his head cut off. . . .

The kingdom of youth and love and poesy—that is, sexual youth and the long hair of Adam and the beard of the body—is the counteragent to both:

> And I am the King of May, which is the power of sexual youth,
> And I am the King of May, which is industry in eloquence and action in
>   amour,
> and I am the King of May, which is long hair of Adam and the Beard of my
>   own body
> and I am the King of May, which is Kraj Majales in the Czechoslovakian
>   tongue,
> and I am the King of May, which is old Human poesy, and 100,000 people
>   chose my name. . . .

As if to resolve any ambiguity about his meaning, Ginsberg had the poem published in a broadside by Oyez Press in 1965, the text flanked by woodcuts of Ginsberg naked except for sneakers, standing inside of obelisks in the form of erect penises.[9]

"Kraj Majales" was a doctrinal statement for the sixties, a rejection of states and politics in favor of being "King of May that sleeps with teenagers laughing." To be sure, sleeping with teenage boys is a far cry from anything that Reich himself countenanced in touting "full geni-

tality." Indeed, a glance at the indices of his major books suggests that
Reich did not acknowledge homosexuality at all, let alone pederasty, as a
vehicle for the "orgasm reflex." But once you've singled out the orgasm
as the sine qua non of mental health, to extend that axiom to voluntary
coupling of any kind seems no more than a simple extrapolation from
first principles.

IV. Dictatorship of the Poetariat

It is easy enough to dismiss the theorem that sex ordains politics as
romantic, untestable, and downright simple-minded. But that does not
rule out the possibility that there may be some natures for whom it is
true. What is impossible for most of us may be mandatory for others.
The fusion of sex and politics in Ginsberg reminds us of no one so much
as Reich himself, and the insistence on the sexual realm as the prototype
of the political and therefore a window of therapeutic intervention is not
only a Reichian idea but the outgrowth of a similar nature, one that has
globalized sexuality and made it a touchstone for all other forms of
relationship.

But the proposition that sex ordains politics urges us to have a second
look at Ginsberg's values and to ask whether they are precisely as we have
usually taken them to be: libertarian, egalitarian, fraternal, adhesive—in
short, Enlightenment values raised to the nth power by homosexuality
and anarchism. For the sex, when it is made explicit, looks more like a
tableau from the Marquis de Sade than an argument out of Mill's *On
Liberty.* The model of sexuality that Ginsberg presents in his poetry is
commonly one of mastery and submission, in which violence or the
threat of it enhances the erotic frisson. Images of this are scattered
throughout the *Collected Poems,* from the "best minds of my generation"
who "let themselves be fucked in the ass by saintly motorcyclists, and
screamed with joy" to the abject entreaties, in the 1968 poem "Please
Master," to be treated in love like a dog.

> Please master call me a dog, an ass beast, a wet asshole,
> & fuck me more violent, my eyes hid with your palms round my skull
> & plunge down in a brutal hard lash thru soft drip-fish
> & throb thru five seconds to spurt your semen heat
> over & over, bamming it in while I cry out your name I do love you please
>   Master.[10]

Ginsberg spoke bluntly about the sexual/religious joy of submitting to
power in the *Gay Sunshine* interview, telling Allen Young, "There's a

mysticism when you screw somebody in the ass, or in being screwed. There's a great mysticism in being screwed and accepting the new lord divine coming into your bowels—'Please Master.' "[11]

If Ginsberg's sexual and social metaphysics are of a piece, as I suspect they are, such bedroom politics are bound to have corollaries in his social visions and practices. But what precisely are they? For on the face of them, the politics we are familiar with are apparently unrelated to "please master" sexuality. The familiar politics are those of malediction and of what Reed Whittemore has called "the thirties vogue of super-colossal system damnation."[12] Thirty years of antiwar, anticapitalist, and anti-authoritarian poetry and pronouncements leave us no doubt about what Ginsberg abominates. From the rousing Moloch chant in "Howl" ("Moloch whose soul is electricity and banks") in 1956 through "Kraj Majales" in 1965 to a 1980 jeremiad entitled "Birdbrain" ("Birdbrain is the ultimate product of Capitalism"), Ginsberg's maledictions against organized power of any kind, especially American capitalism, have remained consistent.[13] Ginsberg occasionally changes his emphases, but he never changes his mind. Certainly one line of inquiry invites us to look at the Marxism of Ginsberg's youth, which formed his basic attitudes toward the American Moloch and schooled him in the rhetoric of invective. "America when will we end the human war?/ Go fuck yourself with your atom bomb." In that, Ginsberg, who sometimes gives the illusion of being a social tabula rasa who sprang full grown from a Platonic idea of himself, has been true to the visions of his communist mother and socialist father. "America free Tom Mooney/America save the Spanish Loyalists." In his most fundamental political instincts, Ginsberg retains the Marxist vision of America as the capitalist juggernaut, which may account for the fact that though he celebrates Blake, Whitman, Pound, and Williams as his poetic mentors, an ear sensitive to the marching rhythms of depression-era poetry has no trouble picking up in Ginsberg's line echoes of Kenneth Fearing.

In the sixties, the system damnation and global malediction guaranteed him a friendly reception by college audiences, since it put him in tune with the general revulsion against predatory capitalism that swept the campuses. In Vietnam, the mask of Yankee benevolence (the Marshall Plan, CARE, the Peace Corps) was off and Moloch was the face America showed to the world, and it was not hard to gain converts to the view that the basic American motive was profit and that all operations of American power were the brutal exploits of Daddy Warbucks on the march. In the post-Vietnam era, however, when manifestations of American power have been more ambiguous and when Ginsberg's own politics have been put to the test, his fidelity to the madcap improvisation and egalitarian anarchism of Vietnam Day has been called into question.

Ginsberg's ambiguities were brought into focus in 1975 by an event of near-mythic stature by now in the poetic community, involving Ginsberg, the poet W. S. Merwin, and Ginsberg's spiritual mentor since the early 1970s, Chogyam Trungpa, Rinpoche (Rinpoche being his title, like "the honorable" or "his excellency").[14] Trungpa founded, in 1974, the Naropa Institute in Boulder, Colorado, under whose auspices Ginsberg directs the Jack Kerouac School of Disembodied Poetics. A direct descendant, by a mystical inheritance akin to apostolic succession, of the Kagypa and Karmapa orders of Tibetan Buddhism, Trungpa is to the Dalai Lama more or less what the Archbishop of Canterbury is to Rome. Born in Tibet in 1938 and identified in his infancy by the monks of the Surmang monastery as the eleventh incarnation of Trungpa Tulku, he was raised to be the supreme religious leader of the Karmapa order. When China invaded Tibet in 1959, Trungpa fled across the Himalayas to India and from there to Oxford to study. After leaving Oxford he settled in Scotland, where he founded the Samye-ling meditation center. In 1970, he established the first Tibetan meditation center in America, Tail of the Tiger in Vermont, where he began to make contact with American poets. In 1974, Trungpa moved to Boulder and founded the Naropa Institute, which has become the center of Buddhist teaching and organization in America.

During his travels, Trungpa picked up a number of poet-disciples who interested him in attaching a program in poetics to the Naropa Institute. That eventually became the Kerouac School, whose annual summer program, featuring the brightest stars in America's poetic firmament, is the closest thing we have had to an American Helicon since the closing of Black Mountain College. The relation between Naropa and the Kerouac School has not been without its strains, however, and the *locus classicus* of them was a party held at the Vajradhatu Seminary in Snowmass, Colorado, in 1975. It was a wild and drunken party—Trungpa is a notorious drinker—at which some people were forcibly undressed by Trungpa's bodyguards and Trungpa himself removed his clothes and tied a red scarf around his penis. The poet W. S. Merwin was there with Hawaiian poetess Dana Naone. Appalled at the goings on, they retreated to their room early that evening. Noting their absence, Trungpa ordered his guards to fetch and bring them down, by force if necessary, which led to a smashing down of their door and a violent confrontation between Merwin and the guards. Merwin, a pacifist, attempted briefly to defend himself with a broken beer bottle but was overcome by force and the sight of blood (he cut one of the guards) and submitted at last to the dharma police.

Confronted by Trungpa and surrounded by a crowd of partying acolytes, Merwin and Naone were chastised for their rudeness in declining Trungpa's hospitality. During one exchange, Trungpa threw sake in Merwin's face and made disparaging remarks about Naone's consorting with a white man. Trungpa invited the couple to make amends by disrobing, and when they refused, he ordered his guards to forcibly undress them. Merwin later wrote an account of the event in a letter to Ed Sanders' "investigative poetry group," which conducted and published an inquiry into the incident in 1977.

> They dragged us apart, and it was then that Dana started screaming. Several of them on each of us, holding us down. Only two men, Dennis White and Bill King . . . said a word to try to stop it, on Dana's behalf. Trungpa stood up and punched Bill King in the face, called him a son-of-a-bitch, and told him not to interfere. The guard grabbed Bill King and got him out of there. One of the guards who'd stayed out of it went out and vomited, as we heard later. When I was let go I got up and lunged at Trungpa. But there were three guards in between, and all I could swing at him, through the crowd, was a left, which was wrapped in the towel, and scarcely reached his mouth. It didn't amount to much, and I was dragged off, of course.[15]

The public humiliation of Merwin and Naone apparently satisfied Trungpa and released a pent up hedonism in the others, who then began to disrobe and return to the party. Merwin and Naone fled back to their room but inexplicably stayed on at Vajradhatu for three more weeks of teachings.

The relevance of this event to Ginsberg was that, as Trungpa's disciple and associate, he was presented with a challenge to clarify his values, to reaffirm his commitments to nonviolent and noncoercive relations, and to distance himself from the politics of humiliation and force. His reaction was a disappointment to much of the poetic community.

In an interview with Tom Clark, who had conducted the excellent 1966 interview of Ginsberg for *Paris Review*, Ginsberg spoke candidly about his relations to Trungpa and his views of the Merwin incident and admitted to mixed feelings, though not before admonishing Clark, "You know, you're talking about my love life. My extremely delicate love life, my relations with my teacher."

> It's really complicated. And as all love lives, it's shot through with strange emotions, and self questionings, and paranoias, and impulses. So to reduce

it to discussion with reference to cultural artifacts like the Bill of Rights. . . .[16]

On the one hand, the charge of Buddhist fascism that Merwin would later raise struck a chord in Ginsberg, who ruefully conceded that he may have led the poetic/bardic movement into a cultic trap.

> I accuse myself all the time of seducing the entire poetry scene and Merwin into this impossible submission to some spiritual dictatorship which they'll never get out of again and which will ruin American culture forever. Anything might happen. We might get taken over and eaten by the Tibetan monsters. All the monsters of the Tibetan Book of the Dead might come out and get everybody to take L.S.D.[17]

On the other hand he was not above expressing outrage over Dana Naone's crying out, in a moment of terror, "Call the police," while divine mysteries were being revealed.

> In the middle of that scene, to yell "Call the Police"—do you realize how *vulgar* that was? The Wisdom of the East was being unveiled, and she's going, "Call the police!" I mean, shit! Fuck that shit! Strip 'em naked, break down the door![18]

And rising to bardic levels of invective, Ginsberg condemned nothing less than the principles of liberty, privacy, and individual choice which, alongside those of illumination and transcendence, appear to be the ideologies of a corrupt American theocracy.

> So, yes, it is true that Trungpa is questioning the very foundations of American democracy. Absolutely. . . . So he's pointing out that "in God we trust" is printed on the money. And that "we were endowed with certain inalienable rights, including life, liberty and the pursuit of happiness." That Merwin has been endowed by his *creator* with certain inalienable rights, including life, liberty and the pursuit of happiness. Trungpa is asking if there's any deeper axiomatic basis than some creator coming along and guaranteeing his rights.
>
> Because one of the interesting things that the Buddhists point out is that there's always a sneaking God around somewhere, putting down these inalienable rights. Urizen is around somewhere. And they're having to deal not only the with communists and the fascists and the capitalists, they also have to deal with the whole notion of God, which is built right into the Bill of Rights. The whole foundation of American democracy is built on that, and it's as full of holes as Swiss cheese.[19]

It isn't just the image of Allen Ginsberg as our leading anarchist that was shattered by these events; so was the Reichian myth of unfettered eros as the guarantor of free and democratic politics. It may be objected that Ginsberg was the wrong test case for a sex-pol morality and that his homosexuality, with its insistent dynamics of mastery and submission and its currents of sadism and masochism was not the brand of sexuality Reich and other sexual millenarians have envisioned. But that won't wash. Sex-pol morality was always, at bottom, a morality of measure, number, and degree that, transubstantiating quantity into quality, implicitly equated the gratifications of frequent orgasm with the creation of a democratic and libertarian spirit. The cornerstone of sex-pol doctrine is that this displacement upward is automatic and that a heightened consciousness flows like water or élan vital from the gonads to the heart and mind. The gratified man, for Reich as for Blake, has no truck with kings or apparatchiks or bankers or rinpoches.

The example of Ginsberg should be enough to shatter that myth once and for all. His religious life and his sexual life would seem to be cut from the same cloth, whether or not Trungpa is, as Ginsberg intimates in the Clark interview, his lover. From those hierarchical power relations has grown a tolerance for spiritual monarchies and a diminished appreciation for such imperfect works of the secular mind as the Bill of Rights.

It is twenty years since the Vietnam Day march, and the spirit of play that animated that event now seems a relic of forgotten innocence, of a belief in the redemption of politics through brightening of the human spirit. Ours is a less optimistic age, and Ginsberg himself, approaching sixty (as of 1985), seems a less optimistic and certainly a less transcendent figure. If he still mesmerizes his audiences with the harmonium, the chants, the finger cymbals, and the Blake songs, he also plies his trade in a three-piece suit, looking as though the dharma had joined forces with the corporation and enlightenment were henceforth to be conducted as a business. (At Naropa, as everywhere else in transcendental America, revelation is run by lawyers and accountants.) Perhaps it is that the poetry has lost some of its authority; certainly no poetry since the cross-country "vortex" poems of the mid- and late sixties is charged with any great force, and force has always been Ginsberg's particular *métier* as a poet. Perhaps too it is that his spiritual life has come to rest in a Buddhism that looks disappointingly mundane to an outsider, undistinguishable from a dozen transient cults that have come and gone since the sixties, all boasting the keys to sacred knowledge and inner peace and all looking remarkably like IBM or the United States Marine Corps in their corporate structures. Or the CPUSA Ginsberg knew as a youngster. It is not beyond speculating that some fatal conjunction of a nostalgia for political authority and craving for sexual authority has bound him to a theocratic institution that he has mistaken for an antidote to an imperfect American democracy.

Ginsberg's distinction for many of us twenty years ago was his appearance of having stepped out of time and taken up residence in a higher world, despite the vehement earthiness of his poems and their insistent tale of pain, confusion, and mortality. But that appearance was an illusion. Even when he was locked in bitter struggle with it, Ginsberg was always quintessentially a man of his era, even if he had to invent that era, as in some measure he did, in order to get in step with it. Now, in the eighties, his acceptance of the discipline, the ritual, and the corporate structure of an organized religion would seem to put him in tune with the Zeitgeist he once appeared to defy. But he defied it, we now see, in much the way a helium balloon defies gravity, by obeying it according to his own nature. And helium now appears to be in short supply.

Our last icon of the sixties, Ginsberg has shown himself to be fallible, like the rest of us, and not finally a moral exemption whose errors are windows of revelation. He is a man rather whose mistakes are symbols of limitation and need—like the rest of us. Our leading transcendental poet, he now comes into focus not through his charms and spells, his rites of the spirit or doctrines of the breath, but through his confusion, his fallibility, and his mortality, as a man of this world, neither more nor less. And that is the best way to think about Ginsberg.

11. The Road of Excess
Philip Roth

Updike and Bellow hold their flashlights out
into the world, reveal the real world as it is *now*.
I dig a hole and shine my flashlight into the
hole.
                                        —Philip Roth

The most basic formula of a highly developed
culture—a formula which transcends all particular contents—may be suggested by designat-
ing it as a crisis constantly held back. . . .
                                        —Georg Simmel

The road of excess leads to the palace of
wisdom.
                                        —William Blake

I. I Always Wanted You to Admire My Burrow; or, Looking at Roth

MY FAVORITE IMAGE of Philip Roth is one supplied by Roth himself. It is
that of the artist at bay, holed up in a burrow, issuing disclaimers,
granting interviews or interviewing himself, protesting his innocence,
justifying his books or his life, responding to critics, rabbis, crusaders,
old Shachtmanites, new conservatives, and other stalkers of the book
world, and denying that his desperate characters are in any way replicas
of himself, even while he is openly plundering his journals, his "feverish
notes" as he calls them in one book, for recollections and *mots justes* out of
which to construct the next round of fictions. The burrow, to be sure, is
not something scratched into the earth with bare claws or pounded out
of loose and sandy soil by an animal's forehead like the burrow in Kafka's
story of that name.[1] It is a rustic Connecticut farmhouse, furnished with
all the bric-a-brac of a well-composed life, including a screened-in
gazebo, a wood stove, an English actress, a fridge laden with tofu and
veal. Up there in the woods on a crisp and silent morning, the sorrows of
Newark are easily forgotten and the baying of the literary hounds is
absolutely inaudible. This is a burrow fit for *House and Garden* magazine,

196

where indeed it appeared not long ago in an illustrated article showing the hounded writer at work, the hounded writer on a hammock alongside his friend Claire Bloom, and a photo of the hounded writer's patron saint, Franz Kafka, providing a kind of tragic European decor.[2] This burrow is, all in all, one of the cozier fortifications on record and as gracious a nest for licking your wounds, or having them licked, as a convalescent could hope for this side of Hans Castorp's magic mountain.

This well-appointed retreat, with its spacious grounds, its invigorating silence, its Franklin Library Memorial Swimming Pool, its soothing distance from the contending egos of literary Manhattan is, nonetheless, a retreat, a place to work in peace and recuperate from the weekly strafing runs known as book reviewing in America. It is, willy nilly, Roth's castle keep, a place of comfort and safety much like the burrow in the Kafka story and an integral part of the myth of Roth that Roth himself has been fostering throughout his life as a writer. That myth has run through two phases now, phases that can be traced neatly enough through his books: the myth of the man in the trap and that of the man who got away. The first encompasses all the books from *Letting Go* in 1962 to *My Life as a Man* in 1974 and the second those from *The Professor of Desire* in 1977 through the end of the Zuckerman cycle, though *The Anatomy Lesson* (1983) suggests that Roth is not so easily done with the man in the trap as we might have hoped. Does the man who got away still hear, like Kafka's burrower, distant subterranean noises signalling the approach of some great beast, or has he found the real thing at last, like E. I. Lonoff's Berkshire home in *The Ghost Writer*—serene, simple, secluded, where a man can turn sentences over and over again to his heart's content until he has gotten them just right?

By myth, I mean a basic narrative, a story told time and again to knit together the fragments of experience, to draw their trajectory, and to explain and justify a way of life. It takes all that is random and bewildering and gives it form and purpose, turning, in effect, an existence into a life story. Myths of self are vital to Roth because he is so much the clinician of his own experience and because, in his undeviating fascination with the ego at bay and its violent thrashings to set itself free, he has had to maintain a steady supply of stories to keep his tireless self-invention from flying off into chaos. Every Portnoy, every Kepesh, every Tarnopol and Zuckerman needs a myth to be credible, and foremost among those Roth has adapted to his purposes have been psychoanalytic tales drawn from Freud: fables of childhood impulse and adult remorse, of offense and restitution, of hidden wounds cauterized by burning confessions, of self-entrapments and self-punishments. Some of his fables are so steeped in Freudian antinomies that they are virtually case histories: The Breast Man, The Liver Man, The Sentence Man, Alex: A Study in Hysteria. But other myths have played their part in Roth's self-invention as well: Kafkaesque myths of original guilt and original defeat, Jewish myths of wandering and homelessness, American myths of seasonal play, pitches and catches, wins and losses.

The won-lost record may be the most fundamental of all, since the ball game vies with the marriage to be Roth's basic metaphor for the human condition. A relationship, according to Roth, or to his books, is a zero-sum game in which someone wins and someone loses, and the basic relationship in the Roth novel is the pitched battle (in marriage, as in baseball, you have a pitcher and a catcher). Roth is on record as the most provoked, and perhaps the most provoking, writer in America, and while he speaks of America as a place where everything goes and nothing matters, he continues to write as though words matter a great deal, that they rend and sooth, inflict pain and relieve it—as though the written word were some indispensable substance, not unlike mother's milk, that could make or ruin a man's life. Roth is the most pugnacious as well as the most vulnerable writer around, and it is this volatile concoction of hardness and vulnerability that creates so much of the tension in his books and arouses so much of the controversy surrounding them. The Jewish publications in particular have had a go at Roth; magazines like *Commentary* and *Midstream* have conducted virtual warfare against him and have not, in the most extreme cases, refrained from accusing him of following Nazi scripts.[3] And since his reputation as a writer and his feelings of embattlement in the tournament of literary-cultural politics are the very subject of much of his later fiction, we might profitably begin a retrospective of his writing by reviewing a case in point of the writer versus his readers and the myth he himself has elaborated around them: that of the misunderstood artist who counts among those whom he has baffled and enraged none other than himself.

II. Our Kulturkampf, or, Socialism Bites Therapy

In a painful scene in *The Anatomy Lesson,* Nathan Zuckerman, stung by a review of his work by Milton Appel, a critic of national eminence, and by Appel's subsequent appeal to him to write something favorable to Israel for the *Times* op ed page, dials Appel on the phone and showers him with insults.

In that bloodthirsty essay you have the fucking gall to call *my* moral stance "superior"! You call my sin "distortion," then distort my book to show how distorted it is! You pervert my intentions, then call me perverse! You lay hold of my comedy with your ten-ton gravity and turn it into a travesty! My coarse, vindictive fantasies, your honorable, idealistic humanist concerns! I'm a sellout to the pop-porno culture, you're the Defender of the Faith! Western Civilization! The Great Tradition! The Serious Viewpoint!

Appel's review in *Inquiry* magazine had caught Zuckerman off guard, all the more so because fourteen years earlier Appel had hailed the young writer's dissections of middle-class Jewish life in his collection of stories, *Higher Education,* as "fresh, authoritative, exact." But now, in the wake of his cause célèbre, the novel *Carnovsky,* all his books seem, as Zuckerman paraphrases Appel, "tendentious junk, the byproduct of a pervasive and unfocused hostility . . . mean, joyless, patronizing little novels, contemptuously dismissive of the complex depths."

Compounding Zuckerman's injury is the fact that some of his books, including the despised *Carnovsky,* owe their slant on Jewish life to an essay by Appel who, as a self-conscious, alienated intellectual in the forties, had expressed the perplexities of second-generation Jewish boys too thoroughly Americanized to rest easily in their parents' Jewish world but too Jewish, too inward, too painfully intellectual to embrace confidently a rude, jostling America. The essay had served Zuckerman as a beacon of thoughtful alienation, and "each time he returned to school from a bruising vacation in New Jersey, he took his copy of the essay out of its file folder ('Appel, Milton, 1918—') and, to regain some perspective on his falling out with his family, read it through again. He wasn't alone. . . . He [was] a social type. . . . His fight [with] his father [was] a tragic necessity. . . ."

Zuckerman might have suffered this rejection by this once-admired father in fretful silence had not Appel, with a curious mordant flourish, prevailed upon a mutual friend, Ivan Felt, to ask Zuckerman to write that op ed piece in defense of Israel, which had just rallied to defeat the combined Egyptian and Syrian armies in the Yom Kippur War. But the phrasing did not lack Appel's customary belligerence:

"Why don't you ask your friend Nate Zuckerman to write something in behalf of Israel for the Times Op Ed page? He could surely get in there. If I come out in support of Israel there, that's not exactly news; it's expected. But if Zuckerman came out with a forthright statement, that would be news of a kind since he has prestige with segments of the public that don't care for the rest of us. Maybe he has spoken up on this, but if so I haven't seen it. Or does he still feel that, as his Carnovsky says, the Jews can stick their historical suffering up their ass?"

Felt, as any friend would, xeroxed the letter and passed it along to Zuckerman who, given his volatile temper, his delicate nerves, his chronic upper back pain (a sharp, persistent pain in the neck), and his fragile self-esteem, erupted in Krakataus of rage, threw a tantrum, and made his call. Appel's answer is measured, austere, and crushing.

> "Mr. Zuckerman, you're entitled to think anything you want of me, and I'll have to try to live with that, as you've managed obviously to live with what I said about your books. What is strange to *me* is that you don't seem to have anything to say about the suggestion itself, regardless of your anger against the person who made it. But what may lie in store for the Jews is a much larger matter than what I think of your books, early or late, or what you think of my thinking."

Properly rebuked, Zuckerman silently sets down the phone. The reply comes only later, after Zuckerman's imagination has taken stock of the situation and devised a symbolic and wholly private response. Flying to Chicago with the idea of entering medical school and high as a cirrus on Percodan, which he takes for his neck, and marijuana, which he takes for pleasure, he introduces himself to a fellow traveller as Milton Appel, publisher of *Lickety Split* magazine and former owner of Milton's Millennia, New York's hottest sex club. Stoned, enraged, and 25,000 feet up somewhere over Lake Michigan he lets his imagination roam freely over the rare possibilities of being Milton Appel the sleaziest man in all New York, the Jewish Larry Flynt.

> My magazine is a mirror and we reflect it *all.* I want my readers to know that they shouldn't feel self-hatred if they want to get laid. If they jerk off it doesn't make them beneath contempt. And they don't need Sartre to make it legit. I'm not gay, but we're starting to run a lot of stuff on it. We help out married men who are looking for quick sex. Today most of the blow jobs are being given by guys who are married. You married?

Neither Roth nor his delirious Zuckerman proposes this wild fantasy of Milton Appel, sleaze king, as a proper answer. It is simply a private release, a device for easing the pain while admitting defeat.

Here is a drama of fathers and sons worthy of Kafka: the son's esteem and efforts at emulation, the father's initial solicitude turned inexplicably to censure and then, whimsically, to truculent and impersonal pleas for solidarity in the name of higher purposes. This son doesn't leap from a bridge or become an insect (or a breast); he merely makes agitated phone calls, suffers excruciating neck aches, and invents exotic imaginary reprisals. Only this isn't a Kafka story, but a true-life misadventure, co-authored by Philip Roth and Irving Howe. This version of the New York intellectual Kulturkampf is as livid with bruises as anything Roth has written. The gabardine of fiction on the body of experience in *The Anatomy Lesson* is no thicker than the legally obligatory changes of name to protect Roth from lawsuit, and there probably isn't a reader east of the Hudson, maybe even the Rio Grande, who missed the allusions.

The essay that so provokes Zuckerman is Irving Howe's "Philip Roth Reconsidered," which appeared in the December 1972 issue of *Commentary,* heralded by Norman Podhoretz's snickering fanfare on the editor's page, "Laureate of the New Class," about which more presently.[4] *Higher Education* is transparently *Goodbye Columbus,* which Howe reviewed in 1959, hailing Roth's arrival as a young writer of note, though in fact it was not so unambiguously laudatory as Appel's review of *Higher Education* is said to be; it introduced many of the reservations that the later "reconsideration" would expand into indictments. The youthful essay on which the young Zuckerman and his University of Chicago compeers nourished their alienated spirits in the 1950s is a remarkable document, in view of Howe's later emergence as a Yiddish scholar and historian of his father's generation. Entitled "The Lost Young Intellectual" and patently a reflection upon his generation's journey from the ghetto of Williamsburg to the land of higher values, it appeared in the October 1946 *Commentary,* and we may suppose that Roth, reading it in later years, did take it to heart and did take it for a voice of intellectual kinship and a guideline for his own writing. The echoes of "The Lost Young Intellectual" in *Portnoy's Complaint* are, to my ear, unmistakable.[5]

As for Appel's plea that Zuckerman speak out in defense of Israel and Zuckerman's phone call with its cascades of invective we can only speculate. Both strike me as consistent with the characters and temperaments of Howe and Roth and therefore plausible.

This incident and its literary refraction claim our attention for several reasons. For one, Roth has endeavored for eleven years to keep his stigmata on show, as though they meant something to him; *The Anatomy Lesson* is just the most recent exhibition of his wounds. For another, the aftershocks of the event have been registered on Roth's books themselves; Roth's grappling with Howe has left its mark on his writing, in the apologetics that have marked Roth's subsequent writing and in the modulations of tone and style that have rippled through it these past eleven years. And finally, because in this skirmish some interior dimension of Jewish intellectual culture in America is opened up for inspection.

Howe's case, scattershot though it was, clustered about a few key points. 1. Roth is a "willful" writer who imposes himself on his characters and denies them any fullness, contour, or surprise. His animus, his free-floating "ressentiment," moreover, invariably reduces them cruelly to caricatures. Roth delights in abusing his characters, as if to deal them what they so richly deserve. 2. Roth lacks all patience for uncertainties, mysteries, and doubts, for negative capability. "Only rarely do his fictions risk the uncharted regions of imaginative discovery; almost all his work drives a narrative toward cognitive ends fixed in advance." 3. He is hampered by a "thin personal culture," lacking a vital culture or tradition to nourish his gifts and curb his egocentricities. 4. Roth is vulgar, both in the conventional sense (though Howe claims not to be put off by Roth's language) and in his overwhelming proclivity "to submit the rich substance of human experience, sentiment, value, and aspiration to a radically reductive levelling or simplification." 5. Roth has surrendered to cultural fashion and chosen to court the gallery as a contemporary, literary "swinger" rather than to walk the lonesome valley of Art. "Flaubert once said that a writer must choose between an audience and readers. Evidently Roth has made his choice."

We needn't contest every one of Howe's premises to see the failure of proportion in his admonition. The trouble was that there was sufficient validity to certain of his accusations to obscure his general insensitivity to any of Roth's virtues and skills. And to be insensitive to Roth's masterful deployment of common language, to his wit, and to his perfect pitch for the psychology of dismay is no small failing in a critic. (Another reminder, if one were needed, that the realm of *values* is not that of *taste*.) Surely there was something ludicrous in Howe's grave supplications to James and Flaubert and his application of discriminations worthy of Edmund Wilson or Sainte-Beauve to, of all books, *Portnoy's Complaint* or to "Eli the Fanatic" and "Defender of the Faith," stories Roth had written at 23 or 24 years of age. Roth's willfulness, his egocentricity, his disposition to punish his characters, and his penchant for caricature instead of ripe and rounded portraiture are commonly agreed on. But, does a "thin personal culture" follow necessarily from that? Or a lack of moral seriousness? Or general failure of imagination and plenitude? Roth's fiction has limitations enough that the less vexed reader will observe, but an impoverished imagination that perennially fails to "risk the uncharted regions of imaginative discovery" is not one of them. Roth's is a literature of risk par excellence, and though one may argue that the risks are not always well taken, it is foolish to accuse him of playing it safe. How as it possible for Howe to miss the comedy and daring of *Portnoy's Complaint* or *The Breast* or mistake Roth's precise social anthropology for simple aggression and wage a crusade of scorn that was the moral equivalent to scolding Milton Berle for not being Sir Laurence Olivier?

De gustibus non disputandum est; Roth is not to Howe's taste, and there is always a portion of taste that is purely personal, no matter how well fortified it appears to be by principles. Taste is character, and Howe, for all his celebrations of the rough-hewn American spirit, is too severe a critic for so raucous and mercurial a writer as Roth. Roth, moreover, is anything but a balm for sore nerves. His writing is nervous and abrasive. Despite the tenderness of his feelings, he is not a warm writer, and his ample wit is dipped in steel. His social judgments are pointed; he mounts frequent melodramatic displays of injured feelings, and his comedy normally rises to mayhem. *Portnoy's Complaint* is a particularly combative book, and no one who has read it with students can fail to note their discomfort, the women in particular. That the anger that lines Roth's books should provoke some readers to fury is understandable, and as the rueful tone of some later books shows, Roth has bruises to show for his offenses.

Still, Howe does not strike without a higher purpose. He is a New York intellectual, after all, and New York intellectuals normally join battle under the standard of high purpose. I doubt that Howe would have cultivated such indignation were there not something basic at stake, something of a social or political nature beyond the scope of the offending books themselves. That is, I think, precisely the case, and here the publication of his polemic in *Commentary* and Norman Podhoretz's strident declamations provide the clue.

Howe and Podhoretz took Roth for a weathervane, if not a Weatherman, of culture. Whatever it was that had gone haywire for them in the sixties was visible in a particularly noxious form in Roth who, with *Portnoy's Complaint* in 1969, had thrown off the lendings of high cultural ambition to run naked with the counterculture (or the "adversary culture" or the "new left" or whatever the cultural opposition of the hour was called). Seen as a document of its time and its "class," *Portnoy's Complaint* was of a piece with Abbie Hoffman's presidential campaign for Pigasus during the wild summer days of 1968, a spell of "épatism" combining Dadaist revelry with revolutionary zeal. *Portnoy's Complaint,* with its spasms of hysteria, did share a common dramaturgy of disburdening with the street politics of the sixties, prompting Howe to complain of "Roth's own feeling that it constitutes a liberating act for himself, his generation, and maybe the whole culture." Podhoretz, unencumbered by any merely textual considerations—Howe, at least, still tangled with the books—drove right to the heart of the *Kulturkampf,* charging *Portnoy's Complaint* with being nothing less than an effusion of "new class" consciousness.

> It does not strike me as fanciful to suggest that Philip Roth owes his centrality to the fact that he so perfectly embodies the ethos of a group which began coming to consciousness of itself as a distinctive social class around the time Roth first appeared on the scene and which has become numerous enough and powerful enough in recent years to move from the margins of our culture into the very mainstream of our political life.

Now, Podhoretz was talking here not of the counterculture but of the "new class," the newly emergent social and technocratic elite in American society that, in the analysis of neoconservative theorists in the sixties, set the cultural fashion and the political agenda for America.[6] But in the demonology of new-class theory, the new class was the soil in which the counterculture grew. The new-classniks were the chic radicals and Park Avenue progressives who sponsored the unrest in Union Square or Harlem, showering it with self-hating congratulation, glowing publicity, and sometimes cash. They had rallied behind George McGovern. As the title of Midge Decter's *Liberal Parents, Radical Children* proposed, the new class of liberal parents bred the New Left of radical children from its very loins.[7] It was not the conflict of generations that spawned the revolutionary upheaval of the sixties but the perverse logic of tolerance, affluence, and Dr. Spock. Sparing the rod, new class parents had spoiled the child.

The specific political context of the assault on Roth, three years after the publication of *Portnoy,* is critical. 1972 was the election year in which Richard Nixon roundly defeated George McGovern, and *Commentary* at the time, though nominally Democratic in its sympathies, was in full revolt against McGovernism and was gloating in its catastrophic failure. To catch a closer glimpse of the politics behind Podhoretz's diatribe on Roth, the reader should compare his "Laureate of the New Class" editorial in the December 1972 issue with Penn Kemble and Josh Muravchik, "The New Politics and the Democrats," also in the December issue, and Podhoretz's "What the Voters Sensed," in the January 1973 issue, his introduction to Earl Raab and Seymour Martin Lipset's "The Election and the National Mood."[8] Roth, it becomes clear, was guilty of being the quintessence of McGovernite sensibility: show-offy, antifamily, soft on drugs and communism, probussing, pro–affirmative action and job quotas, bullying, morally ruthless, and irredeemably radical chic.

Howe himself did not invoke this reasoning, however much he shared the revulsion in which it had taken root; perhaps he understood the obvious, that the new class, *c'est lui-même.* A socialist through it all, he assailed the New Left from a position that he fancied to be somewhere also on the left, sharing its dissent from the Vietnam War and the basic premises of American capitalism yet fearing the eclipse of his own democratic socialist politics by a movement that was more spectacular, more sensual, and more innocent than anything he had to offer. Provoked to dithyrambs of scorn by the apocalytpic fervor of some New Left maneuvers, he discovered in Roth's books their literary counterparts and vented upon them his rage toward events taking place elsewhere in the culture. Howe's voice, rising in crescendos of invective every bit as agitated as Roth's own, need only to leaf through its repertoire of anathemas and choose those that suited Roth. Roth was a piece of contemporary cultural furniture—Jewish modern—in which the element of the modern overwhelmed and obscured the element of the Jewish.

We should not underestimate Howe's exasperation in the sixties. Though he considered himself a partisan of many New Left aims, he was appalled by its rhetoric and tactics and gratified by its swift decomposition. Nearly a third of his essay "The New York Intellectuals" is a jeremiad on the New Left and the counterculture—Howe tended not to distinguish between them—for their arrogance, their theatrics, their innocence, and their weakness for Third World communism.[9] In consequence of his tireless admonishing, he found himself shunned and even at times abused by the youth with whom he sought, in his dyspeptic fashion, to make common cause. His sense of injury went deep. Between tirades about the politics of ressentiment and the psychology of unobstructed need that blurred the distinction between politics and therapy in the sixties, Howe brooded over his missed opportunities to join ranks with the only movement of the postwar era that had a chance of affecting American society in a fundamental way. But it was not Howe's way. The Movement's aftermath left him bitter, and some of the most candid and melancholy passages in his memoir *A Margin of Hope* are those which mull over the injuries he suffered in the sixties.[10]

It is now clear, as it may not have been in 1972, that Roth was by no stretch of the imagination either a literary revolutionist or a spokesman for higher consciousness, neither Allen Ginsberg nor Alan Watts. It is doubtful that any New Leftist read or took counsel from Roth or he from them. As for his relation to the Movement in its cultural aspects, there is little reason to think that Roth encountered it in any form other than through the newspapers or television, where, after all, its most outrageous attempts at propaganda became the standard fare of net-work entertainment. He was then as now a dissenting and distraught son of the New York intellectuals themselves, his dissent grounded firmly in theirs, his language and world view drawn at great pains from them. Like Bellow and Malamud before him, he found an early home in the right magazines, *Partisan Review* and *Commentary,* and attracted early admiration from the right editors and critics. His personal list of modern masters might well have been copied straight from the *Partisan Review* bookshelf, circa 1946. In framing a view of the world and a Jewish identity for himself, he immersed himself in Bellow and Rosenfeld and took the enigmas of Kafka for personal mandates. He even touched base with Howe. And he has become, without the public self-congratulation that normally attends such arrivals, a leading literary anticommunist, though he has arrived at that position by his own routes (his involvement with Eastern European writers) and found expressions for it that are neither polemical nor predictable.

And yet, who can deny that the excesses Roth yielded to in *Portnoy's Complaint, Our Gang,* and *The Great American Novel* were sponsored by a historical moment in which they seemed valiant tokens of resistance to the discontents of civilization? Roth's traumas may have been uniquely his own, but who can doubt that his literary disburdenings in the late sixties were authorized by a culture of desublimation, the culture Lionel Trilling called "modernism in the streets"? Howe was not entirely wrong in taking Roth for a representative figure, insofar as Roth's own surges of anger and cries of pain were consonant with other surges and cries being heard in other quarters. There was indeed a rasping note in Roth's writing that irritated the abrasions Howe had suffered in the 1960s, leaving him bitter and peevish. Who could not be forgiven for taking Alex Portnoy's battle cry, "Let's Put the Id Back into Yid!" for a slogan out of Reich or Norman O. Brown, or for confounding SDS's Days of Rage in Chicago for Alex Portnoy's days of rage in the kitchen, the dining room, the bathroom, the bedroom, and finally the couch in *Portnoy's Complaint?*

But this is not an essay on Irving Howe, who has only a glancing relation to the major themes of the book. If it were, we would be bound to follow our intuition and take up the ironies inherent in his transformation from a fiery revolutionist to a nostalgic socialist, from a storm-bird of iconoclastic modernism to its curator, from an alienated Jewish son to a Yiddish scholar and keeper of his father's culture. We would be inclined to ponder the dialectics of filial prodigality and paternal authority, the chemistry of youthful vulnerability sublimed into midlife rigidity, the mental economy of conversion. At the risk of turning both men into cases, we would probe the *commedia Judaica* that both men have played with furious conviction and ask whether the issues Howe joined in chastising Roth, or those Roth has declaimed in provoking Howe, are issues at all or excuses for waging the brands of Jewish generational combat that Kafka sought to allegorize in his fables and Freud sought to interpret in dreams.

III. Kafka in Search of a Father

In this delectable comedy of fathers and sons, Roth has played his part more cunningly than Howe, for his image of himself as perennial Jewish son has composed from the start his basic polemical strategy: to court, cajole, and provoke from a position of ersatz weakness. That self image may also play into his attachment to Kafka, another Jewish son with a crippling relationship to fathers. "Marrying is barred to me," confesses Roth's Kafka to his father, in the essay-story "'I Always Wanted You to Admire My Fasting'; or, Looking at Kafka," "because it is your domain." But the sons in Roth's fiction differ from Kafka's in one crucial respect: it is not the father's power that condemns them to impotence and bachelorhood, but his weakness. A portion of the terror in Roth's fiction grows from the son's realization that his father is impotent. Roth may even be braced and energized by the condemnation of the Howes and the rabbis, for the father's enmity is preferable to his adoration. The overbearing father may be fought or he may be fled, but there is no escaping the ineffectual father, whose daily failure renews the son's guilt. "Others," confesses a fictional Philip Roth in the Kafka essay, "are crushed by paternal criticism—I find myself oppressed by his high opinion of me!" "Make my father a father," cries Lucy Nelson in *When She Was Good,* and she, a daughter, broadcasts this appeal on behalf of all the Roth sons, before and after.

Roth rewrites the opening sentence of Kafka's *The Metamorphosis* this way: "As Franz Kafka awoke one morning from uneasy dreams he found himself transformed in his bed into a father, a writer, and a Jew." This Kafka is no giant insect flailing jointed legs helplessly before him but a man with three afflictions: Jewishness, genius, and fatherhood, the last, the greatest affliction of all. Imagine a Kafka, or a Roth, trying to love that precocious spawn of his loins known as a son. "Keep him away from me," screams a young Philip Roth in the Kafka piece. Jake Portnoy's bowels answer in frozen rage from the pages of an earlier book. Paternity is a legal fiction in Roth's books, where sons and fathers turn out to be brothers under the skin, locked into generations by an accident of biology. What should Isaac do when Abraham drops the knife and lies down on the altar with him? The son's chief care in Roth's world is not to escape his father's wrath but to stanch his sentimentality; the last thing he wants to do is make his father cry.

With fatherhood in doubt, all other relationships are threatened. Relationships, in Roth's world, are promises of pain. Men and women are biological enemies, like wolves and sheep, cats and mice, who draw blood when they get together. Aunt Rhoda (in "Looking at Kafka") should count her blessings that Dr. Kafka's problem was revealed to her at that Atlantic City Hotel before she decided to commit marriage, for marriage to a man like that is a fate worse than loneliness. In Roth's world, love is a front for aggression, sex is an occasion for failure, childhood is tragedy, adulthood farce. The family, according to Roth, is the transmitter of symptoms. In such a world, to be a child is excruciating, while to be a parent is beyond imagining.

If Roth's books individually read like case histories, the profile of his career resembles a fever chart. It begins with a conventional fiction about straight-laced heroes who fail at some relationship or vital task and manifest their pain in violent symptoms, spontaneous outbreaks of anger, unreason, or vertigo. Mrs. Portnoy calls them "conniption fits." The early books, the *Goodbye Columbus* stories, *Letting Go,* and *When She Was Good,* with their repressed and driven characters, constituted a fiction of failed renunciation. Their heroes are all characters who repress desires which, as we might expect, refuse to go away and keep returning as compulsive and irrational outbursts. In *Letting Go,* the mutual renunciation of Gabe Wallach and Libby Herz (prompted by their mutual reading of *A Portrait of a Lady*) is prelude to six hundred pages of indecision (his), neurasthenia (hers), confusion, and sudden, explosive tantrums (theirs). The praise accorded to Willard Nelson in the opening sentence of *When She Was Good* tells us exactly what is wrong with him. "Not to be rich, not to be famous, not to be mighty, not even to be happy, but to be civilized— that was the dream of his life." (In a later book, *The Ghost Writer,* E. I. Lonoff follows those very sentiments to bitter conclusions.) A man who has renounced so much might find repose in a novel of manners—recall Trilling's John Laskell—but when Jamesian commandments are issued in a Roth novel, the snafu begins. When Roth hears the word *civilization,* he reaches for his discontents. Thus, in *When She Was Good,* Lucy Nelson, having learned from Grandpa Willard the virtues of small-town character armor, reaps its rewards when faced with the demands of pregnancy and abandonment. Her studied reaction-formations are exposed as useless, and she goes berserk with terror and righteousness.

Portnoy's Complaint advertises itself as Roth's emotional breakthrough, the book in which the Yid grapples with repression and lays claim to his id. An oppressive childhood is dragged into the light; wild sexual fantasies make their debut seemingly unguarded by tact or euphemism; the Jewish mother in all her ambiguous radiance replaces the father at stage center; the Jewish son caters himself bar mitzvahs of masturbation; food is revealed to be an agent of both repression and liberation; and eating turns out to have something to do with love and sex. The book ends with nothing less than the primal scream, all ninety-six a's and four h's of it. *Portnoy's Complaint* appears to deliver all the right confessions demanded of an analysis: confessions of bondage to the past and struggles against it, of secret humiliations and secret rages, of crimes against the family, of failures of the body and overcompensations of the will.

In the years immediately following *Portnoy,* Roth entertained us with a peppy choreography of breakthrough books and stories: "On the Air" (*New American Review* 10), a savage and barely controlled saga of one day in the life of Milton Lippmann, talent scout; *Our Gang,* a symbolic slaying of Richard Nixon; *The Breast,* a comic nightmare of a man's transformation into a female breast; " 'I Always Wanted You to Admire My Fasting'; or, Looking at Kafka," a lecture on Franz Kafka coupled with a fantasia on his misadventures in Newark as Philip Roth's Hebrew school teacher; *The Great American Novel,* a four-hundred-page Grossinger's routine employing baseball as a metaphor for the Holocaust; and *My Life as a Man,* a novel about marriage in the fifties. Up until this last book Roth's progress exhibited a common therapeutic form: the pre-*Portnoy* books were the documents of repression, the books immediately after it, witnesses to the return of the repressed. Where Roth began by giving us stoical characters who bore their misfortunes with the sullen nobility of the civilized until overtaken by panic, he later turned to suffusing his compositions with alarm. Where repression had been, there suddenly was rage; in lieu of neurotic symptoms we began to get documents of fury and mayhem.

Starting with *My Life as a Man* (1974) and continuing through *The Professor of Desire* (1977) and the Zuckerman trilogy: *The Ghost Writer* (1979), *Zuckerman Unbound* (1981), and *The Anatomy Lesson* (1983), Roth has produced a writing in which elements of the earlier two stages form an unstable amalgam. Calmer and more conventional in its narrative strategies than that of the breakthrough books, it is nonetheless suffused with their turmoil. If we didn't have *The Anatomy Lesson* to show us just how molten Roth's nerves were still, we might look upon these past ten years as the convalescent era. Certainly through *The Professor of Desire*, *The Ghost Writer*, and *Zuckerman Unbound*, Roth attempted to knit together the world he had shattered in his previous books. *The Anatomy Lesson*, however, with its brittle emotions, its conspicuous sense of injury, and its bursts of fury, gives notice that the process of shattering may not yet have run its course. It is not difficult to see a Hegelian pattern in all this, complete with thesis, antithesis, and synthesis, the last book suggesting that the synthesis hasn't quite taken hold or that a new cycle of reaction has begun to take shape.

IV. Where Ego Was There Id Shall Be

Taken together, as the profile of a man's life, the accumulated work comes into view as a sustained exercise in self-analysis on a scale unknown in American literature since Hawthorne, and Roth has the advantage of Hawthorne in his grasp of neurosis, being a student of both Kafka and Freud. Upon its appearance, *Portnoy's Complaint* was the most spectacular instance of Freudian fiction in postwar American literature, not only due to the boldness of its confessions, but also because of Dr. Spielvogel's summary diagnosis, which challenged readers with its crisp expertise. Alex Portnoy too is up to date on psychoanalytic theory and annotates his alienation with appropriate references to *The Standard Edition* of Freud's writing and *The Collected Papers*. We know that he had read "The Most Prevalent Form of Degradation in Erotic Life" and *Civilization and Its Discontents* and that he suffers from both. We see his furtive sexuality as a failed effort to gratify a clamorous, infantile id and a vigilant, righteous superego. Thus, according to Spielvogel:

> Acts of exhibitionism, voyeurism, fetishism, autoeroticism and oral coitus are plentiful; as a consequence of the patient's "morality," however, neither fantasy nor act issues in genuine sexual gratification, but rather in overriding feelings of shame and the dread of retribution, particularly in the form of castration.

That is a cogent and inclusive sentence and, in fact, the malady, stripped of its cultural paraphernalia and defensive wit, does make sense as a strategy for negotiating conflicts deep within. Moreover, contends Spielvogel, "Many of the symptoms can be traced to the bonds obtaining in the mother-child relationship." The good doctor has saved us some research here, though his labels, like most diagnostic commonplaces, are textbookish and preemptive, and if the analytic sections of *My Life as a Man* are any indication of what Spielvogel sounds like when under a full head of steam, we should be more appreciative of his silences in the earlier book. Still, he has the right idea: the fictional imitation of confession *is* confession, and we as readers have some duty to make sense of what we are being so painfully told.

To set the stage for an analysis of our own we have to set the table, for *Portnoy's Complaint* is an analysis and a vaudeville of the Jewish stomach. Food is to Jewish comedy and Jewish neurosis what drink is to Irish, though only Roth so far as I know has taken the full anthropological plunge into the ethnology of the Jewish digestive tract. Roth's Jews are not a people, a culture, nation, denomination, or persuasion; they are a tribe, which, after its own primitive fashion, obeys arbitrary taboos and performs strange rituals that look like obsessional symptoms. Roth possesses a lucid and unsentimental eye for the forms of irrational behavior, his own included. As he sees it, the kosher laws are as primitive as any Australian fetish or Papuan cargo cult, and the antagonism of milk and meat in the Jewish diet is something, not out of *Leviticus,* but out of *National Geographic.*

Portnoy's morality, not to mention his immorality, begins at the table. Here is *The Law* according to that Moses of Manhattan, the Assistant Commissioner of Human Opportunity for the City of New York, aka Alex Portnoy. "Let the *goyim* sink *their* teeth into whatever lowly creature crawls and grunts across the face of the dirty earth, we will not contaminate our humanity thus." This is the same Portnoy who can say to a woman on the street, "At least let me eat your pussy." It is in that spectrum of possibilities between noble renunciation and insane lapping that the minute moral discriminations of Jewish life come into being, quite as if the word *moral* came down etymologically from the word *oral.*

When a sin is committed in the Portnoy home it is more likely to involve gluttony than lechery, though in the muddled circuits of a complicated and unreliable memory, primal crimes often become confused. "A terrible act has been committed, and it has been committed by either my father or me. The wrongdoer, in other words, is one of the two members of the family who owns a penis. Okay. So far so good. Now: did he fuck between those luscious legs the gentile cashier from the office, or have I eaten my sister's chocolate pudding?" This confusion never does get resolved. In the infantile moral system of this household, shared by young and old alike, pudding and pussy may be equally taboo. Food, of course, is the first medium of love and authority for all of us, and where it retains its original meaning, as it does among the Portnoys, young sinners may be heard to confess: "I'm eight years old and chocolate pudding happens to get me hot." It is understandable then that the table is the field on which Alex's battle for manhood is fought and lost. In this oral, anal, phallic world, the toilet and the bed are also put to strategic uses but they are mere backup systems, and by the time Alex has mastered them, the war is over. Rearguard actions still rage, however, and Alex's prime weapons are all the tricks in his stubborn oral trade: "having a mouth on him," refusing to eat, eating *chazerai* (or lobster or pussy), feeding his parents in turn, or, and herein shines forth his desperate genius, masturbating into his family's dinner.

The politics of food and guilt at the Jewish table have given rise to a unique taboo: *chazerai*. *Chazerai* is not necessarily unkosher food formally proscribed by the dietary codes; neither the pizza nor the cupcake is anathematized by name in *Leviticus*. But *chazerai*, while not *trayf* de jure is certainly so de facto. It is cheap, processed, mass-produced snack food, gotten outside the home, behind one's mother's back. Its true purpose, as every Jewish mother knows, is to ruin her son's appetite for dinner. Thus, the eating of snacks after school is a betrayal, and the boy who stops for a burger and fries at fourteen will, at thirty, be stopping after work for a shikse, thus ruining his appetite.

For the son, *chazerai* means freedom, sexual freedom, thus Alex Portnoy's dietary analysis of the difference between himself and his libidinous friend Smolka. "He lives on Hostess cupcakes and his own wits. I get a hot lunch and all the inhibitions thereof." But for ultimate aphrodisiacal virtue there is the lobster, a terror beyond *chazerai*, an unambiguous threat to sanity and life. Sophie Portnoy's historic bout with lobster, paralysis, and an Irish insurance salesman is textbook hysteria. "See how I'm holding my fingers?" she instructs her son, a neophyte in primitive religious phenomena, "I was throwing up so hard, they got stiff just like this, like I was *paralyzed. . . .*"

Sophie's symptons are prophecies for her son. Within an hour of eating a lobster with brother-in-law Morty at Sheepshead Bay, Alex has his cock out on the 107 bus, "aimed at a *shikse*." It is to protect him from such madness that a mother must keep up her dietary vigilance. Naturally this education in taboo-by-diet falls to the mother, for she understands better than anyone how food, love, power, and possession are related.*

Is it any wonder then that this same Sophie invites Jake's new cashier from the office for a nice, home-cooked Jewish meal? Hardly, for once Anne McCaffrey has dined chez Portnoy she is hooked, and not on Jake but on his wonderful *haimische* family. "This is your real Jewish chopped liver, Anne. Have you ever had real Jewish chopped liver before?" So much for that affair, for if lobster is the Spanish fly of the Jews, real chopped liver is their saltpeter, the all-inhibiting cold hors d'oeuvre of the constipated husband. Could Jake be slipping it to that new cashier on the side? Not after that meal. For this is a totem feast, and that is *his* liver they're passing around. We needn't wonder that a man in such a fix should suffer from a recalcitrant bowel. A battle lost at one end of the alimentary track may spell trouble at the other end. Jake Portnoy's inability to move his bowels at will is his brand of impotence, and we needn't guess at what his wife has in mind in boasting that she could have married "the biggest manufacturer of mustard in New York."

So, it is not just a happy conjunction of libido and opportunity that sets Alex to violating that fresh liver behind the billboard *on his way to a bar mitzvah lesson.* It is another symbol of Alex's private war. What price such conquest? To have your mother serve up the conquest two hours later, healthy as milk, dry as matzo, warm and safe as your own Jewish childhood. In other words, defeat.

If Alex is telling the truth—and who would invent a cock-and-liver story like that?——his mother's intentions are plain and menacing. She wants nothing less than complete annexation of her son, the full possession of and control over his manhood, and she'll have it by gaining command over the table, the maternal equivalent of taking the high ground. That is why mealtime is the prime time for Alex to make that libidinal lunge for the toilet, for as long as he dines at home, his mouth belongs to mama (because mama she treats it so well?). When his manhood droops, he seeks refuge in the sure successes of boyhood love, determined to win praise at least as a good eater. Similarly, in *My Life as a Man*, it is appropriate that Nathan Zuckerman tries to face down his boyish disgust and demonstrate to Lydia Ketterer that he is a good man

---

*Roth isn't the first Jewish writer to make this connection. Isaac Rosenfeld, in an essay entitled "Adam and Eve on Delancy Street," argued that the Jewish food taboos are also sexual taboos, and Roth, in writing *Portnoy's Complaint*, simply adopted and dramatized Rosenfeld's argument.

and a proper lover by eating her. The ability to eat anything is one of the many definitions of manhood that Roth's heroes try on for size.

That food and love should be so consistently mistaken for each other is no mystery. The connection is built into our mammalian heritage, and the job of learning the difference is an ordinary childhood task that we all perform more or less badly. The natural history of that task is spelled out by Roth in two of his titles, *The Breast* and *Letting Go*, which stand for the primal situations between which his characters must strike a modus vivendi. For these characters, letting go is a dire need, for entrapment, in the form of either captivity or self-repression, is their common condition. Alex Portnoy's final scream is a spasm of letting go that is native to the Roth novel, where the tantrum is a moral statement. In *My Life as a Man*, Peter Tarnopol's tantrum is a moment of truth: it finds him donning his wife's panties and bra in order to show her, he later explains, that "I wear the panties in this family." In *Portnoy*, it constitutes Alex's final statement, the last desperate demand before Spielvogel interrupts to commence the analysis.

Holding on and letting go are terrors because they first were wishes, and it is in the struggle between those wishes that Alex is paralyzed. That conflict, nourished by a Jewish family that does not itself know when to let go, can ramify into the alimentary insanity of Alex Portnoy's love life. Every odd libidinal adventure of his is an attempt to gratify those two needs and to be a man and a baby at the same time. Recall his fantasies of Thereal McCoy, the perfect prostitute, who calls him "Big Boy" and offers up a nipple the size and shape of a tollhouse cookie. What more could the infantile rebel ask for than milk and cookies on the same dish? In the jungle of love it is eat or be eaten.

Every character of Roth's is struck with this obligation, to satisfy deep-seated but contrary needs at once: to grow up and to regress, to let go and to hold on, to be autonomous and dependent, a man and a child. Totalists that they are, they cannot find and occupy a human middle ground on which self-reliance need not be isolation or love entrapment. Alex Portnoy steers clear of love by laying sexual traps for himself, insuring that his experiments in love will always end in defeat. His episodes of sexual boredom and his bouts with impotence are strategically timed. It is Peter Tarnopol who, seemingly on Alex's behalf, tries to break out of the circle of sexual isolation by getting married, and manages, not unpredictably, to marry a woman he fears and despises. To be sure, Maureen Johnson is a fearsome woman, but that is why Peter wants her. He married her in order to injure her, and while any woman will do for that, it is a nice point of conscience that she should seem to deserve what she is bound to get.

This same dilemma underlies that odd little book *The Breast,* which Roth wrote some time between *Portnoy's Complaint* and *My Life as a Man* and which reads like a footnote to both. In fact, it is my guess that it is an appendix to *Portnoy's Complaint* and one of those dreams that Alex Portnoy must have produced in analysis but somehow failed to report to us. The book's hero, David Kepesh, is something of a primary process version of Alex, his repressed infant perhaps, his latent content. Surely, the process of unmanning that began with the wandering of Alex Portnoy's ball around the inguinal canal—his testicular insurrection—is a prelude to David Kepesh's hormonal revolution. Kepesh appears to be the disguised fulfillment of Alex's most primitive desire, to undo his ill-starred birth altogether in favor of a generational merger, to become, not just an infant, but his own mother in order to raise himself. Such merger permits him to hold on and let go at the same time, to *have* his mother without *having to deal* with her and to bring himself up according to his own laws. In such a blissful state, the dreamer is at last on his own, self-contained, androgynous, and pleasantly autoerotic, indulging himself forever at the sacred found of life without two sets of dishes. (The breast confounds the kosher laws by being *both milchig and flayshig.*) As a breast, moreover, *he* should do the feeding. But since this dream is also a story by Roth and this fantasy ostensibly a true story, its fulfillment is bound to incur a penalty. Luck would have it that the dream of a mammary Eden is also the nightmare of tender imprisonment and the fairy tale of self-sufficiency the cautionary lesson of total isolation. Kepesh suffers both extremes at once—the total absorption into the mother leaves him more isolated and alienated than ever before. Helpless as an infant, he must be fed, intravenously at that, an ordeal of forced nutrition beyond anything that happens to Alex Portnoy. Bravely, Kepesh takes his medicine.

Reminiscent though it may be of Kafka's "The Metamorphosis," this situation has small dramatic potential. Cocooned in his garden of flesh, Kepesh can only lie there and suffer and, in the end, grow ironic, demanding, and tiresome. Accordingly, while *Portnoy's Complaint* is a protest novel and a brief in behalf of letting go, *The Breast* is a conservative fable about the virtues of holding on. It hands us the dilemma of civilization and its discontents at the most primitive infantile level and comes out foursquare for self-control. Alex, with his temper, is a tiger of wrath; Kepesh, with his Shakespeare and his Rilke, is a horse of instruction. But he may have no choice; all he can do is want, and want, and behave himself when he doesn't get. Unlike Portnoy, who is too busy being hysterical (or is it vivid?) to pay attention to the finer points of social etiquette, David Kepesh speaks in perfect sentences, as if his rage and fear were all the more manageable if his grammar and style were sedate and orderly. He is exceptionally well bred. That may be why *The Breast* is so unsettling a book, for to us, Kepesh's "mature" prescriptions of a daily anesthetic to reduce his polymorphous appetites reinforced by therapeutic doses of Shakespeare seem like a strategy for a meager endurance. We want a magical release from breasthood, and Kepesh gives us, English majors all, the ersatz magic of poetry. We want the primal scream, and he lectures on Mr. Reality. He is unique among the likes of Ozzie Freedman, Gabriel Wallach, Lucy Nelson, Alex Portnoy, Peter Tarnopol, and Nathan Zuckerman; he never throws a tantrum. Mammary or no he is an overachiever, a good boy, a mad professor, and a cockeyed gentleman.*

V. Life as a Man

The therapeutic novel in America has been, as often as not, the divorce novel, the miseries of the marriage bed being to modern fiction what the anticipated delights were once to Elizabethan comedy. To the contemporary writer, the dramaturgy of courtship and union is not half so appealing as that of divorce, and between the chapel and the courtroom falls the analysis. Roth's *My Life as a Man* bears something of the same relation to this writing that *Herzog* and *The Last Analysis* bear to Bellow's and *After the Fall* to Arthur Miller's. It is a testament of freedom, a memorial to trauma, a report card on psychoanalysis, and an exorcism of the ex-wife.

Peter Tarnopol of *My Life as a Man* is thirty-four-year-old writer— author of the celebrated *A Jewish Father*—widower, neurotic, narcissist, teacher, and outpatient who has squandered his talent and manhood in a marriage that has left him frantic, suspicious, over his head in debt and guilt, and barely able to salvage from this wreckage material for a book. That book is *My Life as a Man* itself, a novel in three parts: two stories or

---

**The Breast seems to be a favorite of Roth's, for he rewrote and republished it in 1980. A quick perusal suggests that the new edition is not all that different and that only minor alterations of phrasing distinguish the second edition from the first. An amateur at analysis might be forgiven for imagining that the real significance of this event was Roth's desire to have a second breast.

"useful fictions," "Salad Days" and "Courting Disaster (or Serious in the Fifties)," and an autobiographical novella, "My True Story," a confession of a young writer's marital desperation cleverly rendered as a "True Confession." Due partly to the ironbound divorce laws of New York State and partly to the tenacity and cunning of Maureen Johnson Tarnopol, formerly Mezik, formerly Walker, Tarnopol's marriage could be dissolved only by Maureen's death. It had been a trumped-up affair from the start, founded upon a false pregnancy, a faked urine sample, and a phony abortion, for which a Jewish boyfriend had paid through the nose. Three years into this marriage, in the heat of the daily brawl, this one over Tarnopol's affair with an undergraduate student, Maureen feigns a suicide attempt and threatens to expose her professor-husband to the university, and he reacts by firing off the last salvo in his emotional arsenal, a tantrum. He tears off his clothes and dons Maureen's underclothes. Confronted by her husband feminized and in tears, Maureen relents and confesses her original sin and, as such things go in stalled marriages, turns her confession into an instrument of further coercion: "If you forgive me for the urine, I'll forgive you for your mistress," a quid pro quo that only a mugger could love. Now, 1967, four years after Tarnopol's flight from Maureen and a year after Maureen's death in a car crash, he is finally writing the novel, episode by bloody episode, in the monastic isolation of the Quahsay writer's retreat in Vermont.

Like *The Breast, My Life as a Man* is largely a dissertation on entrapment, a disclosure of how a man can find himself so irredeemably beyond the pleasure principle just when he had so much pleasure to expect. As Roth conducts it, the inquiry is less philosophical than accusatory. The two forms of inquiry differ as "how?" differs from "who?" or a Bellow novel differs from a Roth novel, for where Moses Herzog and Artur Sammler presume evolutionary conditions behind their predicaments and pose such questions as "What is this life?" and "What is the heart of man?" the likes of Portnoy, Kepesh, and Tarnopol presume transgression, guilt, and blame, and tend to ask, "Why is *she* doing *that* to *me*?" and "Where did I screw up?" Tarnopol is quick to accuse the culture. He was deceived into making that vain and calamitous gesture of a marriage, he believes, by the moral climate of the fifties, in which decade,

> Decency and Maturity, a young man's "seriousness," were at issue precisely because it was thought to be the other way around: in that the great world was so obviously a man's, it was only within marriage that an ordianry woman could hope to find equality and dignity. Indeed, we were led to

believe by the defenders of womankind of our era that we were exploiting and degrading the women we *didn't* marry, rather than the ones we did.

Augmenting that moral climate for a young English graduate student was the great tradition of literary high seriousness, a tradition epitomized for Tarnopol by an epigram from Thomas Mann that he had appended to *A Jewish Father* (and Roth himself had used in *Letting Go*): "All actuality is deadly earnest, and it is morality itself that, one with life, forbids us to be true to the guileless unrealism of our youth." Such a courtship of cultural superegos has always been the English major's stock-in-trade, and Tarnopol suffers an English major's catastrophe—to have been ruined by the tight-lipped austerities of the great Protestant tradition and by those smothering lessons about duty, renunciation, and endurance that adorn a literary education. "To live properly," saith the superego, especially one nurtured upon Dostoevsky, Conrad, Hawthorne, Leavis, Trilling, and Irving Howe, "is to suffer." The great dialogue of Western Man says precious little about the morality of pleasure.

The ubiquitous Spielvogel, who is Tarnopol's analyst too, sees it differently. What Tarnopol had taken for cultural coercion, he sees as the victim's collusion, as the "acting out" of his ambivalence, narcissism, and libidinized aggression, which he had initially directed toward a "phallic mother" but eventually displaced onto his wife. What Spielvogel sees is not a man victimized by an era that placed a premium on self-sacrifice and moral accountability but a tactical arrangement between two people out to enjoy some upscale misery. So taken is Spielvogel with his own diagnosis and the insight it gives him into the dynamics of creativity that he publishes a paper on it while Tarnopol is still under his care.

Behind Spielvogel's jargon about libidinized aggression and phallic mothers is the suggestion that the marriage had its purposes for Tarnopol and that Maureen's duplicity not only posed a threat to him but opened up opportunities as well. On Maureen's part, the signs of wanting something more than "true love" are there from the start: she courts punishment with all the conviction of a journeyman welterweight out to prove he can still take a punch. Even before the marriage, when she attacks Peter with her purse and he threatens in his harmless way, "CLIP ME WITH THAT, MAUREEN, AND I'LL KILL YOU," she responds, "Do it! Kill me! Some man's going to—why not a 'civilized' one like you!"

Though readers are in no position to disentangle the byzantine strategies of a marriage gone sour, they may observe that Maureen's death plea is in earnest and that Peter, in marrying her, had homed in on her self-destructiveness. Guilt, submission, intimidation, and sudden moral collapse had all played their part in leading Tarnopol to the altar, and yet one suspects that such marriages tend to befall a special class of man: those who bear a grudge against women. Maureen had an instinct for finding such men: Mezik, the saloonkeeper who made her go down on his buddy while he watched, and Walker, the homosexual who broke his promise to give up boys. Tarnopol has more in common with such company than he imagines. All three found in Maureen the right type of woman, one for whom their misogyny could seem a just and reasonable hatred. Indeed, the circumstances surrounding Maureen's death are ambiguous enough to suggest that it is Walker at last who kills her, for he was driving the car in which she died.

The news of Maureen's death has hardly arrived when Peter finds himself contemplating his newest problem, girlfriend Susan McCall, who, until then, had merely been a sweet burden: a helpless, mildly neurotic, leggy heiress who is incapable of an orgasm but cooks a marvelous *blanquette de veau* and spikes her fruit salads with kirsch. In short, she is not morally challenging enough for an aspiring young hunger artist who must take off for Quahsay and sexual quarantine, to a life of hard work, regular hours, calisthenics, a hot breakfast, and a simple boy's lunch, to relive the easy ascetic triumphs of those salad days when to finish your homework and clean your plate were the only evidence needed that you were a good boy.

If *My Life as a Man* offers less immediate gratification than *Portnoy,* that may be because it is a more labored and more intricately woven book than the spontaneous *Portnoy* and the ad-libbed *Our Gang* and *The Great American Novel.* Its mixed styles and shifting perspectives reflect thick infoldings and elaborate overdubbings—they reflect seven years of work and doubt. But for all its intricacy and "art," the book strikes deeper than *Portnoy,* whose formulas for the sources of Alex Portnoy's complaint come down to a couchful of theories and notions from Freud, Otto Fenichel, Isaac Rosenfeld, and others, brilliantly applied though they may be. *My Life as a Man* is a book of uncertainties which suggests that the truth, if one exists, lies beyond the scope of psychoanalysis in its customary forms. *The mother* scarcely makes an appearance; *the phallic mother* is only a figment of Spielvogel's imagination. The point of Tarnopol's quarrel with Spielvogel over the latter's interpretation of his truant sexuality is that there are no privileged explanations, only points of view. Spielvogel is granted one, Tarnopol's brother Morris another, sister Joan yet another, Maureen still another. Even Frannie Glass of J. D. Salinger's *Frannie and Zooey* is permitted a neurasthenic word on the subject. By means of his "useful fictions," Tarnopol plies himself with alternatives, making *My Life as a Man* a lesson in the varieties of interpretive experience. The book may even be understood as Roth's answer to Spielvogel, his explanation of why psychoanalysis finally fails as a basic and comprehensive guide to motives and why fiction, with its freedom, its variousness, and its possibility, is far more faithful to life than case history. No single interpretation, the book warns us, will explain the mess Tarnopol is in, and nothing less than a symposium on the subject can begin to approach it.

In *My Life as a Man,* Tarnopol's, and the reader's, doubts about Spielvogel's judgment and about the integrity of the entire analytic process are brought to a head by Spielvogel's paper on Tarnopol, "Creativity: The Narcissism of the Artist," in which the latter is thinly disguised as "a successful Italian-American poet in his forties." Tarnopol's dismay at the essay stems largely from the fact that while the history is familiar, if distorted, the interpretation strikes him as entirely fanciful. "I could not read a sentence in which it did not seem to me that the observation was off, the point missed, the nuance blurred—in short, the evidence rather munificently distorted so as to support a narrow and unilluminating thesis at the expense of the ambiguous and perplexing actuality."

Spielvogel's analysis *is* couched in a distressing jargon. Adverting to Tarnopol's "enormous ambivalence" about leaving his wife, his "castration anxiety vis-à-vis a phallic mother figure," his "acting out with other women," and "reducing all women to masturbatory sexual objects," it so reduces Tarnopol's tangled motives to catch-phrases that Tarnopol himself is filled with wonder that the man to whom he has poured out his soul could conceive of that outpouring in so mechanical a fashion. There is simply no relationship between that language and his life, and Tarnopol, his confidence shattered, is poised to forsake analysis for Quahsay and isolation to apply to himself the one therapy he can trust for nuance, if not results: writing.

Indeed, the distinction *My Life as a Man* enjoys as a modern psychological novel lies in the analysand's battle with analysis by refusing the ritualized explanations offered by Spielvogel. "Does your wife remind you of your mother?" Spielvogel asks Tarnopol in one of their first sessions, causing Tarnopol to balk and number all the differences between them, an enumeration that benefits the mother. The scenes of angry rejoinder between Tarnopol and Spielvogel, though not always the freshest writing in *My Life as a Man,* cast a critical light on psychoanalysis itself: on the reductiveness of its diagnostic terminology and its power to intimidate the skeptical patient simply by charging him with resistance. Initially, upon getting wind of Spielvogel's bias, Tarnopol challenges Spielvogel's textbook interpretations, but as time passes he begins to question his own recollections of a blessed childhood, calling up in their stead "rather Dickensian recollections of my mother as an overwhelming and frightening person."

A charge commonly levied against psychoanalysis that it bullies the patient into accepting interpretations that violate memory is tellingly illustrated here, as Tarnopol learns in analysis to dislike his mother, even as he suspects that the diagnosis Spielvogel has given him "revealed more about some bête noire of his than of my own." And yet, despite that realization, the desperate need to be cured rather than any conscious assent to the doctor's findings keeps Tarnopol in analysis for three years and drives him through bouts of sullenness with his mother whom, until entering analysis, he believed he adored.

This episode reflects back on *Portnoy's Complaint,* a book whose very slant on Alex Portnoy's childhood takes its cues from psychoanalysis. The myth on which the book rests—when in pain, *cherchez la mère*—is now suggested to be a delusion foisted upon Alex Portnoy by his analyst, the selfsame Spielvogel. *My Life as a Man* is, it seems, the first of several novels written contra-*Portnoy,* a son's plea that it was Freudian doctrine or the Zeitgeist or the great books that led him astray, not his mother.

My Life as a Man is, all in all, Roth's best book. Its prose is pungent and aquiver with the asperities of a sour marriage, the jargon of the clinic, the argot of the street. Roth reproduces the language around him better than any American writer today, and when he is listening well his prose is gratefully free of his characteristic mannerisms: those of precocious insight and those of high purpose. And it is the sensitivity to language, I believe, that explains the final assessment of psychoanalysis in this book, for it is language at last that drives a wedge between Tarnopol and Spielvogel and sends the latter back to Quahsay and his typewriter for a session of autotherapy that may produce, if not good feelings, at least good books. Spielvogel, in contributing his "useful fiction" to the symposium on Tarnopol, violates not just a code of professional ethics but one of style. The analysis goes swimmingly until the analyst bursts into the artist's medium and reveals his own inadequacy with words. By breaking into prose, the one domain over which his patient is master, he demystifies himself and de-authorizes his craft. The mask of omnicompetence is off and the writer/patient, finding himself a character in a routine case history that goes from formula to banal formula with dull predictability, must quit the analysis. He'd given Spielvogel his best lines and Spielvogel had botched them. In *My Life as a Man,* Roth takes his lines back and takes charge of his own story, laboring to show how, with sensitivity, imagination, and a flair for *le mot juste,* it might properly be told.

VI. The Convalescence, or The Man Who Got Away

By contrast, *The Professor of Desire* (1977) is a mopping-up operation, a recapitulation of second-hand themes at reduced levels of panic. It is a transition piece between the mayhem-filled breakthrough books and the relatively modulated *The Ghost Writer,* a convalescence novel, that tracks the flight of an emotion from illness to health and features a hero who is discharged from analysis, not because he has successfully completed therapy but because he no longer needs it. Though Kafka and entrapment crop up as motifs in *The Professor of Desire,* the book finally puts away Kafkaesque determinism and testifies to the medicinal properties of simple love, and while Kepesh is haunted by transformations to come, *The Professor of Desire* on its own terms gives reason to believe that there are second acts in Jewish-American lives.

David Alan Kepesh, in a pre-breast incarnation, experiences his bleak marital strife with Helen Baird, a Southern California coed manqué who had spent seven years as an international seductress and femme fatale before returning home to marry, and torment, a young Jewish English professor. The marriage, the affliction, the conviction that fate possesses an imagination not unlike Franz Kafka's are tediously familiar to the reader of Roth: they are the threads of domestic Sturm und Drang that draw *The Professor of Desire* into the company of *Letting Go, When She was Good,* and *My Life as a Man* as a novel of that magnificent Roth obsession: marriage. What is new, however, is the countertheme, which finds Kepesh being rescued from his agony and his impotence by Claire Ovington, a warm, patient, doting woman of twenty-four, whose very physicality provides him, as if by sheer weight, with the emotional ballast he lacks. Peter Tarnopol may justly complain to Spielvogel that his wife does *not* remind him of his mother, but even the staunchest antagonist to Freudian doctrine is bound to observe in Claire a decidely maternal addition to David Alan Kepesh's life. *The Professor of Desire* makes scant sense unless we assent to the proposition that Kepesh is plucked from depression and released from psychoanalysis by expert mothering.

The Professor of Desire, then, is a novel of rebirth, that Bellovian theme. Roth's version of it, however, could not be more different, for where

Bellow's characters are reborn to themselves and stake out their new lives as isolates and even, as in *The Last Analysis,* as enemies of the family, a Roth character is reborn to love and brought back into the family. Through his love of Claire, Kepesh is also reunited with his father, who discovers in Claire a lifeline to his son. What Kafka, what Bellow, could have conjured up such a scene as the one in this book that finds the Jewish father embracing in both arms the prodigal son and prodigal son's shikse girlfriend with tears of appreciation gleaming in his eyes. What ever happened to alienation? To Kafka? This is borscht, served with Wonder Bread, perhaps, but borscht all the same. *The Professor of Desire* signals Roth's turn from outrage to *poshlost* and from Kafka to Catskill, where all trials are resolved in sobs of forgiveness. But if *The Professor of Desire* is Yiddish theater, it is Yiddish theater suburbanized, eroticized, and brought up to date by sweet dreams of healing miscegenation.

It is noteworthy that the books of convalescence that depict the Roth hero as getting better should also feature a turn toward the illnesses of history. History replaces individual pathology in these books, and the basic strategy of postwar fiction is reversed. *The Professor of Desire* and, more centrally, *The Ghost Writer* are history-laden books: the Jewish past weighs heavily upon them. In *The Professor of Desire,* the past is implied through the metaphor of Kafka; in *The Ghost Writer* it breaks through in Nathan Zuckerman's dream that a young woman whom he meets at the house of E. I. Lonoff is in actuality Anne Frank. Kafka, it seems, does dual service for Roth, standing as a metaphor for marital entrapment and sexual failure in some writing (see " 'I Always Wanted You to Admire My Fasting,' or Looking At Kafka" and *The Breast)* and elsewhere as a metaphor for life under totalitarianism.

But in *The Professor of Desire,* the shift of gears from the personal to the historical is incomplete: the novel seems to have been conceived in one frame of mind and completed in another. *The Professor of Desire* is a not a novel but an assemblage of moments and reflections, some of them flat, others rising to crescendos of tenderness. Themes rise but never converge, and we never know for certain what Herbie Bratasky, Kepesh's boyhood idol who is a *tummler* at Abe Kepesh's Hungarian Royale resort in the Catskills and did "Petomaine" routines for David Kepesh's private delectations, has to do with Helen Baird or Claire Ovington or the mystique of Kafka or with what appears to be the book's grand theme: Kepesh's initiation into love.[11]

The Professor of Desire is Roth's tenderest book, the one in which he takes the greatest risks of love. It dispenses almost entirely with irony, crisis, moral intricacy, and the comic strategies of self-defeat, and attempts to make a simple statement of the power of tenderness to mend what is broken in a life. But Roth as a writer is not a practiced hand at sweetness and for the most part doesn't know how to package it as anything but effusion. The book stumbles over its own gratitude. Tenderness only becomes charged with imagination when it is the father, rather than Claire, upon whom it is lavished. Abe Kepesh, widower and retired owner of Kepesh's Hungarian Royale resort, is the ubiquitous, voluble Roth father, whose fears and obsessions all wrapped in a charming immigrant naiveté, come pouring forth in an unrelenting stream of blessings and non sequiturs, pushcart nostrums and dizzy flights of diaspora fancy. He has a warm heart that secretes affection—even if you do not prick him he bleeds love. He and Claire, creatures of untutored love, are spontaneously drawn together, recognizing in each other the simplicity of heart with which each is endowed.

Simplicity of heart! What in the world is that doing in a Roth novel, where doubt, unreason, cunning, and panic are the stocks-in-trade of all characters, all *except* the father, who is always, everywhere, untainted? In a fallen world, he is the prelapsarian patriarch, a bewildered Adam who has shlepped innocently into the wrong garden and knows no more of evil than the failure of his own business. Through the years, in many books, from *Portnoy's Complaint* through *The Breast* (where Abe Kepesh is ostensibly the same) through the marvelous story " 'I Always Wanted You to Admire My Fasting'; or Looking at Kafka" to *The Professor of Desire*, this portrait of paternity-with-a-human face has been the counterweight to the Kafkaesque nightmares of entrapment and impotence that these Roth sons invariably suffer. For though the father is himself trapped and hemmed in, he meets his fate with dignity and provides the distraught son with an emotional safety valve. The love between them would seem to go deep. In later books, *The Ghost Writer* and *Zuckerman Unbound,* their bond of blood and wacky conversation which amounts to verbal love will unravel, but up through *The Professor of Desire*, it will prove to be the most powerful and sentimental bond of all, making all others, including those of sexual love, seem fragile and tentative by comparison.

Hegel's parable of the honest soul giving way in the modern world to the disintegrated consciousness finds its image in Roth in the simple father raising the neurotic son who then struggles to get back to a lost and elusive simplicity. But even as Kepesh remarks on his great fortune in having found Claire and contentment, he awakes from bad dreams filled with portents of disasters to come and lets us know that contentment is only provisional, if only because, we may surmise having read this book, it provides him with too little material.

Perhaps this book is a boundary marker for Roth's talents, an indication of what his imagination can*not* encompass, for there does not seem to be enough aggression or despair or irony in Kepesh's predicament to bring into play Roth's full talent, a talent so completely keyed to incipient panic that it appears to be the imaginative equivalent of Georg Simmel's definition of a highly developed culture: a crisis constantly held back. One finally sees *The Professor of Desire* as a book between books, an unfinished project, a rough beast, its hour come round at last, slouching toward Zuckerman and a trilogy.

VII. Epilogue: Zuckerman III

> Like a patient etherized upon a table.
> —T. S. Eliot

If Roth's books are not precisely autobiographies, neither are they fictions in quite the same manner that Shakespeare's plays or Dickens's novels are fictions. They are, rather, fables of identity, variations upon the theme of the self designed to heighten and refine essential elements, highlight basic terms of being, and dramatize recurring conflicts. "He used to wonder how all the billions who didn't write could take the daily blizzard," muses Zuckerman in *The Anatomy Lesson*, "all that beset them, such a saturation of the brain, and so little of it known or named. If he wasn't cultivating hypothetical Zuckermans he really had no more means than a fire hydrant to decipher his existence." These fables are experiences laundered in the pools of the imagination and given form, so that each Roth novel, for all its invention, develops a fairly limited idea, one that can be captured, at times, in a single phrase. We might call *The Ghost Writer* a fable of the artist as a martyr to language; *Zuckerman Unbound,* a fable of the artist as a martyr to his fame; *The Anatomy Lesson,* one of the artist as a martyr to his critics. (And, might not *My Life as a Man* be the artist as a martyr to marriage; *The Breast,* the man as a martyr to his own desires; *Portnoy's Complaint,* the boy as a martyr to the family; and *The Great American Novel,* the team as a martyr to history?) None of these books is a perfectly neat rendering of an idea, and yet the ease with which such captions come to mind does suggest two things about the turn of Roth's imagination: that for all its wild improvisations it tends to be thesis-bound and that it is prodded into invention by feelings of martyrdom.

The censure Roth has endured has played into that sense of martyrdom, and it stands to reason that he would periodically bow to the chorus and tailor his books to humor it, or worse, to plead the case that he was, all along, not so frightening a fellow as his books let on but just an author plying his trade. It was also inevitable, given his image of himself as a man torn between his ethical impulses and his appetites, that he would hush the unsocialized self for a moment to permit his more measured and circumspect inclinations to have their say, even if the voice in which they spoke was shaking with silent laughter. Thus it was, I suspect, that *The Ghost Writer* was conceived, a book in which Roth affected a studied modulation of voice that muted the trademarks of his personal style: the brashness, the mordant wit, the self-advancement. His reward for such a sacrifice was a quieting of the gallery and a modicum of critical respect that had previously eluded him. That Roth, having courted the critics' deference is determined to live without it is demonstrated in his most recent novel (as of 1984), *The Anatomy Lesson,* in which he explodes in rage against his Jewish antagonists, the elders of Zion, and then impales Zuckerman upon a Jewish gravestone, breaking his jaw and demonstrating conclusively to the kibbitzers at *Commentary* that they were right about him all along.

In *The Ghost Writer* a twenty-three-year-old Jewish writer, already on the way to becoming anathema to his parents and their middle-class Jewish community because of his story "Higher Education," which hung family wash out in public, seeks the advice, counsel, and patronage of E. I. Lonoff, a novelist-recluse who lives in a retreat in the Berkshires and covets no life other than to write his elegant fables unto the nth draft and to turn sentences around and around until he has gotten them right. Lonoff is a martyr to words; he is their master but also their captive, and his freedom in Connecticut is more apparent than real.

Upon first stepping into Lonoff's retreat Zuckerman is struck by its prevailing civility and composure and decides, as well a young man from Newark might, "This is how I will live." What he believes he sees is a life pared down for work and stripped of inessentials, including inessential passions. And so it is, though such a life has its penalties. Lonoff has either repressed the fire in him or has no fire to repress. He is a man with "autumn in his heart and spectacles on his nose"—Isaac Babel's definition of the Jewish writer. As another character in *The Ghost Writer* observes, he is as "unimpressive as he is unimpressed." This lack of a spark is intolerable to the women in his life, and during the course of Zuckerman's visit Lonoff's wife, who "cannot take any more moral fiber," darts off into the Berkshire winter, while Lonoff's student assistant, Amy Bellette (whom Zuckerman dreams might be Anne Frank) leaves in disappointment that Lonoff will not elope with her to Florence. Lonoff does one thing only: "I turn sentences around. That's my life. I write a sentence and then I turn it around. Then I look at it and I turn it around again." It occurs to the reader, though not to the starstruck Zuckerman, that Lonoff's studied composure is a symptom of vast egotism, and that to be unimpressive as he is unimpressed is to be so full of himself that nothing can penetrate his shield of self-conceit. As a Reichian would say, Lonoff is ferociously armored and primed to either suffer explosions or to provoke them in others, which is precisely what he does in this book. Whatever other blunders Zuckerman commits in the novels subsequent to *The Ghost Writer,* he does not become a protégé of E. I. Lonoff; he is too turbulent, too hot-blooded, for that.

The Ghost Writer is widely praised as Roth's masterwork, the book in which he withdrew sufficiently from his own irritations to compose a stirring little tableau of the writer's vocation and some of its liabilities: Nathan Zuckerman's first encounter with the voices of disapproval from his own community and Lonoff's martyrdom to his own Jamesian canons of renunciation. But in controlling his instinct for complaint, Roth also placed his gift for mad improvisation into escrow and created in Lonoff a saint of prohibition whose sainthood is most admirable from afar. Lonoff secretes renunciations the way an assembly line secretes cars. Just once does the Rothian imp peep out of the polished Lonovian mask. As Zuckerman sits up late into the night in Lonoff's study, his snooping through Lonoff's books is interrupted by provocative voices from Amy's bedroom above. What is he to do but stand on Lonoff's desk, atop a volume of Henry James's stories, and apply his ear to the ceiling? What he overhears are Amy's efforts to lure her "Dad-da" into bed. But Dad-da is steadfast, and even when she sheds her nightgown to stand naked before him, he remains firm and sensible. He is a married man and will not hear of an affair. ("I've had the bed," he confides elsewhere to Zuckerman.) Yet he does momentarily let down his guard when she cries out, "Oh, tell me a story. Sing me a song. Oh imitate the great Durante, I really need it tonight." And he does. But like a flasher on the subway, Lonoff quickly tucks this routine away before it gets him into trouble and slides back into the old prohibitive formulas, which are tedious enough to drive Amy away. Zuckerman praises him as "the Jew who got away," though it is only New York and the rancor of urban intellectual life that he has escaped; he is otherwise as much the man in the trap as any of the others.

Lonoff is a technical problem that Roth didn't satisfactorily solve. His vitality is reserved for the pen which, twenty-seven drafts per story notwithstanding, is his lone avenue of expression, and yet, apart from giving us some story titles ("Life is Embarrassing," "Eppes Essen"), Roth gives us nothing of Lonoff's writing, effectively keeping whatever appeal he has for Zuckerman under wraps. And since the man himself in propria persona is cold brisket, those segments of the book devoted to him come to life only sporadically. And yet, Lonoff embodies Roth's own immersion in language, and if it does not bring life in the conventional sense of causing the world about him to blossom, it nonetheless is life to the writer, perhaps even the only life he has. Lonoff's vocation *is* an erotic pursuit, though it is an Eros so private and so sublimated that it is available only at a distance. It is no accident that Amy Bellette, his dedicated reader, is enthralled by him, and no accident too that she should be sent packing when she dares to unbutton her blouse. It is his wife, Hope, whom Lonoff trudges out into the snow to retrieve, doubt-less because as a wife of thirty-five years she no longer taxes his intri-cately calibrated equilibrium or competes with his fantastic tracery of words and dreams. Lonoff writes—all writers do—to excite readers to admiration, even to love, though should he succeed it may cost him everything he has to keep his admirers at bay. Lonoff does that by retreating to his burrow and being unimpressive, his need for affection being fed entirely by whatever tributes arrive in the morning mail. If life withers on such a diet, sentences nevertheless grow ripe.

Perhaps this property of words to arouse sexual interest tells us some-thing too about Zuckerman's fascination with Amy Bellette, whom he wildly supposes to be Anne Frank, alive and incognito. It is not simply to astound his parents, Judge Wapter, and the Newark Jewish community that he imagines marrying the Holocaust's most famous martyr, but to join forces with a great martyred writer, joining in matrimony their respective martyrdoms (as if the trivial could become noble if wedded to the tragic) and their prose styles. The mystique of Amy Bellette for Zuckerman is precisely that of Lonoff for Amy, the sensual magnetism of the superior writer. These erotics of writing are developed later on in *The Anatomy Lesson,* where Nathan Zuckerman, by then a writer of note and a martyr to neuralgia brought on, he imagines, by hostile reviews, has four women coming regularly to his apartment to stroke his ego and lick his feathers.

Zuckerman Unbound lacks the ambition of *The Ghost Writer.* It does not flirt with tragic history—the Holocaust or Anne Frank. Its tragic moments, such as they are, are entirely domestic. And it has no Lonoff to make a desert of the emotions in the name of Flaubertian ideals. Rather, it has Alvin Pepler, escapee from Newark, ex-Marine, ex–quiz show contestant, egotist, bully, amateur extortionist, and idiot savant who has the trivia of a generation at his fingertips. Like Zuckerman, he has a raconteur's instincts; like Zuckerman he is unhinged; like him he collects grievances in much the same spirit as he collects facts: he adds them up and keeps a running total. Zuckerman sees Pepler as his "pop self," as perhaps Lonoff was his Weimar self. In these fables of identity, the supporting characters tend to be facets of Zuckerman, essentialized and given voice as if to see how his proclivities, pushed to extremes, might produce monsters. Recalling Roth's myth of himself as a man torn between the measured and the reckless, the civilized and the untamed, we might think of Lonoff and Pepler as bookends, examples of what can happen when either side takes full command. Lonoff is a monk of the sentence, Pepler "another contending personality for ringside at Elaine's." What, then, is Zuckerman himself, for all his antics and his *Carnovsky,* but an appeal for sanity—if not quite a demonstration of it— and the best of both worlds? (All of which is thrown overboard in the last novel, *The Anatomy Lesson,* in which all balances are dispensed with and Zuckerman out-Peplers Pepler for grievance, spite, and personal invective.) The difference between *The Ghost Writer* and *Zuckerman Unbound,* then, corresponds to Roth's choice of monsters, and the book with the more spirited monster is the livelier of the two.

Zuckerman Unbound bears resemblances to Saul Bellow's *Seize the Day.* It possesses a similar maniacal verve and sardonic humor, and has in Zuckerman a character who, like Tommy Wilhelm, is dispossessed of a wife—Zuckerman has recently left her—a father, and a family, and in Pepler a cunning little madman and a word-intoxicated gonif, like Tamkin. It even comes equipped with a father's curse, the elder Zuckerman's dying word to his son: "bastard." But this resemblance is mostly tonal: an occasional flurry of repartee, a breakneck pace, and a shared vision of the scalded nerves and blasted hopes of urban life. Pepler lacks the dimension that renders Tamkin so authentic a figure of the urban phantasmagoria, that of the popular shaman and philosopher-charlatan, the professional healer-stealer. He is finally just another plaintiff in Roth's serialized court of appeals. Trying to "do" Bellow as he had elsewhere "done" Kafka, Roth nonetheless had his own preoccupations to work out: the penalties of success, not failure, success beyond expectation, and to examine that in its most critical domain Roth needed more than just a phantom heckler. He needed an injured family, and it is in the family feud that develops over Zuckerman's writing that his success takes on its proper meaning.

The source of Zuckerman's notoriety is his novel, *Carnovsky*, a recent *succès de scandale* (this is 1969) that has catapulted him into fame and fortune and made him a national celebrity and the most snickered about writer in America. *Carnovsky*, a novel about a young man's masturbations and his battles to become a man against the determined opposition of his mother, has brought him unwanted attention, opened a breach between his family and himself and made him a spectacle on the streets of New York. Strangers accost him: "Hey, careful, Carnovsky, they arrest people for that!" The Fifth Avenue bus comes alive when he gets on. A woman steps into his path: "You need love, and you need it all the time. I feel sorry for you." The man from Con Ed: "Hey, you do all that stuff in that book? With all those chicks? You are something else, man." But of all Zuckerman's admirer-assailants, it is Pepler who captures his, and Roth's, imagination. A landsman and a maniac, the Ancient Mariner of the marginal, he stoppeth Zuckerman in a deli, commandeering his sandwich and demanding an audience for his tale of woe.

Pepler had been a quiz show prodigy in the 1950s, starring for three weeks on the rigged TV sensation "Smart Money" before the producers pulled the plug on him because, as he believes, a Jewish champion was bad for their ratings. His unhinged life ever since has been devoted to baring his stigmata and demanding justice, and he wants Nathan to help him write the book, claiming in fact to have a broadway producer, Marty Paté, interested in the story. (Paté only goes after big projects, having an option on the Six Day War for a musical, with Yul Brynner as Moshe Dayan.) As things unfold, he becomes a crank phone caller, who threatens to kidnap Zuckerman's mother unless he is paid a king's ransom. There are suggestions, as one reviewer of *Zuckerman Unbound* shrewdly noted, that Pepler is a latter day Alex Portnoy, with whom he shares initials, an obsession with past injustices, a history of dealings with a rigged television quiz program, and an instinct for the polemics of masturbation.[12] His last, desperate acts are to accuse Zuckerman of having stolen *Carnovsky*, which is *his* life's story, and to leave in Zuckerman's mailbox a handkerchief, which Zuckerman had loaned him, in which he has masturbated. Are we to take it that this is what might happen to Alex Portnoy if analysis fails? If it succeeds? This erosion of boundaries between art and life and between one book and the other, as Roth's books and characters become embedded as fictions within other fictions, presents the reader with a hall of mirrors. His books begin to collide like subatomic particles, throwing off exotic fragments. *Zuckerman Unbound* points us back in one direction toward *Portnoy's Complaint* (it takes place in 1969, the year *Portnoy's Complaint* is published), in another toward *The Ghost Writer,* and looks ahead toward *The Anatomy Lesson,* in which Zuckerman Peplerizes himself and becomes a lunatic assailant and a dangerous grievant, dangerous in the main to himself.

If *The Ghost Writer* is a book about the penalties of art, then *Zuckerman Unbound* is about those of fame. Zuckerman enjoys a one-night stand with the actress Caesara O'Shea (who is also being wooed by Fidel Castro), who is reading Kierkegaard's *The Crisis in the Life of an Actress,* in which she has marked this passage: "And she, who as a woman is sensitive regarding her name—as only a woman is sensitive—she knows that her name is on everyone's lips, even when they wipe their mouths with their handkerchiefs." Such fame resembles Zuckerman's own, his name on everyone's lips even as they wipe their mouths with their handkerchiefs, with, indeed, *his* handkerchief, as Pepler does after finishing Zuckerman's sandwich. (It is the same handkerchief Pepler later returns impregnated with his semen, a token of fame that not even Kierkegaard's actress was likely to receive. Or was she?) With *Carnovsky,* Zuckerman has been thrust into such public attention, which he experiences as gossip and invasion, since people take his books for confessions or declarations which demand angry or intimate responses.

But though Roth tries to show how painful this public assault can be he makes it look equally diverting. He receives threats and protests but he also gets proposals and propositions. He becomes a target for the fantasies of others which, however trying they may be, always fall short of being lethal. Even Pepler, for all his antics, is only a spectral emanation of fractured Newark sensibility who doesn't captivate Zuckerman so much as circumnavigate him, firing in salvos from way offshore.

The public side of fame, then, is a divertissement from what is central to the book; Zuckerman's crime against his parents by the writing of *Carnovsky.* At the very height of the uproar over *Carnovsky,* Zuckerman's father suffers a killing stroke. Once a vigorous man, he now lies helplessly in bed while members of the family troop past to pay their respects. As he lies on his deathbed, barely conscious and unable to speak, Nathan eschews the opportunity to say a simple, loving farewell. He is an artist, after all, and wedded to the elaborate, the indirect, the metaphorical, and he narrates to his father instead the "big bang" theory of the universe, telling him about "the universe expanding outward . . . the galaxies all rushing away, out into space, from the impact of that first big bang. And it will go on like this, the universe blowing outward and outward, for fifty billion years." Now, that may be a metaphor for love (orgasms don't come any bigger than the big bang), but it is also a fatuous routine which Nathan's father, mustering his remaining strength, damns with his last word, the barely audible but painstakingly pronounced "Bastard!"

Zuckerman Unbound's conclusion finds Nathan in black Newark, reconnoitering his old neighborhood, now blasted by riot and neglect. Zuckerman has gone there to contemplate whatever there was to contemplate, mainly, Zuckerman being Zuckerman, himself. A black man with a shaven head steps out of a house and stares at him.

> "Who you supposed to be?"
> "No one," replied Zuckerman, and that was the end of that. You are no longer any man's son, you are no longer some good woman's husband, you are no longer your brother's brother, and you don't come from anywhere anymore, either.

This is one of Roth's bleaker conclusions, but does Zuckerman deserve it? Does a man get this for just writing a shocking book? To be bombarded by the Peplers of the world or gang-tackled by the Irving Howes, Norman Podhoretzes, Marie Syrkins, and Joseph Epsteins comes with the literary territory: you take your lumps. But to be lost in the stars like some ricochet from the big bang? Surely it is to be wondered that Zuckerman, for all the blows he suffers for *Carnovsky*, gets small pleasure from his money or his fame, and experiences the latter only as a curse. After the burial of the father, Zuckerman's brother turns on him with this withering indictment:

> "You *are* a bastard. A heartless conscienceless bastard. What does loyalty mean to you? What does responsibility mean to you? What does self-denial mean, *restraint*—anything at all? To you everything is disposable! Everything is *exposable*! Jewish morality, Jewish endurance, Jewish wisdom, Jewish families—everything is grist for your fun-machine. Even your shiksas go down the drain when they don't tickle your fancy anymore. Love, marriage, children, what the hell do you care? To you it's all fun and games. *But that isn't the way it is to the rest of us.*"

A reader would be pardoned for taking this for a mea culpa, Roth's admission that he had provoked a scandal with *Portnoy's Complaint* and done some damage in the family (though Roth's own father, we are told, is a fan of his son's writing). He would seem to have taken his Jewish critics to heart, conceding that his revolt in the name of the cerebellum was ill-conceived. And it does seem as though *Zuckerman Unbound,* following the lead of *The Professor of Desire* and *The Ghost Writer,* is another contra-*Portnoy* book, more nakedly than the others, and a rueful concession that he'd been a bad boy after all.[13] If so, then let the scolding truly begin, for what artist in his right mind these days asks the world to honor him for being a gentleman? What advantage accrues to the imagination when the artist publicly repents his days as a brat? Zuckerman's outburst in *The Anatomy Lesson,* then, becomes clear as Roth's reminder that decorum, tact, and order have their place, but not in his novels.

What do we make of *The Anatomy Lesson,* this refrain of rancor and grief, this return to the agonies of being oneself punctuated by the usual bursts of fury at the unfairness of it all? In part, this question is subsumed by a larger one: what do we make of Roth?—a simple question only for those who are already poised to dismiss him out of hand, but a more perplexing one for those of his readers who continue to enjoy his books but are rather in doubt about the value of what it is they are enjoying. In reviewing *Zuckerman Unbound* for *The Nation,* Richard Gilman recalled being asked by a bewildered Flannery O'Connor why a writer like Norman Mailer was displaying himself, rather than letting his work speak for itself. Gilman's answer had obvious application to Roth:

> I remember saying, wholly unsure of my argument, that like other gifted Jewish writers Mailer, as a historical outsider, saw writing, at least in part, as an embattled "way in," that for many such writers language was a social weapon and a means of justification. Their dwelling so much on their own situations, rather than on the possibilities of language as invention, didn't mean that their work was necessarily inferior but only that it was more tied to contingency, that it was more utilitarian, so to speak, and more deliberately seductive; such writing sought love and power more nakedly.[14]

An explanation of this kind is appealing because it depersonalizes the issue, turning it into one of culture and history. It even de-ethnicizes it, since to be an outsider one needn't be a Jew. These posturings and plays for attention are simply the gyrations of the arriviste who has dispensed with the protocols of social initiation and just put his rough shoulder to the door. Roth's books, like those of his fellow Newarker, Leroi Jones/Baraka, are as rude as the streets, though their rudeness is calculated, designed to stir up disapproval and gather in the rewards of scandal. Still, this explanation tells us less than we want to know about why certain books ask greater indulgence of their readers than others. Why, we might ask, after *The Professor of Desire* and *The Ghost Writer,* is *The Anatomy*

Lesson so punishing a book? Why this belated overflow of powerful feelings recollected in what we are constantly assured is tranquility? Four plausible answers come immediately to mind: The Offense, The Agenda, The Dialectic, The Demonstration.

The Offense. After 12 years, the offense still rankled.

The Agenda. *The Anatomy Lesson* was simply the next item on Roth's my-life-as-an artist agenda. *The Ghost Writer* was set in 1956; *Zuckerman Unbound* in 1969; *The Anatomy Lesson* in 1973, and after the publication of *Portnoy/Carnovsky*, the Howe attack was the next shattering event. By then, Roth had no marriage to chafe against and only indignant reviews to suffer. Having made Zuckerman roughly a reflection of his own life, Roth was not about to pass up the opportunity to make l'affaire Howe his next item.

The Dialectic. Having played the Sensitive Jewish Boy in the three prior novels, Roth felt pressed to dust off the Jewboy in the Zuckerman finale and bare his fangs. (For which liberty Zuckerman's fangs get knocked out.) Once he had given himself over to a schematic conception of himself as a man torn between the civilized and the primitive, he began testing the roles, now donning one, now the other, as an actor might play Othello one night and Iago the next in repertory. Roth's writing is an extension of his mimicry, and his role-playing comes into keener focus if we see his entire oeuvre as a repertory theater in which he has cast himself in a series of parts based on the vicissitudes of being himself. Now he is Portnoy, now Tarnopol, Kepesh, Lonoff, Pepler, now one of the five flavors of Nathan Zuckerman.

The Demonstration. Roth wanted to establish once and for all that Nathan Zuckerman is not Philip Roth but a moral fable that takes its departure from Rothian premises. How else do we account for the carefully timed encounters with Roth in the news weeklies and the Condé Nast publications (*House and Garden, Vogue*) except as demonstrations that Roth is alive and well and cool and in command in Connecticut, not out of his gourd or walking the wards with Nathan Zuckerman in Chicago? It is noteworthy that a book based so closely upon Roth's life should in the end prove a demonstration of the difference, but Roth wants it clear that his novels place autobiography wholly at the disposal of myth and imagination. If Milton Appel's attack is taken straight from life, Nathan Zuckerman's crackup is sheer invention. The behind-the-scenes profiles, especially those in the upscale monthlies with their beau monde chitchat about Philip and Claire making "tofu runs" to far off groceries, are public relations of a low order, and even the hardhats at *Commentary* would be pardoned for smirking at these inside exclusives instructing the credulous that Roth is not out making crank calls or heading for the woodwork with an apple in his back but right at home where he belongs, doing his homework and keeping a high profile.

In a larger sense, though, this fine tuning of the public image, which began in the sixties with Roth's postpublication interviews and self-interviews (see *Reading Myself and Others*) and has since spread to the soft-glow stories about his travels, his domesticity, his friendships, is itself a product of the same mythmaking imperative that has shaped his books.[15] The backstage glimpses are entirely of a piece with the costumes: images of a man who wishes to be known as basically sane, cordial, and of regular habits and who, in the interests of getting along better with people, relegates to his books all the disruptive emotions that are forbidden to daily life. "These books," the image admonishes, "are not written with my entire being." The image brings to mind an epigram from Flaubert that Peter Tarnopol in *My Life as a Man* places on his desk as a lesson in the proper relation between life and art: "Be regular and orderly in your life like a bourgeois, so that you may be violent and original in your work."

Whether what we're seeing is a man divided irreparably aginst himself and courting the bourgeois life in order to write unseemly and scandalous books is uncertain: we have only Roth's word for it. What *is* certain is that Roth wishes to be seen that way and has taken great pains to make sure we've got the proper image. *The Anatomy Lesson,* then, is a way of restoring the visible balance, even as Roth trims in the other direction by summoning reporters to his Berkshire nest for white wine and cold veal.

Such considerations take us far afield from Roth's books, except as they lend *The Anatomy Lesson* a plausible raison d'être: to redress an imbalance. Prior books had flirted with sweetness, arousing in Roth a need for a bracing howl at the moon, or at the Jewish fathers—excepting, of course, his actual father. (A Kafka by proxy, he allows himself to be oppressed only by proxy fathers.) During the Percodan-powered diatribe in which he parades as Milton Appel, pornographer, Nathan Zuckerman chatters away about the indecencies of being nice, and though he is playacting it is the sort of play that permits him to romp carelessly through his imagination. "Nice. I don't care what my kid grows up to be, I don't care if he grows up wearing pantyhose as long as he doesn't turn out *nice*. You know what terrifies me more than jail? That he'll rebel against a father like me, and that's what I'll get. Decent society's fucking revenge: a kid who's very very very nice—another frightened soul, tamed by inhibition, suppressing madness, and wanting only to live with the rulers in harmonious peace." And curious though it may appear, Zuckerman, in casting off the polyesters of the bourgeois, is heeding the words of the fathers, for it was Lonoff who observed to a rather abashed young writer:

> "You're not so nice and polite in your fiction. You're a different person."
> "Am I?"
> "I should hope so."

And it was Howe who, castigating Roth for his ressentiment and whining, called for a "good clean hatred that might burn through" or "the fury of social rebellion." *The Anatomy Lesson* is nothing if not a hatred that burns through, though it is Roth himself who takes the heat.

If illness and recovery are our metaphors for the larger design of Roth's career, and if Roth himself led us to think of *The Professor of Desire* and *The Ghost Writer* as symbols of convalescence, then what is *The Anatomy Lesson?* A relapse novel? A return of the repressed? A dropping of the mask? A tutorial in the "secondary gains" of illness, as Zuckerman's analyst proposes? *The Anatomy Lesson* is a rude and dissonant book, a nightmare of a novel, really, and the most pugnacious of Roth's books since *Our Gang.* Zuckerman's call to Appel, with its choruses of insult, is particularly painful to read, not least because the reader feels the humiliation from which Zuckerman himself, doped to the nostrils against pain, is insulated. Yet for all that, *The Anatomy Lesson* possesses a vibration and a daring far beyond a book like *Our Gang* and is a performance to be reckoned with. (Performance is, I think, the proper word here, since Roth himself rather than the events in the book draws our attention.) The sheer force of being in it demands consideration. Roth does not always write with taste or with grace—why should he?—but he writes with power, power generated by turning himself inside out and summoning the hidden, the recessive and the shameful, quite as though he were acting on Isaac Rosenfeld's precept that "the sooner we strike shame, the sooner we draw blood."

Such a willingness to strike shame is, in Roth as it was in Rosenfeld, fueled by a moral imperative. One does not write books like *Portnoy's Complaint* or *The Anatomy Lesson* for the simple joy of letting go. There is little of hedonism or sensuality in them, or, rather, such hedonism as there is is mere material and far removed from purpose. Roth's purposes are invariably moralizing: behind every erotic fantasy or sexual act, behind every provocation, screed, and fantastic monologue lurks a program of self-improvement. (Roth, having given up on the conceptual framework of psychoanalysis, has nevertheless clung to its basic morality.) The basic morality of *The Anatomy Lesson,* then, is the morality of striking deep, diving to the floor of the imagination and searching for insight and health, like pearls, in the darkest recesses. It is symptomatic of the moment in which the book is set that marijuana and Percodan are Zuckerman's royal roads to the unconscious. But behind Zuckerman's drugged consciousness stands the iron suzerainty of Roth's conscience, demanding that Zuckerman stop beating around the Lonovian bush and face the tough issues: his profession, his eventless life, his pain, himself. "Had he kept a pain diary," Zuckerman notes, "the only entry would have been one word: myself." *The Anatomy Lesson,* then, is not a book that panders to any ready-made audience. Lacking the sexual comedy and inventive gusto of *Portnoy's Complaint* while being every bit as self-punishing, to whom could it appeal? Answer: to Roth himself. It is his own approval that Roth is always courting, the approval not of the instincts, which neither condemn nor bless but only want, but of a strict code of conduct that comands him to tell the truth, to plumb the depths, *to be fearless.*

There are many standards against which a writer may be judged, and I'm not persuaded that Roth has always been subjected to the most illuminating of them. Clearly, one doesn't apply to Roth the standards of Tolstoy or Flaubert, let alone Sholom Aleichem. Even Kafka, for all Roth's efforts to emulate him, belongs to another world. But there are other standards, all American, by which Roth might be profitably measured: Hawthorne, whom he resembles in degree of torment, in motive hunting, in moral allegory; Whitman, with whom he shares an unending self-recital; Bellow, from whom he has learned something about the desperate monologue, the aromas of the city, and the psychopathologies of everyday life. And there is one other who might provide the most relevant yardstick of all: Isaac Rosenfeld, with whom he shares a sense of humor (Rosenfeld was also a gifted mimic), an overbearing superego, a dynamism of suffering, a heart bursting with chicken fat and gall, and a longing to break out.

Roth writes with his whole being, as Rosenfeld often expressed the desire to. He holds nothing back, endeavoring with all his skill to reach beyond skill toward power. The effort has been only fitfully successful— I account *Portnoy's Complaint* and *My Life as a Man* as those of his books that come closest to being powerful novels. *The Anatomy Lesson,* by contrast, achieves at best a kind of force, which is the application of power without grace. And yet *The Anatomy Lesson* exposes the drive, the heat, and the ready irritability that propel Roth's imagination and make him so hard a writer to settle in with. Roth's own refusal to settle, to be ingratiating and "nice," which is constantly at war with his artist's instinct for form, style, and grace, is the basic drama of his writing.

Roth's, then, is not a settled career, its very volatility being the promise of his continuing invention. Roth walks a high wire with each book, not with Mailer's swagger and bravado, but with the artisan's sense of balance and touch, placing one foot carefully before the other, testing the line for tautness and sway, checking his footing as he goes. We would be foolish not to cheer him on his way.

12. Conclusion

As I APPROACHED the completion of this book, I sent chapters to a friend whose own writing examines much of the same period and features the same cast of characters as my own. What, he wanted to know, was my conclusion, broadly conceived? Was it Allen Tate's thesis, in his essay on Emily Dickinson, that art emerges from the breakup of old faiths? I hadn't been quite prepared to stretch my ideas on so broad a frame, but that was certainly consistent with ideas I was groping toward as my argument had taken shape. Tate had written eloquently of Dickinson's poetry as the product of an intelligence that was steeped in Puritan lore but had suffered the Emersonian fall and therefore been released to play Puritan melodies without yielding to Puritan stringencies. "[Her poetry] comes out of an intellectual life towards which it feels no moral responsibility."[1] I had been heedful throughout of Irving Howe's observation that his own generation did its best work only after its Marxist faith had begun to decompose. Released from the prison house of the sect but still possessing the lingo, the history, the combative posture, and the habit of dialectic, they wrote brilliant allegories of their own uncertainty and commentaries on an intellectual life from which they continued to draw inspiration but toward which they felt no moral responsibility. "Ideology crumbled, personality bloomed," observes Howe. "Perhaps there was a relation between the two?"[2] The conclusion is difficult to avoid, that there was a flowering of both the critical intelligence and the creative impulse during the twilight of American Marxism, as the conversion of intellectuals from sectarians to individuals released geysers of creative and intellectual power.

However, the apostasy from Marxism was, we remember, a cycle within a cycle, a fall within a fall, and therefore represented a second stage of shock and emancipation. The first fall was the long, slow disengagement from Judaism that was for some a personal mission and for others a donnée of existence, presented to them as an accomplished fact by prior generations. The revolutionism that was to be abandoned in the late thirties and early forties was itself a surrogate Judaism, with its own ceremonies and myths, its own canonical texts and Talmudic interpretations, its own messianic expectations.[3] The history of Jewish intellectual life in America might well be described as a series of apostasies, losses, and disillusionments, each leave-taking and each disillusionment opening new doors of insight and unlocking fresh reserves of inspiration.

Indeed, to these we must add a third fall, one that seared the consciousness of all these writers but which, for all the terror it occasioned, went curiously unexamined except by Isaac Rosenfeld: the Holocaust. In contrast to the Marxist experience, which left visible stigmata, the Holocaust was for most a hidden wound, shrouded in darkness and suffered in silence, felt everywhere but confronted virtually nowhere. That the Jewish writers should for the most part have been reticent to deal with it is one of the curious sidelights of this history, but one which the scope of this book does not permit us to explore. Surely Howe was correct in observing that the New York intellectuals came on the scene at a moment "when there [was] a strong drive not only to break out of the ghetto but also to leave behind the bonds of Jewishness entirely," which may tell us something about why the failures of socialism galvanized their imaginations so much more than the disasters that befell the Jews.[4] But even at their most estranged they were not insensible of the fact that only an ocean divided them from those who died at Auschwitz and that but for an accident of birth and the vagaries of immigration they themselves were the victims of the Final Solution. Apostates from the Jewish community, they were not unaware that history had a way of seeing through their apostasies.

Such reflections bring us back to the figure of Isaac Deutscher's non-Jewish Jew, who, by becoming a heretic and stepping beyond the boundaries of Jewish thought partook of a great and time-honored Jewish tradition that runs from Spinoza through Freud and Einstein and encompasses the great Jewish revolutionaries from Marx to Luxemburg to Trotsky.[5] And Deutscher in turn looks back to the ethnographers of marginality, Robert Park and Thorstein Veblen, who earlier in this century extolled the apostate Jew as the prototypical stranger, cosmopolite and disturber of the intellectual peace—the pioneer, in a phrase, of contemporary alienation and modern thought.[6] Veblen wrote in 1919:

> It appears to be only when the gifted Jew escapes from the cultural environment created and fed by the particular genius of his own people, only when he falls into the alien lines of gentile inquiry and becomes a naturalized, though hyphenate, citizen in the gentile republic of learning,

that he comes into his own as a creative leader in the world's intellectual enterprise. It is by loss of allegiance, or at the best by force of a divided allegiance to the people of his origins, that he finds himself in the vanguard of modern thought.

The figures with whom this book mainly deals are all variants on the Veblenian hyphenate, non-Jewish Jews who by divided allegiance and uncertain loyalty generated a dynamism of thought out of the disparities in their experience and became "pathfinders and iconoclasts in science, scholarship and institutional growth and change."

This book would be no more than a reprise of familiar themes, however—the intellectual as the non-Jewish Jew, the Jewish writer as hyphenate, as cosmopolitan, as restless modernist—were it not for the extra dimension of voluntary self-transcendence that set the agenda for so many Jewish writers and intellectuals of the postwar generation. What matters is not simply that they lived in divided worlds, but that they invented the divisions by which they lived. The distinguishing feature of this generation was the conversion that transformed so many from Jews to Americans or from revolutionists to convalescents, a conversion that was commonly mediated by some brand of radical therapy that took on for a brief period something like scriptural authority in the life of the writer. That Wilhelm Reich and orgonomy should have provided the scripture by which many of these conversions took place should come as no surprise. In the struggle to overcome the shaping conditions of one's past and dictate the terms for a radically different future, discovering that one had a body—coming from a culture in which the body is virtually ignored as a part of the moral self—was a crucial step toward becoming a new self.

Though group labels are treacherous to propose—and finally every group designation is a convenient fiction—one finally thinks of these writers as elective Marranos or Conversos, men who, without an Inquisition to force a conversion upon them, hastened to tear away the gabardines of tradition and strip down to the fig leaves of new Adamism. (These terms obviously do not apply to Lionel Trilling, the Sartor Resartus of his generation.) But these conversions came equipped with a reserve clause, the irrevocable past, which, hidden though it might be behind veil after veil of illusion, bides its time and awaits its moment to return in some new and strange and surprising form. Thus it is that Trilling should have wound up a rabbi of Victoriana, Ginsberg a Buddhist rebbe of dharmic Hasidism, Bellow the comic anthropologist of Chicago Jewry, Rosenfeld a martyr to survivor's guilt, Mailer the perverse celebrant of "ancient evenings" in Egypt—the Old Country and then some—Kazin the hagiographer of the New York Jew, Howe the mythographer of his father's world, and Roth the spiritual stepchild of Franz Kafka and promoter of writers from "the other Europe." These ambivalent converts are the icons of our time and testaments to what commonly befalls the new Adam when he reaches middle age and starts ransacking the attic for antiques and souvenirs, hoping to find an item of old clothing that might fit him. It is not exactly his grandfather's threadbare gabardine, which has been spit upon once too often, that he hopes to find, but something at once suitably dark and yet smartly tailored that can be worn with a talith or a long overcoat, or even a sarape, but will be, however it is worn, recognizàbly, ineluctably, unmistakably Jewish in its styling.

Notes

1. Introduction

1. Vivian Gornick, "Why Do These Men Hate Women?" reprinted in *Essays in Feminism* (New York: Harper & Row 1978), 189–99.

2. Leslie Fiedler, "The Jew in the American Novel," *To The Gentiles* (New York: Stein and Day, 1972), 112.

3. "Our Country and Our Culture," *Partisan Review* 19 (May–June 1952): 283–326; 19 (July–August 1952): 420–50, and 19 (September–October 1952): 562–597.

4. *Partisan Review* 19 (May–June): 287.

5. Irving Howe, "This Age of Conformity, Notes on an Endless Theme, or, A Catalogue of Complaints," *Partisan Review* 21 (January–February 1954): 7–33.

6. As attractive as that prospect was, to locate models for a contemporary dissent in classic American texts, it had the disturbing feature of having been anticipated by the Popular Front, which treated our native radical tradition not as an alternative to fellow travelling but as its naive precursor: Melville pointing the way to Lenin. In 1949, Dwight Macdonald would recall with savage delight F. O. Matthiessen's address to the "Cultural and Scientific Conference for World Peace" at the Waldorf Hotel, where Matthiessen "talked about Emerson, Thoreau, Whitman and Melville as the Henry Wallaces of their day (high point was the reference to Captain Ahab as a 'common man'), and praised Emerson's dedication to 'the organizing of liberty' as pretty good considering that Lenin hadn't yet come along to show us how to do the job right." Dwight Macdonald, "The Waldorf Conference," *Politics* (Winter 1949): 32A–32D.

7. See, for example, Walter Rideout, " 'O Workers' Revolution . . . The True Messiah,' The Jew as Author and Subject in the American Radical Novel," *American Jewish Archives* 11 (April 1959): 157–75, and Daniel Aaron, "Some Reflections on Communism and the Jewish Writer," *Salmagundi* 1 (Fall 1965): 23–36.

8. Philip Rieff, *The Triumph of the Therapeutic: Uses of Faith After Freud* (New York: Harper & Row, 1966).

9. See R. W. B. Lewis, *The American Adam* (Chicago: University of Chicago Press, 1978).

10. Isaac Deutscher, "The Wandering Jew as Thinker and Revolutionary," *Partisan Review* 25 (Fall 1958): 556. The essay is reprinted as "The Non-Jewish Jew" in Deutscher, *The Non-Jewish Jew and Other Essays* (New York: Oxford University Press, 1968).

2. The Paradox of the Fortunate Fall

1. George Steiner, "The Archives of Eden," *Salmagundi* 50/51 (Fall 1980/ Winter 1981): 85.

2. Steiner, 86.

3. Steiner, 86.

4. Saul Bellow, *Herzog* (New York: Viking Press, 1964), 169.

5. Cesar Graña, *Modernity and Its Discontents: French Society and the French Man of Letters in the Nineteenth Century* (New York: Harper and Row, 1967), 19–20.

6. Irving Howe, "The Lost Young Intellectual," *Commentary* 2 (October 1946): 152–163. Reprinted in *Mid-Century: An Anthology of Jewish Life and Culture in Our Times*, ed. Harold U. Ribalow (New York: Beechhurst Press, 1955).

7. See Sidney Hook on the "semantic beacons" of the forties: "Intelligence and Evil in Human History: An Answer to Intellectual Defeatism," *Commentary* 3 (March 1947): 210

8. Alfred Kazin, "Under Forty," *Contemporary Jewish Record* 7 (February 1944): 11.

9. Harold Rosenberg, "Professors of Man Estranged," in *Discovering the Present* (Chicago: University of Chicago Press, 1973), 182.

10. Lionel Trilling, *Sincerity and Authenticity* (Cambridge: Harvard University Press, 1971), 104–105.

11. Bellow, *Herzog*, 75.

12. Norman Podhoretz, *Making It* (New York: Random House, 1967), 170.

13. Joseph Epstein, "A Conspiracy of Silence," *Harper's* 255 (November 1977): 77–92.

14. Hilton Kramer, "The Revenge of the Philistines: Tom Wolfe & Avant-Garde Chic," *Commentary* 59 (May 1975): 35. See also Kramer, "Modernism and Its Enemies," *The New Criterion* 4 (March 1986): 1–7.

15. Gerald Graff, *Literature against Itself: Literary Ideas in Modern Society* (Chicago: University of Chicago Press, 1979).

16. David Hollinger, "Ethnic Diversity, Cosmopolitanism and the Emergence of the American Liberal Intelligentsia," *American Quarterly* 27 (May 1975): 133.

17. On the neoconservative assault on homosexuality see especially Norman Podhoretz, "Culture of Appeasement," *Harper's* 255 (October 1977): 25–32, and Midge Decter, "The Boys on the Beach," *Commentary* 70 (September 1980): 35–48.

18. The literature of alienation by now is so vast and the uses of the word so Byzantine that to even begin to examine it would demand an essay of its own, and rather than do that here I've allowed its meanings to emerge from the particular uses to which writers put it and the attitudes they struck while under its influence. That will have to do for now. The best historical survey of alienation is Richard Schacht, *Alienation* (New York: Doubleday & Co., 1970).

19. Norman Mailer, "The Man Who Studied Yoga," in *Advertisements for Myself* (New York: G. P. Putnam's Sons, 1959), 154.

20. Philip Rahv, "Disillusionment and Partial Answers," *Partisan Review* 15 (May 1948): 526.

21. Lionel Trilling, "Art and Fortune," in *The Liberal Imagination* (New York: Viking Press, 1950), 265.

22. "A frequent theme of 1950s fiction was the depression at the top. William H. Whyte's *The Organization Man* (1956) furnished sociological documentation, and such novels as Sloan Wilson's *The Man in the Gray Flannel Suit* (1955) and Cameron Hawley's *Executive Suite* (1952), dramatized the paradox; freedom lay in the poverty-stricken, wartorn past; repression and corporate back-stabbing in the affluent present. The price paid for success was the loss of self-restraint, each achievement of security and status demanded even greater personal or moral abasement." Leo Braudy, "Realists, Naturalists, and Novelists of Manners," in *Harvard Guide to Contemporary American Writing*, ed. Daniel Hoffman (Cambridge: Belknap Press, 1979), 143.

23. "Our Country and Our Culture: A Symposium," *Partisan Review* 19 (May–June 1952): 282–326; 19 (July–August 1952): 420–50; 19 (September–October 1952): 562–97.

24. "A hundred years after the *Manifesto*," reported Leslie Fiedler in his contribution to the *Partisan Review* symposium "Our Country and Our Culture," "the specter that is haunting Europe is—Gary Cooper!" *Partisan Review* 19 (May–June 1952): 294.

25. Judith N. Shklar, "The Romanticism of Defeat: The Unhappy Consciousness Today," in *After Utopia: The Decline of Political Faith* (Princeton: Princeton University Press, 1957).

26. Morris Dickstein, *Gates of Eden: American Culture in the Sixties* (New York: Basic Books, 1977).

3. The Aftermath of Socialism

1. The literature of this deconversion is vast, but see especially John P. Diggens, *Up from Communism: Conservative Odysseys in American Intellectual History* (New York: Harper & Row, 1975), and Peter Steinfels, *The Neoconservatives: The Men Who Are Changing America's Politics* (New York: Simon and Schuster, 1979).

2. A spectacular instance of these smoldering hostilities erupting some thirty or more years after the precipitating events is the exchange of accusations between Hellman, a lapsed Stalinist, and McCarthy, an ex-Trotskyist, after the publication of Hellman's *Scoundrel Time* (Boston: Little Brown and Co, 1976). McCarthy's statement, on the Dick Cavett show in January, 1980, that Hellman was "terribly overrated, a bad writer and a dishonest writer," provoked Hellman to sue her for $1.75 million and brought half of literary New York into the fray. See John Simon, "Literary Lionesses," *National Review* 32 (May 16, 1980): 614–16 and Norman Mailer, "An Appeal to Lillian Hellman and Mary McCarthy," *New York Times Book Review* 85 (May 11, 1980): 3, 33.

3. Alan Trachtenberg, "Intellectual Background," in *Harvard Guide to Contemporary American Writing*, 4–5.

4. Howe, *Politics and the Novel* (New York: Avon Books, 1967), 203.

5. Rosenberg, *Discovering the Present*, 215.

6. Louis Francis Budenz, *This Is My Story* (New York: McGraw-Hill, 1947); Granville Hicks, *Where We Came Out* (New York: Viking Press, 1954); Elizabeth Bentley, *Out of Bondage* (New York: Devin-Adair, 1952); Whittaker Chambers, *Witness* (Chicago: New York: Random House, 1952); Freda Utley, *Lost Illusions* (London: Allen & Unwin, 1949); Benjamin Gitlow, *I Confess: The Truth about American Communism* (New York: E. P. Dutton, 1940), and *The Whole of Their Lives* (New York: Charles Scribner's Sons, 1948); *The God That Failed*, ed. Richard Crossman (New York: Harper & Row, 1950); Eric Bentley, *Thirty Years of Treason: Excerpts from Hearings before the House Committee on Un-American Activities, 1939–1968* (New York: Viking Press, 1971).

7. "Our Country and Our Culture," *Partisan Review* 19 (May–June, 1952): 309.

8. The major texts of this campaign to bring literature into line with healthy sentiments were Archibald MacLeish, "The Irresponsibles," in *A Time to Speak* (Boston: Houghton, Mifflin, 1941), and Van Wyck Brooks, "What Is Primary Literature?" and "Coterie-Literature," first delivered as an address at Columbia University in 1941 and printed in Brooks, *Opinions of Oliver Allston* (New York: E. P. Dutton and Co., 1941), 211–46. A handy source of these essays along with Dwight Macdonald's stinging reply, "Kulturbolschewismus Is Here," is *The Survival Years: A Collection of American Writings of the 1940s*, ed. Jack Salzman (New

York: Pegasus Books, 1969), 173–212. See also Bernard De Voto, *The Literary Fallacy* (Boston: Little, Brown, 1944), and John Chamberlain's screed against the image of the businessman in contemporary fiction, "The Businessman in Fiction," *Fortune* 38 (November 1948): 134–46.

9. From a letter to *Time* (December 5, 1938), quoted by Macdonald in "Kulturbolschewismus," Salzman, 208.

10. Dickstein, *Gates of Eden*, 40.

11. Malcolm Cowley, *The Literary Situation* (New York: Viking Press, 1954), 57.

12. Alfred Kazin, *On Native Grounds* (New York: Harcourt, Brace, 1942). Quote is from the 1956 Anchor edition, p. 116.

13. Irving Howe, "The New York Intellectuals," *Decline of the New* (New York: Horizon Press, 1970), 216.

14. Kazin, *New York Jew* (New York: Alfred A. Knopf, 1978), 4–5.

15. Kazin, 8.

16. Lionel Trilling, "Manners, Morals, and the Novel," in *The Liberal Imagination* (New York: Viking Press, 1950), 211.

17. Mary McCarthy, "Philip Rahv, 1908–1973," in *Philip Rahv: Essays on Literature & Politics, 1932–1972*, ed. Arabel J. Porter and Andrew J. Dvosin (New York: Houghton Mifflin, 1978), vii. McCarthy's memoir of Rahv originally appeared in *New York Times Book Review* (February 17, 1974), 1–2.

18. Renato Poggioli, *The Theory of the Avant Garde* (Cambridge: Harvard University Press, 1968), 90.

19. Saul Bellow, "Machines and Storybooks: Literature in the Age of Technology," *Harper's* 249 (August 1974): 54.

20. Quoted in Poggioli, 110.

21. Delmore Schwartz, "I Am to My Own Heart Merely a Serf," in *Summer Knowledge* (Garden City: Doubleday, 1959), 71.

22. Quoted in Kazin, *New York Jew*, 26.

23. From Schwartz's poem "The Sin of Hamlet," in *Summer Knowledge*, 35.

24. From "The Kingdom of Poetry," in *Summer Knowledge*, 188.

25. Kazin, *New York Jew*, 25.

26. Malcolm Cowley, *Exile's Return* (New York: Viking Press, 1951), 47.

27. William Barrett, *The Truants: Adventures among the Intellectuals* (Garden City: Anchor Press/Doubleday, 1982), 23.

28. Howe, "The Lost Young Intellectual," 155. See ch. 2, n.6.

29. James Joyce, *Ulysses* (New York: Viking Press, 1961), 377.

30. Trilling, "Under Forty," *Contemporary Jewish Record* 7 (February 1944): 15–17.

4. From Socialism to Therapy, I: Sigmund Freud

Abbreviations: SE = Sigmund Freud, *The Standard Edition of the Complete Psychological Works of Sigmund Freud*, ed. James Strachey, Anna Freud, Alix Strachey, and Alan Tyson, 24 vols. (London: the Hogarth Press and the Institute of Psychoanalysis, 1953–1966).

1. See Frederick J. Hacker, "Freud, Marx & Kierkegaard," in *Freud and the Twentieth Century*, ed. Benjamin Nelson (Cleveland: Meridian, 1957), 130. In the same spirit, Trotsky's biographer, Isaac Deutscher, in the course of defining the "non-Jewish Jew" as the characteristic revolutionary figure in modern European culture, had no difficulty in likening Freud's theory of dreams, jokes, and slips of the tongue to Marx's laws of historical development as equivalently radical, and *Jewish,* determinisms, revelations of the basic regularities of life. See Deutscher, "The Wandering Jew as Thinker and Revolutionary," *Partisan Review* 25 (Fall

1958): 62. The essay is reprinted as "The Non-Jewish Jew," in Deutscher, *The Non-Jewish Jew and Other Essays* (New York: Oxford University Press, 1968).

2. For these notes on Felix Morrow, I am indebted to Alan Wald for kindly letting me see his unpublished manuscript on the American Trotskyist movement, "The New York Intellectuals."

3. Trilling, "The Fate of Pleasure," *Beyond Culture* (New York: Viking Press, 1968), 73.

4. Philip Roth, *The Ghost Writer* (New York: Farrar Straus & Giroux, 1979), 77.

5. Saul Bellow, *Dangling Man* (New York: Vanguard Press, 1944), 10.

6. Sigmund Freud, "A Difficulty in the Path of Psychoanalysis," *SE* 17:143.

7. Freud, *Leonardo da Vinci and a Memory of his Childhood, SE* 11:115.

8. These amendments to Freud's theory of mind appeared, respectively, in *Beyond the Pleasure Principle* (1920) and *The Ego and the Id* (1923), though their implications for the theory of man and society were not spelled out until *Civilization and Its Discontents* in 1930.

9. For the political backgrounds to Freud's thought, see Carl Schorske, "Politics and Parricide in Freud's *Interpretations*," in *Fin-de-Siècle Vienna* (New York: Knopf, 1979), 181–203.

10. Freud, *Civilization and Its Discontents, SE* 21:112.

11. Erich Fromm, *Escape from Freedom* (New York: Holt, Rinehart & Winston, 1941).

12. Max Eastman, *Reflections on the Failure of Socialism* (New York: Devin-Adair, 1955), 108. On the biological-reductionist side of Eastman's later thought, see Diggens, 226.

13. Trilling, "Art and Fortune," in *The Liberal Imagination*, 264.

14. Arthur Schlesinger, *The Vital Center: The Politics of Freedom* (Boston: Houghton, Mifflin, 1949), 40.

15. James Burnham, *Suicide of the West* (New York: John Day Co., 1964), 154.

16. Arthur Miller, *After the Fall* (New York: Viking Press, 1964). All quotes in this chapter are from the 1965 Bantam paperback, pp. 4, 162.

5. Psychoanalysis and Liberalism: The Case of Lionel Trilling

1. Lionel Trilling, *The Liberal Imagination* (New York: Viking Press, 1950), xi. All subsequent references are abbreviated as *TLI*.

2. Trilling, *The Middle of the Journey* (New York: Viking Press, 1947), reprinted with an introduction by Trilling, Avon Books, 1975. Critical study of Trilling abounds, though there are just a few books on him and little solid biographical material. The most comprehensive critical study to date is William M. Chace, *Lionel Trilling: Criticism and Politics* (Stanford: Stanford University Press, 1980). See also Robert Boyers's monograph, *Lionel Trilling: Negative Capability and the Wisdom of Avoidance* (Columbia: University of Missouri Press, 1977). These studies will shortly be supplemented by Mark Krupnick's book, *Lionel Trilling and the Fate of Cultural Criticism*, forthcoming from Northwestern University Press. Though that book has not appeared as of the time this manuscript was being completed, I have profited greatly from an exchange of views and chapters with Professor Krupnick as we both worked on the same subject. I am also indebted to Alan Wald for details about Trilling's early political affiliations in the 1930s and to Wald's study, "The *Menorah* Group Moves Left," *Jewish Social Studies* 38 (Summer–Fall 1976): 289–320, for details of the social and political circle in which Trilling began his intellectual career. Another biographical study is Diana Trilling, "Lionel Trilling, A Jew at Columbia," *Commentary* 67

(March 1979): 40–46. A sound collection of critical essays may be found in *Salmagundi* 41 (Spring 1978) and a partial bibliography of Trilling's writings and critical studies of him in Marianne Gilbert Barnaby, "Lionel Trilling: A Bibliography, 1926–1972," *Bulletin of Bibliography* 31 (January–March 1974): 37–44. Finally, for portraits, not always complimentary, of Trilling as an intellectual presence, see Kazin, *New York Jew,* 42–47 and 191–93, and Norman Podhoretz, *Making It* (New York: Random House, 1967), passim, and *Breaking Ranks: A Political Memoir* (New York: Harper & Row, 1979), 276–304 and passim.

3. *TLI,* xiv.

4. Trilling's conception of Freudian man evolved throughout his career as he persistently returned to the subject of psychoanalysis and the character of Freud as his most abiding themes. The earliest essays are "Freud and Literature" and "Art and Neurosis" in *TLI,* but Trilling consistently revised and darkened the image. His major statements after *TLI* are in "Freud: Within and Beyond Culture," *Beyond Culture* (New York: Viking Press, 1968), 89–118 and *Sincerity and Authenticity* (Cambridge: Harvard University Press, 1972), 140–68. See also Trilling, "Last Years of a Titan," review of volume 3 of Ernest Jones's *Life of Freud,* in *The Griffin* 6 (December 1957), and introduction to *The Life and Work of Sigmund Freud* (New York: Basic Books, 1961), an abridgement of the three volume work by Ernest Jones, edited with Steven Marcus.

5. *Sincerity and Authenticity,* 27–34 and passim.

6. This is a persistent theme of *TLI,* but see especially the preface, "Reality in America," and "Freud and Literature."

7. *Matthew Arnold* (New York: W. W. Norton & Co., 1939).

8. Edmund Wilson, *The American Jitters: A Year of the Slump* (New York: Charles Scribner's Sons, 1932), revised and purged of its Marxist effusions as *The American Earthquake: A Documentary of the Twenties and Thirties* (Garden City: Doubleday, 1958).

9. The introduction to Tess Slesinger's *The Unpossessed* also appeared as "Young in the Thirties," *Commentary* 41 (May 1966): 43–51.

10. Introduction to Avon edition of *The Middle of the Journey* (1975). In subsequent references, the book is abbreviated as *TMJ.*

11. *TMJ,* 55.

12. *TMJ,* 59.

13. *TLI,* 264, 266.

14. *TLI,* xv.

15. *TLI,* 45, 174.

16. *TLI,* 179.

17. Steven Marcus, "Lionel Trilling, 1905–1975," in *Art, Politics, and Will,* ed. Quentin Anderson, Stephen Donadio, and Steven Marcus (New York: Basic Books, 1977), 265.

18. *TLI,* 50.

19. Saul Bellow, "Machines and Storybooks: Literature in the Age of Technology," *Harper's* 249 (August 1974): 59.

20. Frederick Crews, "The Future of an Illusion," *New Republic* 192 (January 21, 1985): 30.

21. Trilling, "Freud: Within and Beyond Culture," in *Beyond Culture* (New York: Viking Press, 1968).

22. Marcus, 270.

23. Trilling, "Last Years of a Titan," *The Griffin* 6 (December 1957): 9. *The Griffin* was the publication of The Reader's Subscription. Its editorial Board from 1952 to 1959 featured Trilling, Jacques Barzun, and W. H. Auden.

24. *Sincerity and Authenticity,* 156, 158.

25. Trilling, "The Poet as Hero: Keats in His Letters," *The Opposing Self* (New York: Viking Press, 1955), 3–49. All subsequent quotes from that essay are from pages 19–22.

26. Dickstein, *Gates of Eden*, 263.

6. From Socialism to Therapy, II: Wilhelm Reich

1. Robert Michels, *Political Parties: A Sociological Study of the Oligarchical Tendencies of Modern Democracy* (1915), trans. Eden Paul and Cedar Paul (New York: Free Press, 1962).

2. Wilhelm Reich, *The Mass Psychology of Fascism*, trans. Theodore P. Wolfe (New York: Orgone Institute Press, 1946), 265.

3. Reich, *Mass Psychology*, ix.

4. Reich, *Mass Psychology*, 25.

5. Frederick Crews, "Anxious Energetics," in *Out of My System: Psychoanalysis, Ideology, and Critical Method* (New York: Oxford University Press, 1975), 148.

6. Paul Goodman, "The Political Meaning of Some Recent Revisions of Freud," *Politics* 2 (July 1945): 197–202.

7. Norman Mailer, *Barbary Shore* (New York: Holt, Rinehart & Winston, 1951). Quote is from the Signet edition, p. 199.

8. Goodman, 201.

9. C. Wright Mills and Patricia J. Salter, "The Barricade and the Bedroom," *Politics* 2 (October 1945): 314.

10. Reich, *Reich Speaks of Freud*, ed. Mary Higgins and Chester M. Raphael (New York: Farrar Straus & Giroux, 1967), 44.

11. The wavelike undulations of the earthworm were among Reich's favorite metaphors for unarmored and uninhibited motion, but in a pinch almost any invertebrate pulsation would do, from the amoeba to the jellyfish—the more primitive and less self-conscious the better. See Reich's definitions of the orgasm reflex in *The Function of the Orgasm*, trans. Theodore P. Wolfe (New York: World Publishing Co., 1971), 243ff, and Wilhelm Reich, "The Expressive Language of Living," in *Selected Writings* (New York: Farrar, Straus & Giroux, 1973), 136ff.

12. Reich's ordeal at the hands of the Federal Drug Administration has been documented in ample detail by Jerome Greenfield in *Wilhelm Reich vs. the U.S.A.* (New York: W. W. Norton, 1974). See also Myron Sharaf, *Fury on Earth: A Biography of Wilhelm Reich* (New York: St. Martin's Press, 1983), 360ff.

13. Allen Ginsberg, "America," in *Howl and Other Poems* (San Francisco: City Lights, 1956), 34.

14. The journals of Isaac Rosenfeld, the most dedicated of his generation's literary Reichians, have nothing of self-congratulation in them but plenty to say about therapy as a prod to balky imaginations. See the excerpts from Rosenfeld's journals in *Partisan Review* 47: 1 (1980): 9–28 and *Salmagundi* 47 (Spring 1980): 30–47.

15. Alfred Kazin's phrase in his evocative and tender portrait of Rosenfeld in *New York Jew*, 47–53.

16. Interview with Saul Bellow in *Writers at Work: The Paris Review Interviews, Third Series* (New York: Viking Press, 1968), 183.

7. Preserving the Hunger: Isaac Rosenfeld

1. Selections from Isaac Rosenfeld's journals have been published, with introductions by Mark Shechner, in *Partisan Review* 47:1 (1980): 9–28, and

Salmagundi 47 (Spring 1980): 40–47. Most of the subsequent quotes from his journals are from those selections, though a few are published here for the first time.

2. Saul Bellow, "Isaac Rosenfeld," *Partisan Review* 23 (Fall 1956): 567.

3. Isaac Rosenfeld, *Passage From Home* (Cleveland: World Publishing Co., 1946); *Alpha and Omega* (New York: The Viking Press, 1966); *An Age of Enormity*, ed. Theodore Solotaroff (Cleveland: World Publishing Co., 1962), hereinafter *Age*.

4. Kazin, *New York Jew*, 47–53 and Irving Howe, *A Margin of Hope* (New York: Harcourt Brace Jovanovich, 1982), 109–13, 133–34.

5. The only novel to be completed and published was *Passage from Home* (1946), his account of his painful adolescence. A subsequent novel, *The Enemy*, was to prove unpublishable, and an "Indian" novel, *The Empire*, was abandoned after years of work. Rosenfeld contemplated at least two other novels, a Dostoevskian novel for which he took notes under the title, *Mother Russia*, and a Greenwich Village novel. So far as I know, neither progressed beyond the stage of random notes. Most of the stories are collected in *Alpha and Omega*, and even the Yiddish stories have recently been translated and published. See Isaac Rosenfeld, "Yiddish Fables," *Prooftexts* 2 (May 1982): 131–45.

6. *Alpha and Omega*, 3–18.

7. *Alpha and Omega*, 122–52.

8. *Age*, 134.

9. "The Situation of the Jewish Writer," *Age*, 69.

10. *Age*, 280.

11. *Age*, 56.

12. *Age*, 195.

13. Reich, *Character Analysis*, 2d ed., trans. Theodore P. Wolfe (Orgone Institute Press, 1945).

14. *Age*, 178.

15. *Age*, 52.

16. *Partisan Review* 17 (September 1949): 951.

17. *Age*, 151.

18. *Age*, 111–14.

19. *Age*, 115–18.

20. *Age*, 119–22.

21. *Age*, 138–43.

22. Review of *Insight and Outlook*, by Arthur Koestler, *Kenyon Review* 11 (Spring 1949): 323.

23. *Age*, 37.

24. "The World of the Ceiling," *Midstream* 2 (1956): 35. This fantasy of Yevgenia Borisovna is based no doubt on the real Sophia Perovskaya, a member of the Narodnaya Volya terrorist group that conspired to assassinate Czar Alexander II in 1881.

25. "Adam and Eve," *Age*, 182–87; "David Levinsky," *Age*, 273–81.

26. *Partisan Review* 16 (February 1949): 206–11.

27. *Age*, 198.

28. *Age*, 206–09.

29. *Getseltn* (Tents) was published from 1945 to 1948 under the editorship of Eliezer Greenberg and Elias Schulman. During its brief existence, it published such notable writers as Jacob Glatstein, I. I. Trunk, Melekh Ravitch, and Reuben Iceland. Greenberg would later become known for his collaborations with Irving Howe on anthologies of Yiddish writing in translation; Schulman is currently editor of the Yiddish review *Der Wecker* (The Awakener) and Adjunct Professor of Yiddish at the Queens College campus of CUNY. See Isaac Rosenfeld, "Yid-

dish Fables," *Prooftexts* 2 (May 1982): 131–45.

30. *Age*, 246–57.

31. See Robert Cromie, *The Great Chicago Fire* (New York: McGraw-Hill, 1958).

32. See, for example, "In the Monastery," *Kenyon Review* 13 (1951): 394–413, and "The Brigadier," *Alpha and Omega*, 101–109.

33. *Age*, 296.

34. "King Solomon," *Alpha and Omega*, 171–213; "Life in Chicago," *Age*, 323–47.

8. Down in the Mouth with Saul Bellow

In the interest of not cluttering the chapter with footnotes or page numbers, and in the belief that most readers will have no reason to want to look up these passages anyway, I've eliminated references to the books immediately under discussion and footnoted only secondary references or the works of other writers. The books by Bellow under discussion are the following: *Dangling Man* (New York: Vanguard Press, 1944); *The Victim* (New York: Vanguard Press, 1947); *The Adventures of Augie March* (New York: Viking Press, 1953); *Seize the Day* (New York: Viking Press, 1956); *Henderson the Rain King* (New York: Viking Press, 1959); *Herzog* (New York: Viking Press, 1964); *The Last Analysis* (New York: Viking Press, 1965); *Mr. Sammler's Planet* (New York: Viking Press, 1970); *Humboldt's Gift* (New York: Viking Press, 1975); *The Dean's December* (New York: Harper & Row, 1982).

1. Reich, *The Function of the Orgasm*, 271.

2. Delmore Schwartz, "A Man in His Time," a review of *Dangling Man*, *Partisan Review* 11 (Summer 1944): 348–49.

3. Irving Howe, "Down and Out in New York and Chicago," *The Critical Point* (New York: Dell, 1973), 127.

4. "The Trip to Galena," *Partisan Review* 17 (November–December 1950): 779–94.

5. See ch. 3, n.8.

6. Trilling, *TLI*, 277.

7. Frederick Perls, Ralph Hefferline, and Paul Goodman, *Gestalt Therapy: Excitement and Growth in the Human Personality* (New York: Dell, 1951), 19.

8. Richard Stern, "Henderson's Bellow," *Kenyon Review* 21 (1959): 655–61.

9. Wilhelm Reich, *Selected Writings: An Introduction to Orgonomy* (New York: Farrar, Straus and Giroux, 1973), 147.

10. Notes on the production of *The Last Analysis* along with a text of the play can be found in Marilyn Stasio, *Broadway's Beautiful Losers* (New York: Delacorte Press, 1972), 177–262. The text of the play is in many particulars different from the version published in 1965 by Bellow himself, suggesting that the text as it appears in Stasio is closer to the stage version of the play than Bellow's edited edition.

11. Edmund Wilson, "Morose Ben Jonson," *The Triple Thinkers*, rev. ed. (New York: Oxford University Press, 1948), 213–32.

12. Mark Shechner, "Jewish Writers," *The Harvard Guide to Contemporary American Writing*, ed. Daniel Hoffman (Cambridge: Harvard University Press, 1979), 239.

9. Memoirs of a Revolutionist: Norman Mailer in the '50s

1. I am indebted for most of this information to unpublished chapters of a book-in-progress on the cultural Cold War by sociologist Stephen Longstaff. I've

also drawn from Dwight Macdonald's account of the Waldorf conference in *Politics* (Winter 1949) and Joseph P. Lash, "Weekend at the Waldorf," *New Republic* (April 18, 1949): 10–14.

2. Marvin Mudrick, "Mailer and Styron," in *On Culture and Literature* (New York: Horizon Press), 184.

3. Macdonald announced, grandly, "I choose the West," during a debate with Mailer at Mount Holyoke College in winter, 1952, though he was prompt to add, "I support it critically. . . ." See Stephen J. Whitfield, *The Politics of Dwight Macdonald* (Boston: Archon Books, 1984), 89.

4. Eric Goldman, *The Crucial Decade—and After: America, 1945–1960.* (New York: Random House, Vintage Books, 1960), 262.

5. Documentation of the Hollywood purges is so vast that one can only scratch the surface of it. But see especially Eric Bentley, ed., *Thirty Years of Treason: Excerpts from Hearings before the House Committee on Un-American Activities, 1938–1968* (New York: Viking Press, 1971); Stefan Kanfer, *A Journal of the Plague Years* (New York: Atheneum, 1973); Bruce Cook, *Dalton Trumbo* (New York: Charles Scribner's Sons, 1977); David Caute, *The Great Fear: the Anti-Communist Purge under Truman and Eisenhower* (New York: Simon and Schuster, 1978); Victor S. Navasky, *Naming Names* (New York: Viking Press, 1980); Nancy L. Schwartz and Sheila Schwartz, *The Hollywood Writers' Wars* (New York: Alfred A. Knopf, 1982).

6. Norman Mailer, *The Deer Park* (New York: G. P. Putnam's Sons, 1955), frontispiece.

7. These and other quotes in this section are from "Fourth Advertisement for Myself: The Last Draft of *The Deer Park*," in *Advertisements for Myself* (New York: G. P. Putnam's Sons, 1959). All references are to the 1971 Perigee paperback edition.

8. This particular phrase is from the introduction to *Advertisements*, Mailer's "First Advertisement for Myself," but the more detailed account of his trials on publisher's row are in the "Fourth Advertisement."

9. Some of the details of Cerf's whispering campaign against *The Deer Park* can be found in the "Fourth Advertisement"; others, in Peter Manso, ed. *Mailer: His Life and Times* (New York: Simon and Schuster, 1985), 211.

10. A brief account of this episode can be found in Manso, 185–87.

11. Andrew Gordon, in his psychoanalytic study of Mailer, has covered the ground of Mailer's psychological ideas and models with admirable thoroughness. See his *An American Dreamer: A Psychoanalytic Study of the Fiction of Norman Mailer* (Cranbury, New Jersey: Associated Universities Press, 1980), especially Chapter 1, "Mailer, Freud, and Reich: The Novelist as Psychoanalyst."

12. "The White Negro, Superficial Reflections on the Hipster," *Dissent*, 5 (Summer 1957): 276–93. Reprinted in *Advertisements*, 299–320.

13. The most detailed account of this transformation, which argues that the psychoanalytic movement was forced to repress its own history as a result of fascism and the fears and pressures of exile, is Russell Jacoby, *The Repression of Psychoanalysis* (New York: Basic Books, 1983). See also the chapter "Freud and Reich," in Richard King, *The Party of Eros: Radical Social Thought and the Realm of Freedom* (Chapel Hill: University of North Carolina Press, 1972), 51–77.

14. Robert Lindner, *Rebel without a Cause* (New York: Grune and Stratton, 1944) and *Must You Conform?* (New York: Holt, Rinehart and Winston, 1955).

15. See especially "Come over Red Rover," in *The Fifty-Minute Hour: A Collection of True Psychoanalytic Tales* (New York: Rinehart & Company, 1955), and "Political Creed and Character," in *Must You Conform?*

16. That Mailer helped Lindner with some of his writing is recalled by Mailer's then-wife, Adele Morales, in Manso, 321.

17. Lindner, *Must You Conform?* 108.

18. Lindner, 100.

19. Mailer, "The White Negro," *Advertisements*, 309.

20. See Jean Malaquais, "Reflections on Hip," in *Advertisements*, 320–26.

21. See Richard Gilman, "Norman Mailer: Art as Life, Life as Art," *The Confusion of Realms* (New York: Random House, 1969), 84.

10. Allen Ginsberg: The Poetics of Power

1. See Allen Ginsberg, "Berkeley Vietnam Days" and "To the Hell's Angels," *Liberation* (January 1966): 42–47. The poem appeared in the *Berkeley Barb* as "To The Angels" and is reprinted in Hunter S. Thompson, *Hell's Angels* (London: Penguin, 1967), 258–65.

2. Allen Ginsberg, *Collected Poems, 1947–1980* (New York: Harper & Row, 1984). Hereafter abbreviated *CP.*

3. See Mark Shechner, review of *Journals: Early Fifties, Early Sixties; As Ever: The Collected Correspondence of Allen Ginsberg and Neal Cassady;* and *Mind Breaths;* by Allen Ginsberg, *Partisan Review* 46:1 (1979): 105–112. Revised and reprinted in Lewis Hyde, ed., *On the Poetry of Allen Ginsberg* (Ann Arbor: University of Michigan Press, 1984), 331–41.

4. George Dennison, "Remarks from a 'Symposium on the Writer's Situation,'" *New American Review* 9 (April 1970): 105–12. Reprinted in Hyde, 451.

5. Interview with Allen Ginsberg, *Writers at Work: The Paris Review Interviews, Third Series* (New York: Viking Press, 1968), 279–320. The passages on the Blake vision are reprinted in Hyde, 120–30.

6. The search for definitions would have to start with Ginsberg's own journals, the *Indian Journal: March 1962–May 1963* (San Francisco: Dave Hasselwood Books and City Lights Books, 1970) and *Journals: Early Fifties, Early Sixties*, ed. Gordon Ball (New York: Grove Press, 1977).

7. See the dedication to *Indian Journal*, p. 4.

8. In addition to the journals there are Ginsberg and William Burroughs, *The Yage Letters* (San Francisco: City Lights, 1963); *Allen Verbatim: Lectures on Poetry, Politics, Consciousness*, ed. Gordon Ball (New York: McGraw-Hill, 1974); Ginsberg, *Gay Sunshine Interview with Allen Young* (Bolinas: Grey Fox Press, 1974), and *As Ever: The Collected Correspondence of Allen Ginsberg & Neal Cassady*, ed. Barry Gifford (Berkeley: Creative Arts Book Company, 1977).

9. This broadside is reproduced in *CP*, p. 355.

10. *CP*, 94–95.

11. Ginsberg, *Gay Sunshine Interview*, 37.

12. Reed Whittemore, "From 'Howl' to Om," review of *Indian Journals*, *New Republic* 163 (July 25, 1970): 17–18. Reprinted in Hyde, 200–202.

13. "Howl," *CP*, 126–33; "Kraj Majales," *CP*, 353–55; "Birdbrain," *CP*, 738–39.

14. There are several versions of this event and accounts of Trungpa and his operation. The first and most thoroughly documented is *The Party: A Chronological Perspective on a Confrontation at a Buddhist Seminary*, prepared and written by members of the Investigative Poetry Group under the direction of Ed Sanders (Woodstock, New York: Poetry, Crime and Culture Press, 1977). Others are Tom Clark, *The Great Naropa Poetry Wars* (Santa Barbara: Cadmus Editions, 1980); Peter Marin, "Spiritual Obedience," *Harper's* 258 (February 1979): 43–58; Eliot Weinberger, review of *The Party and the Great Naropa Poetry Wars*, *Nation* 230 (April 29, 1980): 470–76.

15. *The Party*, 86.

16. Clark, 53.

17. Clark, 54.

18. Clark, 60.
19. Clark, 65–66.

11. The Road of Excess: Philip Roth

As in the chapter on Saul Bellow, quotes from Roth's books will not be footnoted nor will page numbers be provided in the text. Books and stories by Roth under discussion here are *Portnoy's Complaint* (New York: Random House, 1969); *The Breast* (New York: Holt, Rinehart & Winston, 1972); "'I Always Wanted You to Admire My Fasting'; or, Looking at Kafka," in *Reading Myself and Others* (New York: Farrar, Straus & Giroux, 1975); *The Professor of Desire* (New York: Farrar, Straus & Giroux, 1977); *The Ghost Writer* (New York: Farrar, Straus & Giroux, 1979); *Zuckerman Unbound* (New York: Farrar, Straus & Giroux, 1981); *The Anatomy Lesson* (New York: Farrar, Straus & Giroux, 1983). In the interests of writing something less than an entire book on Roth, I've omitted any discussion of *Goodbye Columbus, Letting Go, When She Was Good, Our Gang,* and *The Great American Novel.* The epilogue to the Zuckerman trilogy, "The Prague Orgy," which is bound with the three Zuckerman novels as *Zuckerman Bound* (New York: Farrar, Straus & Giroux, 1985), appeared too late to be included.

1. See Roth's story, "'I Always Wanted You to Admire My Fasting'; or, Looking at Kafka," in *Reading Myself and Others,* 247–70.

2. Jesse Kornbluth, "Zuckerman Found? Philip Roth's One-Man Art Colony," *House and Garden* 155 (December 1983): 122–31.

3. See particularly: Norman Podhoretz, "Laureate of the New Class," *Commentary* 54 (December 1972): 4, 7; Irving Howe, "Philip Roth Reconsidered," *Commentary* 54 (December 1972): 69–77, reprinted in Howe, *The Critical Point* (New York: Delta, 1973), 137–57; Marie Syrkin, "The Fun of Self Abuse," *Midstream* 15 (April 1969): 64–68; Bruno Bettelheim, "Portnoy Psychoanalyzed," *Midstream* 15 (June–July 1969): 3–10. See also Syrkin's letter to the editor of *Commentary* in March 1973, complaining that Howe had let Roth off too easily and accusing Roth of reveling in *Rassenschande* (racial defilement) "right out of the Goebbels-Streicher script." The diminished footnote to such roundhouse assaults is Joseph Epstein, "What Does Roth Want?" *Commentary* 77 (January 1984): 62–67. For an instructive contrast, see also Robert Alter's more thoughtful, ambivalent, and finally more illuminating discussion of anti-Semitism in Ernest Lehman's filmed version of *Portnoy's Complaint,* "Defaming the Jews," *Commentary* 55 (January 1973): 77–82.

4. See note 3 above.

5. Howe, "The Lost Young Intellectual." See ch. 2, n. 6.

6. It was this "new class" that C. Wright Mills studied in *White Collar* (1951). But whereas Mills approached it with sympathy, seeing it as a new beleaguered proletariat, neoconservatives have tended to anathematize it as a morally reckless bourgeoisie. In the sixties and early seventies, the new class became something of a fetish among post-Marxist sociologists who believed they had found in the concept the final nail in the coffin of Marxism. See especially the symposium on the new class in B. Bruce Briggs, ed., "Is There a New Class?" a special issue of *Social Science and Modern Society* 16 (January–February 1979). Contributors include Seymour Martin Lipset, Michael Harrington, Daniel Bell, Irving Louis Horowitz, Jeane J. Kirkpatrick, Aaron Wildavsky, Andrew Hacker, and Briggs. See also David T. Bazelon, "How Now 'The New Class'?" *Dissent* (Fall 1979), 443–49.

7. Midge Decter, *Liberal Parents, Radical Children* (New York: Coward, Mc-Cann & Geohagen, 1975).

8. Penn Kemble and Josh Muravchik, "The New Politics and The Democrats," *Commentary* 54 (December 1972): 78–84; and Seymour Martin Lipset and Earl Raab, "The Election and the National Mood," *Commentary* 55 (January 1973): 43–50.

9. Irving Howe, "The New York Intellectuals," in *Decline of the New* (New York: Horizon Press, 1970), 211–65. One might ask why Howe, in "The New York Intellectuals" and elsewhere, expended so much effort excoriating the New Left and the new sensibility and so little protesting the Vietnam War. Two answers suggest themselves. One is that the Vietnam War was purely a political fact for him, not a cultural one, and therefore had no place in his cultural polemics. A second and less charitable one is that the war did not arouse in him the same degree of personal anguish as the follies of the Left. Calling upon New York writers in 1969 to make a "sustained confrontation with the new sensibility," Howe said nothing about the war that had stunned that sensibility into being. But then, for the leftist, the enemy is always *à gauche*. And that is the subject for another essay.

10. Irving Howe, *A Margin of Hope: An Intellectual Autobiography* (New York: Harcourt Brace Jovanovich, 1982), 291–327.

11. "Le Petomaine" was a French entertainer at Le Moulin Rouge in the early years of this century who had trained his anus to make noises on demand, play musical instruments, and even drink water.

12. Edward Rothstein, review of *Zuckerman Unbound*, in *New York Review of Books* 28 (June 25, 1981): 21.

13. That was the conclusion George Stade drew in reviewing *Zuckerman Unbound* in the *New York Times Book Review* (May 24, 1981). "I do wish Mr. Roth would stop apologizing for *Portnoy's Complaint*. Its bite sinks deepest into the soft spot of something more American than it is Jewish. The custodians of our high literary culture are as retrograde and feminizing as they were over a hundred years ago. The ghosts of Mr. Roth's *Landsmanner*, Fenny Cooper, Nate Hawthorne, Hermie Melville and Sammy Clemons [sic] are nodding approval. Who cares what the momma's boys think?"

14. Richard Gilman, review of *Zuckerman Unbound*, *Nation* (June 13, 1981), 736.

15. The growing literature of Philip Roth at home includes James Atlas, "A Visit with Philip Roth," *New York Times Book Review* 84:35 (September 2, 1979), 1, 12–13; Richard Stern, "Roth Unbound," *Saturday Review* 8 (June 1981): 27–31; David Plante, "Conversations with Philip," *New York Times Book Review* (May 4, 1981) 3, 30–31; Cathleen Medwick, "A Meeting of Arts and Minds," *Vogue* 175 (October 1983): 530–31, 603–604; Jesse Kornbluth, "Zuckerman Found? Philip Roth's One-Man Art Colony," *House and Garden* 155 (December 1983): 122–31.

12. Conclusion

1. Allen Tate, "Emily Dickinson," in *Essays of Four Generations* (Chicago: Swallow Press, 1968), 298.

2. Irving Howe, *A Margin of Hope: An Intellectual Autobiography* (New York: Harcourt Brace Jovanovich, 1982), 133.

3. See Daniel Aaron, "Some Reflections on Communism and the Jewish Writer," *Salmagundi* 1 (Fall 1965): 23–36, and Will Herberg, "From Marxism to Judaism," *Commentary* 3 (January 1947): 25–32.

4. Irving Howe, "The New York Intellectuals," in *Decline of the New* (New York: Horizon Press, 1970), 214–15.

5. For Deutscher, see ch. 1, n. 9.

6. Thorstein Veblen, "The Intellectual Pre-Eminence of Jews in Modern Europe," *Political Science Quarterly* 34 (1919): 33–42. Robert E. Park, "Human Migration and the Marginal Man," *The Journal of American Sociology* 33 (May 1928): 881–93.

Index

Aaron, Daniel, 243, 255
Abbott, Jack Henry, 159, 179
Adam, The New, 12, 176, 188, 241–42. *See also* Lewis, R. W. B.
Adams, J. Donald, 40, 163
Aleichem, Sholom, 54, 56, 112, 114, 237
Alienation, 5, 10, 14, 16, 17
Alter, Robert, 44, 254
Anderson, Quentin, 248
Anderson, Sherwood, 56
Anthroposophy. *See* Steiner, Rudolf
Ardrey, Robert, 66
Arnold, Matthew, 46–48, 55, 57, 71, 73, 75, 82, 86
Arvin, Newton, 4
Atlas, James, 50, 255
Auden, W. H., 50, 248
Austen, Jane, 78–79, 82–83, 89

Babel, Isaac, 83, 114, 226
Ball, Gordon, 253
Baraka, Imamu Amiri (LeRoi Jones), 233
Barnaby, Marianne Gilbert, 248
Barrett, William, 53, 246
Barzun, Jacques, 4, 248
Baudelaire, Charles, 50–51, 62, 153, 177
Bazelon, David, 254
Beckett, Samuel, 48
Bellow, Saul: 3, 6, 15, 18, 31, 44–48 *passim,* 52–53, 57, 60, 62, 83, 101, 104, 106, 111–15 *passim,* **121–58,** 196, 206, 223, 229, 237, 241–250 *passim; Dangling Man,* 2, 26, 29, 30, 43, 45, 61–62, **124–26,** 128, 131–33, 140, 157–58, 247, 251; *The Victim,* 26, 29, 43, 45, 123–24, **126–29,** 131–33, 251; *The Adventures of Augie March,* 41, 100, 115n, 125, **130–33,** 135, 148–49, 151, 250; *Seize the Day;* 60, 100, 124, 126, **132–34,** 137, 151, 157, 229, 251; *Henderson the Rain King,* 60, 100, 123, **134–38,** 140, 148–49, 151, 157, 251; *Herzog,* 15–16, 30, 47, 55, 91, 95, 115n, 123–24, 128, **140–45,** 147–49, 151–54, 157, 216, 251; *The Last Analysis,* 100, 124, **138–141,** 152–53, 216, 251; *Mr. Sammler's Planet,* 124, 128, **146–49,** 154–55, 251; *To Jerusalem and Back,* 30; *Humboldt's Gift,* 115n, 124, 129, 138, **149–54,** 157, 251; *The Dean's December,* 124, 149, 151–52, **154–58,** 251; *The Crab and the Butterfly,* 129; "Looking for Mr. Green," 129; "The Trip to Galena," 129
Bentley, Elizabeth, 39
Bentley, Eric, 40, 245, 252
Bergson, Henry, 121
Berkeley Barb, The, 182–83
Berlin Blockade, 160
Bernstein, Leonard, 177
Bettelheim, bruno, 254
Bialik, Nahum, 15
Blake, William, 135, 181, 184–85, 190, 196
Bloom, Claire, 197
Borges, Jorge Luis, 48
Bourke-White, Margaret, 39
Boyers, Robert, 247
Brando, Marlon, 174
Braudy, Leo, 244
Briggs, B. Bruce, 254
Brooks, Van Wyck, 40–42, 130–31, 245
Brown, Norman O., 63, 206
Browning, Robert, 89
Budenz, Louis, 39–40, 245
Burnham, James, 32, 68, 247
Burroughs, William, 48, 253
Buscaglia, Leo, 65n
Byron, Lord, 89

Cahan, Abraham, 114
Caldwell, Erskine, 39
Calverton, V. H., 56
Camus, Albert, 28, 43
Capote, Truman, 3
Carlyle, Thomas, 72
Cassady, Neal, 185
Caute, David, 252
Cerf, Bennett, 171, 252
Chace, William, 247
Chamberlain, John, 41, 163, 246
Chambers, Whittaker, 32, 37, 39, 76, 80, 245
Chase, Richard, 4
Chekhov, Anton, 48, 127
Clark, Tom, 192, 253–54
Cohen, Elliot, 20, 56

257

Coleridge, Samuel Taylor, 73
Commentary, 4, 10, 20–21, 28, 53, 56, 103–104, 198, 201–206 *passim,* 226, 235
Conrad, Joseph, 218
Communist Party. *See* CPUSA
Cook, Bruce, 252
Copeland, Aaron, 160
Coué, Emil, 131
Cowley, Malcolm, 42, 53, 246
CPUSA, 40
Crews, Frederick C., 85, 93–94, 248–49
Cromie, Robert, 118, 251
Crossman, Richard, 40
Cultural Freedom: American Committee for, 160; Congress for, 160
Czechoslovakia: communist coup in, 160; Allen Ginsberg in, 188

Dean, James, 174, 177
Decter, Midge, 204, 244, 254
Dennison, George, 184, 353
Deutscher, Isaac: 12, 246; "The Non-Jewish Jew," 12, 240, 243, 247
DeVoto, Bernard, 40, 163, 246
Dickens, Charles, 121, 146, 167, 221, 225
Dickinson, Emily, 239
Dickstein, Morris, 30, 41–42, 89, 245–46, 248
Diderot, Denis, 73
Diggens, John P., 245
Dissent, 10, 174
Doctorow, E. L.: 55; *The Book of Daniel,* 2, 91
Donadio, Stephen, 248
Dos Passos, John, 32
Dostoevskian. *See* Dostoevsky
Dostoevsky, Fyodor: 27, 43, 45, 48, 55, 67, 103, 111–12, 125–26, 129–30, 140, 218; *The Eternal Husband,* 126–27
Dubois, W. E. B., 160
Dupee, F. W., 46
Durkheim, Emil, 27
Dvosin, Andrew, 246

Eastman, Max, 32, 63, 66, 247
Einstein, Albert, 160, 240
Eliot, George, 78
Eliot, T. S., 38, 48–51 *passim,* 80, 103, 126, 135
Encounter, 4, 10
Engels, Friedrich, 48, 92
Epstein, Joseph, 18, 232, 244, 254
Erhard, Werner, 97

Fadayev, A. A., 161
Falwell, Rev. Jerry, 20
Fascism, 66, 92
Fast, Howard, 38, 160
Faulkner, William, 56, 121
Fearing, Kenneth, 190

Fenichel, Otto, 219
Fiedler, Leslie: 3–4, 47, 52–53, 56, 60, 62, 243, 245; *Love and Death in the American Novel,* 6
Fischer, Louis, 40
Fitzgerald, Scott, 38, 164
Flaubert, Gustav, 79, 202, 235, 237
Forster, E. M., 55, 71, 75, 78–79, 82, 86
Freud, Sigmund, 10–11, 44, 47–48, **59–70,** 71–90 *passim,* 92, 96–97, 99, 121–22, 138, 155, 173–74, 197–98, 210, 219, 240, **246–47,** 248, 252
Freudianism. *See* Freud
Fromm, Erich, 65n, 66, 78, 92, 247

Gandhi, 99, 118
Getseltn, 117
Gide, Andre, 40, 108, 112
Gifford, Barry, 253
Gilman, Richard, 177, 233, 253, 255
Gilmore, Gary, 179
Ginsberg, Allen: 53, 56, 60, 62, 98–99, 101, 123, **180–95,** 205, 241, 249, **253–54;** "Howl," 29
Ginsberg, Louis, 184
Ginsberg, Naomi, 184
Gitlow, Benjamin, 39, 245
Glazer, Nathan, 103
Gold, Herbert, 29
Gold, Michael, 29
Goldman, Eric, 164, 252
Goodman, Paul: 5, 60, 65n, 78, 92, 95, 99, 100–101, 123, 133, 178, 186, 249, 251; *The Empire City,* 29; "The Breakup of Our Camp," 29
Gordon, Andrew, 252
Gornick, Vivian: "Why Do These Men Hate Women?" 3, 243
Graff, Gerald, 19, 244
Graña, Cesar, 16, 244
Greenberg, Clement, 33
Greenberg, Eliezer, 250
Greenfield, Jerome, 249
Griffin, The, 248

Hacker, Andrew, 254
Hacker, Frederick, 246
Hardy, Thomas, 56
Harrington, Michael, 254
Hawley, Cameron, 244
Hawthorne, Nathaniel, 210, 218, 237
Hefferline, Ralph, 133, 251
Hegel, G. W. F., 47, 71, 73, 176, 210, 224
Hegelian. *See* Hegel, G. W. F.
Heidegger, Martin, 27, 141
Heller, Joseph: *Something Happened,* 2
Hellman, Lillian, 32, 245
Hell's Angels, 181–82
Hemingway, Ernest, 38, 62, 108, 112, 174

Herberg, Will, 32, 255
Hesse, Hermann, 112
Hicks, Granville, 32, 39, 245
Higgins, Mary, 249
Hipster, the. *See* Mailer, Norman
Hiss, Alger, 32, 34, 36, 76, 163
Hitler, Adolf: 64; non-aggression pact with Stalin, 8
Hoffman, Abbie, 203
Hoffman, Daniel, 251
Hollinger, David, 244
Hollywood, purges in, 164–69
Holocaust, the, 116, 127, 147, 240
Hook, Sidney, 32, 161, 244
Horney, Karen, 58
Horowitz, Irving Louis, 254
House and Garden magazine, 196, 234
Howe, Irving, 3–6, 16–17, 37, 45, 53–56, 104, 115, 125, 239–46 *passim,* 250–55 *passim;* "The Lost Young Intellectual," 16–17, 54, 244, 246; and Philip Roth, 201–207, 218, 232–36 *passim*
HUAC (House Committee on Un-American Activities), 8, 35, 40, 164, 171
Hubbard, Elbert, 131
Hurwitz, Henry. See *Menorah Journal*
Huxley, Aldous, 37
Huysmans, Joris-Karl, 50
Hyde, Lewis, 253

Isherwood, Christopher, 108, 164

Jacoby, Russell, 252
James, Henry, 56, 71, 78, 80, 82, 89
Janov, Arthur, 97
Jarrell, Randall, 26
Jaspers, Karl, 27
Jones, Ernest, 248
Jones, Leroi. *See* Baraka, Imamu Amiri
Jonson, Ben, 121–22, 146–47
Joyce, James, 43, 45, 48, 50, 54, 57, 78, 112, 121, 126–27
Judaism, 239–42
Jung, Carl G., 60, 121

Kafka, Franz, 24, 27, 43, 45, 48, 53, 62, 104, 111–16 *passim,* 196–98, 200–201, 207–208, 210, 215, 223–24, 229, 237, 242
Kazin, Alfred: 3, 17, 31, 42, 45–47, 51–57 *passim,* 62, 104, 111, 115, 242–50 *passim; On Native Grounds,* 5, 46
Keats, John, 75, 78, 82, 86–88
Kemble, Penn, 205, 255
Kennedy, Jack, 179
Kerouac, Jack, 123
Khrushchev, Nikita, 163–64
Kierkegaard, Soren, 27, 67, 231
King, Richard, 252
Kirkpatrick, Jeanne, 254

Koestler, Arthur, 37, 40, 60, 250
Korea, war in, 163
Kornbluth, Jesse, 254, 255
Kramer, Hilton, 19, 244
Kristol, Irving, 32, 103
Krupnick, Mark, 247
Kundera, Milan, 15

Lash, Joseph P., 252
Lawrence, D. H., 112
League of American Writers, The, 32
Leavis, F. R., 218
Lenin, V. I., 48, 92
Lewis, R. W. B.: *The American Adam,* 243
Liben, Meyer, 29, 43
Lindner, Robert, 26, 174–79, 252–53
Lipset, Seymour Martin, 204, 254
Longstaff, Stephen, 251
Lorenz, Konrad, 66
Lowell, Robert, 26
Lueger, Karl, 64
Luxemburg, Rosa, 240

Macdonald, Dwight: 5, 94, 110, 161, 163–64, 167, 243, 245–46, 252; *Politics* magazine, 33, 60, 95
MacLeish, Archibald, 40–41, 131, 245
Mailer, Norman: 3–6 *passim,* 24, 53, 60, 62, 78, 92, 95, 99, 101, 122, 153, 157, **159–79,** 184, 233, 238, 241, 245, 249, **251–53;** *The Naked and the Dead,* 28, 159–60, 165, 166–67, 169; *Barbary Shore,* 5, 24, 28–29, 31, 44–45, 94, 159, **162–63,** 166, 170–72; *The Deer Park,* 29, 44, 159, **163–73;** *Advertisements for Myself,* 24, 31, 100, 167–68, 170–71, **172–78;** *An American Dream,* 169, 173n; *Why Are We in Vietnam?,* 169, 173n; *The Executioner's Song,* 169, 173n; *Tough Guys Don't Dance,* 10, 169; "The White Negro," 159, 174–79; "The Time for Her Time," 163; "The Man Who Studied Yoga," 24, 163, 244; the hipster, *see* "The White Negro"
Malamud, Bernard: 43–44, 206; *The Assistant,* 2, 29; *The Natural,* 29
Malaquais, Jean, 5, 157, 160, 162, 176–77, 253
Malenkov, Georgi, 163
Mandelstam, Osip, 15
Mann, Thomas, 62, 218
Manso, Peter, 252
Marcus, Steven, 82, 85, 248
Marin, Peter, 253
Markfield, Wallace, 29
Marx, Karl, 45, 48, 55, 59n, 66, 86, 92, 96–97, 240
Marxism, 58, 79, 91, 99, 106, 145, 159–79 *passim,* 182, 190, 239–40
Matthiessen, F. O., 161, 243

McCarthy, Mary, 32, 48, 161, 245–46
McCarthy, Sen. Joseph, 35–36, 163–65
McCullers, Carson, 26
McGovern, George, 204
Medwick, Cathleen, 255
Meese, Edwin, 181
Melville, Herman, 48
Menorah Journal, 56
Merwin, W. S., 191–93
Michels, Robert, 91, 249
Midstream, 198
Mill, John Stuart, 48, 55, 71–75 *passim*, 79–82 *passim*, 189
Miller, Arthur: 60, 62, 161, 247; *Death of a Salesman*, 22, 26, 29; *After the Fall*, 67–70, 216
Miller, Henry, 109
Mills, C. Wright, 4, 5, 96, 249, 254
Milton, John, 180–81
Modern Quarterly/Modern Monthly, 56
Morrow, Felix, 60, 247
Moscow Trials, 8, 9, 76
Mudrick, Marvin, 162, 252
Mumford, Lewis, 40
Muravchik, Joshua, 204, 254

Nabokov, Vladimir, 48
Naone, Dana, 191–93
Nation, The, 56, 104
New Leader, The, 4, 10, 104
New Republic, The, 56, 104
New Yorker, The, 110
Niebuhr, Reinhold, 63
Nietzsche, Friedrich, 67, 115–17, 130, 141, 155, 174, 179
Nixon, Richard, 34, 36

O'Connor, Flannery, 233
O'Hara, John, 109
Odets, Clifford, 29, 70, 161
Orgone/Orgonomy. *See* Reich, Wilhelm
Ortega y Gasset, José, 113
Orwell, George, 37, 82–83, 117–18

Paris Review, 184, 192
Park, Robert, 240, 256
Partisan Review: 1, 4, 10, 28, 48–49, 51, 60, 104, 129, 131, 206; symposium on "Our Country and Our Culture," 4–5, 27, 148, 160, 162–63, 243, 245
Patchen, Kenneth, 109
Péguy, Charles, 71
Peretz, Isaac Leib, 54, 112–16 *passim*
Perls, Frederick (Fritz), 65n, 97, 133, 251
Phillips, William, 4–5
Plante, Richard, 255
Podhoretz, Norman, 3, 18, 201–204 *passim*, 232, 244, 248, 254
Poggioli, Renato, 48, 246
Politics magazine. *See* Macdonald, Dwight

Popular Front, 4, 160, 165, 169
Porter, Arabel, 246
Pound, Ezra, 51, 112, 190
Presley, Elvis, 174
Progressive Party, The, 160
Proust, Marcel, 43, 51, 62, 78, 112
Psychoanalysis: **71–90** *passim;* as a social idea, 11. *See also* Freud, Sigmund
Public Interest, The, 10

Raab, Earl, 204, 254
Rahv, Philip, 3–5, 25, 31, 40, 46, 48, 52, 55, 102, 110–11, 244
Raphael, Chester, 249
Reed Club, The John, 32
Reich, Wilhelm, 63, **91–101**, 102–23 *passim*, 126, 132, 135–39 *passim*, 148–49, 167, 174, 176, 178, 188–89, 206, 227, 241, **249**, 250–52
Reichianism, 11, 60, 79, 155, 186, 195. *See also* Reich, Wilhelm
Rembar, Charles, 171n
Reporter, The, 10
Ribalow, Harold U., 244
Rideout, Walter, 243
Rieff, Philip: *The Triumph of the Therapeutic*, 10, 81, 98, 138, 243
Riesman, David, 26, 174–76
Rimbaud, Arthur, 45, 48, 51
Robbe-Grillet, Alain, 48
Rolf, Ida, 97
Roosevelt, Theodore, 132
Rosenberg, Harold, 3, 5, 18, 33, 39, 244–45
Rosenberg, Julius and Ethel, 32, 34, 36
Rosenfeld, Isaac: 14, 31, 43–44, 47, 53, 60, 62, 78, 100, **102–20**, 129–30, 213n, 219, 236–37, 240–41, **249–51;** *Passage from Home*, 29, 118
Roth, Philip: 3, 101, 154, **196–238**, 242, **254–55;** *Goodbye Columbus*, 201, 208, 254; *Letting Go*, 197, 208, 214, 218, 254; *When She Was Good*, 207–209, 254; *Portnoy's Complaint*, 2, 203, 206, 208, **210–15**, 218, 221, 224–25, 230–31, 234, 236–37, 254; *The Breast*, 203, 209, **214–16**, 217, 224–25, 254–55; *The Great American Novel*, 111, 206, 209, 219, 225; *Our Gang*, 206, 209, 219, 254; *My Life as a Man*, 197, 209, 211, 213, 215, **216–22**, 225, 235, 237; *Reading Myself and Others*, 235, 254; *The Professor of Desire*, 197, 209–10, **222–25**, 233, 236, 254; *The Ghost Writer*, 61, 208–10, 222–24, **225–29**, 231–36 *passim; Zuckerman Unbound*, 209–10, 224–25, **229–33**, 234, 254, 255; *The Anatomy Lesson*, 197–201, 209–10, 225–26, 228, 231, **233–37**, 254; "On the Air," 209; "I Always Wanted You to Admire My Fasting," 207–209, 224, 254
Rothstein, Edward, 255

Sade, Marquis de, 189
Salinger, J. D., 219
Salter, Patricia, 249
Salzman, Jack, 245
Sandburg, Carl, 131
Sanders, Ed, 192, 253
Sartre, Jean-Paul, 27–28, 43
Schacht, Richard, 244
Schapiro, Meyer, 33
Schlesinger Jr., Arthur, 4, 67, 74n, 247
Schorske, Carl, 247
Schorer, Mark, 5
Schulberg, Budd, 164
Schulman, Elias, 250
Schwartz, Delmore: 4, 31, 44, **49–52,** 57, 60, 111–12, 125, 131, 246, 251; "The World is a Wedding," 29; as a character in *Humboldt's Gift,* 151
Schwartz, Nancy and Sheila, 252
Scott, Sir Walter, 89
Seide, Michael, 29, 43
Shachtman, Max, 32, 106
Shakespeare, William, 48, 52, 57, 121, 225
Sharaf, Myron, 249
Shaw, Irwin, 38, 109, 112
Shechner, Mark, 249, 251, 253
Shelley, Percy Bysshe, 89, 180
Shklar, Judith, 28, 245
Shostakovich, Dmitri, 161
Silone, Ignazio, 32, 40
Simmel, Georg, 196, 225
Simon, John, 245
Singer, Isaac Bashevis, 2
Slesinger, Tess, 74, 248
Smedley, Agnes, 161
Solotaroff, Theodore, 105, 113, 115, 250
Sorel, George, 67
Spanish Civil War, 9, 76, 165–66
Spartacus Youth League, 9, 106, 157
Spender, Stephen, 40
Spengler, Oswald, 141, 144, 159
Spinoza, Baruch, 240
Spock, Dr. Benjamin, 204
Stade, George, 255
Stalin, Josef, 163, 165, 167
Stasio, Marilyn, 251
Steiner, George, 14, 243–44
Steiner, Rudolf, 149–52 *passim*
Steinfels, Peter, 245
Stendahl, 79
Stern, Richard, 135, 251, 255
Stevenson, Adlai, 90
Stone, I. F., 161
Styron, William, 26, 252
Sweezy, Paul, 161
Swift, Jonathan, 78
Swinburne, Algernon, 89, 155
Syrkin, Marie, 232, 254

Tate, Allen, 239, 255
Tennyson, Alfred, 72, 89
Thackeray, William, 78
Thompson, Hunter S., 253
Tolstoy, Leo, 48, 79, 112, 118, 237
Trachtenberg, Alan, 35, 245
Trilling, Lionel: 3–4, 18, 26, 29, 31, 38, 46–48, 52–62 *passim,* 66, **77–90,** 110–11, 125, 132, 157, 206, 218, 241, 244, 246, **247–48,** 251; *The Middle of the Journey,* 37, 61, 72, 74n, **75–81;** *The Liberal Imagination,* 72–74; *Sincerity and Authenticity,* 148
Trilling, Diana, 32, 247
Trotsky, Leon, 54, 56, 97, 99, 162, 240, 246
Trotskyism, 4, 99, 157, 160–61
Trungpa, Rinpoche Chogyam, 191–94, 253
Twain, Mark, 48, 66, 111

Ulysses. See James Joyce
Updike, John, 196
Utley, Freda, 39, 245

Valery, Paul, 62
Veblen, Thorstein, 240–41, 256
Vegetotherapy. *See* Reich, Wilhelm
Vidal, Gore, 3
Vietnam Day, 1965, 181–83, 194
Village Voice, The, 100, 173, 177
Vogue, 234

Wahl, Jean, 47
Wald, Alan, 247
Waldorf Conference, 160–61
Wallace, Henry, 90, 160–61, 243
Warshow, Robert, 103
Watts, Alan, 205
Weber, Max, 84
Weil, Simone, 114, 118, 119
Weinberger, Eliot, 253
West, Nathaniel, 164–65
Whitfield, Stephen, 252
Whitman, Walt, 131, 155, 190, 237
Whittemore, Reed, 180, 253
Whyte, William H., 244
Wildavsky, Aaron, 154
Williams, William Carlos, 190
Wilson, Edmund, 14, 33, 48, 74, 81, 202, 248, 251
Wilson, Sloan, 244
Wolfert, Ira, 161
Woolf, Virginia, 121
Wordsworth, William, 72
Wright, Richard, 28, 40

Young, Allen, 190
YPSL (Young People's Socialist League), 6, 106

MARK SHECHNER is professor of English at SUNY-Buffalo and author of *Joyce in Nighttown: A Psychoanalytic Inquiry into Ulysses.*